Lecture Notes in Computer Science 14389

Founding Editors

Gerhard Goos
Juris Hartmanis

The series Lecture Notes in Computer Science (LNCS), including its subseries Lecture Notes in Artificial Intelligence (LNAI) and Lecture Notes in Bioinformatics (LNBI), has established itself as a medium for the publication of new developments in computer science and information technology research, teaching, and education.

LNCS enjoys close cooperation with the computer science R & D community, the series counts many renowned academics among its volume editors and paper authors, and collaborates with prestigious societies. Its mission is to serve this international community by providing an invaluable service, mainly focused on the publication of conference and workshop proceedings and postproceedings. LNCS commenced publication in 1973.

Vladimir Voevodin · Sergey Sobolev ·
Mikhail Yakobovskiy · Rashit Shagaliev
Editors

Supercomputing

9th Russian Supercomputing Days, RuSCDays 2023
Moscow, Russia, September 25–26, 2023
Revised Selected Papers, Part II

 Springer

Editors
Vladimir Voevodin (iD)
Research Computing Center (RCC)
Moscow State University
Moscow, Russia

Sergey Sobolev (iD)
Research Computing Center (RCC)
Moscow State University
Moscow, Russia

Mikhail Yakobovskiy (iD)
Russian Academy of Sciences (RAS)
Keldysh Institute of Applied Mathematics
Moscow, Russia

Rashit Shagaliev
Russian Federal Nuclear Center
Sarov, Russia

ISSN 0302-9743   ISSN 1611-3349 (electronic)
Lecture Notes in Computer Science
ISBN 978-3-031-49434-5   ISBN 978-3-031-49435-2 (eBook)
https://doi.org/10.1007/978-3-031-49435-2

This Springer imprint is published by the registered company Springer Nature Switzerland AG
The registered company address is: Gewerbestrasse 11, 6330 Cham, Switzerland

Paper in this product is recyclable.

Preface

The 9th Russian Supercomputing Days Conference (RuSCDays 2023) was held during September 25–26, 2023. The conference was organized by the Supercomputing Consortium of Russian Universities, the Russian Academy of Sciences, and the Moscow Center of Fundamental and Applied Mathematics. The conference organization coordinator was the Moscow State University Research Computing Center. The conference was supported by platinum sponsors (Cloud.ru, RSC, AMD Technologies, and E-Flops) and silver sponsors (Norsi-Trans and Forsite).

To make the event as safe as possible, the conference was held in a hybrid way, combining offline and online sessions. Every offline session was also available online for remote attendees. There were also several online-only sessions.

RuSCDays was born in 2015 as a union of several supercomputing event series in Russia and quickly became one of the most notable Russian supercomputing international meetings. The conference caters to the interests of a wide range of representatives from science, industry, business, education, government, and academia – anyone connected to the development or the use of supercomputing technologies. The conference topics cover all aspects of supercomputing technologies: software and hardware design, solving large tasks, application of supercomputing technologies in industry, exaflops-scale computing issues, supercomputing co-design technologies, supercomputing education, and others.

All 104 papers submitted to the conference were reviewed by three referees in the first review round. During single-blind peer reviewing, the papers were evaluated according to their relevance to the conference topics, scientific contribution, presentation, approbation, and related works description. After notification of conditional acceptance, a second review round was arranged which aimed at the final polishing of papers and also at the evaluation of authors' work following revision based on the referees' comments. After the conference, the 45 best papers were carefully selected to be included in this volume.

The proceedings editors would like to thank all the conference committee members, especially the Organizing and Program Committee members as well as the referees and reviewers for their contributions. We also thank Springer for producing these high-quality proceedings of RuSCDays 2023.

October 2023

Vladimir Voevodin
Sergey Sobolev
Rashit Shagaliev
Mikhail Yakobovskiy

Organization

Steering Committee

Victor A. Sadovnichiy (Chair)	Moscow State University, Russia
Vladimir B. Betelin (Co-chair)	Russian Academy of Sciences, Russia
Alexander V. Tikhonravov (Co-chair)	Moscow State University, Russia
Jack Dongarra (Co-chair)	University of Tennessee, USA
Alexey I. Borovkov	Peter the Great Saint Petersburg Polytechnic University, Russia
Vladimir V. Voevodin	Moscow State University, Russia
Georgy S. Elizarov	NII Kvant, Russia
Elena V. Zagainova	Lobachevsky State University of Nizhni Novgorod, Russia
Alexander K. Kim	MCST, Russia
Elena V. Kudryashova	Northern (Arctic) Federal University, Russia
Alexander A. Moskovskiy	RSC Group, Russia
Gennady I. Savin	Joint Supercomputer Center, Russian Academy of Sciences, Russia
Alexey S. Simonov	NICEVT, Russia
Victor A. Soyfer	Samara University, Russia
Leonid B. Sokolinskiy	South Ural State University, Russia
Igor A. Sokolov	Russian Academy of Sciences, Russia
Roman G. Strongin	Lobachevsky State University of Nizhni Novgorod, Russia
Alexey R. Khokhlov	Russian Academy of Sciences, Russia
Boris N. Chetverushkin	Keldysh Institute of Applied Mathematics, Russian Academy of Sciences, Russia

Program Committee

Vladimir V. Voevodin (Chair)	Moscow State University, Russia
Rashit M. Shagaliev (Co-chair)	Russian Federal Nuclear Center, Russia
Mikhail V. Yakobovskiy (Co-chair)	Keldysh Institute of Applied Mathematics, Russian Academy of Sciences, Russia
Thomas Sterling (Co-chair)	Indiana University, USA
Sergey I. Sobolev (Scientific Secretary)	Moscow State University, Russia

Happy Sithole	Centre for High Performance Computing, South Africa
Alexander V. Smirnov	Moscow State University, Russia
Hiroyuki Takizawa	Tohoku University, Japan
Michela Taufer	University of Delaware, USA
Vadim E. Turlapov	Lobachevsky State University of Nizhni Novgorod, Russia
Eugeny E. Tyrtyshnikov	Institute of Numerical Mathematics, Russian Academy of Sciences, Russia
Vladimir A. Fursov	Samara University, Russia
Thorsten Hoefler	Eidgenössische Technische Hochschule Zürich, Switzerland
Boris M. Shabanov	Joint Supercomputer Center, Russian Academy of Sciences, Russia
Lev N. Shchur	Higher School of Economics, Russia
Roman Wyrzykowski	Czestochowa University of Technology, Poland
Mitsuo Yokokawa	Kobe University, Japan

Industrial Committee

A. A. Aksenov (Co-chair)	Tesis, Russia
V. E. Velikhov (Co-chair)	National Research Center "Kurchatov Institute", Russia
A. V. Murashov (Co-chair)	Russian Foundation for Advanced Research Projects, Russia
Yu. Ya. Boldyrev	Peter the Great Saint Petersburg Polytechnic University, Russia
M. A. Bolshukhin	Afrikantov Experimental Design Bureau for Mechanical Engineering, Russia
R. K. Gazizov	Ufa State Aviation Technical University, Russia
M. P. Lobachev	Krylov State Research Centre, Russia
V. Ya. Modorskiy	Perm National Research Polytechnic University, Russia
A. P. Skibin	Gidropress, Russia
A. B. Shmelev	RSC Group, Russia
S. V. Strizhak	Institute for System Programming, Russian Academy of Sciences, Russia

Educational Committee

Vl. V. Voevodin (Co-chair)	Moscow State University, Russia
L. B. Sokolinskiy (Co-chair)	South Ural State University, Russia
Yu. Ya. Boldyrev	Peter the Great Saint Petersburg Polytechnic University, Russia
K. A. Barkalov	Lobachevsky State University of Nizhni Novgorod, Russia
A. V. Bukhanovskiy	ITMO University, Russia
R. K. Gazizov	Ufa State Aviation Technical University, Russia
I. B. Meerov	Lobachevsky State University of Nizhni Novgorod, Russia
V. Ya. Modorskiy	Perm National Research Polytechnic University, Russia
S. G. Mosin	Kazan Federal University, Russia
N. N. Popova	Moscow State University, Russia
O. A. Yufryakova	Northern (Arctic) Federal University, Russia

Organizing Committee

Vl. V. Voevodin (Chair)	Moscow State University, Russia
B. M. Shabanov (Co-chair)	Joint Supercomputer Center, Russian Academy of Sciences, Russia
S. I. Sobolev (Scientific Secretary)	Moscow State University, Russia
A. A. Aksenov	Tesis, Russia
A. P. Antonova	Moscow State University, Russia
A. S. Antonov	Moscow State University, Russia
K. A. Barkalov	Lobachevsky State University of Nizhni Novgorod, Russia
M. R. Biktimirov	Russian Academy of Sciences, Russia
Vad. V. Voevodin	Moscow State University, Russia
T. A. Gamayunova	Moscow State University, Russia
O. A. Gorbachev	RSC Group, Russia
V. A. Grishagin	Lobachevsky State University of Nizhni Novgorod, Russia
V. V. Korenkov	Joint Institute for Nuclear Research, Russia
I. B. Meerov	Lobachevsky State University of Nizhni Novgorod, Russia
D. A. Nikitenko	Moscow State University, Russia
I. M. Nikolskiy	Moscow State University, Russia
N. N. Popova	Moscow State University, Russia

Contents – Part II

Contents – Part I

Distributed Computing

Benchmarking DAG Scheduling Algorithms on Scientific Workflow Instances

Oleg Sukhoroslov[1]([✉]) and Maksim Gorokhovskii[2]

[1] Institute for Information Transmission Problems of the Russian Academy of Sciences, Moscow, Russia
sukhoroslov@iitp.ru
[2] HSE University, Moscow, Russia
magorokhovskiy@edu.hse.ru

Abstract. Many real-world applications executed on distributed computing systems are organized as directed acyclic graphs (DAGs) of tasks. The algorithm employed for scheduling these tasks across the system has a substantial impact on the achieved performance. Despite the numerous DAG scheduling algorithms proposed by researchers, there is a lack of benchmarks that evaluate the performance of such algorithms on a set of real application instances in realistic conditions. Thus developers of runtime systems often resort to the use of simple but inefficient algorithms. In this work we aim to fill this gap by proposing a benchmark for evaluating DAG scheduling algorithms based on a set of 150 real-world workflow instances with up to 1695 tasks and 10 realistic cluster configurations with multi-core machines. We apply this benchmark for evaluation of 16 scheduling algorithms including the well-known static algorithms and the commonly used in practice dynamic algorithms. The obtained results demonstrate that the proposed benchmark allows to clearly separate and compare the algorithms performance from different angles and to make important observations.

Keywords: DAG scheduling · Task graph · Workflow · Distributed computing · Simulation · Benchmark

1 Introduction

Many real-world applications that run on distributed computing environments are organized as a series of standalone tasks with data dependencies. For instance, within the realms of science and technology, applications are frequently described and executed as workflows [9]. In this context, a workflow task entails the execution of an independent software package which reads input files, conducts necessary computations and data processing, and generates output files. The definition of the workflow links the output and input files of the tasks, establishing producer-consumer relationships. The execution of the workflow is automated through special runtime systems overseeing resource allocation, task

V. Voevodin et al. (Eds.): RuSCDays 2023, LNCS 14389, pp. 3–20, 2023.
https://doi.org/10.1007/978-3-031-49435-2_1

scheduling, and data management [10]. This structured approach is not confined to scientific workflows but extends to various domains including distributed data processing, microservice applications, and build systems. In essence, all such applications can be represented as directed acyclic graphs (DAGs), where the vertices correspond to the application tasks and the edges signify the dependencies between them.

A significant hurdle encountered by runtime systems in executing such applications is task scheduling. This involves determining when and on which resource each task should be executed. These scheduling decisions must align with user-defined objectives and constraints, which may encompass factors like performance, cost-effectiveness, energy efficiency, reliability, and more. The selection of a scheduling algorithm, as frequently noted, including in this study, has a substantial impact on the actual performance in relation to these specified objectives. This work considers the most widely used objective of minimizing the application's execution time.

Extensive effort has been dedicated to devising algorithms for scheduling DAGs. The problems of scheduling of task graphs with precedence constraints has been thoroughly examined for both homogeneous and heterogeneous multiprocessor systems [15,22,27]. It's important to note that in the general case, these problems are NP-complete [13], with polynomial-time solutions known only for specific restricted instances. Consequently, most of research has been devoted to devising heuristics that can produce high-quality solutions in a reasonable time. The proposed heuristics are based on several techniques, such as list scheduling, task clustering, duplication, guided random search, etc. Among these techniques, list scheduling is the most widely adopted one, as it tend to yield better results in less computational time [27].

The rise of distributed computing infrastructures, cloud platforms, and workflow management systems [4,9] has sparked the subsequent research on scheduling of workflow applications [1,3,14,16,20]. These works refine the examined models and assumptions to capture the practical issues related to efficient execution of workflows in modern systems. For instance, in scenarios involving data-intensive workflows, it becomes crucial to factor in network congestion alongside the data placement and transfer strategies [24]. Objectives and constraints are also expanded, encompassing considerations such as the monetary cost of execution in cloud environments [18], or energy consumption [12]. Nevertheless, a majority of workflow scheduling algorithms still draw on ideas from the preceding works on DAG scheduling. Recent research has also delved into the application of reinforcement learning for DAG scheduling [17,19].

Despite the large body of research on DAG scheduling algorithms, the existing workflow runtime systems often rely on simple task scheduling strategies that may lead to significant performance loss [7]. This disconnect between research and practice is caused by several reasons. First, research results are often based on simplified models and assumptions that may not hold in a real execution environment. For example, ignoring network contention or assuming accurate estimates of task execution times. Second, the evaluation of scheduling algorithms by researchers is done in an ad-hoc manner on different sets of problem instances and using different performance metrics. The lack of a common benchmark makes it hard to compare the algorithms against each other on a unified basis. Furthermore, published so far algorithm evaluations use only a small set of real-world DAG instances of small size or even only synthetic instances. The used system configurations can also be far from the production systems. For example, our previous study [26] used a limited set of synthetic DAG instances with 100 tasks each based on real workflow applications [5], and assumed that each machine can execute only one task at a time. These issues do not allow to asses the potential effectiveness of these algorithms in practice.

In this work we address the mentioned issues by proposing a benchmark for evaluating DAG scheduling algorithms based on a set of 150 real-world workflow instances with up to 1695 tasks and 10 realistic cluster configurations with multi-core machines. The evaluation is performed by simulating the execution of each workflow instance on a given system using the schedule generated by each algorithm. Several algorithm performance metrics are collected for each execution. As a demonstration, we apply this benchmark for evaluation of 16 scheduling algorithms including the well-known static algorithms and the commonly used in practice dynamic algorithms. For better comparison of algorithm performance we employ the performance profiles technique [11], which is novel in the context of evaluating DAG scheduling algorithms. We hope that this work will serve as a foundation for better evaluation of DAG scheduling algorithms, including the new ones, and their applicability in practical runtime systems.

The subsequent sections of the paper are structured as follows. Section 2 outlines the DAG scheduling problem under consideration, introduces the application and system models, and details the evaluated scheduling algorithms. Section 3 introduces the main parts of the proposed benchmark – selected workflow instances, system configurations, and algorithm performance metrics. Section 4 briefly describes DSLab DAG, a simulation library used for benchmark execution. Section 5 presents and analyzes the benchmark results obtained for the evaluated scheduling algorithms. Finally, Sect. 6 concludes and outlines the future work.

2 DAG Scheduling

2.1 Problem Statement

An application can be represented as a directed acyclic graph $G = (T, D)$, where T denotes the set of tasks (vertices) and D signifies the set of dependencies between these tasks (edges). If $(i, j) \in D$ it implies that task t_j relies on data produced by t_i, establishing t_i as a parent task for t_j. A task lacking parent tasks is termed an entry task, while a task without children is referred to as an exit task. The weight assigned to an edge, denoted as d_{ij}, indicates the volume of data transferred from task t_i to task t_j. The tasks operate in isolation, lacking communication during their execution. Task outputs become available after the task completion. A task is eligible for execution on a specific machine only after all of its parent tasks have been completed, and their respective outputs have been transmitted to the machine.

The system used for task execution can be represented as a set of machines M linked via a network, such as a computing cluster. Each machine m_k is equipped with c_k CPU cores of identical performance. In a homogeneous system, all machines possess the same number of cores and exhibit identical performance characteristics. Conversely, in a heterogeneous system, machines vary in their specifications. It is assumed that each task utilizes a single CPU core throughout its execution, and a machine is incapable of running more than c_k tasks concurrently. Every task must be executed in its entirety on a single machine. Task execution is non-preemptive and can be overlapped with data transfers between machines.

The execution time $ET(t_i, m_k)$ for each task t_i on each machine m_k can be explicitly provided, or alternatively, calculated as follows. Each task is assigned a weight w_i representing the required amount of computations, while each machine is characterized by a CPU core performance p_k. Consequently, the task's execution time is computed as $ET(t_i, m_k) = w_i/p_k$. In this paper, we adopt the latter approach, employing the number of floating-point operations as the task weight, and the floating-point operations per second as the measure of CPU core performance.

Before a task t can start its execution on machine m, its inputs (generated by t's parent tasks) must be transmitted to m. Once the task concludes its execution, its outputs are stored on m. In cases where the parent and child tasks are executed on the same machine, the parent's output becomes immediately accessible. Alternatively, if the tasks are executed on different machines, the data must be transmitted via the network from the machine that executed the parent task. The duration of such data transfer between tasks t_i and t_j is calculated as $DTT(t_i, t_j) = L + d_{ij}/B$, where L signifies the network latency and B represents the network bandwidth. The used network model assumes no contention, i.e. each data transfer utilizes the full network bandwidth.

Considering the outlined application and system models, the DAG scheduling problem involves determining the assignment of application tasks to machines such as to minimize the overall application execution time, often referred to as the *makespan*.

2.2 Algorithms

DAG scheduling algorithms fall into two main categories: static and dynamic. *Static* algorithms assign all tasks to machines prior to the DAG execution. These algorithms rely on estimates of task execution and data transfer times. The assignments made by a static algorithm remain unchanged throughout the execution. *Dynamic* algorithms, in contrast, assign tasks incrementally as the DAG is executed. A dynamic algorithm is called multiple times, either upon completion of previously scheduled tasks or at regular intervals, and each time can output new scheduling decisions. Unlike static algorithms, dynamic ones have the ability to adapt the schedule during execution to accommodate errors in time estimates, respond to machine failures or system reconfigurations, etc. However, static algorithms are generally better at accounting for the whole DAG's structure. A hybrid approach, combining the strengths of both static and dynamic algorithms, involves initially constructing a schedule using a static algorithm and then dynamically adjusting it during runtime.

Irrespective of their type, most DAG scheduling algorithms employ the list scheduling technique, which involves two steps. In the first step, known as task selection, the algorithm identifies the next task for scheduling. This is made using a ranking function or some predetermined criterion. In the subsequent step, referred to as resource selection, the algorithm determines the resource for execution of the previously chosen task. Again, this selection is based on a designated criterion. These two steps are iteratively carried out until all tasks are scheduled.

Dynamic List Scheduling (Dynamic): A family of dynamic algorithms employing typical list-scheduling heuristics to assign tasks to machines at runtime [7]. In the task selection step, only unscheduled tasks whose parents have already been completed are considered. The selection process employs one of the following criteria:

1. Select the task with the largest amount of computations,
2. Select the task with the largest amount of input and output data,
3. Select the task with the largest number of children tasks,
4. Select the task with the largest bottom-level (see the task rank in HEFT algorithm below).

During the resource selection step, only machines with available cores are taken into consideration. The selection process employs one of the following criteria:

1. Select the machine with the fastest CPU cores,
2. Select the machine with the largest amount of task input data stored locally,
3. Select the machine with the most idle cores.

This results in 12 algorithms implementing all possible criteria combinations. For example, algorithm *Dynamic(1,2)* uses criteria 1 and 2 for task and resource selection steps respectively. Note that some task selection criteria require the estimates of task computational and data sizes.

Dynamic-Level Scheduling (DLS): A static algorithm that utilizes the *dynamic level* metric calculated for each task-machine pair [21]:

$$DL(t_i, m_j) = SL(t_i) + \Delta(t_i, m_j) - EST(t_i, m_j),$$

where $SL(t_i)$ represents the *static level* of task t_i, defined as the largest sum of median execution times of tasks along any directed path from t_i to the exit task. $\Delta(t_i, n_j)$ denotes the difference between the median execution time of task t_i on all machines and $w_{i,j}$. $EST(t_i, m_j)$ indicates the earliest start time of task t_i on machine m_j. During each iteration, the algorithm evaluates all ready tasks, selecting a task-machine pair with the highest DL value. It then updates the list of ready tasks and recalculates the DL values.

Heterogeneous Earliest Finish Time (HEFT): A well-known static DAG scheduling algorithm for heterogeneous systems [27]. The tasks are scheduled in descending order of their rank computed as

$$rank(t_i) = \overline{w_i} + \max_{t_j \in children(t_i)} \left(\overline{DTT(t_i, t_j)} + rank(t_j) \right),$$

where $\overline{w_i}$ represents the average execution time of task t_i across all machines, and $\overline{c_{i,j}}$ denotes the average data transfer time between tasks t_i and t_j across all pairs of machines. Each task is assigned to machine with the earliest expected task completion time. The rank function establishes a valid topological order, ensuring that, similar to DLS, a task is scheduled only after its parent tasks, and allowing for the computation of required earliest start time estimates.

Lookahead: A static algorithm that can be viewed as an extension of HEFT [6]. It employs the same ranking function for task selection. However, in resource selection step, Lookahead schedules the subsequent tasks using HEFT and then selects a machine that minimizes the maximum task completion time. Consequently, a task's completion may be delayed if it leads to a reduction in the overall makespan, making the algorithm less greedy. The examined subsequent tasks can include only immediate children of a task, recursive children up to a certain depth, or all remaining tasks. In this work, we adopt the latter variant, which exhibits superior solution quality albeit at the cost of high computational complexity.

Predict Earliest Finish Time (PEFT): A static algorithm that aims to capture the advantages of Lookahead while maintaining a lower computational complexity [2]. To achieve this, PEFT precomputes the values of the Optimistic Cost Table (OCT) for each task-machine pair as

$$OCT(t_i, m_k) = \max_{t_j \in children(t_i)} \min_{m_n \in M} (OCT(t_j, m_n) + ET(t_j, m_n) + DTT(t_i, t_j, m_k, m_n)),$$

which estimates the remaining execution time without considering machine availability. Tasks are selected in decreasing order of the mean OCT value across all machines. The selected task is assigned to machine that minimizes the sum of task completion time and OCT.

3 Benchmark

3.1 Workflow Instances

Workflows is a popular approach to describe and execute computational and data processing pipelines in science and technology [9]. As was discussed previously, workflow execution is an important area for application of DAG scheduling algorithms. Therefore it is crucial to test these algorithms on realistic workflow instances.

In the proposed benchmark, we employ a set of 150 real-world scientific workflow instances, which correspond to 9 distinct workflow applications spanning various domains. These instances have been derived from the logs of real workflow executions and are made available through the WfCommons project [8]. From 170 available instances we excluded 5 instances executed by Nextflow runtime system due to the lack of files information and 15 extremely large instances.

A workflow instance represents as a JSON file adhering to the WfCommons JSON Schema. It contains information about the workflow tasks (task name, task execution time, input and output files, machine on which the task was executed) and the execution environment (machines and their specifications, including core count and performance). This data is sufficient to reconstruct the corresponding DAG instance, including with the weights associated with its vertices and edges, in accordance with the outlined model.

Below we briefly overview each of the featured workflow applications.

1000Genome: This bioinformatics workflow identifies mutational overlaps using data from the 1000 genomes project. It consists of three levels: two wide levels with many parallel tasks separated by a single data merge task.

BLAST: This bioinformatics workflow is named after a toolkit for finding regions of similarity between biological sequences. The workflow runs BLAST against large reference databases by splitting the reference file into parts, running BLAST on each part and merging the results of BLAST executions. It has a simple fork-join structure with depth 3. The number of parallel BLAST tasks depends on the input query size and the number of sequences per split.

BWA: This bioinformatics workflow is named after a package for mapping low-divergent sequences against a large reference genome, such as the human genome. Similar to BLAST, this workflow is aimed to parallelize BWA execution on large reference databases by splitting the reference file into parts and running BWA on each part in parallel. This results in a similar simple fork-join structure with depth 3, the only difference is two entry tasks instead of one.

Cycles: This agroecology workflow computes the agroecosystem model with daily time step simulations of crop production and the water, carbon and nitrogen cycles in the soil-plant-atmosphere continuum. The workflow is composed of 7 types of tasks and has four levels of parallel tasks, with the widest level containing about the half of the tasks.

Epigenomics: This bioinformatics workflow implements a data processing pipeline for executing various genome sequencing operations. It splits the DNA sequencing data into chunks to be processed in parallel, filters them to remove noisy and contaminating segments and maps into the correct location in a reference genome. Finally, a global map of the aligned sequences is generated and the sequence density at each position in the genome is calculated. The workflow is composed of 14 types of tasks and has 9 levels including multiple parallel fork-join subgraphs followed by a global merge.

Montage: This astronomy workflow allows to re-project, background correct and add astronomical images into custom mosaics. The workflow is composed of 8 types of tasks and has 8 mono-type levels. The workflow structure is formed from three identical parallel branches corresponding to different bands (red, blue, and green). Each branch contains three waves of parallel tasks and five sequential split and merge tasks.

Seismology: This seismology workflow implements cross-correlation of sequences of measurements from multiple seismic stations. It has the simplest structure with two levels. The first level consists of parallel tasks where each task processes a pair of signals. The second level consists of a single task which merges and processes the results of all previous tasks.

SoyKB: This bioinformatics workflow implements a genomics pipeline that re-sequences soybean germplasm lines selected for desirable traits such as oil, protein, stress resistance, etc. The workflow is composed of 14 types of tasks and has 11 levels. The workflow structure is formed from several parallel branches which results are combined by several parallel tasks, similar to MapReduce model.

SRA Search: This bioinformatics workflow performs alignment of high throughput sequencing data from Sequence Read Archive (SRA) database. The workflow is composed of four types of tasks and has three or four levels. The first two wide levels are formed by parallel tasks which number correspond to the number of input data items. The remaining one or two levels are formed by tasks that merge the obtained results.

Table 1. Characteristics of workflow instances used in the benchmark

Workflow	#	Tasks	Depth	Width	Parallelism	CCR	Max work/data
1000Genome	22	52–902	3	28–572	13–152	47–487	2.14/75.62
BLAST	15	43–303	3	40–300	34–269	0.02–6.5e5	42.87/5119
BWA	15	104–1004	3	100–1000	4–26	32–105	3.78/57
Cycles	16	67–1091	4	32–540	5–62	2265–7741	0.9/7.77
Epigenomics	26	41–1695	9	9–420	5–97	684–2373	1.17/12.7
Montage	11	58–1312	8	18–936	10–79	234–1055	3.08/17.42
Seismology	10	101–1001	2	100–1000	27–116	36694–78748	0.02/0.02
SoyKB	10	96–676	11	50–500	2.5–7.8	62–174	6.03/2.88
SRA Search	25	22–104	3–4	11–51	5–24	775–3092	5.64/78.87

Table 1 provides an overview of the characteristics of the employed workflow instances. The number of tasks per instance varies from 22 to 1695. The most of workflows have fixed depth (number of levels) while their width (maximum number of tasks per level) can vary significantly from instance to instance based on the input data and parameters. The relatively small DAG depths and extensive widths suggest that these instances are well-suited for parallel execution. The degree of parallelism is estimated by the ratio of the total computational workload (task sizes) to the critical path length (excluding data transfers). The BLAST and Seismology instances have the highest parallelism, while the SoyKB instances have the lowest one, which correlates with their depth. The computation-to-communication ratio (CCR), which is defined as the ratio of the total computational workload (in Gflops) to the total size of data transfers (in GBytes), helps to identify data-intensive applications and estimate the sensitivity of application performance to data transfer costs. The Seismology and Cycles workflows have the highest CCR values (i.e. CPU intensive), while the BWA and SoyKB workflows have the lowest CCR values (i.e. I/O intensive). Interestingly, BLAST instances have a very wide spectrum of CCR values covering the both cases. The maximum values of work (measured in hours of execution on a 10 Gflop/s machine) and total size of files (in GB) are also reported for each application.

As it can be seen, the used workflow instances have diverse characteristics, which allows to perform a comprehensive evaluation of scheduling algorithms.

3.2 System Configurations

The considered workflow applications are commonly executed on commodity clusters comprised of multicore machines linked by Ethernet network. To obtain a diverse set of environments for benchmarking algorithms, we employed 10 distinct cluster configurations, as detailed in Table 2. These configurations vary

Table 2. System configurations used in the benchmark

System	Machines	Homogen.	Cores	Performance	Network
cluster-hom-4-32	4	Y	32	128 Gflop/s	10GbE
cluster-hom-4-64	4	Y	64	256 Gflop/s	10GbE
cluster-hom-8-64	8	Y	64	256 Gflop/s	10GbE
cluster-hom-8-128	8	Y	128	512 Gflop/s	10GbE
cluster-hom-8-128-100g	8	Y	128	512 Gflop/s	100GbE
cluster-het-4-32	4	N	32	320 Gflop/s	10GbE
cluster-het-4-64	4	N	64	640 Gflop/s	10GbE
cluster-het-8-64	8	N	64	640 Gflop/s	10GbE
cluster-het-8-128	8	N	128	1280 Gflop/s	10GbE
cluster-het-8-128-100 g	8	N	128	1280 Gflop/s	100GbE

in terms of cluster size, heterogeneity, performance capabilities of machines, and network speed. Each machine is equipped with 4-24 CPU cores with 2-6 Gflop/s performance per core. The machines are connected by either a 10GbE or 100GbE network.

3.3   Algorithm Comparison Metrics

The comparison of DAG scheduling algorithms is based on the following metrics.

Makespan: The primary performance metric for a scheduling algorithm s on a problem instance $p = (workflow, system)$ is $makespan_{s,p}$ which denotes the DAG execution time with the schedule generated by the algorithm. However, when evaluating the algorithm's performance on a set of problem instances with varying characteristics, it becomes imperative to employ some normalization of the makespan values.

Normalized Makespan (NM): A common approach is to normalize the makespan to a lower bound [15,27]. However, while the previous work estimated the lower bound using the critical path length $LB_{path} = \sum_{t_i \in CP_{MIN}} min_{m_k \in M} ET(t_i, m_k)$, we propose to use a more accurate estimate.

First, another lower bound can be computed based on the total work and the aggregate system performance:

$$LB_{volume} = \frac{\sum_{t_i \in T} w_i}{\sum_{m_k \in M} p_k}.$$

This bound can be more accurate for wide DAGs, such as the ones found in scientific workflows, where the execution time can be bounded by the system throughput. Second, the bound can be improved by taking into account the input and output data transfer times:

$$LB_{imp} = LB_{input} + \max(LB_{path}, LB_{volume}) + LB_{output},$$

where LB_{input} is the minimum time needed to transfer input data across all entry tasks, and LB_{output} is the minimum time needed to transfer output data across all exit tasks. Finally, we can take into account the edge cases with extremely large input and output data transfers dominating the makespan as follows:

$$LB = \max(LB^*_{input}, LB_{imp}, LB^*_{output}),$$

where LB^*_{input} is the maximum time needed to transfer input data across all tasks reading the DAG inputs, and LB^*_{output} is the maximum time needed to transfer output data across all tasks writing the DAG outputs.

Using the described lower bound, the normalized makespan for an algorithm s on a problem instance p is computed as $NM(s, p) = makespan_{s,p}/LB(p)$.

Degradation from Best (DFB): Another frequently used approach is to calculate the relative difference between the makespan achieved by the algorithm and the best makespan obtained for this problem instance:

$$DFB(s,p) = \frac{makespan_{s,p} - \min\{makespan_{s,p} : s \in S\}}{\min\{makespan_{s,p} : s \in S\}}.$$

This metric is easier to calculate than NM, however, in contrast to NM, its values depend on the set of used algorithms.

Performance Profile: The previously described metrics evaluate the algorithm's performance on a single problem instance and should be aggregated, e.g. averaged, in case of multiple instances. Performance profiles [11] is an alternative approach to compare the performance of several algorithms on a set of problem instances. Initially introduced for evaluating the performance of optimization software, performance profiles offer a general method for aggregating and visualizing benchmark results.

The performance profile for an algorithm is essentially the cumulative distribution function for the performance ratio

$$\rho_s(\tau) = \frac{1}{n_p}\text{size}\{p \in P : r_{p,s} \leq \tau\},$$

where $n_p = |P|$ is the number of problem instances, $r_{p,s}$ is the performance ratio of algorithm s on problem instance p:

$$r_{p,s} = \frac{makespan_{s,p}}{\min\{makespan_{s,p} : s \in S\}}.$$

Algorithm Running Time: The running time of an algorithm is the amount of time it takes to compute the schedule for a given DAG. For static algorithms this is the duration of a single algorithm call, while for dynamic algorithms this is the total duration of all algorithm's calls. This metric reflects the computational cost associated with using the algorithm. The algorithms with low running time are preferred for practical use, while the algorithms which running time is comparable with achieved makespans should be avoided. We can take this into account by adding the algorithm running time to the makespan to obtain the *effective makespan* and compare the algorithms using it. Note that this metric is less informative for dynamic algorithms since their execution may be overlapped with the application execution.

4   Simulation Model

The benchmarking of DAG scheduling algorithms is carried out through simulation. For each problem instance and algorithm a separate simulation run in performed to model the execution of the workflow on the system using the schedule generated by the algorithm. The simulation stops when all workflow tasks are completed, and the resulting makespan is recorded.

The durations of task executions and data transfers in the simulation exactly match the estimations used by the algorithms. Consequently, for static algorithms, the achieved makespan coincides with the one anticipated by the algorithm. The incorporation of errors in estimations used by the algorithms is left for future work.

The simulations are performed by means of DSLab DAG[1] [25], a library designed for exploring DAG scheduling algorithms, implemented in the Rust programming language. This library facilitates the description of a DAG and enables the simulation of its execution within a specified distributed system, employing included or user-defined scheduling algorithms.

The distributed system is modeled in DSLab DAG as a set of computing resources connected with network. Each resource is described by the number of CPU cores, their speed in flop/s and amount of memory. Resources can execute compute tasks described by the amount of computations in flops, the minimum and maximum number of used cores, and the amount of used memory. This model is more general and realistic than the one described in Sect. 2.1 by supporting multi-core tasks and memory requirements, which we plan to investigate in the future work.

The library supports two network models – the constant model in which each data transfer receives the full network bandwidth and the shared model in which concurrent data transfers share the network bandwidth. The constant model is used in this work to avoid the influence of network contention on benchmark results. Considering network contention is left for future work.

The DAG is modeled in DSLab DAG as a set of tasks and inter-task dependencies based on *data items*. Each task can produce one or more data items (task outputs) and consume (as task inputs) data items produced by other tasks. Entry tasks consume separate data items corresponding to the DAG inputs. The data dependencies between the tasks define constraints on task execution – a task cannot start its execution on some resource until all its inputs are produced (parent tasks are completed) and transferred to this resource. This model is similar to the model described in Sect. 2.1 but refines it by introducing data items which correspond to files in scientific workflows. The used workflow instances contain the information about input and output files of each task.

The scheduling of DAG tasks is performed by an implementation of *Scheduler* interface. This interface includes two callback methods which are called at the start of DAG execution and on every task state change respectively. Each method can return one or multiple actions corresponding to decisions made by the scheduling algorithm (assign task to resource, transfer data item between resources, etc.). This approach allows to implement and test arbitrary static or dynamic scheduling algorithms. The implementations of the evaluated algorithms are included in DSLab DAG.

---

[1] https://github.com/osukhoroslov/dslab/tree/main/crates/dslab-dag.

5   Benchmark Results

We conducted a total of 24000 simulations corresponding to 16 runs, one per each algorithm, of the described benchmark consisting of 15000 problem instances (150 workflow instances × 10 systems). The simulations were run in parallel on a single VM instance with 32 cores and 32 GB of RAM, which took less than 6 h.

The benchmark results are presented in Table 3. The number of instances where the algorithm performed the best or the worst, and the average values of the performance metrics (the median value of normalized makespan is also presented in brackets) are reported. The distributions of normalized makespan values are presented on Fig. 1.

Table 3. Benchmark results sorted by normalized makespan (NM).

Algorithm	Best	Worst	NM	DFB,%	Run.time
Lookahead	1386	0	1.10 (1.02)	0.03	364.35
HEFT	735	1	1.11 (1.03)	0.55	0.07
DLS	743	0	1.11 (1.03)	0.74	8.89
Portfolio	52	0	1.16 (1.06)	5.50	1.82
PEFT	371	64	1.19 (1.12)	8.18	0.08
Dynamic(4,1)	28	41	1.21 (1.07)	9.4	1.05
Dynamic(1,1)	20	69	1.25 (1.10)	12.66	0.16
Dynamic(4,2)	22	50	1.25 (1.09)	13.00	0.16
Dynamic(2,1)	18	75	1.28 (1.18)	15.51	0.34
Dynamic(1,2)	16	105	1.30 (1.13)	17.49	0.12
Dynamic(3,1)	0	122	1.32 (1.23)	19.63	0.11
Dynamic(2,2)	15	163	1.34 (1.22)	21.28	0.32
Dynamic(3,2)	5	164	1.38 (1.27)	25.33	0.10
Dynamic(4,3)	10	94	1.42 (1.29)	28.38	0.61
Dynamic(1,3)	4	133	1.44 (1.32)	31.02	0.13
Dynamic(2,3)	0	371	1.49 (1.40)	35.32	0.33
Dynamic(3,3)	0	498	1.52 (1.42)	38.49	0.11

As it can be seen, Lookahead outperforms other algorithms in terms of makespan by achieving the best result in 92% of cases. The median NM value for Lookahead is 1.02, which means that in 50% of cases its makespan is within 2% from the lower bound. However these results come at the price of significantly higher running time. The median running time of Lookahead is 13 s, while for other algorithms it is less than a second. HEFT and DLS perform very close to

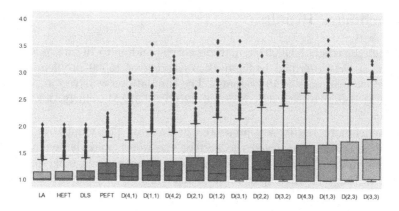

Fig. 1. Distribution of normalized makespan values.

Lookahead. However, from the average metric values and even metric distributions it is hard to see the difference. We will address this issue further by using the performance profiles. PEFT performs the worst among the static algorithms.

Among the dynamic algorithms the ones using the task selection criteria 4 (largest bottom-level) and 1 (largest amount of computations) perform the best in average. Among the resource section criteria the best is 1 (fastest CPU cores), while 3 (most idle cores) demonstrates the worst results. Based on the mixed results of dynamic algorithms (e.g. many worst counts) it is reasonable to assume that in different cases the best makespan is achieved by different algorithms. To confirm this hypothesis we have combined the results of dynamic algorithms into a single virtual algorithm *Portfolio*. For each case this algorithm takes the best

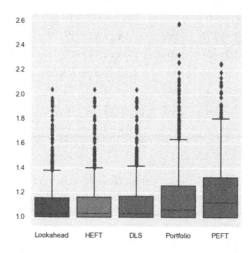

Fig. 2. Distribution of normalized makespan values (after combining dynamic algorithms into Portfolio).

result among all dynamic algorithms following the algorithm portfolio approach proposed in [7]. The results of Portfolio indeed are significantly better and even outperform PEFT.

The distribution of normalized makespan values after combining the dynamic algorithms into Portfolio is presented on Fig. 2. To better visualize the difference in performance of Lookahead, HEFT and DLS we use performance profiles plotted on the left side of Fig. 3. Indeed, the Lookahead curve lies above and is clearly separated from the ones of the two other algorithms. The curves of HEFT and DLS closely follow each other with a slight advantage of HEFT. This means that their performance on benchmark instances is nearly identical.

To quantify the impact of algorithm running time, we have computed for each run effective makespan including the algorithm running time. The performance profiles for effective makespans are presented on the right side of Fig. 3. The situation has dramatically changed from the original curves plotted on the left side. Lookahead has lost its competitiveness due to prohibitively high running times and is outperformed by other algorithms. Similarly, the DLS curve now is moved far below HEFT. The clear winner is HEFT due to its both efficient and low-complexity heuristic. Note that the running time of Lookahead can be improved by limiting its depth, e.g. considering only task children. Investigating whether this will allow to outperform HEFT in terms of effective makespan is left for future work.

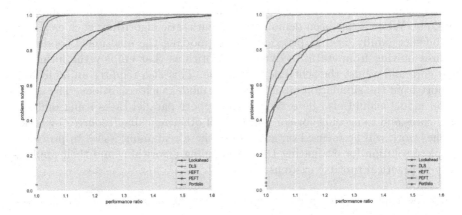

Fig. 3. Performance profiles (left – for original makespan, right – for effective makespan including the algorithm running time).

6   Conclusion

Currently there is a gap between research and practice related to efficient execution of DAGs such as workflows in distributed computing environments. Workflow runtime systems often resort to simple strategies instead of implementing advanced scheduling algorithms proposed by researchers. This is caused by the lack of common benchmarks for evaluation of such algorithms on real-world application instances and in realistic conditions similar to production systems.

In this paper we have addressed the first part of this problem by proposing a simulation-based benchmark for evaluating DAG scheduling algorithms based on a large set of real-world workflow instances and realistic cluster configurations with multicore machines. The benchmark files and documentation are published on GitHub[2]. We applied this benchmark for evaluation of several well-known static and dynamic algorithms. The obtained results demonstrate that the proposed benchmark allows to clearly separate and compare the algorithms' performance from different angles such as schedule length and running time, and to make important observations. In particular, static algorithms can significantly outperform dynamic ones on benchmark instances, performing within 3% of the lower bound in 50% cases and achieving the mean DFB below 1%. However, the algorithm running time of some static algorithms may be prohibitive for practical use. We hope that this benchmark will serve as a foundation for better evaluation of DAG scheduling algorithms, including the new ones, and their potential use in real-world systems.

To completely connect research and practice, we also need to incorporate in this benchmark the realistic conditions present in production systems as discussed in [7]. These conditions include different aspects of uncertainty and dynamicity such as the lack of accurate estimations of task execution or data transfer times, network contention, machine failures and system reconfigurations, etc. While it has been demonstrated that static algorithms such as HEFT can be successfully used in practice [23], supporting the mentioned conditions requires moving from static to dynamic algorithms that employ the former in their core and adjust the schedule in runtime. This also requires an additional support from the simulation environment to model such conditions. The application model should also be extended to support parallel tasks using multiple CPU cores and to account for consumption of other machine resources by tasks. Further work will be focused on addressing these remaining issues to provide a complete solution for evaluating DAG scheduling algorithms and their applicability in practical runtime systems.

Acknowledgments. This work is supported by the Russian Science Foundation (project 22-21-00812).

References

1. Adhikari, M., Amgoth, T., Srirama, S.N.: A survey on scheduling strategies for workflows in cloud environment and emerging trends. ACM Comput. Surv. (CSUR) **52**(4), 1–36 (2019)
2. Arabnejad, H., Barbosa, J.G.: List scheduling algorithm for heterogeneous systems by an optimistic cost table. IEEE Trans. Parallel Distrib. Syst. **25**(3), 682–694 (2014)

---

[2] https://github.com/osukhoroslov/wf-scheduling-benchmark.

3. Arya, L.K., Verma, A.: Workflow scheduling algorithms in cloud environment-a survey. In: 2014 Recent Advances in Engineering and Computational Sciences (RAECS), pp. 1–4 (2014)
4. Badia Sala, R.M., Ayguadé Parra, E., Labarta Mancho, J.J.: Workflows for science: a challenge when facing the convergence of HPC and big data. Supercomput. Front. Innov. **4**(1), 27–47 (2017)
5. Bharathi, S., Chervenak, A., Deelman, E., Mehta, G., Su, M.H., Vahi, K.: Characterization of scientific workflows. In: 2008 Third Workshop on Workflows in Support of Large-Scale Science, pp. 1–10. IEEE (2008)
6. Bittencourt, L.F., Sakellariou, R., Madeira, E.R.M.: DAG scheduling using a lookahead variant of the heterogeneous earliest finish time algorithm. In: 2010 18th Euromicro Conference on Parallel, Distributed and Network-Based Processing, pp. 27–34, February 2010
7. Casanova, H., Wong, Y.C., Pottier, L., da Silva, R.F.: On the feasibility of simulation-driven portfolio scheduling for cyberinfrastructure runtime systems. In: Job Scheduling Strategies for Parallel Processing (2022)
8. Coleman, T., Casanova, H., Pottier, L., Kaushik, M., Deelman, E., da Silva, R.F.: WfCommons: a framework for enabling scientific workflow research and development. Futur. Gener. Comput. Syst. **128**, 16–27 (2022)
9. Deelman, E., Gannon, D., Shields, M., Taylor, I.: Workflows and e-science: an overview of workflow system features and capabilities. Futur. Gener. Comput. Syst. **25**(5), 528–540 (2009)
10. Deelman, E., et al.: Pegasus, a workflow management system for science automation. Futur. Gener. Comput. Syst. **46**, 17–35 (2015)
11. Dolan, E.D., Moré, J.J.: Benchmarking optimization software with performance profiles. Math. Program. **91**, 201–213 (2002)
12. Durillo, J.J., Nae, V., Prodan, R.: Multi-objective energy-efficient workflow scheduling using list-based heuristics. Futur. Gener. Comput. Syst. **36**, 221–236 (2014)
13. Garey, M.R., Johnson, D.S.: Computers and Intractability, vol. 174. Freeman, San Francisco (1979)
14. Gupta, A., Garg, R.: Workflow scheduling in heterogeneous computing systems: a survey. In: 2017 International Conference on Computing and Communication Technologies for Smart Nation (IC3TSN), pp. 319–326. IEEE (2017)
15. Kwok, Y.K., Ahmad, I.: Benchmarking the task graph scheduling algorithms. In: Proceedings of the First Merged International Parallel Processing Symposium and Symposium on Parallel and Distributed Processing, pp. 531–537. IEEE (1998)
16. Liu, J., Pacitti, E., Valduriez, P., Mattoso, M.: A survey of data-intensive scientific workflow management. J. Grid Comput. **13**, 457–493 (2015)
17. Luo, J., Zhou, Y., Li, X., Yuan, M., Yao, J., Zeng, J.: Learning to optimize DAG scheduling in heterogeneous environment. arXiv preprint arXiv:2103.06980 (2021)
18. Mao, M., Humphrey, M.: Auto-scaling to minimize cost and meet application deadlines in cloud workflows. In: Proceedings of 2011 International Conference for High Performance Computing, Networking, Storage and Analysis, pp. 1–12 (2011)
19. Orhean, A.I., Pop, F., Raicu, I.: New scheduling approach using reinforcement learning for heterogeneous distributed systems. J. Parallel Distrib. Comput. **117**, 292–302 (2018)
20. Rodriguez, M.A., Buyya, R.: A taxonomy and survey on scheduling algorithms for scientific workflows in IaaS cloud computing environments. Concurr. Comput. Pract. Exp. **29**(8), e4041 (2017)

21. Sih, G.C., Lee, E.A.: A compile-time scheduling heuristic for interconnection-constrained heterogeneous processor architectures. IEEE Trans. Parallel Distrib. Syst. **4**(2), 175–187 (1993)
22. Sinnen, O.: Task Scheduling for Parallel Systems. Wiley, New York (2007)
23. Sukhoroslov, O.: Supporting efficient execution of workflows on everest platform. In: Voevodin, V., Sobolev, S. (eds.) Supercomputing: 5th Russian Supercomputing Days, RuSCDays 2019, Moscow, Russia, 23–24 September 2019, Revised Selected Papers 5, vol. 1129, pp. 713–724. Springer, Cham (2019). https://doi.org/10.1007/978-3-030-36592-9_58
24. Sukhoroslov, O.: Toward efficient execution of data-intensive workflows. J. Supercomput. **77**(8), 7989–8012 (2021)
25. Sukhoroslov, O., Gorokhovskii, M., Ilgovskiy, R., Kuskarov, T., Semenov, Y., Vetrov, A.: Towards a general framework for studying resource management in large scale distributed systems. In: 4th International Workshop on Information, Computation, and Control Systems for Distributed Environments (ICCS-DE 2022), pp. 79–96 (2022)
26. Sukhoroslov, O., Nazarenko, A., Aleksandrov, R.: An experimental study of scheduling algorithms for many-task applications. J. Supercomput. **75**, 7857–7871 (2019)
27. Topcuoglu, H., Hariri, S., Wu, M.Y.: Performance-effective and low-complexity task scheduling for heterogeneous computing. IEEE Trans. Parallel Distrib. Syst. **13**(3), 260–274 (2002)

Classification of Cells Mapping Schemes Related to Orthogonal Diagonal Latin Squares of Small Order

Eduard Vatutin[1] and Oleg Zaikin[2]([✉])

[1] Southwest State University, Kursk, Russia
`evatutin@rambler.ru`
[2] ISDCT SB RAS, Irkutsk, Russia
`oleg.zaikin@icc.ru`

Abstract. Volunteer computing is a cheap yet efficient type of distributed computing, where desktops of private persons are united into projects. Some of these projects are aimed at finding new mathematical objects based on orthogonal systems of Latin squares. In 2021, new systems of orthogonal diagonal Latin squares of order 10 were found in a volunteer computing project. This was done using cells mapping schemes related to extended self-orthogonal diagonal Latin squares. In the present study, a classification of such schemes is proposed. The classification is built upon a structure of a multiset of cycle lengths, when a scheme is considered a permutation. For orders 1–9, the classification is constructed completely on a computer, while for order 10 only some classes are determined via volunteer computing. Finally, for order 10 new orthogonal systems were investigated using the cells mapping schemes and a SAT solver on a computer. It is described how the latter results can lead to finding the remaining classes for order 10 via volunteer computing.

Keywords: Computational combinatorics · Latin square · MOLS · Cells mapping scheme · Volunteer computing · SAT

1 Introduction

Distributed computing is a powerful method for solving computationally hard problems which can be divided into independent or slightly dependent subproblems. In general, computational resources of various types are leveraged to solve the obtained subproblems: supercomputers, servers, desktops, etc. Suppose that only idle computational resources of desktops owned by private persons are at hand, and these resources are managed by a server owned by a scientific group. By managing it is meant that the desktops periodically request jobs from the server and report results to the server via the Internet. This type of distributed computing is called volunteer computing [1]. The first volunteer computing project was launched back in 1996, and since that time numerous scientific results in medicine, astronomy, earth sciences, and mathematics have been

V. Voevodin et al. (Eds.): RuSCDays 2023, LNCS 14389, pp. 21–34, 2023.
https://doi.org/10.1007/978-3-031-49435-2_2

obtained in dozens of volunteer computing projects. As a rule, such projects are created on the basis of some middleware that includes server software, project web site, and client software for main operating systems. At the present moment, the most popular middleware of this type is BOINC [1]. If a project is maintained properly and volunteers' feedback is taken into account, then huge computational resources can be gathered.

Combinatorics is a area of mathematics aimed at finding, counting, and enumerating finite mathematical structures. One of the most well-studied structures of this type is Latin square [6]. A Latin square of order N is a square table of size $N \times N$ filled with N different elements in such a way that each row and each column contains all the elements. In other words, there is no repetition of elements in each row and each column of the square. A Latin square is diagonal if additionally both its main diagonal and main anti-diagonal have the same described feature. Perhaps the most significant relation between two Latin squares of the same order is orthogonality. Consider two Latin squares of order N. Construct one more square (not Latin one), where each cell contains an ordered pair of the corresponding elements from the Latin squares' cells. If the constructed square contains all N^2 different ordered pairs of elements (i.e. no pair occurs more than once), then two Latin squares are orthogonal. If a Latin square is orthogonal to its transpose (in this case the Latin square without loss of generality is considered matrix), then it is self-orthogonal. In [11], extended self-orthogonal Latin square was proposed. Such a Latin square is orthogonal to some Latin square from the same main class. A main class in turn is an equivalence class, where row and columns are simultaneously permuted in a certain sense [11]. Since for any Latin square its transpose is in the same main class, then self-orthogonality is a special case of extended self-orthogonality.

The present paper is an improvement of the paper [15], where it was proposed to search for systems of orthogonal diagonal Latin squares via cells mapping schemes. In fact, such a scheme describes how a Latin square can be mapped to another Latin square. The present paper proposes a classification of types of cells mapping schemes that correspond to extended self-orthogonal Latin squares. This classification is built upon a structure of a miltiset of cycle lengths when a scheme is considered a permutation. For orders 1–9, the classification is presented completely. A for order 10, the corresponding problem is time-consuming. For this order, only some classes are determined via volunteer computing. Finally, for some schemes new systems of orthogonal diagonal Latin squares are found via the SAT approach. According to this approach, a considered combinatorial problem is reduced to the Boolean satisfiability problem (SAT) by constructing a nonlinear equation $F = True$, where F is a propositional Boolean formula. Then a solution of this equation is found (if any) via a SAT solver.

The paper's structure is as follow. Preliminaries on orthogonal Latin squares, cells mapping schemes, and SAT are given in Sect. 2. Section 3 proposes the classification of cells mapping schemes related to extended self-orthogonal Latin squares and presents the complete results for orders 1–9 and partial results for order 10. Section 4 describes how new orthogonal systems of order 10 are found by reducing to SAT and using SAT solvers.

2   Preliminaries

This section briefly gives preliminaries on orthogonal Latin squares.

2.1   Mutually Orthogonal Diagonal Latin Squares

Hereinafter $MO(D)LS$ stands for a set of *mutually orthogonal (diagonal) Latin squares*, i.e. such a set of (diagonal) Latin squares, where all possible pairs of squares are orthogonal. Consider two Latin squares A and B. A MOLS is formed if A is orthogonal to B. Now consider three Latin squares A, B, and C. In this case they form a MOLS if A is orthogonal to B, A is orthogonal to C, and B is orthogonal to C.

A standard approach to finding MOLS is the Euler-Parker method [8], where for a given square all its transversals are constructed, and then all orthogonal mates (if any) are found based on the transversals. This problem can be efficiently reduced to the exact cover problem. The latter is NP-complete, so no polynomial algorithm for its solving is known (though, it can exist), but any presented solution (a cover) can be verified in polynomial time. However, many interesting instances of the exact cover problem can be efficiently solved by DLX, a dancing-links-based implementation of the algorithm X [3]. When the Euler-Parker method is applied along with DLX, all MODLS for about 900–1000 DLSs of order 10 can be found per second. If symmetrically placed transversals in a LS are put in place of the main diagonal and main anti-diagonal by rearranging rows and columns, then the rate is increased to 8000–9000 DLSs per second because it is not needed to construct a set of transversals for each DLS separately within the corresponding main class of LS. Meanwhile, generators of LS/DLS of a certain type (e.g., symmetric squares) have much higher rate—about 6.6 million DLSs per second when implementations based on nested loops with specified order of cells' filling along with bit arithmetic are used [5]. In some cases, a search space may decrease by 3–4 orders by dividing into equivalence classes of some type.

A promising direction is to find all MODLS of a special type with the rate close to the DLS generators. The simplest known example of this idea is based on *self-orthogonal Latin square* (SOLS), a Latin square that is orthogonal to its transpose (when the square is considered a matrix) and For diagonal case SODLS is defined similarly. It is clear, that transversals are not needed in this case to find MOLS/MODLS. Since transposing is an extremely fast operation, the rate of finding MOLS/MODLS is very high. However, very limited number of MOLS/MODLS can be found in such a way. To overcome this issue, in [11] *extended self-orthogonal Latin square* (ESOLS) was introduced. It denotes a Latin square that is orthogonal to some Latin square from the same main class [11]. ESODLS is defined similarly for diagonal case. *Main class isomorphism* is an equivalence relation on the set of (diagonal) Latin squares [12]. According to this relation, all (diagonal) Latin squares can be divided into *main classes*, where any (diagonal) Latin square can be obtained by applying equivalent transformations to any other (diagonal) Latin square [12] (main classes for LS and DLS formally are not same, but have similar definitions). There are two types of such transformations for DLS called *M-transformations*. According to the first one, two middle-symmetrical columns are permuted, and then two rows with the same indices are permuted as well. The second type permutes two columns in the left half of a square, permutes two middle-symmetrical columns in the right part, and finally the permutation is done for rows with the same indices. In combination with the rotation, reflection, and transpose transformations, they form a complete set of equivalent transformations, used in practice to construct main classes and to form ESODLS CMSs for a selected order. Note that ESOLS/ESODLS is a generalization of SOLS/SODLS.

2.2   Cells Mapping Schemes

String representation of a Latin square is a string where square's elements are listed left-to-right and top-to-bottom. Consider string representations of two Latin squares A and B of order N. A *cells mapping scheme* (CMS) for an ordered pair (A, B) is a permutation p of N^2 integer numbers from $0, \ldots, N^2 - 1$ such that $p[i] = j, 0 \le i, j \le N^2 - 1$ iff $A[i] = B[j]$. In other words, a CMS maps one Latin square to another. An example of two Latin squares of order 10 and a matching CMS is shown in Fig. 1.

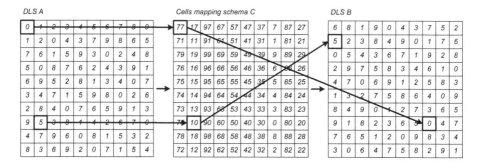

Fig. 1. An example of CMS of order 10.

For some CMSs there are no matching MOLS. An example is *trivial CMS* that maps a Latin square onto itself. Any permutation can be represented by its cycles. *Canonical CMS* of order N has N 1-cycles and $N^2 - N$ 2-cycles. A canonical CMS can be easily constructed given any pair of MOLS.

If a CMS is applied many times, a cycle of MO(D)LS $L_0 \rightarrow L_1 \rightarrow \ldots L_{n-1} \rightarrow L_0$ can be obtained. In this cycle, some MO(D)LS can be equivalent to each other up to the normalization, so the length of the cycle of normalized MO(D)LS may be a multiple less than the length of the obtained cycle of MODLS of the general type.

3   List of Distinct Multisets of Cycle Lengths

Consider a trivial CMS for a given Latin square's order N and apply all possible combinations of M-transformations to it. As a result, a set of ESODLS CMS with the cardinality of $4 \times 2^m \times m!$ is obtained, where $m = \lfloor \frac{N}{2} \rfloor$. For example, for order 10, it was calculated in [15] that there are 15 360 ESODLS CMSs. For small order, multisets of cycle lengths, which correspond to the obtained set of ESODLS CMS, are presented below. Tables 1, 2, 3, 4, 5 and 6 present data for orders 4, 5, 7, 8, 9, 10. If there is a pair of matching MODLS for a multiset, then in the column MODLS the corresponding structure name from [13] is given, otherwise it is "-". In the column CMS, the corresponding CMS are mentioned (if any).

Table 1. List of multisets of cycle lengths for ESODLS CMS of order 4.

No.	Multiset	MODLS	CMS
1	{1:16}	-	trivial CMS 0
2	{1:4, 2:6}	once, 1 CF	canonical CMS 1
3	{2:8}	-	-
4	{4:4}	once, 1 CF	CMS 3

Table 2. List of multisets of cycle lengths for ESODLS CMS of order 5.

No.	Multiset	MODLS	CMS
1	{1:25}	-	trivial CMS 0
2	{1:5, 2:10}	once, 1 CF	canonical CMS 1
3	{1:1, 4:6}	once, 1 CF	CMS 13
4	{1:1, 2:12}	-	-
4	{1:9, 2:8}	-	-

For order 1, there is only one multiset {1:1} that corresponds to trivial CMS 0, and there is a matching pair of MODLS. The multisets for order 2 are as follows:

- {1:4};
- {1:2, 2:1};
- {2:2};
- {4:1}.

For order 3 the multisets are

Table 3. List of multisets of cycle lengths for ESODLS CMS of order 7.

No.	Multiset	MODLS	CMS
1	{1:49}	-	trivial CMS 0
2	{1:7, 2:21}	once, 1 CF	canonical CMS 1
3	{1:1, 4:12}	clique-4, 1 CF	CMS 3
4	{1:9, 2:20}	-	-
5	{1:3, 2:23}	-	-
6	{1:1, 3:16}	-	-
7	{1:1, 3:2, 6:7}	once, 1 CF	CMS 9
8	{1:1, 12:4}	clique-4, 1 CF	CMS 59
9	{1:25, 2:12}	-	-
10	{1:15, 2:17}	-	-
11	{1:1, 2:24}	-	-
12	{1:1, 6:8}	-	-
13	{1:9, 4:10}	-	-
14	{1:3, 2:3, 4:10}	-	-
15	{1:5, 2:10, 4:6}	-	-
16	{1:1, 2:4, 4:10}	-	-

- {1:9};
- {1:3, 2:3};
- {1:1, 4:2};
- {1:1, 2:4}.

For both order 2 and 3, the first two multisets correspond to trivial CMS 0 and canonical CMS 1, respectively, while there are no matching pairs of MODLS at all (it is well known that DLS are not exist for orders 2 and 3).

Note, that since the least common multiple (LCM) of 1, 3, and 6 is 6, for multiset 7 and order 7, an expected structure is the cycle of length 6, but a 1 CF once is found instead. In fact, in the found cycle the lengths of 6 MODLS are equal every second time to the normalization. It means that the LCM's value does not guarantee that a cycle of MODLS of this length will be obtained. The latter can have less length which is a multiple of LCM.

For order 6, there are following multisets:

- {1:36};
- {1:6, 2:15};
- {2:18};
- {4:9};
- {1:4, 2:16};
- {3:12};
- {3:2, 6:5};

Table 4. List of multisets of cycle lengths for ESODLS CMS of order 8.

No.	Multiset	MODLS	CMS
1	{1:64}	-	trivial CMS 0
2	{1:8, 2:28}	bipartite graph 4-4, 2 CF	canonical CMS 1
3	{2:32}	-	-
4	{4:16}	N8HUGE824, 657 CF	CMS 3
5	{1:16, 2:24}	-	-
6	{1:4, 3:20}	N8HUGE824, 657 CF	CMS 536
7	{1:2, 2:1, 3:2, 6:9}	N8HUGE824, 657 CF	CMS 33
8	{2:2, 6:10}	N8HUGE824, 657 CF	CMS 488
9	{4:1, 12:5}	N8HUGE824, 657 CF	CMS 35
10	{1:36, 2:14}	-	-
11	{1:12, 2:26}	-	-
12	{1:4, 2:30}	-	-
13	{2:2, 3:12, 6:4}	-	-
14	{2:2, 3:4, 6:8}	-	-
15	{8:8}	N8HUGE824, 657 CF	CMS 133
16	{1:4, 6:10}	-	-
17	{2:8, 4:12}	-	-
18	{1:4, 2:6, 4:12}	N8HUGE824, 657 CF	CMS 309
19	{1:16, 4:12}	-	-

- {6:6};
- {12:3};
- {1:16, 2:10};
- {1:8, 2:14};
- {1:4, 4:8};
- {1:2, 2:1, 4:8};
- {2:2, 4:8};
- {1:4, 2:6, 4:5}.

Only the first two of them correspond to CMSs: trivial CMS 0 and canonical CMS 1, respectively. There are no matching MODLS for all multisets (it is well known that MODLS are not exist for order 6).

As for order 10, there are 43 multisets, and for most of them the matching MODLS have not been found yet. The multisets with known matching MODLS are presented in Table 6.

The remaining multisets are as follows in the format "multiset's number, multiset":

- 3, {2:50};
- 7, {1:4, 2:6, 3:2, 6:13};

Table 5. List of multisets of cycle lengths for ESODLS CMS of order 9.

No.	Multiset	MODLS	CMS
1	{1:81}	-	trivial CMS 0
2	{1:9, 2:36}	3LOOPS4, 2 CF	canonical CMS 1
3	{1:1, 4:20}	once, 1 CF	CMS 3
4	{1:25, 2:28}	-	-
5	{1:5, 2:38}}	-	-
6	{1:9, 3:24}	triple, 1 CF	CMS 8
7	{1:3, 2:3, 3:2, 6:11}	clique-6, 1 CF	CMS 9
8	{1:1, 4:2, 12:6}	61824N374064M198C, 198 CF	CMS 19
9	{1:1, 2:40}	-	-
10	{1:49, 2:16}	-	-
11	{1:21, 2:30}	-	-
12	{1:1, 2:4, 3:16, 6:4}	552N720M5C, 5 CF	CMS 104
13	{1:3, 2:3, 3:6, 6:9}	113616N675264M177C, 177 CF	CMS 106
14	{1:1, 8:10}	113616N675264M177C, 177 CF	CMS 108
15	{1:9, 6:12}	552N720M5C, 5 CF	CMS 112
16	{1:1, 2:12, 4:14}	113616N675264M177C, 177 CF	CMS 157
17	{1:5, 2:10, 4:14}	-	-
18	{1:25, 4:14}	-	-
19	{1:1, 2:4, 6:12}	clique-6, 1 CF	CMS 296
20	{1:9, 2:8, 4:14}	bipartite graph 4-4, 2 CF	CMS 308

- 8, {2:8, 6:14};
- 9, {4:4, 12:7};
- 10, {1:4, 4:24};
- 11, {1:2, 2:1, 4:24};
- 12, {2:2, 4:24};
- 13, {5:20};
- 14, {5:2, 10:9};
- 15, {10:10};
- 16, {20:5};
- 17, {1:4, 2:48};
- 18, {2:8, 3:12, 6:8};
- 21, {1:8, 2:46};
- 22, {1:4, 2:6, 3:20, 6:4};
- 23, {1:4, 2:6, 3:4, 6:12};
- 24, {1:4, 8:12};
- 25, {1:2, 2:1, 8:12};
- 26, {2:2, 8:12};
- 27, {4:1, 8:12};

Table 6. List of multisets of cycle lengths for ESODLS CMS of order 10 such that matching MODLS are found or their absence is proven.

No.	Multiset	MODLS	CMS
1	{1:100}	-	trivial CMS 0
2	{1:10, 2:45}	once, 1 CF	canonical CMS 1
4	{4:25}	cycle-4, 1 CF	CMS 47
5	{1:36, 2:32}	-	-
6	{1:16, 3:28}	-	-
19	{1:64, 2:18}	-	-
20	{1:16, 2:42}	-	-
28	{1:16, 6:14}	-	-
38	{1:36, 4:16}	-	-
39	{1:24, 2:38}	-	-
41	{1:16, 2:10, 4:16}	-	-

- 29, {2:8, 3:8, 6:10};
- 30, {3:12, 4:4, 12:4};
- 31, {3:2, 4:4, 6:5, 12:4};
- 32, {4:4, 6:6, 12:4};
- 33, {1:4, 2:6, 12:7};
- 34, {1:4, 2:16, 4:16};
- 35, {1:6, 2:15, 4:16};
- 36, {2:18, 4:16};
- 37, {1:4, 2:6, 4:21};
- 40, {1:4, 2:6, 6:14};
- 42, {1:8, 2:14, 4:16};
- 43, {1:8, 2:28, 4:9}.

For all cases when MODLS were found, examples of DLSs which are part of these MODLS are presented below in the string representation. For each DLS, its order and multiset number in accordance to the tables are given.

- N = 4, multisets 2 and 4: 0123230132101032.
- N = 5, multisets 2 and 3: 01234234014012312340340 12.
- N = 7, miltisets 2 and 7: 01234562365041425016364123051153462030465 125601234.
- N = 7, miltisets 3 and 8: 01234562315640564012340623156201534153 40 623456201.
- N = 8, miltiset 2: 0123456723016745476503216547210332105476745612 305674301210327654.
- N = 8, miltiset 4: 0123456723107645547610326754320176325410326701 544501672310452376.

- N = 8, miltisets 6, 8, and 18: 01234567230167454567012367452301321076541032547676543210547610 32.
- N = 8, miltisets 7 and 9: 01234567230167454510762356743012673254017456123030652174124703 56.
- N = 8, miltiset 15: 01234567123074565072634136142705436152702507163474563012674501 23.
- N = 9, miltiset 2: 01234567823067814586715430214586702335421078667803245178642153 04215038675037862 14.
- N = 9, miltiset 3: 01234567812358674053472108634567280148103726527610845386721053 4750864312608453 127.
- N = 9, miltiset 6: 01234567812368754048570132670145683263487201557613820484026315 7358024761267510 483.
- N = 9, miltiset 7: 01234567823508176478640325152713084637865410246172803585327641 0640817523104562 387.
- N = 9, miltiset 8: 01234567823568071442610835757086243110745382664301728585472610 3368271540781534 062.
- N = 9, miltisets 12 and 15: 01234567826317085440562813767081254312853470635406728183670142554 7286310781453062.
- N = 9, miltiset 13: 01234567824810673562543801716078435275406128348725316030157284687 3610524536827401.
- N = 9, miltisets 14 and 16: 01234567812806473535682140778340615257021834686153702443718256060475 3281245670813.
- N = 9, miltiset 19: 01234567823547680182415376078063415264851032740128753657680124315376 2084367028415.
- N = 9, miltiset 20: 01234567812308654754783012647851306220576841336120478563012785485467 1230786452301.
- N = 10, miltiset 2: 0123456789120487953676593804219836047215348210569763752910485741638 9024968712350251 09648738097523164.
- N = 10, miltiset 4: 0123456789120679834536798425104085237196594836027178640139526452179038951 76048232390581 4678731925604.

Consider a CMS with more than N fixed points, i.e. a multiset of the kind $\{1{:}X,\dots\}$, where $X > N$. For such a CMS no matching pair of MODLS exists because there are only N pairs of elements $(0,0),(1,1),\dots,(N-1,N-1)$ [15]. The number of distinct multisets of cycle lengths in the CMS is the following integer sequence: 1, 4, 4, 4, 5, 15, 16, 19, 20, 43, ... which is not yet presented in the On-Line Encyclopedia of Integer Sequences (OEIS) [9].

To find cycles of MODLS of order 10, which match ESODLS CMS of order 10, small set of computing experiments were held in the volunteer computing project Gerasim@home [14]. Within these experiments, one of the CMSs was randomly selected, 8–10 its cells were filled using random values, the rest were filled by exhaustive search with time limit. As a result, several cycles from MODLS were found, and it turned out that all of them have either length 2 or 4. An exhaustive search is needed to find rare combinatorial structures of MODLS of order 10, which comprise cycles of MODLS of distinct lengths, or to prove that no ESODLS compared to known 33 240 ones exist (see numerical series A309210 in OEIS[1]).

---

[1] https://oeis.org/A309210.

4 Searching for MODLS of Order 10 via ESODLS CMS and SAT

Any combinatorial problem can be efficiently reduced to the Boolean satisfiability problem (SAT [16]). In SAT, an arbitrary propositional Boolean formula F over n Boolean variables is considered. In its decision form, SAT is to determine if there exists an assignment of variables' values such that F evaluates to True. If there is at least one such *satisfying assignment*, then F if *satisfiable*, otherwise it is *unsatisfiable*. In the search form, SAT is to find a satisfying assignment if F is satisfiable, and to prove unsatisfiability otherwise. The decision form is NP-complete, while the search form is NP-hard. It means that at the moment no polynomial algorithm for solving SAT is known. While in theory any propositional Boolean formulas are considered, in practice usually the Conjunctive Normal Form (CNF), that is a conjunction of disjunctions, is used for this purpose.

The main complete algorithm for solving SAT is Conflict-Driven Clause Learning (CDCL) [7]. Recently, a CDCL solver was applied to find pairs of MODLS of order 10 such that the squares match given ESODLS CMS [15]. In particular, CMS 1234, 3407, and 4951 were considered, and only for the first two of them pairs of MODLS were found. Apparently, no pair of MODLS matches CMS 1234, but it was not proven in [15]. As for CMS 3407 and 4951, the search was not exhaustive, so not all pairs were found.

In the present paper, it was decided to improve the results from [10]. In [10], the notion of *X-based partially filled diagonal Latin squares* was introduced. In such partially filled Latin squares, both the main diagonal and main anti-diagonal are known, while values of the remaining cells are unknown. New equivalence classes were formed in [10]. First, all distinct partially filled Latin squares with known main diagonal and anti-diagonal are formed. Then all possible M-transformations (see Subsect. 2.1) are applied to them and the obtained partial Latin squares are normalized by the main diagonal. As a result, in these X-based partially filled diagonal Latin squares, the main diagonal has values $0, \ldots, N-1$, while the main anti-diagonal is also known, but it may have any values. Finally, lexicographically minimal representatives are chosen, and each of them corresponds to an equivalence class (there are 67 equivalence classes for DLSs of order 10). Each diagonal Latin square can be transformed to the one of 67 lexicographically minimal X-based partial fillings form. Such representatives are called *strongly normalized* DLSs.

All three CNFs, constructed in [15] were taken. They encode the search for pairs of MODLS of order 10 which match CMS 1234, 3407, and 4951. In these CNFs, the most non-trivial part is the orthogonality condition. The naive encoding of this condition (see, e.g., [4]) was implemented in the CNFs. Based on each CNF, a family of 67 CNFs was constructed by assigning values of the corresponding X-based partially filled diagonal Latin squares to the first square. Then on the obtained 201 CNFs the sequential CDCL solver KISSAT [2] of version 3.0.0 was run on a computer, equipped with AMD 3900X, in the single-threaded mode. As a result, all 67 CNFs based on CMS 1234 turned out to be unsatisfiable.

It means that it was proven via the SAT approach that there is no pair of MODLS of order 10 such that any of two squares is strongly normalized, and they match CMS 1234. As for the runtime, on 58 CNFs it took a fraction of a second, while on the remaining 9 CNFs the average runtime was 1 h 16 min. The same approach was applied to CMS 3407 and 4951. In both cases, 39 CNFs out of 67 were very simple for the SAT solver, while on the remaining 28 CNFs the runtime was about 20 min–1 h 20 min. All CNFs turned out to be unsatisfiable as well. So the non-existence of matching pairs of MODLS of order 10 was also proven for CMS 3407 and 4951.

Finally, the same approach was applied to CMS 5999. The runtime on the corresponding 67 CNFs was similar to that on the first 3 CMSs, but here 1 CNF turned out to be satisfiable—the one that corresponds to the following 6th X-based partially filled diagonal Latin square:

$$
\begin{pmatrix}
0 & - & - & - & - & - & - & - & - & 1 \\
- & 1 & - & - & - & - & - & - & 0 & - \\
- & - & 2 & - & - & - & - & 3 & - & - \\
- & - & - & 3 & - & - & 2 & - & - & - \\
- & - & - & - & 4 & 6 & - & - & - & - \\
- & - & - & - & 7 & 5 & - & - & - & - \\
- & - & - & 8 & - & - & 6 & - & - & - \\
- & - & 9 & - & - & - & - & 7 & - & - \\
- & 5 & - & - & - & - & - & - & 8 & - \\
4 & - & - & - & - & - & - & - & - & 9
\end{pmatrix}.
$$

Moreover, all 8 solutions for the corresponding CNFs were found. It means that there are 8 pairs of MODLS of order 10 such that any of the squares is strongly normalized, and the squares match CMS 5999. One of the found pairs is as follows

$$
\begin{pmatrix}
0\,2\,5\,7\,9\,4\,8\,6\,3\,1 \\
3\,1\,6\,4\,5\,8\,7\,9\,0\,2 \\
5\,8\,2\,6\,1\,7\,9\,3\,4\,0 \\
9\,4\,7\,3\,6\,0\,2\,8\,1\,5 \\
8\,3\,1\,9\,4\,6\,5\,0\,2\,7 \\
2\,9\,8\,1\,7\,5\,0\,4\,6\,3 \\
1\,7\,3\,8\,0\,2\,6\,5\,9\,4 \\
6\,0\,9\,2\,3\,1\,4\,7\,5\,8 \\
7\,5\,4\,0\,2\,9\,3\,1\,8\,6 \\
4\,6\,0\,5\,8\,3\,1\,2\,7\,9
\end{pmatrix}
\begin{pmatrix}
3\,8\,1\,2\,0\,4\,6\,9\,5\,7 \\
9\,2\,3\,1\,5\,0\,8\,7\,6\,4 \\
8\,4\,5\,6\,3\,9\,2\,1\,7\,0 \\
5\,9\,7\,4\,8\,2\,0\,3\,1\,6 \\
7\,0\,9\,3\,6\,5\,4\,8\,2\,1 \\
1\,6\,2\,8\,4\,7\,9\,5\,0\,3 \\
0\,5\,6\,9\,7\,3\,1\,2\,4\,8 \\
4\,1\,8\,7\,2\,6\,3\,0\,9\,5 \\
6\,3\,0\,5\,9\,1\,7\,4\,8\,2 \\
2\,7\,4\,0\,1\,8\,5\,6\,3\,9
\end{pmatrix}.
$$

In the future it is planned to process all 15 360 ESODLS CMS of order 10 in the sense it was described above. Since there are 67 X-based fillings for each such CMS, it naturally gives 1 029 120 SAT instances. Of course, some of them are very easy and will be solved on the prepossessing stage. However, it is expected that a few hundred thousand instances will remain unsolved. Since all such instances form a time-consuming experiment, it is planned to use volunteer computing to solve them. Optionally additional parallelization will be applied because in some cases it takes a modern SAT solver up to 2 h to solve an instance, while for volunteer computing about 5 min is a much more optimal limit.

5   Conclusions

The present paper proposes a classification of cells mapping schemes based on extended self-orthogonal diagonal Latin squares. For orders 1–9, the classification is fully presented, while for order 10 some parts are to be filled in the future. Some experiments for order 10 were held in a volunteer computing project. Finally, preliminary results on finding MODLS of order 10 via SAT and ESODLS CMS are given. Based on these results, it is planned to start a large-scale experiment in a volunteer computing project.

Acknowledgements. Authors are grateful to volunteers who provided their computational resources to Gerasim@home. Oleg Zaikin was funded by the Ministry of Education of the Russian Federation, project No. 121041300065-9.

References

1. Anderson, D.P.: BOINC: a platform for volunteer computing. J. Grid Comput. **18**(1), 99–122 (2020)
2. Biere, A., Fleury, M.: Gimsatul, IsaSAT and Kissat entering the SAT Competition 2022. In: Proceedings of SAT Competition 2022 - Solver and Benchmark Descriptions, pp. 10–11 (2022)
3. Knuth, D.E.: Dancing Links. Millenial Perspectives in Computer Science, pp. 187–214 (2000)
4. Kochemazov, S., Zaikin, O., Semenov, A.: The comparison of different SAT encodings for the problem of search for systems of orthogonal Latin squares. In: Proceedings of the International Conference on Mathematical and Information Technologies, pp. 155–165 (2017)
5. Kochemazov, S., Zaikin, O., Vatutin, E., Belyshev, A.: Enumerating diagonal Latin squares of order up to 9. J. Integer Seq. **23**(1), 20.1.2 (2020)
6. Laywine, C., Mullen, G.: Discrete Mathematics Using Latin Squares. Wiley-Interscience, New York (1998)
7. Marques-Silva, J.P., Sakallah, K.A.: GRASP: a search algorithm for propositional satisfiability. IEEE Trans. Comput. **48**(5), 506–521 (1999)
8. Parker, E.T.: Orthogonal Latin squares. Proc. Natl. Acad. Sci. U.S.A. **45**(6), 859–862 (1959)
9. Sloane, N.J.A.: The on-line encyclopedia of integer sequences. Electron. J. Comb. **1** (1994)
10. Vatutin, E.I., Belyshev, A.D., Nikitina, N.N., Manzuk, M.O.: Usage of X-based diagonal fillings and ESODLS CMS schemes for enumeration of main classes of diagonal Latin squares. Telecommunications **1**(1), 2–16 (2023)
11. Vatutin, E., Belyshev, A.: Enumerating the orthogonal diagonal Latin squares of small order for different types of orthogonality. In: Proceedings of the 6th Russian Supercomputing Days, pp. 586–597 (2020)

12. Vatutin, E., Belyshev, A., Kochemazov, S., Zaikin, O., Nikitina, N.: Enumeration of isotopy classes of diagonal Latin squares of small order using volunteer computing. In: Proceedings of the 4th Russian Supercomputing Days, pp. 578–586 (2018)
13. Vatutin, E., Titov, V., Zaikin, O., Kochemazov, S., Manzuk, M., Nikitina, N.: Orthogonality-based classification of diagonal Latin squares of order 10. In: Proceedings of the VIII International Conference on Distributed Computing and Grid-Technologies in Science and Education, pp. 282–287 (2018)
14. Vatutin, E., Zaikin, O., Kochemazov, S., Valyaev, S.: Using volunteer computing to study some features of diagonal Latin squares. Open Eng. **7**, 453–460 (2017)
15. Vatutin, E., Zaikin, O., Manzyuk, M., Nikitina, N.: Searching for orthogonal Latin squares via cells mapping and BOINC-based Cube-and-Conquer. In: Proceedings of the 7th Russian Supercomputing Days, pp. 498–512 (2021)
16. Zhang, H.: Combinatorial designs by SAT solvers. In: Biere, A., Heule, M., van Maaren, H., Walsh, T. (eds.) Handbook of Satisfiability - Second Edition, Frontiers in Artificial Intelligence and Applications, vol. 336, pp. 819–858. IOS Press (2021)

Comparative Analysis of Digitalization Efficiency Estimation Methods Using Desktop Grid

Alexander Bekarev[1]([✉])[iD] and Alexander Golovin[2][iD]

[1] Laboratory of Digital Technologies in Regional Development, Karelian Research Centre of RAS, Petrozavodsk, Russia
bekarev@krc.karelia.ru
[2] Institute of Applied Mathematical Research, Karelian Research Centre of RAS, Petrozavodsk, Russia
golovin@krc.karelia.ru

Abstract. In this paper we apply distributed computing to comparative analysis of digitalization efficiency estimation methods tailored to aquaculture. A modified method of digitalization efficiency estimation is presented and discussed. Numerical experiments are performed to demonstrate the capabilities of the novel approach.

Keywords: Distributed computing · Digitalization efficiency estimation · Numerical experiments

1 Introduction

As an affordable and convenient computing framework, Desktop Grids are used in various areas of the economy and economic research. Financial institutions such as banks, insurance companies and investment firms use grid computing to perform complex financial analyses, market forecasting, risk modeling and portfolio optimization [7,12]. In the oil and gas industry, grid computing is used to model and simulate the processes of petroleum exploration [22]. Desktop Grids are actively employed in modern economy driving fields such as bioinformatics. Examples include volunteer computing [15] and enterprise-level [8] projects on virtual screening. These are just a few examples of economic sectors that are using Desktop Grids, but the potential for its use is expanding to cover more and more sectors of the economy. The flexibility, efficiency and scalability of Grid systems make them an important tool for solving complex problems [1]. At the same time, to the best of our knowledge, there are no papers that suggest or apply Desktop Grids in the field of applied Regional Economy studies. The latter, however, is a very important subject of studies within the national economy. We hope that the present paper is the first contribution in this direction.

One of the key drivers of the Regional Economy is digitalization [4]. Digitalization is one of the basic components of the digital transformation of enterprises

V. Voevodin et al. (Eds.): RuSCDays 2023, LNCS 14389, pp. 35–47, 2023.
https://doi.org/10.1007/978-3-031-49435-2_3

and service companies. In this regard, digitalization of particular business processes need to be considered within the study of digitalization of the enterprise as a whole [3]. One of the ways of studying the effects of digitalization is based on the notion of *economic efficiency*.

The definition of economic efficiency as a complex characteristic allows us to consider in a single key and by common metrics both the effectiveness of a specific software developed for a specialized application area, and the effectiveness of the digitalization of the enterprise as a whole, taking into account the financial, economic and social goals of a potential customer. Determining economic efficiency of digitalization of processes is an important problem faced both by commercial enterprise and governmental organizations [6].

Classical methods of evaluating the effectiveness of software suggest the need to measure revenues and costs directly related to the implementation of software, but the main problem and difficulty lies in measuring the results (effects) from the implementation of such business processes, which may not directly participate in the formation of the final revenue component of the enterprise, but support the business processes of resource management in the process economic activity, which forms the result.

The fishing industry is one of the main branches of the economy of the Republic of Karelia, which is due to the favorable location of the region for the industrial cultivation of commercial fish, including trout. The Republic of Karelia occupies a leading position in the production of commercial trout in the Russian Federation, more than 70% of Russian garden trout are grown in the region. In the field of fish farming, there are 56 farms in the region that grow commercial products, fish planting material and carry out primary processing of fish. The Republic of Karelia also retains its position in terms of the volume of aquaculture cultivation among the subjects of the North-Western Federal District, where it ranks first in 2018.

Digitalization of agriculture and aquaculture is a novel trend due to introduction of the aqua(agri)culture 4.0 concept implemented irregularly in the world [14]. However, to the best of our knowledge, there are no methods of measuring the efficiency of digitalization tailored to aquaculture industries, which results in erroneous estimates of its effects, mainly due to a very specific set of gains and risks that are present in the industry. In particular, among the key risks that are mitigated by digitalization are the biological risks (e.g. related to the water treatment quality and water parameters control, water supply management) which are significant for raceway aquaculture and critical for the so-called recirculating aquaculture systems (RAS). At the same time, those factors are not taken into account by conventional digitalization efficiency estimators. Thus, the key novelty of the present paper is in introduction of the modified method to handle specificity of the aquaculture.

To demonstrate the effectiveness of the new method, we perform a series of numerical experiments. Due to a large number of experiments needed to gain statistical data, and independent runs that are performed, we select the Desktop Grid system as a basic computing mechanism. The BOINC system together with RBOINC package may be used to run numerical experiments and obtain the results. Application of BOINC-based Desktop Grid in the field of applied Regional Economy studies is the second key contribution of the present paper.

The structure of the paper is as follows. In Sect. 2 we perform a brief survey of the existing methods of digitalization efficiency estimation and highlight their key properties, which is needed to advocate the need of a novel method introduction. In Sect. 2.1 the novel (modified) method of digitalization efficiency estimation is introduced and discussed. Section 3 is dedicated to numerical comparison of the methods. The paper is finalized with a conclusion in Sect. 4.

2 Digitalization Efficiency Estimation Methods

In the general variety of approaches to assessing the efficiency of digital technologies, we relied on the approach of classification of methods from the point of view of the authors of [2], but since fishing enterprises are becoming increasingly involved in the process of digitalization of the economy [19], and digital products are subject to the effect of rapid obsolescence, we drew attention to more modern approaches in terms of classification of applied methods that are currently used, which in our opinion is the most reasonable, this example is reflected in the research [10]. Based on the fact that approaches to the broad definition of the term "efficiency" and the specifics of the scope of the assessment vary greatly, and the approaches themselves to assessing the efficiency of digitalization are also diverse, the authors propose a classification of methods depending on the scope of application [10].

– Evaluation of the efficiency of digital transformation projects [20], used in the fuel and energy complex. The method consists in evaluating the final result of the implementation of an innovative project and evaluating an innovative project depending on the life cycle of an innovative project (based on the calculation of classical indicators of the evaluation of an investment project: the return on investment, simple and discounted payback period of investments, the investment efficiency coefficient, net discounted income, project profitability, internal rate of return on investment);
– Evaluation of the efficiency of the digital transformation strategy [16], used in business, implemented as a system-dynamic model for evaluating the digital transformation strategy;
– A systematic approach to assessing the efficiency of digitalization [18], used for small and medium-sized manufacturing enterprises, consists in calculating the profitability of digital technologies in statics and dynamics, taking into account the time factor as the ratio of potential benefits from the introduction of digital technologies to the costs of their implementation;
– The methodology of comparative analysis in assessing the economic efficiency of the investment project [11] is used for evaluation at agricultural enterprises. The essence of the method is to compare the costs of two projects and calculate the net discounted income and payback period;

– Methodological approach to evaluating the efficiency of digital investment projects [13], a comprehensive methodological approach based on the assessment of economic efficiency and technical efficiency using the author's algorithm, including the calculation of the multidimensional average of the technical characteristics of the project and its interpretation on the scale of E.S. Harrington;
– An approach to assessing the efficiency of the implementation of smart city elements [21]. The scope of this method is urban and municipal economy. The method is implemented in three stages, as an assessment of efficiency through the urban economy digitalization efficiency index based on the calculation of the ratio of the difference between the actual and minimum time to the difference between the maximum and minimum time, an assessment through the ratio of effect to cost and an assessment through a point-rating evaluation system (based on the calculation of the average value);
– Evaluation of the efficiency of the digital ecosystem [9]. The method is used for various types of enterprises and consists in evaluating the efficiency of the digital ecosystem using fuzzy logic apparatus. As performance indicators, the author suggests 5 groups of indicators that characterize the efficiency of the marketing strategy, financial, production, organizational and branding strategy of the company.

From the presented classification, we see that the essence of the techniques varies greatly. A similar pattern is observed not only in [10], but also in the earlier classification introduced in [2]. In our opinion, this aspect depends not so much on the scope of the evaluation method, as on the tasks of digitalization in a specific area on the basis of which the evaluation method is built, this can be expressed as a conditional equality when a set of specific digitalization tasks with an understanding of the effects obtained is equal to the set of measurement points of the effects obtained from digitalization reflected in the structure of the method. Accordingly, the specifics of our method will be based on the measurement points of the effects obtained, implemented in a specific digitalization object with an architecture in the form of a general structure of business processes at aquaculture enterprises with a full set of measurement points in the form of a set of parameters for key risks and benefits.

2.1 Modified Method of Digitalization Efficiency Estimation

In this section we introduce and describe the modified method of digitalization efficiency estimation, which is based on the approach introduced in [2]. The key distinctive features of the method are related to the specificity of the aquaculture production and are based on calculation of indexes and estimation of risks that are specific to the aforementioned production field. From the practical point of view, the modified method addresses the most significant worries of the potential customer and is focused on the key points of digitalization implementation in the aquaculture industry. We note that it is impossible to directly apply the methods even from the most similar fields such as agriculture, due to dramatic difference of the business processes specificity in these two fields.

As the basis for the development of the modified efficiency estimation method, we selected the most capacious (in terms of the set of approaches used) and applicable method, Rapid Economic Justification (REJ), proposed by Microsoft. The essence of the method is a simple economic justification of investments in digitalization. The scheme of the method is presented as follows:

- Understanding business: correlation of business indicators and business processes with planned changes in the implementation of digital solutions;
- Choosing the solution itself;
- Detailed analysis of business processes;
- Profiling of all benefits of the project;
- Assessment of changes in monetary terms;
- Risk analysis;
- Calculation of financial metrics.

The methodology does not strictly regulate the choice of methods for performing each stage. The disadvantages of the method are: focus on financial metrics and lack of focus on infrastructure and strategic benefits.

The capacity of the methodology is due to a more detailed implementation of the well-known applied method "Total Cost of Ownership" (TCO) in combination with the possibility of using classical economic tools at the stage of calculating financial metrics, such as the "Payback Period" (PP) and others. It should be noted that the lack of strict regulation of the choice of methods when performing each of the stages of the REJ method makes it very convenient for applications.

Using REJ method, we have the opportunity to compare two methods at once, TCO - without taking into account the risks, and REJ itself (by taking into account the risks). The PP may be used as an additional financial indicator that directly affects the process of making a management decision (e.g. to implement or not to implement). Now we suggest the modification of the REJ method tailored to the specificity of the aquaculture field. However, we stress that the modified method can, after appropriate changes, be applied to various field requiring digitalization as well.

The modified method structure has the following steps:

1. calculation of a simple (non-discounted) *Payback Period* which answers the customer's question from the point of view of the return of the costs incurred for digitalization,

$$PP = IC/Proc,$$

where PP is the payback period, IC are the initial costs incurred for digitalization, and $Proc$ is the input of the project implementation which is calculated as the amount of actual savings, i.e. the effect;

2. calculation of a group of indicators of the consumer index (*Customer Index*) — answers the question of evaluating the results of digitalization by measuring

the actual savings, i.e. the effect obtained, depending on the tasks where the measurement points are (increase in income, turnover, customer base, cost reduction, minimizing risks and costs for them);
3. calculation of a group of indicators of key risk parameters based on the FERMA (Federation European Risk Management Associations) risk management standard — based on this standard, we answer the question of predictive assessment of the impact of digital technologies on minimizing unacceptable risk factors that can significantly threaten the functioning of fish farming enterprises.

The customer index indicators include those which are specific for the aquaculture field. In particular, the following indicators may be of use for the so-called net cage aquaculture based on natural water usage and fish growing in net cages:

– actual saving of working time;
– actual wage savings;
– actual saving of machine hours and fuel mixture.

The key risks to consider under FERMA methodology are as follows:

– technical failure and data loss;
– failure in the RAS aeration system;
– biological risks.

Thanks to digitalization, the recovery time of data loss in case of a technical failure is minimized, this risk can be determined as acceptable by the level of its impact, i.e. which does not lead to critical consequences and can be estimated in the effect of actual savings of man-hours, or in monetary terms.

Failure in the RAS aeration system and biological risks are identified as unacceptable, because their implementation carries the threat of a complete shutdown of production, i.e. the loss of all investments in fish planting material due to the death of fish both due to technical failure and due to diseases due to improper feeding regime. Automation of data collection and processing of water indicators allows you to minimize this risk by constantly monitoring water data indicators in real time.

To summarize, we note that the input of the project implementation, $Proc$, should take into account not only actual savings, but also the risk minimization and customer indices expressed in monetary terms, which is the key difference of the suggested modification of the method compared to REJ. This method can be used for estimation of the digitalization efficiency of a single company or a group of companies, and, moreover, to optimize the digitalization strategy of a company under given budget and time constraints, which we demonstrate in the next section.

3   Model

In this section we introduce and describe the model of digitalization efficiency estimation using the example of fish farming. Important parameters that characterize the farm are

- the volume of production expressed in monetary terms (denoted as V),
- the cost (capital expenses) for implementation of technical and digital solution (a_i),
- operating expenses, as a percentage per year of the cost, related to implementation and usage of technical or digital solution (b_i),
- the effect that a particular solution gives in reducing the company running costs, mitigating risks, improving customer indices, expressed as a percentage (e_i) of the company's production volume,

where $i = 1, ..., M$ and M is the number of technical and digital solutions available in the market. The farm is faced with the question of which solutions to choose, having restrictions on the available budget for digitalization (denoted as uV, where u is the percentage of the production volume V of the company) and on the acceptable payback period (denoted as t_0). Let the variable x_i be a binary variable, which indicates that the solution i is purchased. Then we can express the problem of maximization of the digitalization efficiency as follows.

$$\sum_{i=1}^{M}(Ve_i - a_ib_i)x_i \rightarrow max, \tag{1}$$

$$\sum_{i=1}^{M} a_i(1 + b_i)x_i \leq uV, \tag{2}$$

$$\frac{\sum_{i=1}^{M} a_ix_i}{\sum_{i=1}^{M}(Ve_i - a_ib_i)x_i} \leq t_0. \tag{3}$$

In expression (1), we maximize the *total effect* of digitalization. Here, Ve_i is the effect of implementation of the solution i, and a_ib_i is the operating expenses of the solution i, expressed in monetary terms. In (2), we restrict the overall annual expenses (capital and operating) for the implementation of the digital solutions. In (3), we limit the payback period for the implemented solutions, i.e. we divide the capital expenses for purchasing the solutions by the total effect of digitalization expressed in monetary terms. Essentially, the optimization problem (1)–(3) is the *knapsack problem* which is known to be NP-complete, which motivates us to use exhaustive enumeration to find the optimal *digitalization strategy* $(x_1, \ldots, x_M)$. However, such a large state space of the model determines the use of BOINC-based Desktop Grids as the key tool for the numerical experiments.

4   Numerical Experiments Based on Desktop Grid

In the present section we perform numerical studies of the proposed method in comparison to the REJ method that does not take into account the payback period. This is done by sensitivity analysis of the optimization problem (1)–(3) to the parameter t_0 with increasing t_0. The maximized total effect is then normalized to the production volume V. The coefficients of the optimizatin problem are defined in Table 1. The production volume V is defined as $19 \cdot 10^6$ RUB obtained in 3-year period (which is typical for aquaculture industry). Such a company can be considered small, with a total production volume about 50 tons.

The experiment is performed as follows. The optimization problem (1)–(3) is solved for the specific acceptable payback period t_0 which varies in the range $[0.1, 1]$ with a step 0.1. The percentage u of the production volume that can be used for digitalization is taken from the list $u = 0.1, 0.2, 0.3$. The corresponding strategies are obtained, and the normalized total effect is calculated. Finally, the results are summarized on Fig. 1. It is interesting to note the following. The normalized total effect increases with increasing acceptable payback period up to some point where the period no more affects the solution. These points may be considered as the transition points to the generic REJ method. Moreover, the upper limit for the total effect is proportional to the available budget for digitalization.

Table 1. Coefficients, a_i, b_i, e_i, of the optimization problem (1)–(3), defined by method of expert estimation, for various technical and digital solutions, $i = 1, \dots, 14$.

Technical/digital solution	Cost, a_i, RUB	Efficiency, e_i, % of V	Operating costs, b_i, % of a_i
automatic feeding systems	43900	6	30
fish counters	170000	3	25
fish sorters	95000	3	25
automatic RAS systems	350000	10	30
autonomous power supply	150000	2	20
BIG DATA technology	1000000	3	17
sediment monitoring	400000	1	5
water quality assessment	70000	10	5
security/video surveillance	24000	3	10
fish pumps/manipulators	250000	5	15
fish farm management software	90000	3	10
CRM systems	30000	3	10
external conditions assessment	10000	1	5
smart transportation systems	195000	10	5

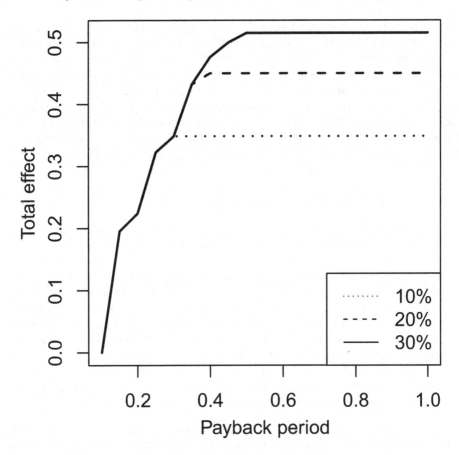

Fig. 1. Normalized total effect vs. payback period for a small-scale aquaculture production subject to digitalization with parameters defined in Sect. 4. The graphs correspond to 10, 20 and 30% of the annual budget of the company under study that are spent annually for digitalization.

4.1   Results and Discussion

It should be noted that the coefficients of the efficiency as well as the (capital/running) costs of the solutions, being the parameters of the model, were defined by means of expert-based estimation. These, however, may need appropriate correction, since the payback period for most of the solutions is unnaturally small.

The amount of computational resources for the experiment presented in this paper is rather small and in such a formulation, it can be solved on a PC using discrete optimization packages (e.g. Gurobi optimizer or Google OR-Tools among many others). However, the method allows one to calculate the effects under assumptions of, say, random production volumes of many companies, random efficiency of digital/technical solutions and other random factors, which provides a large scale experiment over the set of systems with various parameters having many independent subtasks, which is a natural problem statement for the desktop grids, due to the independence of estimates for different companies. Furthermore, we plan to expand the model by introducing the planning horizon and an additional variable, namely the year of purchasing a specific solution, which will undoubtedly result in a substantial increase in the computational complexity of the problem. Thus, we selected BOINC-based Desktop Grid as a natural venue to conduct the calculations. Moreover, the method is BOINC-ready [1] due to the implementation part which is built up with R language [17], and thus it can be run over BOINC by using the RBOINC package [5].

The modified method presented in this paper allows one to solve many tasks, in particular, the following:

- Calculation of the optimal way to digitalize an aquaculture enterprise by performing calculations immediately for the industry, for example at the regional level, which is why we need to perform calculations for a large number of enterprises at once. The need for this calculation is also due to the task of understanding how and to what extent to subsidize digitalization on a regional scale, how to get the total effect from digitalization, therefore, sampling of farms and their parameters is needed. Thus, we come to understand what kind of subsidy budget is needed for the region, so that the digitalization program would be successful and effective;
- Calculation of the total effect on the industry, which allows one to evaluate the effect of digitalization obtained at each specific fish farming enterprise, depending on its production volumes in monetary terms.

Hereafter we name several possibilities to improve the model. Firstly, the effect (efficiency) of a particular digital/technical solution can be expressed in a more detailed way. In particular, a specific risk (say, biological) is mitigated by different solutions in different ways, which gives various contributions to the total effect. Moreover, the effect may be considered as a time-dependent variable.

Another point of improvement of the model is related to "synergistic effects" that can be obtained by simultaneous implementation of several solutions. In particular, implementing analytical software together with, say, RAS automation and automatic feeders allows to dynamically optimize the feeding regimes due to available analytic based on the data obtained, which may hardly be possible if any of the aforementioned three components is missing. This may be treated in the model by means of nonlinear summands in the cumulative effect function (1).

5   Conclusion

In this paper we suggested application of Desktop Grid based distributed computing to comparative analysis of digitalization efficiency estimation methods in the field of aquaculture. A modified method of digitalization efficiency estimation was presented and discussed. Numerical experiments were performed to demonstrate the capabilities of the novel approach. It can be noted that, to the best of our knowledge, the present paper is the first paper where Desktop Grids were suggested for study of the problems in Regional Economy. However, in the present study, the statistics-based models of the business processes involved in aquaculture production, were not studied in detail, and we leave this opportunity for future research.

Currently, we are working on the possibility of taking into account additional variable parameters in our methodology when evaluating the effectiveness of digitalization, which will significantly affect the scope of possible digitalization scenarios. We are trying to use such a parameter as discounting, which will allow us to take into account the risks associated with inflation and the environmental factor as a calculation of the release of pollutants from the intensification of aquaculture production. Taking into account these parameters will allow us to adjust the methodology in accordance with the key accents reflected in the strategy for the development of the agro-industrial and fisheries complex of development until 2030. In the future, we plan to expand the task statement to assess the effectiveness of digitalization in the aggregate for all aquaculture farms in the region, thereby we will be able to assess the effectiveness of digitalization that the state implements by subsidizing this industry. Moreover, efforts are taken in the direction of studying many-year digitalization strategies instead of a single-year planning, as it was done in the present paper. All these options increase the model state space significantly, and thus the need in BOINC-based distributed computing resources is evident.

Acknowledgements. This research is supported by RSF, project No 23-21-00048. The authors thank the reviewers for carefully reading the paper and Alexander Rumyantsev for helpful discussions.

References

1. Anderson, D.: Boinc: a platform for volunteer computing. J. Grid Comput. **18** (2020)
2. Anisiforov, A., Anisiforova, L.: Methods of evaluating the effectiveness of information systems and information technologies in business [Textbook, in Russian]. Saint Petersburg State Polytechnic University, Institute of Engineering and Economics, Department of Information Systems in Economics and Management (2014)
3. Anisiforov, A., Kalyazina, S., Tereshchenko, E.: Digitalization of corporate logistics processes in the architecture of large industrial enterprises. In: Ilin, I., Jahn, C., Tick, A. (eds.) Digital Technologies in Logistics and Infrastructure, pp. 298–308. Springer, Cham (2023). https://doi.org/10.1007/978-3-031-24434-6_28
4. Asalieva, Z.A.: Priorities of digital development in Russian federation regions. Vestnik Plekhanov Russ. Univ. Econ. (6), 78–88 (2022). https://doi.org/10.21686/2413-2829-2022-6-78-88
5. Astafiev, S.N., Rumyantsev, A.S.: Distributed computing of R applications using RBOINC package with applications to parallel discrete event simulation. In: Vishnevskiy, V.M., Samouylov, K.E., Kozyrev, D.V. (eds.) Distributed Computer and Communication Networks: 24th International Conference (DCCN 2021), Moscow, 20–24 September 2021, Revised Selected Papers, pp. 396–407. Springer, Cham (2022). https://doi.org/10.1007/978-3-030-97110-6_31

6. Bekarev, A., Konovalchikova, E., Ivashko, E.: Evaluation of software effectiveness in the production of trout [in Russian]. In: Digital Technologies in Education, Science, Society, pp. 30–33. Petrozavodsk State University (2019)
7. Chang, V., Ramachandran, M.: Financial modeling and prediction as a service. J. Grid Comput. **15**(2), 177–195 (2017). https://doi.org/10.1007/s10723-017-9393-3
8. Ivashko, E.E., Nikitina, N.N., Möller, S.: High-performance virtual screening in a boinc-based enterprise desktop grid. Vestnik Yuzhno-Ural'skogo Gosudarstvennogo Universiteta. Seriya "Vychislitelnaya Matematika i Informatika" **4**(1), 57–63 (2015)
9. Kokhanova, V.S.: Fuzzy logic apparatus as a tool for assessing the effectiveness of digitalization of a company. Vestnik Universiteta (2), 36–41 (2021). https://doi.org/10.26425/1816-4277-2021-2-36-41
10. Kokuytseva, T., Ovchinnikova, O.: Methodological approaches to performance evaluation of enterprises digital transformation in high-tech industries. Creative Econ. **15**(6), 2413–2430 (2021). https://doi.org/10.18334/ce.15.6.112192'
11. Kolmykova, T., Obukhova, A., Grishaeva, O.: Assessment of economic efficiency of digital technologies introduction in agricultural enterprise. Bullet. Agrar. Sci. **2**(89), 129–136 (2021). https://doi.org/10.17238/issn2587-666x.2021.2.129 https://doi.org/10.17238/issn2587-666x.2021.2.129 https://doi.org/10.17238/issn2587-666x.2021.2.129
12. Lin, F.P., Lee, C.F., Chung, H.: Computer Technology for Financial Service, pp. 1341–1379. Springer, New York (2015). https://doi.org/10.1007/978-1-4614-7750-1_49
13. Lyubimenko, D.A., Vaisman, E.D.: Methodical approach to evaluation of effectiveness of the digital investment projects **47**(4), 718–728 (2021). https://doi.org/10.18413/2687-0932-2020-47-4-718-728
14. Monge Quevedo, A., Sandoval, A., Carreño, M., carreño, D.: Aquaculture 4.0 Is the Digital Revolution that Is Not Coming to the Little Mexican Farmers, pp. 70–75 (2021)
15. Nikitina, N., Manzyuk, M., Jukić, M., Podlipnik, Č, Kurochkin, I., Albertian, A.: Toward crowdsourced drug discovery: start-up of the volunteer computing project sidock@home. In: Voevodin, V., Sobolev, S. (eds.) Supercomputing, pp. 513–524. Springer, Cham (2021). https://doi.org/10.1007/978-3-030-92864-3_39
16. Perevoznikova, N., Myznikova, M.: Evaluating the effectiveness of the digital strategy transformations. In: Donetsk Readings 2020: Education, Science, Innovation, Culture and Modern Challenges: Proceedings of the V International Scientific Conference [in Russian], vol. 3, pp. 411–414. Donetsk National University (2020). https://elib.spbstu.ru/dl/2/id20-237.pdf
17. R Core Team. R: A Language and Environment for Statistical Computing. R Foundation for Statistical Computing, Vienna, Austria (2021). https://www.R-project.org/
18. Spatar, A., Shirokova, S.V.: Systematic approach to assess the effectivness of enterprise digital technologies. In: System Analysis in Design and Management: Collection of Scientific Papers of the XXIV International Scientific and Educational-practical Conference, 13–14 October 2020: [in 3 parts]. Part 3 [in Russian], pp. 384–394. Polytech-Press, Saint Petersburg (2020). https://elib.spbstu.ru/dl/2/id20-237.pdf
19. Tropnikova, N.: Provision of qualified personnel for marine industrial fishing enterprises as a reserve for the development of the arctic regions. Manag. Mod. Syst. **2**(26), 55–62 (2020)
20. Trusov, A., Trusov, V., Bochkarev, A.: Evaluating the effectiveness of digital transformation projects. Bullet. Sci. Conf. 106–108 (2019)

21. Tsybareva, M.E., Vasyaicheva, V.A.: Assessment of the effectiveness of implementing "smart city" elements in the process of digitalization of the urban environment. Vestnik of Samara University. Econ. Manag. **11**(2), 83–91 (2020). https://doi.org/10.18287/2542-0461-2020-11-2-83-91
22. Weidong, L., Gaishan, Z., Hailiang, W., Xianghui, X., Yujing, W., Huiqing, Z.: Application of grid computing in petroleum exploration. In: 2006 Fifth International Conference on Grid and Cooperative Computing Workshops, pp. 27–34 (2006)

Diagonalization and Canonization of Latin Squares

Eduard Vatutin[1]([✉]) [iD], Alexey Belyshev[2] [iD], Natalia Nikitina[3] [iD],
Maxim Manzuk[2] [iD], Alexander Albertian[4] [iD], Ilya Kurochkin[4] [iD],
Alexander Kripachev[1] [iD], and Alexey Pykhtin[1] [iD]

[1] Southwest State University, Kursk, Russia
evatutin@rambler.ru
[2] Internet Portal BOINC.Ru, Moscow, Russia
[3] Institute of Applied Mathematical Research, Karelian Research Center of the
Russian Academy of Sciences, Petrozavodsk, Russia
nikitina@krc.karelia.ru
[4] Institute for Information Transmission Problems of the Russian Academy of
Sciences (Kharkevich Institute), Moscow, Russia
assa@4ip.ru

Abstract. Article aimed to the description of equivalent transformations that are allow to get at least one diagonal Latin square (DLS) from all main classes of DLS included in main class of given Latin square (LS) if they are exist. Detailed description of corresponding algorithms for LS of odd and even orders is given. Estimations for time and memory complexities are presented, algorithms are provided with detailed examples. Description of the results of diagonalization and canonization is shown. They allow to get collections of orthogonal diagonal Latin squares in a more efficient way comparing with direct usage of Euler-Paker method using volunteer distributed computing projects Gerasim@Home and RakeSearch on BOINC platform. The possibility of obtaining stronger upper and lower bounds for some numerical series in OEIS connected with DLS using suggested transformations is shown. Prospects for further application of these transformations using distributed software implementation of corresponding algorithms are outlined.

Keywords: Latin squares · Diagonal Latin squares · Orthogonal diagonal Latin squares · Diagonalization · Canonization · Isomorphism classes · OEIS · Gerasim@Home · RakeSearch · BOINC

1 Introduction

One of the widely known types of combinatorial objects is Latin squares (LS) [8,9]. An LS A of order N is a square matrix of size $N \times N$, the cells $A[x, y]$, $x, y = \overline{0, N-1}$ of which are filled with elements of some alphabet U of cardinality $|U| = N$ (for definiteness, $U = \{0, 1, \ldots, N-1\}$) in such a way that the values are not duplicated in the rows and columns of the square (rows and columns are different permutations of the elements of the alphabet U). For diagonal Latin Squares (DLS), an additional requirement is added that prohibits duplication of values on the main and secondary diagonals of the square (DLS diagonals are transversals). A number of open mathematical problems are associated with LS and DLS, such as the enumeration of squares of general and special form [3,12, 14,18,21], the search for squares with an extremal value of one of the numerical characteristics (the number of transversals, intercalates, loops, orthogonal co-squares, etc.) [4,7,13,19], the construction of spectra of numerical characteristics [5], the search for analytical formulas for the corresponding numerical series, the construction of combinatorial structures from LS/DLS on the set of a binary orthogonality relation [20], etc.

When processing low-order squares (usually, $N \leq 7$), at the current level of development of computer technology and telecommunications, it is permissible to use the exhaustive (Brute Force) enumeration method to enumerate LS/DLS of a given type in combination with a corresponding post-processor, for which the computing resources of modern multi-core processors are sufficient. As the dimension of the problem N increases, a "combinatorial explosion" is observed, and the computational complexity of the corresponding algorithms drastically increases, which forces us to use a number of features of the problem (for example, partitioning into isomorphism classes [17]) and develop highly efficient software implementations focused on execution on computing facilities with parallel architectures (computing clusters, supercomputers, grids). From the point of view of parallel programming, combinatorial tasks are weakly-coupled, which allows splitting the original task into independent subtasks (work units, abbr. WU) in accordance with the "bag-of-tasks" principle, followed by their launch on the nodes of grid systems that have received a wide distribution in recent decades due to the active development of the Internet (both in terms of availability and throughput of the corresponding communication channels). The largest example of grid systems today is the BOINC platform [2], which includes several dozen projects from various fields of science, where millions of users (crunchers) participate all over the globe, providing free computing resources of their desktop computers and mobile devices.

In this paper, we address the implementation features of the LS diagonalization and canonization transformations, which work in conjunction with a number of other LS/DLS enumeration and post-processing algorithms, which made it possible to obtain a number of new numerical estimates for the numerical characteristics of the DLS. The corresponding calculations were performed using a computation module oriented to execution under BOINC within the framework of the volunteer distributed computing projects Gerasim@Home[1] and RakeSearch[2].

---

[1] http://gerasim.boinc.ru.
[2] https://rake.boincfast.ru/rakesearch.

2   Basic Concepts and Definitions

In order to preserve the rigor of the presentation of the further material of the paper, it is necessary to introduce a number of concepts and definitions. An *intercalate* in a LS is a LS of order 2×2 standing at the intersection of a certain pair of rows and columns. A *transversal* T_i in a LS is a set of N cells in which all row numbers, all column numbers and all values are different. The set of transversals of a LS will be denoted as T. A *diagonal transversal* in a DLS is a transversal in which there is one element from both main and secondary diagonals (these elements can coincide in the central cell for a DLS of odd order). The *canonical form* (CF) of a DLS is [16] the lexicographically minimal string representation of the DLS within the corresponding main class of the DLS. A pair of LS/DLS A and B is called *orthogonal* (abbr. OLS/ODLS) if all ordered pairs of values $(A[x,y], B[x,y])$, $x, y = \overline{0, N-1}$ in its composition are unique.

The number of transversals, intercalates, ODLSs and other objects in a given square is one of the numerical characteristics that have a minimum and maximum value, as well as the corresponding set (*spectrum*) of possible values. Integer numerical sequences obtained for the selected numerical characteristic with increasing problem dimension N are of fundamental importance and are collected within the framework of the corresponding Online Encyclopedia of Integer Sequences (OEIS) [15].

3   Embedding of LS and DLS Isomorphism Classes

For a LS, it is permissible to use equivalent transformations of *isotopy* which include permutation of rows, columns, and renumbering of elements. These transformations make it possible to set an equivalence relation on the set of LSs and divide them into equivalence classes called *isotopic* ones. The cardinality of the isotopy classes does not exceed $(N!)^3$. Each isotopy class can contain several DLS isomorphism classes (*main classes* of DLS). The main classes of DLS, in turn, can be divided into subclasses, however, in the context of this paper, this issue is of no interest and is not considered. The purpose of the diagonalization transformation considered in the paper is to obtain at least one DLS from each of the main DLS classes for a given initial LS. In order to avoid duplication, DLS obtained during diagonalization are transferred to CF (being canonized), which are subsequently collected.

One of 6 parastrophic transformations can be applied to the squares in the LS isotopy class, as a result of which 6 parastrophic slices (isotopy classes) will be obtained, which together form the *main class* of LS (not to be confused with the main class of DLS considered above). If a LS has generalized symmetries (automorphisms), some parastrophic slices, then LS in the isotopy classes and/or main classes of the DLS may coincide.

Schematically, the hierarchy of isomorphism classes of LS and DLS is shown in Fig. 1.

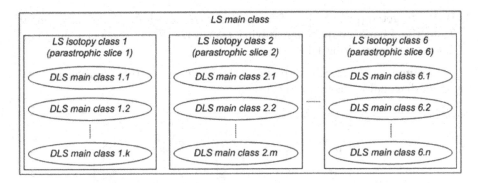

Fig. 1. Hierarchy of isomorphism classes of LS and DLS.

Remark. The depiction of the nested hierarchy of isomorphism classes shown in Fig. 1 is simplified: one main class of DLS can be nested in several paratopy classes of LS, since in the paratopy classes of LS it is not allowed to use rotations or transpositions of the square, unlike the main classes of DLS.

The isomorphism classes considered above are characterized by the presence of various invariants. For example, the invariants of the main class of LS are the number of intercalates, the number of transversals, and the number of OLS, while the invariant of the main class of DLS is the number of diagonal transversals and the number of ODLS. The lexicographically minimal CF of the DLS obtained as a result of the canonization of a given LS, if it exists, is a complete invariant of the main class of LS.

4   Diagonalization and Canonization of Latin Squares

Under the *diagonalization of a LS* we mean the procedure of targeted permutation of rows and columns aimed at obtaining at least one correct DLS from each main class of DLS in the composition of the corresponding isotopy class of LS. The algorithm for performing all possible combinations of permutations of rows and columns has an asymptotic time complexity of the order $t \simeq O((N!)^2)$ and is not applicable for practically important orders of the LS. The diagonalization procedure considered in this paper, as will be shown below, has polynomial time asymptotics both on the order of the square N and on the number of transversals $|T|$.

A schematic description of the diagonalization procedure is given below.

1. Find a pair of transversals T_i and T_j symmetrically placed by Brown [6] in the given LS A.
2. By the targeted permutation of the rows and columns in LS A, set transversal T_i to the main diagonal to obtain LS A'. Transversal T_j in LS A will be transformed into a transversal T_j' in LS A'.

3. By the targeted permutation of the rows and columns in LS A', set transversal T'_j to the secondary diagonal, leaving transversal T_i on the main diagonal, obtaining the resulting DLS A''.

An example schematically explaining the process of setting transversal T_i to the main diagonal is shown in Fig. 2.

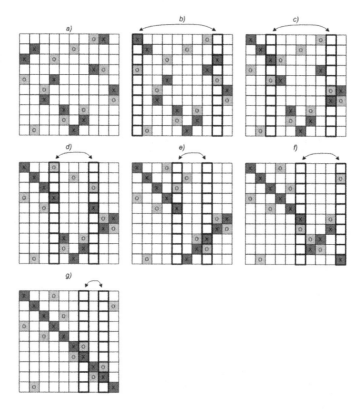

Fig. 2. Setting the transversal T_i of LS A (the elements are indicated by the symbol "x") to the main diagonal by the targeted permutation of the columns to obtain the LS A'.

After setting transversal T_i to the main diagonal, the elements of transversal T_j are located symmetrically with respect to it (see Fig. 2g). An example schematically explaining the process of setting transversal T_j to a secondary diagonal is shown in Fig. 3.

Let us consider the algorithms of the corresponding transformations in more detail. We will say that a cell of LS with coordinates $[x, y]$ belongs to the transversal $T_k \in T$ if $T_k[x] = y$ (the transversal is a one-dimensional array (permutation) in terms of programming languages, see the example in Fig. 4).

The condition that the transversals T_i and T_j are placed symmetrically by Brown can be formulated as follows: for each row x_1 of the LS containing the

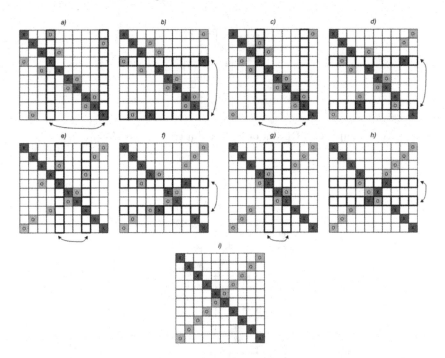

Fig. 3. Setting the transversal T'_j of LS A' (the elements are indicated by the symbol "o") to the secondary diagonal by the targeted permutation of the rows and columns to obtain the DLS A''.

elements $[x_1, T_i[x_1]] = [x_1, y_1]$ and $[x_1, T_j[x_1]] = [x_1, y_2]$ of the considered pair of transversals, there is a row x_2 such that it will contain the elements of the transversals $[x_2, T_i[x_2]] = [x_2, y_1]$ and $[x_2, T_j[x_2]] = [x_2, y_2]$. Moreover, $T_i[x_1] = T_j[x_2] = y_1$ and $T_j[x_1] = T_i[x_2] = y_2$.

In other words, the elements $[x_1, T_i[x_1]]$, $[x_1, T_j[x_1]]$, $[x_2, T_j[x_2]]$ and $[x_2, T_i[x_2]]$ form a rectangle in the LS (see Fig. 5).

The algorithm for checking a pair of transversals for symmetry by Brown is reduced to searching for a row x_2 that satisfies the above condition for a given row x_1 among all rows not yet considered and is presented below.

1. Let the set of considered rows $S := \emptyset$; the number of the first row $x_1 := 0$.
2. If the current first row has already been considered before ($x_1 \in S$), go to step 6.
3. Find row x_2 that satisfies the Brown symmetry condition considered above in a pair with row x_2.
4. If row x_2 was not found, then return the result "the pair of transversals is not symmetric by Brown" ($r := 0$); go to step 9.
5. Mark rows x_1 and x_2 as considered $S := S \bigcup \{x_1, x_2\}$.
6. Consider next row: $x_1 = x_1 + 1$.
7. If $x_1 < N$, go to step 2.

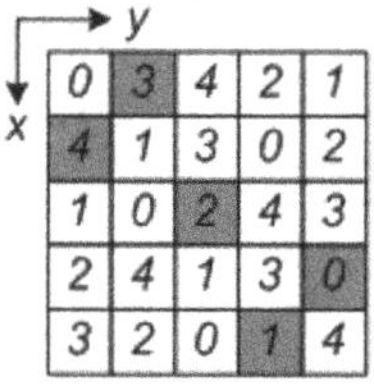

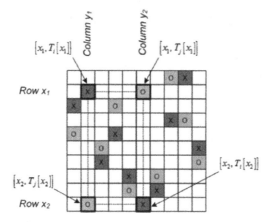

Fig. 4. An example of a DLS of order 5 and a transversal $T_k = [1, 0, 2, 4, 3]$.

Fig. 5. An illustration explaining the condition for the symmetry of a pair of transversals by Brown (a pair of transversals, denoted by the symbols "x" and "o", is taken from the example considered above, see Figs. 2 and 3).

8. Return the result "the pair of transversals is symmetric by Brown" ($r := 1$).
9. End of the algorithm.

When implemented explicitly, the algorithm requires viewing $\frac{N}{2}$ rows x_1 of the LS, for each of which a search is made for the corresponding row x_2 (step 3), performed in linear time, which leads to time asymptotic complexity $t \simeq O(N^2)$. From the above condition $T_j[x_2] = y_1$, it follows that $x_2 = T_j^{-1}[y_1] = T_j^{-1}[T_i[x_1]]$ (another option is $x_2 = T_i^{-1}[y_2] = T_i^{-1}[T_j[x_1]]$ as a consequence of $T_j[x_2] = y_1$), where T_k^{-1} is the permutation inverse to T_k, which allows finding the row number x_2 in time independent of N, and reduces the time complexity of the algorithm to $t \simeq O(N)$, and the algorithm itself can be reduced to checking one of the conditions $T_j[T_i^{-1}[T_j[x_1]]] = y_1 = T_i[x_1]$ or $T_i[T_j^{-1}[T_i[x_1]]] = y_2 = T_j[x_1]$ for all row numbers $x_1 = \overline{0, N-1}$.

It is easy to see that when working with a LS of an even order, transversals placed symmetrically by Brown should not intersect due to the fact that the main and secondary diagonals also do not intersect, for a LS of an odd order there must be exactly one intersection point, which will subsequently be set to the center of the square.

Let us consider the algorithms for setting transversals placed symmetrically by Brown to the diagonal using the example of a LS of even order. As noted above, first it is necessary to set the transversal T_i to the main diagonal to obtain LS A' from the LS A, for which the following formula is used: $A'[l, k] := A[l, T_i[k]], l, k = \overline{0, N - 1}$. The asymptotic time complexity of the algorithm is $t \simeq O(N^2)$. Next, one needs to set the transversal T_j to the secondary diagonal, keeping the main diagonal (the elements of the main diagonal can be interchanged). After setting the transversal T_i to the main diagonal, the elements of the transversal T_j changed their position in the LS A': $T_j[k] \rightarrow T_i^{-1}[T_j[k]]$, and the values stored in them equal $v[k] = A'[k, T_i^{-1}[T_j[k]]]$. The algorithm for the targeted permutation of rows and columns of LS A' in order to obtain DLS A'' is given below.

1. Let the number of the current row $k := 0$.
2. Find column l which contains the value $v[k]$ in the k-th row.
3. Swap columns l and $N - 1 - k$.
4. Swap rows l and $N - 1 - k$.
5. Swap the values $v[k]$ and $v[N - 1 - k]$ in the array of values v.
6. $k := k + 1$. If $k < N$, go to step 2.
7. End of the algorithm.

The algorithm sequentially processes N rows, for each of them a unary search for a suitable column is performed in linear time, therefore, the algorithm as a whole has asymptotic time complexity $t \simeq O(N^2)$.

The processing of an odd-order LS differs in that a pair of transversals placed symmetrically by Brown must have exactly one intersection $[\tilde{x}, \tilde{y}]$, the corresponding element must be set to the center of the square by rearranging rows with numbers $\tilde{x}$ and $\lfloor \frac{N}{2} \rfloor$ and columns with numbers $\tilde{y}$ and $\lfloor \frac{N}{2} \rfloor$, where $\lfloor x \rfloor$ is the operation of rounding down (truncation), $(\lfloor \frac{N}{2} \rfloor, \lfloor \frac{N}{2} \rfloor)$ is the central cell of the square, and then set transversals T_i and T_j to both the main and secondary diagonals in the same way as discussed above.

The transversals are checked for symmetry by Brown for $\frac{|T|(|T|-1)}{2}$ pairs of transversals (upper or lower triangular submatrix with the corresponding graphic representation of the correspondence of transversals to the symmetry condition). Respectively, the asymptotic time complexity of the LS diagonalization algorithm is $t \simeq O(\frac{|T|(|T|-1)}{2}(k_1 N + k_2 N^2 + k_3 N^2)) \simeq O(|T|^2 N^2)$, where k_1, k_2, k_3 are some coefficients. In the algorithms considered above we use, as additional data structures, the mark of already considered rows and information about one of the inverse transversals T_k^{-1}, respectively, the space complexity of the algorithm is $m \simeq O(N)$. At the same time, as initial data, the algorithm operates with the initial LS A ($m \simeq O(N^2)$) and the set of its transversals ($m \simeq O(|T|N)$).

By *canonization* of a LS we mean the procedure of applying parastrophic transformations to a given LS with subsequent diagonalization of the obtained LS and, as a result, obtaining a CF of the DLS for each of the main classes of the DLS in the main class of the LS. In this case, we can restrict ourselves to using only 3 parastrophic transformations out of 6, since transposition is an equivalent transformation for the main classes of DLS and does not lead to new main classes of DLS. An example of a LS and the result of its canonization to obtain a DLS is shown in Fig. 6.

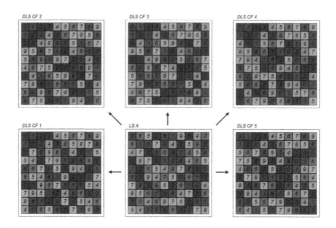

Fig. 6. An example of the original LS A and the results of its canonization (up to normalization and combinations of M-transformations): in total, LS A is diagonalized to 347 main classes of DLS, the CF of five of which are shown in the figure.

5   Practical Application of Canonization and Diagonalization

The canonization procedure can be effectively used in a random search for CF of ODLS, when from a given initial random LS, the CF is constructed from all the main classes of the DLS that are part of the corresponding main class of the LS, and then they are checked for the presence of orthogonal co-squares. The advantage in this case lies in the fact that the construction of the set of transversals is performed only once for the original LS, the sets of transversals for the DLS as part of the corresponding main classes of the DLS can be obtained from it by applying a combination of equivalent transformations (parastrophic transformations, permutations of rows and columns), which is essentially faster than building a set of transversals for each DLS separately. When constructing a list of CF of ODLS of order 10, the use of an appropriate canonizer (the application was developed by A.D. Belyshev and optimized by A.M. Albertyan [1]) makes it possible to increase the effective rate of processed DLS several-fold (see Fig. 7).

When constructing exhaustive lists of CF of ODLS for any order N (at present, the construction of the corresponding lists has been made for dimensions $N \leq 9$), the use of the canonizer does not make sense, because in this case, the initial DLS are formed by exhaustive enumeration, and the gain in the processing rate observed for random DLS will be more than compensated for by the loss either in reprocessing or filtering out of DLS that have already been processed earlier as part of the corresponding main classes of LS. In this case, the use of the classical Euler-Parker method in combination with the dancing links X algorithm (DLX) [10,11] is preferable.

For a number of LS orders, the squares with a record number of transversals are known (see the numerical sequence A090741 in OEIS[3]) [13]. By diagonalizing them, one can obtain DLS with interesting properties (for example, the maximum known number of transversals, diagonal transversals, or ODLS). Thus, a DLS with a record number of diagonal transversals for orders $N \in \{10, 12, 15\}$ and a DLS with a record number of transversals for orders $N \in \{12, 15\}$ were obtained, see Tables 1 and 2.

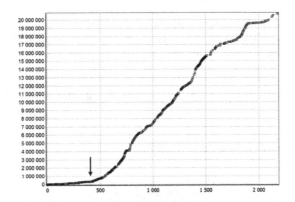

Fig. 7. The dynamics of filling the list of CF of ODLS of order 10 according to the results of calculations in the projects of volunteer distributed computing Gerasim@Home and RakeSearch: days are plotted along the X-axis, the number of CF of ODLS are along the Y-axis, the arrow marks the moment of transition from using the classical Euler-Parker method [10,11] to the canonizer.

In addition, DLS obtained as a result of diagonalization of similar LS of one of the special types (cyclic, Brown DLS, etc., depending on the order of the DLS N) [8], as a rule, form the upper part of the spectra of the corresponding numerical characteristics which seems impossible to be obtained by other methods (see example in Fig. 8).

Diagonalization of cyclic LS of order 11 yielded a number of rare combinatorial structures of ODLS of order 11, not obtained by other methods, and the highest part of the spectra of the number of diagonal transversals in DLS and ODLS of order 11 (Fig. 9).

In combination with heuristic methods for approximating the spectra S of the numerical characteristics of the DLS, based on bypassing the neighborhoods

---

[3]   https://oeis.org/A090741.

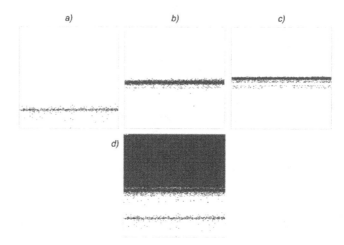

Fig. 8. Examples of spectra of the number of diagonal transversals in the DLS of order 12, obtained by diagonalizing the DLS with 198144, 132096 and 122880 transversals, respectively (a-c) and approximating the spectrum as a whole (d).

of the DLS, the use of diagonalization makes it possible both to increase the cardinality $|S|$ of the corresponding spectra and to strengthen the known upper restrictions on the lower boundary of the spectrum $\inf S$ from 43 979 to 43 093, which cannot be done by other methods.

Fig. 9. Approximation of the spectrum of the number of diagonal transversals in a DLS of order 11 (the part of the spectrum obtained by diagonalizing cyclic LS is highlighted).

6 Conclusion

For DLS of order 12 with a large number of transversals and for the vast majority of DLS of order 13 and higher, a single-threaded software implementation of the diagonalization procedure takes tens of hours at best, which is why its parallel distributed software implementation was developed. Currently, with its use in one of the subprojects of the RakeSearch volunteer distributed computing project, the spectrum of the number of diagonal transversals in the DLS is being expanded to about 13. At the moment, $|S| = 12\,926$, $\inf S = 4\,756$, $\sup S = 131\,106$; about half of the experiment has been completed, the expected time of the computational experiment is about 2 months. In the perspective of further research, we plan to use diagonalization together with methods based on bypassing the DLS neighborhoods to expand the spectra of numerical characteristics of DLS of orders $N \geq 14$.

Table 1. DLS of order N with the maximum number of diagonal transversals obtained using diagonalization (integer sequence A287648 in OEIS (https://oeis.org/A287648.)).

N	DLS	Value of the numerical characteristic	Method
10	0 1 2 3 4 5 6 7 8 9 1 2 3 4 0 9 5 6 7 8 3 4 9 8 2 7 1 0 5 6 6 5 0 1 7 2 8 9 4 3 9 8 7 6 5 4 3 2 1 0 4 0 8 2 3 6 7 1 9 5 8 7 6 5 9 0 4 3 2 1 5 9 1 7 6 3 2 8 0 4 7 6 5 9 8 1 0 4 3 2 2 3 4 0 1 8 9 5 6 7	890	Extending the spectrum of the number of diagonal transversals by going around neighborhoods in combination with diagonalization
12	0 1 2 3 4 5 6 7 8 9 10 11 1 2 3 4 9 8 11 5 10 0 6 7 5 8 10 6 11 4 1 3 9 7 0 2 11 7 5 8 10 2 9 1 3 6 4 0 7 5 8 10 6 3 0 2 4 11 9 1 9 0 1 2 3 7 10 11 5 4 8 6 6 11 7 5 8 1 4 0 2 10 3 9 10 6 11 7 5 0 3 9 1 8 2 4 3 4 9 0 1 6 5 10 11 2 7 8 2 3 4 9 0 10 7 8 6 1 11 5 4 9 0 1 2 11 8 6 7 3 5 10 8 10 6 11 7 9 2 4 0 5 1 3	30 192	Diagonalization of the LS obtained by the composite squares method
15	0 1 2 3 4 5 6 7 8 9 10 11 12 13 14 1 2 0 4 5 3 7 13 9 14 11 12 10 6 8 10 11 12 13 6 7 1 2 4 5 9 14 8 0 3 13 6 7 14 8 9 4 5 12 10 0 1 2 3 11 5 3 4 10 11 12 14 8 1 2 7 13 6 9 0 12 10 11 7 13 6 0 1 3 4 8 9 14 2 5 3 4 5 11 12 10 8 9 2 0 13 6 7 14 1 6 7 13 8 9 14 5 3 10 11 1 2 0 4 12 14 8 9 1 2 0 12 10 7 13 3 4 5 11 6 4 5 3 12 10 11 9 14 0 1 6 7 13 8 2 8 9 14 2 0 1 10 11 13 6 4 5 3 12 7 2 0 1 5 3 4 13 6 14 8 12 10 11 7 9 11 12 10 6 7 13 2 0 5 3 14 8 9 1 4 7 13 6 9 14 8 3 4 11 12 2 0 1 5 10 9 14 8 0 1 2 11 12 6 7 5 3 4 10 13	4 620 434	Partial diagonalization of cyclic LS

Table 2. DLS of order N with the maximum number of transversals obtained using diagonalization (integer sequence A287644 in OEIS (https://oeis.org/A287644.)).

N	DLS	Value of the numerical characteristic	Method

12	`0  1  2  3  4  5  6  7  8  9  10 11`
	`1  2  3  4  5  0  11 6  7  8  9  10`
	`9  8  7  6  11 10 1  0  5  4  3  2`
	`4  5  0  1  2  3  8  9  10 11 6  7`
	`6  11 10 9  8  7  4  3  2  1  0  5`
	`11 10 9  8  7  6  5  4  3  2  1  0`
	`3  4  5  0  1  2  9  10 11 6  7  8`
	`2  3  4  5  0  1  10 11 6  7  8  9`
	`10 9  8  7  6  11 0  5  4  3  2  1`
	`5  0  1  2  3  4  7  8  9  10 11 6`
	`7  6  11 10 9  8  3  2  1  0  5  4`
	`8  7  6  11 10 9  2  1  0  5  4  3`
		198 144	Diagonalization of the LS obtained by the composite squares method

15	`0  1  2  3  4  5  6  7  8  9  10 11 12 13 14`
	`1  2  0  4  5  3  7  13 9  14 11 12 10 6  8`
	`10 11 12 13 6  7  1  2  4  5  9  14 8  0  3`
	`13 6  7  14 8  9  4  5  12 10 0  1  2  3  11`
	`5  3  4  10 11 12 14 8  1  2  7  13 6  9  0`
	`12 10 11 7  13 6  0  1  3  4  8  9  14 2  5`
	`3  4  5  11 12 10 8  9  2  0  13 6  7  14 1`
	`6  7  13 8  9  14 5  3  10 11 1  2  0  4  12`
	`14 8  9  1  2  0  12 10 7  13 3  4  5  11 6`
	`4  5  3  12 10 11 9  14 0  1  6  7  13 8  2`
	`8  9  14 2  0  1  10 11 13 6  4  5  3  12 7`
	`2  0  1  5  3  4  13 6  14 8  12 10 11 7  9`
	`11 12 10 6  7  13 2  0  5  3  14 8  9  1  4`
	`7  13 6  9  14 8  3  4  11 12 2  0  1  5  10`
	`9  14 8  0  1  2  11 12 6  7  5  3  4  10 13`
		36 362 925	Diagonalization of cyclic LS

References

1. Albertian, A.M., Kurochkin, I.I., Vatutin, E.I.: Improving the heterogeneous computing node performance of the desktop grid when searching for orthogonal diagonal latin squares. In: Jordan, V., Tarasov, I., Faerman, V. (eds.) HPCST 2021. CCIS, vol. 1526, pp. 161–173. Springer, Cham (2022). https://doi.org/10.1007/978-3-030-94141-3_13
2. Anderson, D.P.: A platform for volunteer computing. J. Grid Comput. **18**, 99–122 (2020). https://doi.org/10.1007/s10723-019-09497-9
3. Bammel, S.E., Rothstein, J.: The number of 9×9 Latin squares. Discret. Math. **11**, 93–95 (1975). https://doi.org/10.1016/0097-3165(90)90015-O
4. Bedford, D.: Transversals in the Cayley tables of the non-cyclic groups of order 8. Eur. J. Comb. **12**, 455–458 (1991). https://doi.org/10.1016/S0195-6698(13)80096-0
5. Belmonte, A.R., Fiorini, E., Lenard, P., Maldonado, F., Traver, S., Wong, W.H.T.: Spectrum of transversals number in latin squares of order 1–8 (2019). https://oeis.org/A309344
6. Brown, J.W., Cherry, F., Most, L., Most, M., Parker, E.T., Wallis, W.D.: Completion of the spectrum of orthogonal diagonal Latin squares. Lect. Notes Pure Appl. Math. **139**, 43–49 (1992). https://doi.org/10.1201/9780203719916
7. Cavenagh, N.J., Wanless, I.M.: On the number of transversals in Cayley tables of cyclic groups. Disc. Appl. Math. **158**, 136–146 (2010). https://doi.org/10.1016/j.dam.2009.09.006

8. Colbourn, C.J., Dinitz, J.H.: Handbook of Combinatorial Designs, 2nd Edn. (Discrete mathematics and its applications). Chapman & Hall/CRC, Boca Raton (2006). https://doi.org/10.1201/9781420010541

9. Keedwell, A.D., Denes, J.: Latin Squares and Their Applications. Elsevier, Amsterdam (2015). https://doi.org/10.1016/C2014-0-03412-0

10. Knuth, D.E.: Dancing links (2000). arXiv preprint arXiv:cs/0011047v1

11. Knuth, D.E.: The Art of Computer Programming, vol. 4A: Combinatorial Algorithms. Addison-Wesley Professional, Boston (2013)

12. Kochemazov, S., Zaikin, O., Vatutin, E., Belyshev, A.: Enumerating diagonal Latin squares of order up to 9. J. Integer Seq. **23**, article 20.1.2 (2020)

13. McKay, B.D., McLeod, J.C., Wanless, I.M.: The number of transversals in a Latin square. Des. Codes Crypt. **40**, 269–284 (2006). https://doi.org/10.1007/s10623-006-0012-8

14. McKey, B.D., Wanless, I.M.: On the number of Latin squares. Ann. Comb. **9**, 335–344 (2005). https://doi.org/10.1007/s00026-005-0261-7

15. Sloane, N.J.A.: The on-line encyclopedia of integer sequences (2023). https://oeis.org/

16. Vatutin, E., Belyshev, A., Kochemazov, S., Zaikin, O., Nikitina, N.: Enumeration of isotopy classes of diagonal latin squares of small order using volunteer computing. In: Voevodin, V., Sobolev, S. (eds.) RuSCDays 2018. CCIS, vol. 965, pp. 578–586. Springer, Cham (2019). https://doi.org/10.1007/978-3-030-05807-4_49

17. Vatutin, E.I., Belyshev, A.D., Nikitina, N.N., Manzuk, M.O.: Use of X-based diagonal fillings and ESODLS CMS schemes for enumeration of main classes of diagonal Latin squares (in Russian). Telecommunications (1), 2–16 (2023). https://doi.org/10.31044/1684-2588-2023-0-1-2-16

18. Vatutin, E.I., Kochemazov, S.E., Zaikin, O.S.: Applying volunteer and parallel computing for enumerating diagonal latin squares of order 9. In: Sokolinsky, L., Zymbler, M. (eds.) PCT 2017. CCIS, vol. 753, pp. 114–129. Springer, Cham (2017). https://doi.org/10.1007/978-3-319-67035-5_9

19. Vatutin, E.I., Kochemazov, S.E., Zaikin, O.S., Valyaev, S.Y.: Enumerating the transversals for diagonal Latin squares of small order. In: CEUR Workshop Proceedings. Proceedings of the Third International Conference BOINC-based High Performance Computing: Fundamental Research and Development (BOINC: FAST 2017), vol. 1973, pp. 6–14 (2017)

20. Vatutin, E.I., Titov, V.S., Zaikin, O.S., Kochemazov, S.E., Manzuk, M.O., Nikitina, N.N.: Orthogonality-based classification of diagonal Latin squares of order 10. In: CEUR Workshop Proceedings. Proceedings of the VIII International Conference "Distributed Computing and Grid-technologies in Science and Education" (GRID 2018), vol. 2267, pp. 282–287 (2018)

21. Wells, M.B.: The number of Latin squares of order 8. J. Comb. Theory **3**, 98–99 (1967). https://doi.org/10.1016/S0021-9800(67)80021-8

Probabilistic Modeling of the Behavior of a Computing Node in the Absence of Tasks on the Project Server

Khrapov Nikolay[1]([✉]) [ID] and Posypkin Mikhail[2] [ID]

[1] Institute for Information Transmission Problems of the Russian Academy of
Sciences, Moscow, Russia
nkhrapov@gmail.com

[2] Federal Research Center "Computer Science and Control" of the Russian Academy
of Sciences, Moscow, Russia

Abstract. There may be situations where there are no tasks on the
BOINC project for a number of reasons. If a computing node does not
receive a task as a response to a request, then it goes into an idle state for
a while. This publication proposes a probabilistic model of the behavior
of a single computing node in the absence of jobs on the server. The proposed model best describes the processes associated with computing in
local infrastructures, but it is also possible to generalize the methodology
for large-scale voluntary computing projects.

Keywords: BOINC · Voluntary computing · Probabilistic modeling ·
Binary random exponential backoff

1 Introduction

1.1 Related Work

If there are no jobs on the project server, the BOINC client will make periodic
requests, the sequence of which is probabilistic. The query execution logic follows
the principle of *binary random exponential backoff* (BREB) [1].

BREB is widely used for the development of computer network technologies,
including the Ethernet protocol [2]. The specific application of the random exponential backoff principle for network protocols differs from its application in the
BOINC system.

Within the Ethernet protocol, this principle is used to handle collisions
between two computing nodes. An analysis of the BREB principle in the context
of a stability problem specific to computer networks is given in [3]. Within the
BOINC system, the random exponential backoff principle is used to distribute
the load on the calculation server over time, so the problem of node stability is
not relevant.

Also, within the Ethernet protocol, the backoffs are a multiple of a certain
time slot, greater than the transmission time of a network packet, thus time

delays have a clearly discrete nature. However, within the BOINC system, the delay time after an initially unserved request is a random number of seconds between 0 and 300, which is similar to a continuous distribution.

Performance analysis for computer network-specific BREB applications is given in [4]. In this article, the sequence of requests of a network node to a shared resource is considered as a Markov process with fixed transition probabilities between states. After sending a packet, the network card goes into the state of starting to send the next packet. The proposed model is well applicable to describe the operation of network protocols. However, a model built on Markov chains cannot be used to build a delay model in the BOINC system. Within the BOINC system, the probability of the next request depends on previous backoff and on the time of activation of the project. The problem of backoffs becomes less relevant after the computing node transitions from the idle state to the computing state.

The paper proposes methods for obtaining probabilistic characteristics of the behavior of a computing node in the absence of tasks on the server.

Another way to obtain these probabilistic characteristics of the system is simulation modeling [5]. The strength of simulation modeling is its versatility. This makes it possible to build a simulation model of any process, even a very complex one. However, the construction of probabilistic models is more general concerning simulation modeling. An important advantage of the probabilistic approach is the ability to identify patterns in the behavior of both a single node and the entire infrastructure. The probabilistic approach allows a deeper understanding of the causes of various systemic effects. Probabilistic and simulation modeling complement each other: simulation modeling is used to check the correctness of the results obtained using probabilistic models on various examples.

The terminology used in the paper is similar to the terminology of the theory of queuing systems [6]. However, the theory of queuing systems is intended to model the serving system. In this paper, we consider the probabilistic behavior of a separate computing node. And the computing node is the requesting entity, not the serving system. For this reason, the theory of queuing systems cannot be fully applied to the process under consideration.

1.2   Using Random Exponential Backoff in BOINC

A request that has not received a task as a response will be called an *unserved* request. Reasons for not submitting jobs may include:

- the server is turned off for preventive maintenance;
- the server is temporarily out of jobs.

The occurrence of the situation of the absence of tasks will be called the *deactivation* of the project. And the appearance of tasks on the server is the *activation* of the project. An *initial unserved* request is a first unserved request in the sequence. Second, third and subsequent unserved requests will be called *secondary*.

In the BOINC system, the principle of random exponential backoff is implemented as follows:

1. The actual time between requests is equal to the maximum wait time multiplied by a uniformly distributed random number between 0.0 and 1.0.
2. The maximum wait time between requests is increased by a factor of 2 with the next unserved request. The maximum wait time between the first and second requests is 10 min, between the second and third requests is 20 min, and so on.
3. The exact upper limit of the maximum time between requests is 24 h. After reaching this value, the increase will stop, and all subsequent maximum wait intervals will be 24 h.

Random timeout values are generated by the BOINC client in seconds. Similarly, when constructing a probabilistic model, seconds were used as a unit of time. But in this paper, for clarity, when describing the algorithm and considering examples, the time will be indicated in minutes by default.

2   Probabilistic Characteristics of Node Behavior

2.1   Basix Quantities

We introduce the following quantities:

T_{tail} is the time between the compute node's initial unserved request and the activation of the server.

$T_{max} = \{T_1 = 10, T_2 = 20, T_3 = 40, T_4 = 80, T_5 = 160, T_6 = 320, T_7 = 640, T_8 = 1280, T_9 = 1440, T_{10} = 1440, ...\}$ min. It is a vector of values for the maximum time between requests.

The sequence of requests to the project's server will be considered an elementary outcome ω. The set of all elementary outcomes will be considered as the sample space Ω.

$\tau = \{\tau_1, \tau_2, ..., \tau_n\}$ is a vector of random variables of the node's actual waiting time after the i unserved request (including the initial request). The coordinates of the space of elementary events will be denoted by the corresponding letters of the Latin alphabet $t_1, t_2, ...$.

$A_1, A_2, ..$ - sequence of events of execution of the first, second, third, etc. requests:

$$A_n = \{\tau_1 + \tau_2 + ... + \tau_{n-1} < T_{tail}\}, \tau_i \in [0, 10 \cdot 2^{i-1}] \tag{1}$$

The main features of events A_i are:

$$\begin{cases} A_i \subset A_n, \, if \, i < n \\ \\ \overline{A_i} \subset \overline{A_n}, \, if \, i > n \end{cases} \tag{2}$$

$A_1', A_2', ...,$ - events, when the compute node is idle, it will eject accurately n requests. The sequence $A_1, A_2, ...$ forms a complete group of events.

$$\begin{cases} A_i \cap A_j = \varnothing \\ \sum\limits_{i=1}^{\infty} A_i = \Omega \end{cases} \tag{3}$$

Events A_i' will be called *hypotheses*. From the execution of event A_i' follows the execution of events $A_1, A_2, ..., A_{i-1}$:

$$A_j \subset A_i', \ \ if \ \ j < i \tag{4}$$

T_{idle} is the idle time of the compute node. This is the time between the initial unserved request and the first serviced request after the project's activation. The idle time is equal to the total waiting time between requests.

$$T_{idle} = \sum_{i=1}^{n} \tau_i \tag{5}$$

Feature of T_{idle} is $T_{tail} < T_{idle}$.

T_{lose} is a difference between T_{idle} and T_{tail}. This is a time during which the server has tasks, but the compute node is idle.

Consider an example. Let $T_{tail} = 90$ min and $\tau = \{5, 15, 45, 85, 255\}$ min In this case $T_{idle} = 160$ min. This means that for 160 min the server will be active, but the compute node will not have information about it. The time between the initial unserved request and the server's activation is 90 min. But the node begins computation after 255 min after the initial unserved request.

2.2   Method for Calculating the Probability of Query Execution

Elementary outcome can be represented as a random point in a Hilbert parallelotope of dimension n. We will use the term *parallelotope*:

$$\pi^n = \{t = (t_1, t_2, ..., t_n) \in R^n | 0 < t_i < T_i\} \subset R^n \tag{6}$$

Figure within constraints

$$\Delta^n(u) = \{t = (t_1, t_2, ..., t_n) \in R^n | t_1 + t_2 + ... + t_n < u\} \tag{7}$$

we will call *simplex*.

Thus

$$A_n = \pi^{n-1} \cap \Delta^{n-1}. \tag{8}$$

Let us take into account the uniform probability distribution

$$p_i(t_i) = \frac{1}{10 \cdot 2^{i-1}} \tag{9}$$

The probability of the event A_i is equal to the ratio of the generalized volume A to the volume of the parallelotope.

$$P(A_n) = \frac{V^{n-1}(A_n)}{V^{n-1}(\pi^{n-1})} = \frac{V^{n-1}(\pi^{n-1} \cap \Delta^{n-1})}{V^{n-1}(\pi^{n-1})} \tag{10}$$

Methods for calculating multidimensional volumes of intersections of a simplex and a parallelotope are given in the Subsect. 3.2.

Let's consider an example of calculating the probability of 2 or more requests, as well as 3 or more requests for $T_{tail} = 25$ min.

A_1 is a certain event if the initial request is executed. Since $T_{tail} > T_1$, then A_2 is a certain event too.

$$A_3 = \pi^2 \cap \Delta^2(25) \tag{11}$$

Event A_3 is depicted in Fig. 1a as the shaded part of the rectangle. Geometric calculations show that

$$P(A_3) = \frac{S(\pi^2 \cap \Delta^2(25))}{S(\pi^2)} = \frac{S_{t_1+t_2<25}}{T_1 \cdot T_2} = \frac{187.5}{200} = 0.9375 \tag{12}$$

Similarly, the probability of 4 or more requests (Fig. 1) is:

$$P(A_4) = \frac{V^3(\pi^3 \cap \Delta^3(25))}{V^3(\pi^3)} = \frac{S_{t_1+t_2+t_3<25}}{T_1 \cdot T_2 \cdot T_3} = \frac{2020.83}{8000} = 0.2526 \tag{13}$$

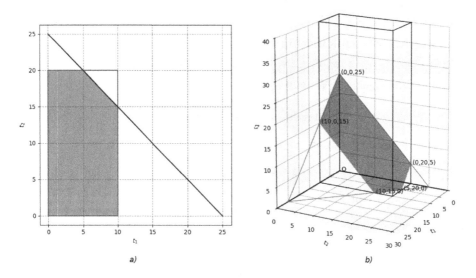

Fig. 1. Estimation of the probability of 3 or more (a) and 4 or more (b) unserved requests.

3   Distribution Function Calculation

3.1   Distribution Function

Consider T_{idle} as a random function depending on the T_{tail} parameter. By definition, the distribution function is equal to the probability of the event $T_{idal} < t$.

$$F(T_{tail}, t) = P\{T_{tail}, T_{idle} < t\} \tag{14}$$

Event $\{T_{tail}, T_{idle} < t\}$ can occur under various mutually exclusive hypotheses $A'_1, A'_2, \dots.$

$$\{T_{tail}, T_{idle} < t\} = \sum_{i=1}^{\infty} \{A'_i \cap \{T_{idle} < t\}\}\big|_{T_{tail}=const} \tag{15}$$

$$F(T_{tail}, t) = \sum_{i=1}^{\infty} P\{A'_i \cap \{T_{tail}, T_{idle} < t\}\} = \sum_{i=1}^{\infty} F_i(T_{tail}, t) \tag{16}$$

$$F_i(T_{tail}, t) = P\{A'_i \cap \{T_{idle} < t\}\}\big|_{T_{tail}=const} \tag{17}$$

$F_i(T_{tail}, t)$ is the unconditional probability of the event that exactly i unserved requests will be executed for a fixed T_{tail} and $T_{idle} < t$ (18). Note that F_i does not correspond to the strict definition of the distribution function, since it has not a limit value equal to 1.

$$\begin{cases} \sum_{i=1}^{n-1} \tau_i < T_{tail} \\ T_{tail} < \sum_{i=1}^{n} \tau_i < t \\ 0 < \tau_i < 10 \cdot 2^i \end{cases} \tag{18}$$

Let's consider an example of calculating F_1, F_2, F_3, F_4 for $T_{tail} = 15$ min and $t = 25$.

Since $T_{tail} > T_1$, then the probability of exactly one request is 0.

For the hypothesis of exactly two queries, the conditions (18) will be:

$$\begin{cases} \tau_1 < 15 \\ 15 < \tau_1 + \tau_2 < 25 \\ 0 < \tau_1 < 10 \\ 0 < \tau_2 < 20 \end{cases} \tag{19}$$

In graphical form, the set of elementary outcomes that satisfy the constraints is shown Fig. 2. The desired probability is equal to the ratio of the area that satisfies the conditions to the area of the rectangle of elementary events.

$$F_2(T_{tail} = 15, t = 25) = P\{\tau_1 + \tau_2 > 15, \tau_1 + \tau_2 < 25\} = \\ = \frac{S_{satisfied}}{S_{rect}} = \frac{87.5}{200} = 0.4375 \tag{20}$$

Similarly, for the hypothesis of exactly three queries, the conditions will be:

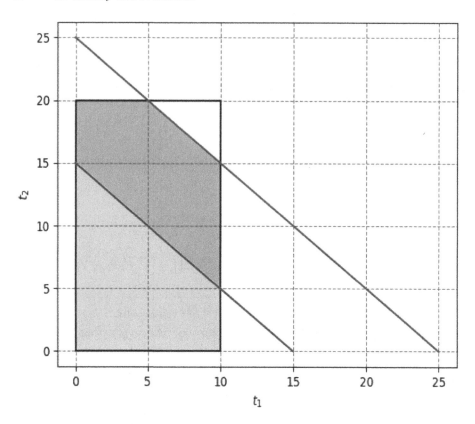

Fig. 2. Constraints for exact two requests (blue color). Conditions for three and more requests (pink color). (Color figure online)

$$\begin{cases} \tau_1 + \tau_2 < 15 \\ 15 < \tau_1 + \tau_2 + \tau_3 < 25 \\ 0 < \tau_i < 10 \cdot 2^{i-1}, i = 1, 2, 3. \end{cases} \tag{21}$$

In graphical form, the set of elementary events that satisfy the constraints is shown in the Fig. 3. The desired probability is equal to the ratio of the volume that satisfies the conditions to the volume of the cuboid of elementary outcomes.

Consider the method of calculating F_i in the general case. To do this, we will consider the random variable τ as the sum of random variables τ_i.

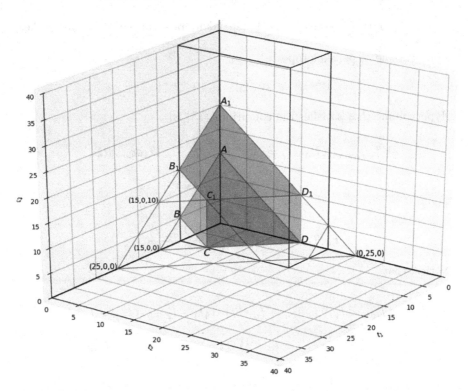

Fig. 3. Bounds of restrictions within the framework of the hypothesis of three requests. The faces of the cuboid correspond to the constraints $\tau_1 < 10, \tau_2 < 20, \tau_3 < 40$ min. The constraint $\tau_1 + \tau_2 + \tau_3 < 25$ min corresponds to the face $A_1 B_1 C_1 D_1$ (indicated in blue). The constraint $\tau_1 + \tau_2 + \tau_3 > 15$ min corresponds to the face $ABCD$ (indicated in pink). The constraint $\tau_1 + \tau_2 < 15$ min corresponds to the face CC_1D_1D (indicated in grey). (Color figure online)

$$F_i(T_{tail}, t) = P\{A_i' \cap \{T_{idle} < t\}\}\big|_{T_{tail}=const}$$

$$= P\{\tau_1 + \tau_2 + ... + \tau_i < t\}\big|_{T_{tail}=const}$$

$$= \int \cdots \int_{\substack{t_1+t_2+...t_{n-1}<T_{tail} \\ T_{tail}<t_1+t_2+...t_{n-1}<t}} p(t_1, t_2, ..., t_n) dt_1 dt_2 ... dt_n \qquad (22)$$

$$= \int \cdots \int_{\substack{t_1+t_2+...t_{n-1}<T_{tail} \\ T_{tail}<t_1+t_2+...t_{n-1}<t}} p_1 \cdot p_2 \cdot .... \cdot p_n \ dt_1 dt_2 ... dt_n$$

$$= \frac{1}{10} \cdot \frac{1}{20} \cdot .... \cdot \frac{1}{10 \cdot 2^{n-1}} \int \cdots \int_{\substack{t_1+t_2+...t_{n-1}<T_{tail} \\ T_{tail}<t_1+t_2+...t_{n-1}<t}} dt_1 dt_2 ... dt_n$$

The probability densities (9) of independent random variables were taken into account.

Hypervolume of parallelotope is:

$$V^n(\pi^n) = 10 \cdot 20 \cdot ... \cdot 10 \cdot 2^{n-1} \tag{23}$$

Hypervolume that satisfies the conditions (18) is:

$$V^n_{restrictions}(T_{tail}, t) = \int \cdots \int_{\substack{t_1+t_2+...t_{n-1}<T_{tail} \\ T_{tail}<t_1+t_2+...t_{n-1}<t}} dt_1 dt_2...dt_n \tag{24}$$

Thus

$$F_n(T_{tail}, t) = \frac{V^n_{restrictions}(T_{tail}, t)}{V^n(\pi^n)} \tag{25}$$

Notice, that

$$\left\{\pi^n \cap \{T_{tail} < t_1 + t_2 + ... + t_n < t\} \cap \{t_1 + t_2 + ...t_{n-1} < T_{tail}\}\right\}$$

$$= \left\{\pi^n \cap \{t_1 + t_2 + ... + t_n < t\} \cap \{t_1 + t_2 + ...t_{n-1} < T_{tail}\}\right\}$$

$$-\left\{\pi^n \cap \{t_1 + t_2 + ... + t_n < T_{tail}\}\right\}$$

Therefore, the hypervolume that satisfies the constraints can be represented as:

$$V^n_{restrictions} = \int \cdots \int_{\substack{t_1+t_2+...t_{n-1}<T_{tail} \\ t_1+t_2+...t_{n-1}<t}} dt_1 dt_2...dt_n - \int \cdots \int_{t_1+t_2+...t_n<T_{tail}} dt_1 dt_2...dt_n \tag{26}$$

The calculation of multiple integrals is possible by recursive integration (Sect. 3.2).

Distribution functions and distribution density for $T_{tail} = 30, 60, 90, 120$ min were constructed based on the proposed method. Figure 4a displays a plot of the distribution functions and Fig. 4b displays a plot of the distribution density.

For example, from Fig. 4a, it can be estimated that with $T_{tail} = 90$ min (blue line), with a probability of 0.6, the idle time will be less than 150 min, and with a probability of 0.82, the idle time will be less than 200 min. Similarly, it can be determined that with $T_{tail} = 120$ min (raspberry line), with a probability of 0.6, the idle time will be less than 150 min, and with a probability of 0.81, the idle time will be less than 200 min.

According to graph Fig. 4b, one can see the stepwise distribution density, where the presence of sections close to horizontal is explained by the uniform distribution of waiting intervals between requests.

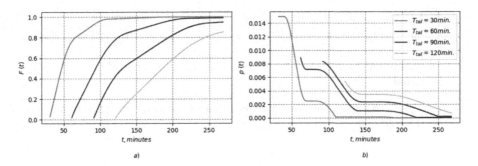

Fig. 4. Distribution function (a) and distribution density function (b) of system inactivity time at $T_{tail} = 30\,\text{min}, 60\,\text{min}, 90\,\text{min}, 120\,\text{min}$. (Color figure online)

3.2 Recursive Way to Calculate Multiple Integrals

Constraints (18) for a fixed value of t_1 to similar (invariant) constraints of lower dimension.

$$\begin{cases} \sum_{i=1}^{n-1} t_i < T_{tail} \\ T_{tail} < \sum_{i=1}^{n} t_i < t \\ 0 < t_i < 10 \cdot 2^i, i = 1, .., n \end{cases} \xrightarrow{t_1=const} \begin{cases} \sum_{i=2}^{n-1} t_i < T_{tail} - t_1 \\ T_{tail} - t_1 < \sum_{i=2}^{n} t_i < t - t_1 \\ 0 < t_i < 10 \cdot 2^i, i = 2, .., n \end{cases}$$

This allows us to calculate n-tuple integrals (26) recursively. Recursive calculations are possible both numerically and analytically.

The integral sum for numerical calculation is:

$$\int \cdots \int_{\substack{t_1+t_2+...t_{n-1}<T_{tail} \\ t_1+t_2+...t_{n-1}<t}} dt_1 dt_2...dt_n = \sum_{i=1}^{N} \left(\int \cdots \int_{\substack{t_2+...t_{n-1}<T_{tail}-t_{1i} \\ t_1+t_2+...t_{n-1}<t-t_{1i}}} dt_2...dt_n \right) \Delta x \qquad (27)$$

N is a number of integration steps.
$\Delta x = T_1/N$ is an integration step.
$x_i = \Delta x \cdot i$
The inner integral is calculated similarly. The criterion for stopping the recursion is an integral of dimension 2, which can be calculated using geometry formulas.

Analytic recursive integral evaluation is more accurate and computationally more efficient. The analytical method for computing a n-tuple integral is based on the assertion that the inner integral is a polynomial of degree n:

$$\left. \int \cdots \int_{\substack{t_2+...t_{n-1}<T_{tail}-t_1 \\ t_2+...t_{n-1}<t-t_1}} dt_2...dt_n \right|_{T_{tail}=const} = a_{n-1}t_1^{n-1} + a_{n-2}t_1^{n-2} + ... + a_0 \qquad (28)$$

Due to space limitations we omit the proof. Thus, to calculate the integral, it is necessary:

1. Calculate the value of the internal integral for n values of t_1.
2. Construct an interpolation polynomial, i.e. calculate coefficients a_{n-1}, a_{n-2}, ..., a_0.
3. Analytically calculate the value of the definite integral of the interpolation polynomial.

We apply a recursive approach to calculating the volume of a figure that satisfies the following restrictions:

$$\begin{cases} \tau_1 + \tau_2 < 15 \\ \tau_1 + \tau_2 + \tau_3 < 25 \\ 0 < \tau_1 < 10, 0 < \tau_2 < 20 \end{cases} \tag{29}$$

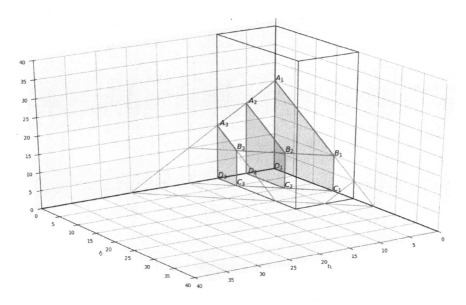

Fig. 5. Using a recursive approach to calculate the volume of a three-dimensional figure $A_1 B_1 C_1 D_1 A_3 B_3 C_3 D_3$. The face $A_1 B_1 B_3 A_3$ corresponds to the constraint $t_1 + t_2 + t_3 < 25$. The face $B_1 C_1 C_3 B_3$ corresponds to the constraint $t_1 + t_2 < 15$.

$$V = \int_0^{T_1} S(t_1) dt_1 \tag{30}$$

$S(t_1)$ - cross-section area within $t = const$ (Fig. 5). According (28)

$$S(t_1) = a_2 t_1^2 + a_1 t_1 + a_0 \tag{31}$$

Interpolate the polynomial of the second sequence by three values t1 = 0, 5, 10 as the area of the trapezoid:

$$\begin{aligned} S(t_1 = 0) &= 262.5 \\ S(t_1 = 5) &= 150 \\ S(t_1 = 10) &= 62.5 \end{aligned} \qquad (32)$$

Let's make an interpolation Lagrange polynomial for these points:

$$S(t_1) = 0.5t_1^2 - 25t_1 + 262.5 \qquad (33)$$

The volume of $A_1B_1C_1D_1A_3B_3C_3D_3$ will be equal to a certain integral t_1 of the cross-sectional area:

$$V = \int_0^{T_1} S(t_1)dt_1 = \int_0^{10} \left(0.5t_1^2 - 25t_1 + 262.5\right)dt_1 = 1541.(6) \qquad (34)$$

Note that the specificity of constraints (1) allows for the presence of silent points of the cross-section function. In these cases, it is necessary to divide the interval $[0, t_1]$ into smooth sections. And the final generalized volume is calculated as the sum of integrals for smooth sections. The calculation of the coordinates of the silent points can also be carried out recursively. Initially, take t_1 equal to 0 and find all the silent points, solving a problem of smaller dimensions. Then take T1 = t1 and count the points for this case, etc.

4   Mathematical Expectation

Let us consider methods for calculating the mathematical expectation of the node idle time for a fixed parameter T_{tail}. This value is relevant when calculating the average values of processor time losses for several computing nodes with a close T_{tail} value. An example of such a situation is a large number of nodes making initial requests in a relatively short time. Another example would be a fixed latency replay situation for a single node. In general, the mathematical expectation can be calculated by integrating the product of the time value with its distribution density.

$$M(T_{tail}) = \int_{T_{tail}}^{\infty} tp(t)dt \qquad (35)$$

This method of calculation involves the numerical calculation of the improper integral. The computational complexity of calculating the values of the distribution function implies a high computational complexity of calculating the mat. expectations. If the mathematical expectation's score must be carried out in real time, then another method of the score is preferred. For a more efficient estimate, we represent the total mathematical expectation as the sum of expectations of unconditional random variables. Subject to the execution of the i-th unserved request mat. expectation will be:

$$M_i = \frac{T_i}{2} = \frac{10 \cdot 2^{i-1}}{2} = 10 \cdot 2^{i-1} \tag{36}$$

Consider a discrete random variable that takes into account that an A_i event may or may not occur. This random variable characterizes the mathematical expectation.

$$\mu_i = \begin{cases} 0, & if \ \overline{A_i} \\ M_i, & if \ A_i \end{cases} \tag{37}$$

Based on this random variable, we obtain a generalized mathematical expectation:

$$M_i' = M(\mu_i) = 0 \cdot P\{\overline{A}\} + M_i \cdot P\{A_i\} = M_i \cdot P\{A_i\} \tag{38}$$

Then the total mathematical expectation of the idle time of the computing node can be represented as

$$M = \sum_{i=1}^{n} M_i' = \sum_{i=1}^{n} M_i \cdot P\{A_i\} \tag{39}$$

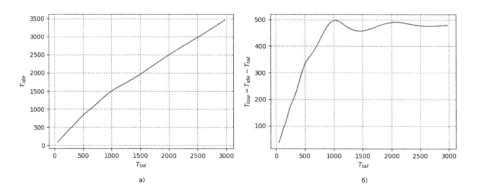

Fig. 6. Dependence of the mathematical expectation of the idle time of the node T_{idle} (a) and the losses of the processor T_{lose} (b) from T_{tail}.

The method of calculating $P\{A_i\}$ was considered earlier as the ratio of a part of a multidimensional brick bounded by conditions to the volume of the entire parallelotope. Methods for calculating such volumes are discussed in Subsects. 3.2. The result of the constructed dependence is shown in Fig. 6. This dependence shows that:

1. With large (a day or more) T_{tail}, the time of processor time loss reaches a ceiling of 450–500 min. This is because the maximum waiting time after the 8th request ceases to increase and will be $T_{maximum} = 1440$.
2. For T_{tail} not exceeding 500 min the average dependence of processor time losses is close to linear. Calculations with high accuracy showed that the dependence on this site is not strictly linear. The presence of quasi-linearity is explained by the fact that for $T_{tail} > 10$, the first n requests satisfying the condition will be guaranteed to be executed. In addition, the quasi-linear view is influenced by linear areas of the increasing volume of the part of the part of the parallelepiped satisfying the constraints (8).

Extrapolation by the linear function $M(T_{tail}) = a \cdot T_{tail} + b$ using the least squares method on a quasi-linear section of 10–500 min provided us with the following coefficients:
For $M(T_{tail})$:

$$
\begin{aligned}
a &= 1.6536 \\
b &= 5.2303 \\
r^2 &= 0.9999
\end{aligned}
\tag{40}
$$

For $M(T_{lose})$:

$$
\begin{aligned}
a &= 0.6536 \\
b &= 5.2303 \\
r2 &= 0.9998
\end{aligned}
\tag{41}
$$

where r^2 is the correlation coefficient.

This means that if the T_{tail} increases by 10 min, the average CPU time loss will increase by 16.5 min. Parameter b = 5.23 min the mate is explained waiting for 5 min, due to the primary unserved request, which is guaranteed to be executed. I.e. for T_{tail} within 1 min the mathematical expectation will be close to 5 min.

5   Conclusions

The article presents methods for obtaining probabilistic characteristics of the behavior of an individual computing node. These methods can be used for the construction of probabilistic models of the behavior of computing infrastructures. This is necessary to pre-plan a preventive server suspension policy to minimize overhead. Also, the results can be useful for a posteriori analysis of the reasons for the behavior of computing nodes after the server's suspension.

In local computing infrastructures, it is possible to control both the operation of the project server and the operation of computing nodes. This makes it possible to coordinate the request policy with the specifics of the project. To fine-tune public projects, the BOINC developers offer some options that affect the behavior of the computing node when the server is suspended.

In the best way, the proposed approaches model the behavior of a computing node that is connected to only one project and does not accumulate tasks. Within the framework of individual studies, it is possible to adapt the proposed approaches to describe the behavior of a computing node in infrastructures of various types.

References

1. Anderson, D., Korpela E., Walton R.: High-performance task distribution for volunteer computing. In: Conference: e-Science and Grid Computing. IEEE Xplore (2005). https://doi.org/10.1109/E-SCIENCE.2005.51
2. Aldous, D.J.: Ultimate instability of exponential back-off protocol for acknowledgment-based transmission control of random access communication channels. IEEE Trans. Inf. Theory **33**(2), 219–223 (1987). https://doi.org/10.1109/TIT.1987.1057295
3. Song, N.-O., Kwak, B.-J., Miller, L.E.: On the stability of exponential backoff. J. Res. Natl. Inst. Stand. Technol. **108**, 289–297 (2003). https://doi.org/10.6028/jres.108.027
4. Kwak, B., Song, N., Miller, L.: Performance analysis of exponential backoff. IEEE/ACM Trans. Netw. **13**(2), 343–355 (2005). https://doi.org/10.1109/TNET.2005.845533
5. Ivashko, E., Nikitina, N., Rumyantsev, A.: Discrete event simulation model of a desktop grid system. Commun. Comput. Inf. Sci. **1331**, 574–585 (2020). https://doi.org/10.1007/978-3-030-64616-5_49
6. Solnyshkina, I.: Queueing Theory. KnASU, Komsomolsk-on-Amur (2015)

Using Virtualization Approaches to Solve Deep Learning Problems in Voluntary Distributed Computing Projects

Ilya Kurochkin[1,2(✉)] [iD] and Valeriy Papanov[2]

[1] Institute for Information Transmission Problems of Russian Academy of Sciences, Moscow, Russia
qurochkin@gmail.com
[2] The National University of Science and Technology MISIS, Moscow, Russia

Abstract. The task of training deep neural networks on a large amount of data requires a lot of resources. The solution of such a problem is often impossible to carry out on one computing device in an adequate time. Distributed computing systems can be used to solve deep learning problems. Such systems may consist of heterogeneous computing nodes with different computing power. To implement deep learning on a distributed heterogeneous system, it is necessary to solve the problem of utilization of all available resources. The solution to this problem is to configure the task delivery system of a distributed system. And to expand the number of computing nodes involved, it is necessary to use virtualization. The article discusses two types of virtualization for grid systems when solving deep learning problems. The features of the implementation of computational applications for training deep neural networks for solving the problem of image classification are discussed. The results of distributed deep learning on a public grid system are discussed. A comparative analysis of two virtualization approaches is given.

Keywords: Deep Learning · Distributed Deep Learning · Desktop Grid · Voluntary Distributed Computing · Virtualization · Docker · BOINC

1 Introduction

The high popularity of machine learning methods and deep neural networks for solving various applied problems determines the development of not only software, but hardware. Most of the modern high-performance computing systems are adapted to solve deep learning problems. The use of video cards and special processors significantly increases the capabilities of high-performance systems. But at the same time, there is a shortage of computing power to solve deep learning problems with a large amount of data. Deep neural network training on a large dataset in an adequate time is possible on high-performance systems and distributed computing systems.

Distributed computing systems have a certain features [1]:

- heterogeneity of computing nodes,
- high overhead costs for data transmission between system nodes,
- autonomy of computing nodes,
- possible errors in calculations and data transmission.

Even with these features, distributed solution of deep learning problems is possible. Combining all available heterogeneous resources in a distributed system makes it possible to solve large-scale problems.

To unify the running of computing tasks on nodes of distributed systems, various virtualization options are often used. Running computational tasks in a virtual environment allows you to expand the number of compatible nodes of a distributed system. But at the same time, part of the resources is spent on providing virtualization. Recently, there has been a tendency to use cloud resources to expand the capabilities of a distributed system. Using cloud resources allows you to increase the number of reliable computing nodes with a high degree of availability. Cloud resources are characterized by the use of virtualization technologies. Some distributed systems can be deployed only on cloud resources and data center resources.

There are a certain number of platforms for deploying distributed systems with a wide range of types of connected nodes (BOINC [2], HTCondor [3], Grid Engine [4], etc.). But when combining cloud resources and data center resources, Hadoop MapReduce [5], Apache Spark [6], Apache Hive and Apache Storm [5] can be used.

2 Distributed Deep Learning

There are quite a large number of approaches to distributed deep learning [7]. There are various classifications of these methods. Here are some of them:

Classification 1: data separation/model separation.

The model separation approach is rarely used in distributed learning. In this case, the same dataset is used on each node, and the neural network model or hyperparameters of this model are changed. In the data-partitioning approach, the same deep neural network model is used at different nodes of a distributed system, and the dataset is divided into local datasets.

For the data separation approach, an additional division into synchronous and asynchronous approaches is possible [7]. The approaches differ in the synchronous and asynchronous way of updating the global neural network model. In the synchronous approach, iterations of distributed learning are clearly expressed. Among the disadvantages of this approach, we can single out possible long synchronization delays in the presence of "weak" nodes with large tasks.

Classification 2 (by the presence of a parametric server): with parametric server (global model)/decentralized training (without global model).

The presence of a global model in distributed learning depends on the architecture of a distributed system and can be both a plus and a minus. At the same time, the implementation of decentralized distributed learning can be implemented even on desktop grid systems [8].

Classification 3 (based on restrictions on data dissemination): federative learning/learning with a common dataset.

The need to create large datasets for solving applied problems has revealed the problem of limiting the distribution of a number of data. One of the ways to overcome this problem is the distributed learning approach [9], when a local neural network model is trained on private data located only on this node. As a rule, private data sets will be unbalanced and vary greatly in size. In this case, a mixed approach can be used, in which not only private data, but also parts of the general dataset are used when training a local model.

The problem of image classification is taken as a test problem for distributed training of a deep neural network. The MNIST reference dataset was chosen as the dataset – a set of images of handwritten digits. It consists of 70,000 black and white images of the same size – 28 × 28 pixels.

A convolutional neural network with 7 layers and a total of 258794 weights was selected. Deep neural network training was carried out using the Adam (Adaptive Moment Estimation) algorithm [10].

The choice of one of the most common MNIST reference datasets and a relatively small convolutional neural network was due to the need for low computational complexity of the distributed deep learning task. Since it was assumed a large number of repetitions of distributed learning in different conditions and with different parameters. In addition, the low complexity of the local model training subtask made it possible to make the calculation time comparable to the time of deploying virtual machines and allowed to increase the share of overhead costs for data transfer between network nodes.

The type of distributed deep learning was chosen with data separation (classification 1), with a parametric server (classification 2) and a shared dataset (classification 3). The data exchange between the parametric server and the computing nodes of the distributed system is shown in the Fig. 1.

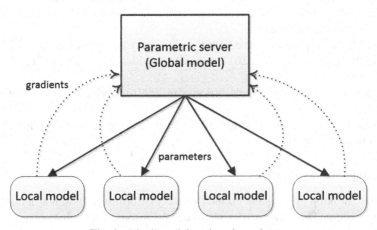

Fig. 1. Distributed deep learning scheme.

3 Voluntary Distributed Computing

At the moment, more than 30 voluntary distributed computing (VDC) projects are active in multiple fields of science and many institutes [11].

About a million devices are actively involved in projects on them. These devices together provide a performance of more than 100 PetaFLOPS. If we compare this performance value with the performance of modern supercomputers, then this would put the VDC in 6 place in the Top500 ranking [12], which consists of the 500 most productive supercomputers in the world.

Features of VDC systems that are superimposed on top of the features of distributed systems [1]:

- All computing nodes are anonymous, unreliable and uncontrolled
- Some or all computing resources are provided by volunteers
- In order to receive resources, it is necessary to recruit and retain volunteers. This requires incentives such as volunteer teams, points for calculations performed and the design of screensavers.
- The scale of VDC systems is larger than grid systems: there can be millions of nodes and millions of tasks per day.

3.1 Distributed Computing Platforms

- BOINC (Berkeley Open Infrastructure for Network Computing) is a widely used platform for distributed and voluntary distributed computing. Developed at the University of California at Berkeley, USA. Most of the VDC projects currently use it [2];
- HTCondor, a platform created at the University of Wisconsin in Madison, USA, was used in 2021 to create a JupyterHub back-end web service for the JupyterNotebook development environment [3];
- XtremWeb-CH, a platform created at the University of Applied Sciences of Western Switzerland, was used in 2011 to design a grid system for studying dosing in radiotherapy;
- Xgrid, a platform created by Apple, was used in 2009 to develop software for modeling fractals;
- Grid MetaProcessor is a platform created by United Devices, in 2003 it implemented protein folding modeling.

3.2 Desktop Grid System

A test public desktop grid system on the BOINC platform was chosen as a distributed computing system. This made it possible to use the resources of volunteers and ensure a high level of heterogeneity.

Figure 2 shows the diagram of the BOINC server. The stages that have been modified for this work are shown in red:

- validator – element for checking the results for correctness;
- assimilator – an element for processing results after validation;

- aggregator is a new element in the system. Its purpose is the aggregation of local gradients from nodes, as well as the implementation of a system of iterations – changes in the global model.

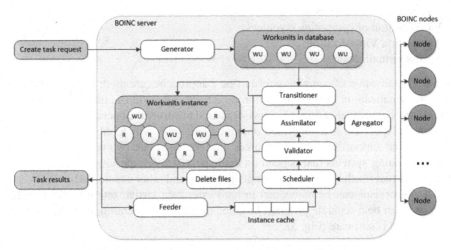

Fig. 2. Diagram of the BOINC project for deep learning.

The test public desktop grid system is a voluntary distributed computing project. In this case, any computing node can connect or disconnect from the grid system at any time. This means that the number of active nodes in the grid system changes over time. Computation errors and data transmission errors may occur. It is assumed that personal computers, laptops, servers, as well as cloud infrastructure resources are connected to the desktop grid system. A certain part of computing nodes has limitations on the use of memory and hard disk.

4 Virtualization

Virtualization technologies appeared quite a long time ago. However, it was only with the development of datacenters and cloud infrastructures that virtualization technologies became widespread. The advantages of virtualization include:

- Efficient use of existing resources;
- Reduction of financial costs for the support of computing infrastructure;
- Increased flexibility and responsiveness to emerging changes;
- Ensuring continuous operation of applications;
- Facilitating backup and recovery processes.

Virtualization involves the separation of software and hardware levels. The interaction of applications with hardware is carried out only through the operating system using standardized methods. When using virtualization technologies, applications can be run in isolation from other applications. This allows each application to form a specific environment.

There are several levels of virtualization:

- Network virtualization;
- Data storage virtualization;
- Virtualization of computing resources;
- Application Virtualization;
- Access virtualization.

For virtualization of computing resources, 2 approaches are used: full virtualization and paravirtualization. Full virtualization requires more resources than paravirtualization. During paravirtualization, a hypervisor is used to ensure the operation of virtualized resources. Hypervisor is a simplified operating system in which only the functions of providing and supporting virtual resources are left. There are two types of virtualization of operating systems that depend on the hypervisor. A hypervisor is an entity that manages virtual machines – their startup, operation, and other events [13].

The hypervisor can be embedded in hardware, then virtualization is called hardware, or it can be a separate program installed on the main operating system, and then virtualization is software (Fig. 3).

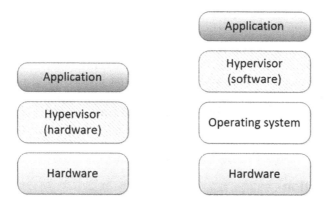

Fig. 3. Two type of hypervisor.

Examples of hardware hypervisors are:

- VMware vSphere/ESXI – the most popular in the commercial sphere, also has a free version;
- KVM (Kernel-Based Virtual Machine) – is open source and can be added to most Linux distributions, such as Ubuntu, SUSE and Red Hat Enterprise Linux;
- Hyper-V is a hypervisor from Microsoft, available only with certain versions of Windows Pro and Enterprise (sometimes Hyper-M is referred to as hybrid hypervisors).

Examples of software hypervisors are:

- VMware Workstation;
- Oracle VirtualBox – a hypervisor used mainly for educational and individual purposes. It has an open source code.

The most common approaches to virtualization in distributed computing systems are (Fig. 4):

1. Virtual machines;
2. Containers.

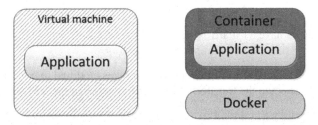

Fig. 4. Features of the application for 2 types of virtualization.

Using virtual machines allows you to create an environment of one or more computing applications with a specific operating system. As a rule, "compact" operating system images are selected for virtual machines to simplify the transfer of virtual machine images over the network.

Using containers allows you to set all dependencies, libraries, and data for a computing application. In this case, the container will use the kernel of the operating system existing on the host through a special "engine". Currently, Docker is a fairly popular software for organizing work with containers [14, 15].

To implement these two approaches, we can use type 2 hypervisors, for example, Virtual Box.

4.1 Virtualization in the Desktop Grid on BOINC

By default, BOINC provides the ability to send the binary file of the application and other files necessary for its operation. When a node accepts and launches a task in the BOINC client, the application associated with the accepted task is automatically executed.

To organize calculations using containers, a solution has been created – boinc2docker. Boinc2docker is a BOINC application that can run Docker containers, thereby simplifying the development and deployment of applications for BOINC [2]. The application works by combining two things – boot2docker and vboxwrapper. Boot2docker is a Linux operating system distribution that is made specifically for running Docker containers. This distribution works exclusively at the expense of RAM, takes about 24 MB and runs for about 5 s. The boot2docker distribution works in RAM, as it is based on TinyCoreLinux, a minimalistic Linux distribution.

Vboxwrapper is an application for BOINC that allows a node to run virtual machines using the VirtualBox program. This provides the following advantages:

- There is no need to develop applications for different platforms that nodes may have. Development takes place in the selected environment, for example, Ubuntu Linux, and then the virtual machine will run it for all platforms. This allows you to reduce the time and work on creating and maintaining applications if they were made for all operating systems.
- The virtual machine provides the most secure environment, since the application does not have access to it and cannot change anything in the host system.

For Vboxwrapper, the implementation of the checkpoint and restart mechanism is optional, since BOINC in this case provides it itself. However, using Vboxwrapper also has disadvantages associated with VirtualBox:

- not all volunteers have VirtualBox installed;
- VirtualBox only runs on x86-compatible processors.

In boinc2docker, the ISO-file from boot2docker was modified to be compatible with vboxwrapper and execute the transferred Docker image when the VM starts (Fig. 5).

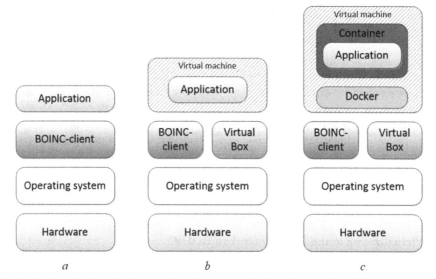

Fig. 5. Application launch schemes: (a) without virtualization; (b) virtual machine; (c) container.

A project with boinc2docker at the task generation stage downloads a given image from the Docker cloud, then the image is divided into layers, each of which is archived and sent to the node. A file is also generated vbox_job.xml, which specifies the settings for the VM being created by vboxwrapper and boinc_app. The boinc_app file unzips the layers on the node, forms the image again, and launches the container. After the container is launched, the commands specified in boinc_app are passed to it, which allow interacting with this container.

The layers for image formation are sent to the node only once, which does not cause additional overhead for data transmission when solving tasks again.

4.2 Application Virtualization

With the help of a pure virtual machine, we can also organize calculations. At the same time, the VBoxwrapper program is used again. This solution involves transferring a VM file, not an ISO-file, as with the boinc2docker approach, but a VDI-file (Virtual Disk Image) – a virtual hard disk that is used in VirtualBox.

However, before that, you need to prepare this VDI-file:

1. install the operating system;
2. install the Guest Additions provided by VirtualBox on it;
3. implement automatic login for a specific user;
4. implement a system in which, after logging in for a certain user, the script necessary to work with BOINC – boinc_app is run;
5. the boinc_app script should allow the developer to cancel the script execution, otherwise it will be impossible to change the VM;
6. the script should connect a shared folder inside the folder with BOINC, and just for this you need Guest Additions;
7. upload libraries or files that will be used for calculations.

5 Results and Discussion

5.1 Configure the BOINC-Server

Due to the specifics of the type of computational task, it is necessary to set the parameters of the created tasks for the project (Table 1), which differ from the default ones.

The most important option in the project is replication (the number of task instances created), which is responsible for computing redundancy. Given the specifics of the computational task, for the purpose of training the model, it is not so critically important to solve some specific project tasks.

The task in the project is to train a local node model on a random part of the dataset. To train a global model, it is enough to go through the entire data set, even if all the generated tasks were not solved, or some of them returned to the server with an error. This is contrasted with projects in which it is necessary to solve all tasks, for example, projects with data search. An example of such a project is the GIMPS (Great Internet Mersenne Prime Search) project for searching for a special kind of prime numbers – Mersenne numbers. In it, it is necessary to perform every task related to a prime number, since it is likely that it will allow you to find a new Mersenne number [16].

Thus, replication is set to a minimum value – 1, which actually means the rejection of redundancy calculations [17]. In the project, the deadline for solving the problem is set different from the default settings. To motivate nodes to solve tasks on time, a task deadline is set that corresponds to the iteration time, otherwise the results obtained are useless for the project. The iteration_start parameter was introduced in order not to wait for all tasks to be completed. This is done for several reasons. Firstly, as it was written earlier, it is not necessary to complete all generated tasks in order to fulfill the learning goal. Secondly, more tasks are created in case some nodes allocate more time to solve problems than usual, or more nodes connect to the system. This allows you to use the resources that are in the system more efficiently, not allowing them to stand idle.

Table 1. BOINC-server parameters.

Parameter	Description	Value
min_quorum	Minimum number of results required for validation	1
target_nresults	Replication Parameter	1
max_error_results	Maximum allowable number of erroneous results	1
max_success_results	The maximum allowed number of correct results	1
delay_bound	Workunits deadline	$t_{iteration}$
iteration_start	Acceptable percentage of aggregated results for a new iteration	50
max_wus_in_progress	Maximum number of workunits per node at a time	$t_{iteration}/t_{wu}$
daily_results_quota	The maximum number of workunits a node can receive in 24 h	$24/t_{wu}$

The max_wus_in_progress parameter is useful in order to prevent one node from taking all instances of tasks without letting other nodes solve them. The daily_results_quota parameter helps to control the maximum number of tasks that are sent to the node for calculation, reducing them if the node often produces erroneous results.

5.2 Experiment with Virtual Machine Approach

The computational experiment was carried out using the pure virtual machine approach. The server settings are set according to Table 1. 300 tasks were created at each iteration. The experiment lasted about 68 h. After the end of the experiment, statistics were collected through SQL queries to the project database. The number of users differs from the number of nodes, since people who have, on average, two devices to work in the application participated in the experiment. The Table 2 also shows the total number of tasks that were solved successfully, that is, the results were validated and assimilated by the project, as well as the number of erroneous tasks that failed for some reason and did not affect the global model.

Table 2. Statistics on nodes and number of tasks.

Parameter	Value
The number of nodes in the experiment	75
The number of users in the experiment	38
Number of completed iterations	64
Number of successful tasks	19 000
Number of erroneous tasks	1 027
Percentage of successful tasks	94.87

Table 2 shows the values associated with solving problems on nodes that are randomly distributed. This is the number of tasks solved by the node, including erroneous tasks. The task execution time was indicated in the table, excluding erroneous tasks, since they can give a strong deviation in time. Solving one problem precisely because of errors can take up to tens of hours. On average, the task execution time was approximately 9 min. This corresponds to the expected execution time, since with a given number of training epochs on a node, the task execution time on a single CPU core should take about 10 min on average. The iteration time in the experiment averaged 11 min, that is, it was during this time that 150 tasks needed to update the global model were solved and aggregated.

Figure 6 shows the dependence of the number of tasks completed successfully on time. The experiment started on May 28 at 17:41 UTC and ended on May 31 at 13:29 UTC. In total, it lasted about 68 h.

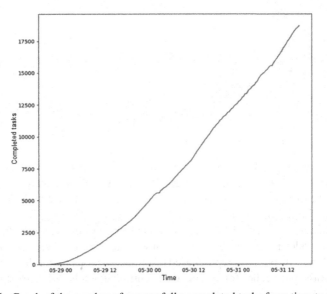

Fig. 6. Graph of the number of successfully completed tasks from time to time.

Figure 7 shows the distribution of task execution time. Only successful tasks were taken into account, since erroneous ones would give a strong outlier. The chart has peaks in the range from 250 to 500 s. This means that a significant number of tasks were solved on devices in which two or more CPU cores were allocated for the task. Also on the chart there is a local peak in the range from 800 to 1300 s. The delay in the execution of tasks was probably caused by:

- solving the problem on one dedicated core;
- suspending a task for a while;
- employment of the CPU core for other purposes.

As a result of the experiment, more than 70 nodes took part in the calculations. In 68 h, almost 20 thousand tasks were solved, more than 90% of them were calculated correctly.

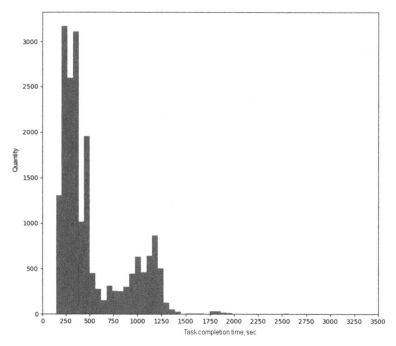

Fig. 7. Histogram of task execution time distribution.

The tasks were solved at different times of the day with similar intensity. This can be explained by the different time zones of the volunteers, or by active nodes that allocated their resources throughout the day.

Many volunteers in the project had computing resources in an amount that exceeded the average for nodes in the desktop grid. Such volunteers most likely joined the project to accumulate BOINC points and purchased resources specifically for these conclusions.

Virtualization approaches for solving deep learning tasks have been tested (Table 3).

Table 3. Comparison of virtualization approaches.

Parameter	Docker	Virtual Box
Approach	Container	Virtual machine
RAM usage, GB	7	2
Download data, MB	517	5 120
Average unzipping time after download, sec	–	305
Storage space usage, MB	517	10 240
Average startup time of virtual machine	62	135

Based on the results of testing, a comparison of these approaches was carried out and the following conclusions were obtained:

- The VirtualBox approach is the best for use in an open grid system in which there are computing nodes of volunteers, the average configuration of which consists of 11 GB of RAM and at least 10 GB of memory on a drive allocated for BOINC. This approach is better in this case, since it has lower costs for using RAM, and the memory costs on the drive are acceptable;
- The boinc2docker approach is the best for a closed grid system, for example, using cloud resources - that is, in systems where the nodes may have plenty of RAM, and a strict restriction is imposed on the memory on the drive.

6 Conclusion

One of the ways to simplify the launch of a computing application in a desktop grid system can be one of two types of virtualization. This is especially true for the tasks of training deep neural networks. Since training a local model on a desktop grid node requires configuration of dependencies. The use of any kind of virtualization requires certain resources. But at the same time, it becomes possible to use almost all nodes on which VirtualBox is installed. The formation of sufficiently complex computational tasks for nodes will reduce the share of virtualization costs and reduce the amount of data transferred between desktop grid nodes. The results of numerical experiments have shown that both virtualization approaches can be used in a desktop grid system to solve distributed deep learning problems.

Acknowledgements. This work was funded by Russian Science Foundation (№ 22-11-00317).

References

1. Foster, I., Kesselman, C.: The grid 2: blueprint for a new computing infrastructure (2004)
2. Anderson, D.P.: BOINC: a platform for volunteer computing. J. Grid Comput. **18**(1), 99–122 (2019). https://doi.org/10.1007/s10723-019-09497-9
3. Bockelman, B., Livny, M., Lin, B., Prelz, F.: Principles, technologies, and time: the translational journey of the HTCondor-CE. J. Comput. Sci. **52** (2021). https://doi.org/10.1016/j.jocs.2020.101213
4. Borges, G., et al.: Sun grid engine, a new scheduler for EGEE middleware. In: BERGRID–Iberian Grid Infrastructure Conference (2007)
5. Da, T., Morais, S.: Survey on frameworks for distributed computing: Hadoop, spark and storm. In: Proceedings of the 10th Doctoral Symposium in Informatics Engineering - DSIE'15 (2015)
6. Zaharia, M., et al.: Apache spark: a unified engine for big data processing. Commun. ACM **59**, 56–65 (2016). https://doi.org/10.1145/2934664
7. Ben-Nun, T., Hoefler, T.: Demystifying parallel and distributed deep learning: an in-depth concurrency analysis. ACM Comput. Surv. **52** (2019). https://doi.org/10.1145/3320060
8. Bellavista, P., Foschini, L., Mora, A.: Decentralised learning in federated deployment environments: a system-level survey (2021). https://doi.org/10.1145/3429252

9. Abdulrahman, S., Tout, H., Ould-Slimane, H., Mourad, A., Talhi, C., Guizani, M.: A survey on federated learning: the journey from centralized to distributed on-site learning and beyond. IEEE Internet Things J. **8**, 5476–5497 (2021). https://doi.org/10.1109/JIOT.2020.3030072

10. Kingma, D.P., Ba, J.L.: Adam: a method for stochastic optimization. In: 3rd International Conference on Learning Representations, ICLR 2015 - Conference Track Proceedings (2015)

11. BOINC projects: List BOINC projects. https://boinc.berkeley.edu/projects.php. Accessed 22 May 2023

12. Top 500. https://top500.org/lists/top500/2023/06/. Accessed 01 Aug 2023

13. Watada, J., Roy, A., Kadikar, R., Pham, H., Xu, B.: Emerging trends, techniques and open issues of containerization: a review (2019). https://doi.org/10.1109/ACCESS.2019.2945930

14. Molto, G., Caballer, M., Perez, A., Alfonso, C. De, Blanquer, I.: Coherent application delivery on hybrid distributed computing infrastructures of virtual machines and docker containers. In: Proceedings - 2017 25th Euromicro International Conference on Parallel, Distributed and Network-Based Processing, PDP 2017, pp. 486–490. Institute of Electrical and Electronics Engineers Inc. (2017). https://doi.org/10.1109/PDP.2017.29

15. Chung, M.T., Quang-Hung, N., Nguyen, M.T., Thoai, N.: Using Docker in high performance computing applications. In: 2016 IEEE 6th International Conference on Communications and Electronics, IEEE ICCE 2016, pp. 52–57 (2016). https://doi.org/10.1109/CCE.2016.7562612

16. Garcia, S., Miller, S.: Great internet Mersenne prime search (GIMPS). In: 100 Years of Math Milestones (2019). https://doi.org/10.1090/mbk/121/84

17. Kurochkin, I.I., Kostylev, I.S.: Solving the problem of texture images classification using synchronous distributed deep learning on desktop grid systems (2020). https://doi.org/10.1007/978-3-030-64616-5_55

Workflows of the High-Throughput Virtual Screening as a Service

Natalia Nikitina[1](✉) and Evgeny Ivashko[1,2]

[1] Institute of Applied Mathematical Research, Karelian Research Center of the
Russian Academy of Sciences, 185910 Petrozavodsk, Russia
{nikitina,ivashko}@krc.karelia.ru
[2] Petrozavodsk State University, 185035 Petrozavodsk, Russia

Abstract. The HiTViSc service is a new advanced tool for implementing high-performance virtual screening using cloud computing and distributed computing technologies of the Desktop Grid type based on the Desktop Grid as a Service concept. The paper describes three main workflows implemented by the HiTViSc user. The main workflow is related to the setup, selection of input data and the launch of a virtual screening, which is performed by the user using a special "experiment wizard". Auxiliary workflows are related to the analysis of the results of virtual screening using external programs and the management of computing resources.

Keywords: Distributed computing · Desktop Grid · BOINC · Cloud computing · Software as a Service · Desktop Grid as a Service · HiTViSc

1 Introduction

High-performance computing (HPC) is an important and powerful tool of the modern fundamental and applied research and development. With the help of high-performance computing, many scientific problems can be solved using computer modeling. However, the variety of computational platforms requires a careful choice of an effective tool for a specific computationally heavy problem.

One of such computationally heavy problems is virtual screening. Desktop Grid systems provide high throughput and scalability for virtual screening implementation. However, a Desktop Grid implementation is technically challenging for scientists, and the maintaining of the computing system is not easier. For this reason, the number of existing volunteer computing projects is still low. High-Throughput Virtual Screening as a Service, a cloud-based virtual screening service based on Desktop Grid, built on the principles of Desktop Grid as a Service, can become a solution to this problem.

The presented work continues the project of developing a cloud-based service for performing virtual screening, High-Throughput Virtual Screening as a Service (HiTViSc) based on the Desktop Grid. In the paper, we consider the workflows embedded in HiTViSc and the main models of user's work in the system.

V. Voevodin et al. (Eds.): RuSCDays 2023, LNCS 14389, pp. 91–102, 2023.
https://doi.org/10.1007/978-3-031-49435-2_7

The structure of the paper is as follows. In Sect. 2, we provide basic information about the HiTViSc cloud service and review related work. In Sect. 3, we describe the main workflow of virtual screening (Sect. 3.1), auxiliary workflows of result analysis (Sect. 3.2) and the management of computational resources (Sect. 3.3). Section 4 presents the final conclusions and discussion.

2   HiTViSc Concept and Related Work

The presented paper is devoted to the High-Throughput Virtual Screening as a Service, which is a specialized cloud-based virtual screening service based on highly scalable resources of a Desktop Grid. Desktop Grid is a distributed high-throughput computing system which uses idle resources of non-dedicated geographically distributed computing nodes connected over regular network. Typical computing nodes of a Desktop Grid are Internet-connected computers belonging to volunteers (this approach is called volunteer computing) or locally-connected organizational workstations (this approach is called Enterprise Desktop Grid) [4].

Desktop Grid computing gives a huge computing capacity at low costs but raises new challenges related to high heterogeneity of computing nodes, their low reliability and availability, etc. The potential computational power of volunteer computing has the order of hundreds of ExaFLOPS [1]. There are a number of software systems implementing Desktop Grid technologies: BOINC, Condor, XtremWeb and others (see [11] for the deeper analysis). De-facto, BOINC (Berkeley Open Infrastructure for Network Computing) is the standard and the most popular platform for volunteer computing. BOINC includes the server part that provides storage of all subtasks, their distribution among the computing nodes, collection of intermediate results, processing of errors that occur during the computational process. The client part of BOINC is represented by an installable application available for various software and hardware platforms that provides isolation of computations and interaction with the server. The BOINC architecture is considered in more detail in work [1].

Desktop Grids are limited to "bag-of-tasks" problems that have independent parallelism and low data/compute ratio (the examples are combinatorial problems, parameter sweep optimization, Monte Carlo simulations, and others). One of such problems is virtual screening, one of the main stages of drug development process. Virtual screening comprises the formation of a set of hits (candidate chemical compounds for passing to subsequent stages of development) that potentially have a high required biochemical activity towards the target – a macromolecule associated with the disease development. Hits are sought among small molecules called ligands. In the process of virtual screening, the interaction of ligands with the target is simulated and the probability to form stable molecular complexes is estimated. Ligands with high estimates of this probability become hits. An important feature of virtual screening is that it is not limited to existing libraries of synthesized molecules and can also be used to evaluate compounds that have not been synthesized, as well as molecular fragments. Virtual screening is performed by special computer programs for molecular docking such as AutoDock Vina, CmDock, GOLD, FlexX etc. [14].

The challenge of virtual screening is the need for significant computational resources and time required to evaluate the potential pharmacological properties of a set of molecules and to identify the most prospective ligands. Despite the fact that molecular docking of a single ligand to a predetermined target is quite fast, the volume of ligand libraries leads to the need to use HPC tools for virtual screening. Therefore, services for organizing the virtual screening process using HPC resources are in demand. Recently, such solutions have been proposed based on cloud computing [10,13], on the Chinese National Grid CNGrid [15] and on a supercomputer Tianhe-2 [7].

The work develops research related to the SiDock@home [9] volunteer computing project and the development of the Desktop Grid as a Service [5] concept, according to which HPC resources are provided to the user in the form of a specialized cloud service, High-Throughput Virtual Screening as a Service (HiTViSc). The concept of HiTViSc has been described in paper [8].

HiTViSc implements three levels of functions:

1. The computational level performs high-throughput computing with the use of a Desktop Grid. A Desktop Grid server provides task generation, performs data exchange with computing nodes during the process of task assignment, transfers input data and computational applications to the computing nodes, and performs accounting of the results. An existing Desktop Grid middleware such as BOINC or Condor can be used to implement this level.
2. Virtual screening process is performed on the second level. It provides special functions of virtual screening, such as a target file uploading or selection, specifying the database of ligands, selection of a computational application. It also sets specific project' parameters and performs selection of a protocol for molecular docking and results processing. On the final stage, it allows the selection of external applications for results visualization and final analysis.
3. The user level provides the user space and interfaces to access the cloud application itself. This includes various interfaces to setup and maintain the process of virtual screening, visualize the progress, visualize and analyze the results, as well as administer the computational resources.

The workflows assume that the user, with a graphical interface (at the third logical level), sets up and runs a virtual screening experiment (second level), managing the available computing resources (first level). The computing nodes of the HiTViSc service are Desktop Grid clients that can be of various types and architectures.

The HiTViSc system supports the independent operation of multiple users. Each user can conduct their computational experiments in an isolated environment and, at the same time, deploy the entire resource pool shared among the users by means of a task scheduler.

A computing project does also follow the multi-user approach. Project owner controls what level of access do other users have to the project settings, computing resources and results.

An important feature of HiTViSc is the preservation and flexible management of the generated data of virtual screening. Users can make benefit of the prepared ligand libraries, whole virtual screening setups and the results, provided the author has granted appropriate rights. Such an approach complies with good practices in the field of bioinformatics and, at the same time, with the principles of the volunteer computing community that values open data.

3   Workflows of the HiTViSc

In accordance with its purpose, the HiTViSc service has three main workflows, which are described below: (1) performing virtual screening, (2) performing primary analysis of results, and (3) managing available computing resources. From the user's point of view, virtual screening comprises one or many independent *computational experiments*. A computational experiment is a virtual screening of a given library of ligands against a given target using given software settings.

3.1   Virtual Screening

The main workflow within the HiTViSc service is the execution of a computational experiment of virtual screening, which occurs as follows:

1. *Upload of the target.* The first step in virtual screening is to select and upload a target description file. The standard format at this step is PDB structural model openly provided by the leading database RCSB Protein Data Bank (RCSB PDB) [2]. Following the common practice, the user prepares the target for molecular docking either by direct upload of a PDB file or via the open interface to the RCSB PDB. In the latter case, HiTViSc downloads a PDB file from a remote database using a standard URL such as, for example, https:// files.rcsb.org/download/7FRV.pdb. The target size is about 0.5–5 Mb; it is downloaded on demand and stored in the HiTViSc service database as part of a computational experiment.
2. *Selection of the molecular docking program.* There are many molecular docking programs that differ both conceptually and technically (settings formats, file formats, etc.). Each docking program has its own features associated with the presentation of input and output files, the interpretation of the results. At the current stage, HiTViSc service supports two molecular docking programs: AutoDock Vina (one of the most common and efficient free open source software) and CmDock (an efficient, developing, free open source software). For the latter, the PDB source file is automatically converted to the AS+MOL2+PRM file set.
3. *Selection of the ligand library.* The preparation of a ligand library is an expert task; its result affects the quality of virtual screening. The file format depends on the selected molecular docking program. PDBQT format is used for AutoDock Vina, SDF format for CmDock. Conversion is performed automatically by the HiTViSc service. The selection is made among open libraries available on the Internet or uploaded by the user. Next, the system provides the tools to filter the library, store and address it in specific virtual screening experiments. Moreover, an urgent problem is the support of

customized author-developed libraries that can be annotated and reused by other users of HiTViSc.

4. *Setup of reference ligands.* One can also define a set of reference ligands for the selected target. These ligands are defined in the form of 3D molecular models docked to the target and are used to evaluate the quality of virtual screening results by the estimated binding energy and structural similarity. Typically, a reference ligand has been experimentally confirmed and can thus assist in evaluation of the set of hits. The reference binding energy is a single number that can be used to select hits that are potentially "better" than an experimentally confirmed ligand. The structural similarity between two molecules is a numerical coefficient expressing the "distance" between their binary vector representations (for example, the Tanimoto coefficient). It can be used to characterize and/or cluster the set of hits represented as a set of points in 2- or 3-dimensional space. Finally, the docking pose of the reference ligand can assist in visual inspection of the docked hits.

5. *Setup of the molecular docking protocol.* At this step, the user selects how each single ligand will be docked against the target. Modern programs for molecular docking allow a complex and flexible adjustment of many parameters. Let us consider a basic setting of docking a single ligand against a rigid target and summarize the user-selected parameters in Table 1. The system interface provides a default docking protocol with the possibility to edit the settings.

Table 1. User-selected parameters of the molecular docking protocol for AutoDock Vina and CmDock programs.

Parameters	AutoDock Vina	CmDock
Docking site	Coordinates of the center, box dimensions	Coordinates of the center, sphere volume, number of cavities
Force field	AutoDock4, Vina or Vinardo	—
Docking runs	The number of runs	The number of runs, the number of additional runs

6. *Setup of the computational experiment protocol.* At this step, the user selects how the hits will be defined and when the computational experiment stops.
   - Hit selection criterion – a numerical threshold to mark the ligands as hits if their docking result exceeds this value. It can be (a) binding energy or (b) ligand efficiency (binding energy normalized by atoms count).
   - Experiment stopping criterion – a numerical threshold to stop the computational experiment when the condition is met. It can be (a) the number of screened ligands or (b) the number of retrieved hits.

7. *Selection of the computational resources.* Different experiment settings may require computational resources of different performance. As the proposed

system operates within the Desktop Grid environment, one can also distinguish resources of different reliability. Usually, computers provided by volunteers provide high total throughput but a relatively low reliability. In contrast, a user can add own reliable computers of any performance and, optionally, share them with other users.

8. *Start and stop of the computational experiment.* A user can prioritize their experiments in a flexible way, including pausing one experiment in favor of another. This step of the HiTViSc workflow is important due to the long running time of virtual screening and the need to effectively share computational resources with the tasks of other users.

9. *Progress display of the computational experiment.* A running experiment on virtual screening proceeds over the ligands library and generates hits. The dynamics of such experiment can be represented from two points of view:

    – Computational point of view. The total running time, the count of completed tasks (or the portion of processed molecules from the library) and prediction of the completion time of the computational experiment are displayed. These statistics may be of interest both to the author of the experiment and to the volunteers who provided their computers as Desktop Grid clients.

    – Problem-specific point of view. The count of hits, the library coverage (e.g. number of processed clusters), the chemical diversity of the found hits are displayed. These statistics are typically restricted to the author of the experiment only.

As an example, Fig. 1 demonstrates a screenshot of the progress display of the series of computational experiments carried out in the long-running volunteer computing project SiDock@home. This progress display has the form of the percentage of processed molecules from the library.

The choice of settings for the computational experiment of virtual screening is a sequential workflow, which is implemented in the HiTViSc service using a special "experiment wizard".

3.2 Results Analysis

The results of the virtual screening have the form of a list of hit molecules sorted by their estimates of the binding energy to the target. For each hit, the system stores its structural description, an estimate of the binding energy, and a specific docking conformation corresponding to this estimate and representing a three-dimensional spatial model of this molecule in conjunction with the target macromolecule. Accordingly, a user can analyze the whole set of hits as well as a single selected hit.

Analysis of the Set of Hits. In practice, the analysis and visualization of a set of small molecules is typically performed using dimensionality reduction methods (such as PCA) and clustering. There are plenty of available third-party programs to process sets of molecules with suitable bioinformatics algorithms. 2D

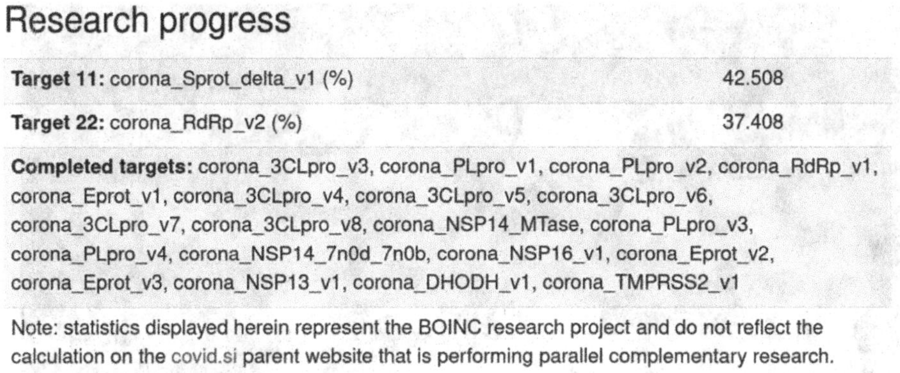

Research progress

Target 11: corona_Sprot_delta_v1 (%)	42.508
Target 22: corona_RdRp_v2 (%)	37.408

Completed targets: corona_3CLpro_v3, corona_PLpro_v1, corona_PLpro_v2, corona_RdRp_v1, corona_Eprot_v1, corona_3CLpro_v4, corona_3CLpro_v5, corona_3CLpro_v6, corona_3CLpro_v7, corona_3CLpro_v8, corona_NSP14_MTase, corona_PLpro_v3, corona_PLpro_v4, corona_NSP14_7n0d_7n0b, corona_NSP16_v1, corona_Eprot_v2, corona_Eprot_v3, corona_NSP13_v1, corona_DHODH_v1, corona_TMPRSS2_v1

Note: statistics displayed herein represent the BOINC research project and do not reflect the calculation on the covid.si parent website that is performing parallel complementary research.

Fig. 1. Example of the progress display of the series of computational experiments in SiDock@home project as of three years of its operation.

visualization is also used in the form of points projected onto a plane (for visual assessment of clustering and chemical diversity). The HiTViSc service offers the following options for 2D visualization of the set of small molecules:

1. Visualization of binding energy and structural similarity in the absence of reference ligands. A set of molecules is projected onto a plane in such a way that the distance between two points is inversely proportional to the structural similarity of the corresponding molecules. Point color corresponds to the value of the binding energy of the given molecule.
2. Visualization of binding energy and structural similarity in the presence of a reference ligand. The set of molecules is represented as points on the plane in such a way that the X coordinate corresponds to the value of the structural similarity between the molecule and the reference ligand, Y to the value of the binding energy.

A user may also perform 3D visualization of a set of hits via third party programs. Figure 2 demonstrates an example of the 3D representation of a set of ligands docked to the target protein.

Finally, the user can filter and upload the results in one of standard formats of molecular representations. The data may then be processed, analyzed and visualized with any third-party independent programs.

Analysis of a Selected Hit. 3D visualization is applied: in the form of molecular structures docked to the target (used for visual evaluation of the molecular docking results and comparison with reference ligands, if any). Third party programs (e.g. PyMOL) or web services (e.g. MolMil) are used. Figure 3 demonstrates an example of the 3D visual comparison of a virtual screening hit to a reference ligand docked to the target protein.

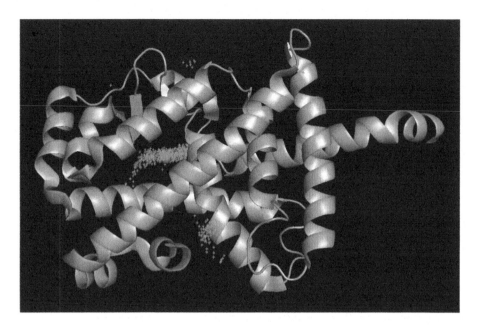

Fig. 2. Example of the visual analysis of a set of hits (depicted by blue markers at the centers of mass of each ligand) docked to the target; the reference ligand is depicted by a blue sphere). The visualization has been performed by PyMOL [12] (Color figure online).

3.3 Management of the Computational Resources

The next workflow consists in the administration of the computational resources. The described service concept assumes three types of computational resources that can be used in virtual screening as computing nodes of the Desktop Grid:

- Test environment. A limited amount of highly available and reliable computational resources to test parameters on a small amount of computations.
- System computing resources shared by volunteers and other users of HiTViSc, deployed to perform general experiments.
- Own and partner computational resources connected to the system, which can be deployed for own experiments, partner projects or provided for general use.

Known issues in Desktop Grid are related to the availability and reliability of computing resources. In volunteer computing, these issues are solved with the help of replication and deadlines [1,3]. However, the problem of fast discovery of reliable results is relevant for test runs of projects, required for debugging and checking virtual screening settings. For this purpose, the HiTViSc service maintains a pool of reliable and accessible computing resources, which can be the nodes of Enterprise Desktop Grid or selected from the general pool of resources connected to the service, having the maximum availability and reliability ratings.

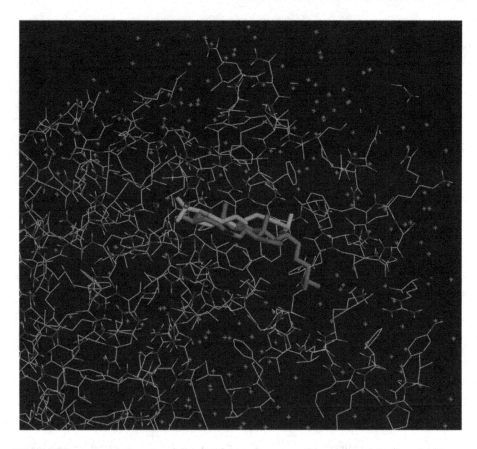

Fig. 3. Example of the visual comparison of a virtual screening hit (in pink) to a reference ligand (in green) docked to the target protein (a fragment is shown). The visualization has been performed by PyMOL [12] (Color figure online).

The user can provide the HiTViSc service with the computational resources available to them in accordance with the principles of volunteer computing. This pool of volunteer computational resources is the main source of resources for performing virtual screening experiments.

The HiTViSc service can be used to conveniently implement virtual screening experiments for which the user has sufficient available resources. One main use case assumes that the pool of volunteer computational resources is used to implement a computational experiment. To fill and expand the pool of available resources, standard volunteer computing methods can be used (ensuring openness, informational attractiveness, organizing competitions, issuing badges, etc. [6]). In addition, a special resource use policy can be developed that ensures greater availability of resources and higher priority for those users who have provided more resources to the common pool of the HiTViSc service.

The registration procedure for new compute nodes in the HiTViSc (Fig. 4) corresponds to the standard registration procedure for BOINC projects and uses the built-in BOINC client and server tools. The process is as follows:

- on the Desktop Grid server, there is a predefined BOINC user account *regnode* with password *regnode*;
- in the "My Resources" section, a "Connection" button is available. When one clicks it, a user prompt *regnode* appears to connect, and a link in the *https://dgaas.org/reg/<id>* style, where the first part of the link is the standard project address for connection, and the second (*<id>*) is the identifier of the user – owner of the resource;
- the user performs a standard connection procedure in his BOINC client by selecting the appropriate menu item, entering the received project link and user credentials *regnode*;
- the HiTViSc server receives a connection request, records the user ID and device ID in the database and passes the request on to connect to the BOINC server;
- The BOINC server performs the standard internal registration procedure.

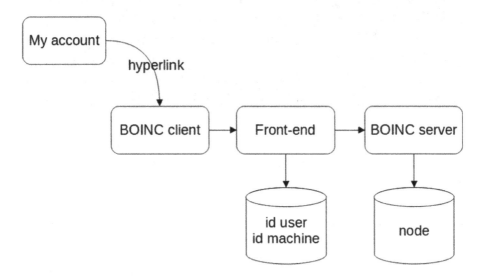

Fig. 4. Registration procedure.

4   Conclusion

The HiTViSc service is a new advanced tool for implementing high-performance virtual screening using cloud computing and distributed computing technologies of the Desktop Grid type based on the Desktop Grid as a Service concept.

The paper describes three main workflows implemented by the HiTViSc user. The main workflow is related to the setup, selection of input data and the launch of a virtual screening, which is performed by the user using a special "experiment wizard". Auxiliary workflows are related to the analysis of the results of virtual screening using external programs, and the management of computing resources.

Built on the basis of accessible, highly scalable Desktop Grid resources (for example, through BOINC), HiTViSc implements the features on their management as well as support for a full cycle of virtual screening.

References

1. Anderson, D.: BOINC: a platform for volunteer computing. J. Grid Comput. **18**, 99–122 (2020). https://doi.org/10.1007/s10723-019-09497-9
2. Berman, H.M., et al.: The protein data bank. Nucleic Acids Res. **28**(1), 235–242 (2000). https://doi.org/10.1093/nar/28.1.235
3. Ivashko, E., Chernov, I.A., Nikitina, N.: A survey of Desktop Grid scheduling. IEEE Trans. Parallel Distrib. Syst. **29**, 2882–2895 (2018). https://doi.org/10.1109/TPDS.2018.2850004
4. Ivashko, E.: Desktop Grid and cloud computing: short survey. In: Voevodin, V., Sobolev, S. (eds.) Supercomputing, pp. 445–456. Springer International Publishing, Cham (2021). https://doi.org/10.1007/978-3-030-92864-3_34
5. Ivashko, E.: Desktop Grid as a service concept. In: Voevodin, V., Sobolev, S., Yakobovskiy, M., Shagaliev, R. (eds.) Supercomputing, pp. 632–643. Springer International Publishing, Cham (2022). https://doi.org/10.1007/978-3-031-22941-1_46
6. Kurochkin, I.I., Yakimets, V.N., et al.: Attraction of volunteers in projects of voluntary distributed computing. Probl. Inf. Technol. (2), 60–69 (2019)
7. Mo, Q., Xu, Z., Yan, H., Chen, P., Lu, Y.: VSTH: a user-friendly web server for structure-based virtual screening on Tianhe-2. Bioinformatics **39**(1), btac740740 (2023)
8. Nikitina, N., Ivashko, E.: Hitvisc: high-throughput virtual screening as a service. In: Malyshkin, V. (ed.) Parallel Computing Technologies, pp. 83–92. Springer Nature Switzerland, Cham (2023). https://doi.org/10.1007/978-3-031-41673-6_7
9. Nikitina, N., Manzyuk, M., Podlipnik, Č, Jukić, M.: Volunteer computing project SiDock@home for virtual drug screening against SARS-CoV-2. In: Byrski, A., Czachórski, T., Gelenbe, E., Grochla, K., Murayama, Y. (eds.) ANTICOVID 2021. IAICT, vol. 616, pp. 23–34. Springer, Cham (2021). https://doi.org/10.1007/978-3-030-86582-5_3
10. Olğaç, A., Türe, A., Olğaç, S., Möller, S.: Cloud-based high throughput virtual screening in novel drug discovery. In: Kołodziej, J., González-Vélez, H. (eds.) High-Performance Modelling and Simulation for Big Data Applications. LNCS, vol. 11400, pp. 250–278. Springer, Cham (2019). https://doi.org/10.1007/978-3-030-16272-6_9
11. Rahmany, M., Sundararajan, A., Zin, A.: A review of Desktop Grid computing middlewares on non-dedicated resources. J. Theor. Appl. Inf. Technol. **98**(10), 1654–1663 (2020)
12. Schrödinger, L., DeLano, W.: Pymol. https://www.pymol.org/pymol

13. Singh, N., Chaput, L., Villoutreix, B.O.: Virtual screening web servers: designing chemical probes and drug candidates in the cyberspace. Brief. Bioinform. **22**(2), 1790–1818 (2021)
14. Torres, P.H., Sodero, A.C., Jofily, P., Silva-Jr, F.P.: Key topics in molecular docking for drug design. Int. J. Mol. Sci. **20**(18), 4574 (2019)
15. Zhang, B., Li, H., Yu, K., Jin, Z.: Molecular docking-based computational platform for high-throughput virtual screening. CCF Trans. High Perform. Comput. **4**, 63–74 (2022)

HPC, BigData, AI: Algorithms, Technologies, Evaluation

3D Seismic Inversion for Fracture Model Reconstruction Based on Machine Learning

Maxim Protasov[1]([✉]) [ID], Roman Kenzhin[1,2] [ID], and Evgeniy Pavlovskiy[2] [ID]

[1] Institute of Petroleum Geology and Geophysics, Novosibirsk, Russia
protasovmi@ipgg.sbras.ru, r.kenzhin@nsu.ru
[2] Novosibirsk State University, Novosibirsk, Russia
e.pavlovskiy@g.nsu.ru

Abstract. The presented paper is devoted to the numerical study of the applicability of 3D inversion for fracture model reconstruction based on machine learning. In practice, geophysicists use seismic inversion for predicting reservoir properties. One-dimensional convolutional model lies in the basis of standard versions of inversion, but geology is more complex. That is why we provide implementation and investigation of the approach for 3D fracture model reconstruction based machine learning, which uses U-net neural network and 3D convolutional model. We provide numerical results for a realistic 3D synthetic fractured model from the North of Russia.

Keywords: 3D Fractured Model · Machine Learning · 3D Convolutional Model

1 Introduction

Faults and fractures can significantly affect the filtration processes in reservoirs. Therefore, the analysis of their spatial structure and its modeling is of high importance in planning the development and operation of oil and gas reservoirs. As a rule, serious errors and limitations accompany the measurement of the geometric characteristics of fracture systems [1]. Therefore, a statistical approach is usually used to describe them. In this paper, we explored the possibilities of reconstructing fracture systems and fracture corridors from seismic data by using discrete fracture network (DFN) model, which requires a specification of the size, spatial position, and orientation of every fracture [2].

In practice, seismic inversion is a standard procedure, the major result of which is a high frequency model of the acoustic impedances, which allows predicting reservoir properties [3, 4]. Usually, geophysicists use seismic inversion as an algorithm that operates with a time or migrated time seismic section [3, 5]. However, one-dimensional convolutional model lies in the basis of seismic inversion that is valid for a horizontally layered medium [3, 5]. The realistic geological models may not satisfy this condition, for example, because it may contain lateral inhomogeneities connected with the fractured zones. To overcome these limitations, we propose to implement inversion algorithms based on two-dimensional and three-dimensional convolutional models.

V. Voevodin et al. (Eds.): RuSCDays 2023, LNCS 14389, pp. 105–117, 2023.
https://doi.org/10.1007/978-3-031-49435-2_8

Nowadays, diffraction images and seismic technologies allowing their construction have great attention of researchers and practical geophysicists. The need to search and develop fractured reservoirs has led to active research and the use of the scattered component of the wave field [6]. Various estimates indicate that fractured reservoirs contain a large percentage of the world's oil and gas reserves. Information about small-scale geological objects is contained in the scattered component of the seismic wave field. Correct processing of this component allows one to identify such geologically interesting objects as fractures, reservoirs, faults, cavernous-fractured zones [7, 8]. Therefore, we propose usage of diffraction images for fracture model reconstruction.

A lot of recent solutions of seismic data processing problems and seismic interpretation problems are based on machine learning methods. Researchers provide investigation and successful application of this method to different seismic data processing problems, such as data enhancement and denoising [9], seismic data interpolation [10], and many others [11]. In seismic interpretation, geophysicists widely used machine learning for classification problems, such as seismic facies analysis [12]. Finally, the machine learning methods have outstanding success in the solution the 1D seismic inversion problems in many real reservoirs [13, 14].

In this paper, we suggest the application of a machine learning methods. We provide implementation and investigation of the approach for 3D fracture model reconstruction. The proposed approach consists of two main components: UNet neural network architecture [15] and 3D depth convolution modeling. 3D convolutional modeling provides the possibility for fast construction of training dataset, and UNet allows reconstruct the fractured model on the basis of the trained dataset. We provide the numerical experiments and results for a realistic 3D synthetic fractured model from the North of Russia.

2   3D Seismic Models and Images

2.1 Discrete Fracture Model

To model a discrete fracture network statistically, we use the scheme described in [2]. We represent fractures as ellipsoids. The average direction of the plane in which the fracture is located we determine by the dip angle value that defines the dip direction. Also, we determine the orientation of the plane via the normal direction. We suppose that the value of the dip angle provides fractures orientation in the vertical plane. For each family of fractures, we provide the distribution of dip directions via defining average dip value and the variance of the dip values of the fracture family. We also determine the distribution of the angle, which describes the deviation of the direction of the main axis from the XY plane. We determine the geometric dimensions of fractures by the dimensions of the main axes. Analogously to the work [2], we provide statistical modeling for the fracture length L (major axis of an ellipsoid). We determine the fracture width W (mean axis value of an ellipsoid) using the simulated fractured length, and determination of the statistical distribution of the relation L/W. Usually, the fractures thickness T (minor axis value of an ellipsoid) is a constant. However, when geometry (sizes and angles) is determined for every fractured we do not need statistical modeling and we use that information directly.

After we do the fractures geometry modeling, then we need to put the fractures on a coarse grid model. The thickness of the fractures is significantly less than the grid step, so a correct solution to the up-scaling problem is necessary. To solve this problem, we use statistical modeling, where in each cell of the sparse grid, we calculate the average value of the indicator function, proportional to the intensity of the fractures. We provide validation of the solution via comparison of ideal seismic images for the models with different grid step.

2.2 3D Seismic Migration and Ideal Images

We use the diffraction imaging algorithm for the localization of fractured zones. The implementation of the algorithm is based on the visualization condition in structural angles [16]:

$$Image(\overline{x}_i; \beta, az) = \int T^{gbs}(\overline{x}_s; \overline{x}_i; \gamma, \theta, \beta, az; \omega)$$

$$\cdot \overrightarrow{T}^{gbr}(\overline{x}_r; \overline{x}_i; \gamma, \theta, \beta, az; \omega) \cdot \overrightarrow{u}^{obs}(\overline{x}_r; \overline{x}_s; \omega) d\overline{x}_r d\overline{x}_s d\gamma d\theta d\omega. \qquad (1)$$

Here $\overrightarrow{u}^{obs}(\overline{x}_r; \overline{x}_s; \omega)$ are multi-component seismic data, and summation weights are calculated on the acquisition surface, which are the Gaussian beam weights in the receivers coordinates and in the sources coordinates:

$$T^{gbs}(\overline{x}_s; \overline{x}_i; \gamma, \theta, \beta, az; \omega), \overrightarrow{T}^{gbr}(\overline{x}_r; \overline{x}_i; \gamma, \theta, \beta, az; \omega). \qquad (2)$$

These weights depend on the structural azimuth and dip angles, as well as the opening angles. Angle domain realization provides a possibility to control the visibility/invisibility of geological objects, and finally provides diffraction images that allow one to find fracture zones [17].

It is shown that the function $Image(\overline{x}_i; \beta, az)$ consists of two linear operators, i.e. it is the superposition of the direct Fourier transform and the "partial" inverse Fourier transform [16]:

$$Image(\overline{x}_i; \beta, az) = \iiint_{X_{par}} F(\omega(\overline{p})) e^{i \cdot \overline{p} \cdot \overline{x}_i} d\overline{p} \iiint_{R_3} f(\overline{y}; \beta, az) e^{-i \cdot \overline{p} \cdot \overline{y}} d\overline{y}, \qquad (3)$$

on the desired perturbation $f(\overline{y}; \beta, az)$ of the macro model. We call the inverse Fourier transform as a "partial" because it is performed only over the subset X_{par} of the entire spectral space. We call X_{par} as the partial reconstruction domain. The function $f(\overline{y}; \beta, az)$ is the scattering potential, and the function $Image(\overline{x}_i; \beta, az)$ is the projection of the scattering potential in the spectral domain, and we call it the ideal image. This is what we can ideally obtain for a given range of seismic frequencies and for a correct migration model and for ideal data with a given acquisition system without noise and without multiples. To calculate an ideal image using formula (3), one must do the Fourier transform of the scattering potential, then project the result onto the partial reconstruction set, and finally do the inverse Fourier transform. We suggest using ideal images for several reasons. The first is obvious: to test the imaging procedure. Another reason is related to the huge computational resources required for numerical modeling of 3D seismic data.

3 Fracture Model Reconstruction Using Machine Learning

3.1 The Dataset for Machine Learning

Physical and numerical experiments show that the presence of fractures in a medium provides the appearance of scattered waves; moreover, the process of seismic waves propagation in a medium with fractures is similar to the process of wave propagation in a medium with localized inhomogeneities of elastic properties. Therefore, many researchers consider fractures on the seismic scale as scatterers/diffractors, which represent the scattered/diffracted part of the model. It is the scatterers/diffractors within the seismic model that are the target that needs to be reconstructed from the depth seismic image, which is the result of seismic data processing. Above we mentioned that alternatively, we can get depth image via 3D convolutional modeling, and it is called 3D ideal image. Thus we suggest to implement and investigate seismic inversion based on the usage of the 3D ideal seismic images because it is a computationally cheap procedure, and therefore it allows to reproduce a lot of seismic images in a fast manner for creating machine leaning dataset. In addition, we create a fairly large number of different 3D models of localized fractures, and easily provide images using fairly small computational resources. This way, we can build a training dataset for a machine learning algorithm within a reasonable computation time.

3.2 The UNet Neural Network for the Machine Learning Algorithm

To predict the fractures, we consider the task as a semantic segmentation of the fractures. The initial hypothesis is to check the capability of some generally used semantic segmentation architecture, like UNet, to reveal the fractures. For that task, the following rule selects the Ground True from the dataset: we label by value 1.0 pixels which correspond to the fractures and value 0.0 for all other pixels. As post-processing after UNet predictions, we apply min-max normalization (4):

$$minmax(x) = \frac{x - \min(x)}{\max(x) - \min(x)} \tag{4}$$

For the machine learning process, we take the standard UNet architecture [15] with small modification: in each double convolution, the first kernel has size 7×7. It has one channel on input and output, see Table 1. For semantic segmentation task, we take the Dice score (5) as a quality measure:

$$Dice\left(x^t, x^p\right) = 2 \frac{\sum_{i,j=1,1}^{150,380} x_{ij}^t * x_{ij}^p}{\sum_{i,j=1,1}^{150,380} x_{ij}^t + x_{ij}^p}, \tag{5}$$

where x^t, x^p – is the ground true and predicted array of pixels correspondingly. The choice of neural network architecture (U-Net) and loss function (Dice-loss) is due to their wide use for solving typical problems of semantic segmentation.

We combine the following loss functions to find the best solution by Dice score: binary-cross entropy (6), dice loss (7), and mean square error loss (8), where σ stands for sigmoid function:

$$\mathcal{L}_{BCE}\left(x^t, x^p\right) = -\frac{1}{N}\sum\nolimits_{i=1}^{N}\left(x_i^t \cdot log\sigma(x_i^p) + (1 - x_i^t) \cdot log\left(1 - \sigma\left(x_i^p\right)\right)\right), \quad (6)$$

$$\mathcal{L}_{Dice}\left(x^t, x^p\right) = 1 - Dice\left(x^t, x^p\right), \quad (7)$$

$$\mathcal{L}_{MSE}\left(x^t, x^p\right) = \frac{1}{N}\sum_{i=1}^{N}\left|x_i^p - x_i^t\right|^2 \quad (8)$$

We use AdamW optimizer [18] with batch size of 20 samples with learning rate 0.001 without scheduling. We implemented the code of training in Python 3.7 with PyTorch library version 1.21.1.

Table 1. Architecture of the UNet. MaxP is MaxPooling2D (kernel = 2x2, stride = 2, padding = 0, dilation = 1), DC(x,y) is Conv2D(in = x, out = y, kernel = 7x7, stride = 1, padding = 3) – BatchNorm – ReLU - Conv2D(in = y, out = y, kernel = 3x3, stride = 1, padding = 1) – BatchNorm – ReLU.

Layer structure	Channels	Size
Input	1	380×151
DC(1,64)	64	380×151
MaxP-DC(64,128)	128	190×75
MaxP-DC(128,256)	256	95×37
MaxP-DC(256,512)	512	47×18
MaxP-DC(512,1024)	1024	23×9
ConvTrans2d(1024,512,2x2,s = 2x2)-DC(1024,512)	512	47×18
ConvTrans2d(512,256,2x2,s = 2x2)-DC(512,256)	256	95×37
ConvTrans2d(256,128,2x2,s = 2x2)-DC(256,128)	128	190×75
ConvTrans2d(128,64,2x2,s = 2x2)-DC(128,64)	64	380×151
Conv2D(64,1,1x1,1)	1	380×151
Output – MinMax[0,1]	1	380×151

4 Numerical Examples

We present numerical examples for 3D realistic model created using real data from North of Russia. This realistic data set contains complete information for construction DFN model, i.e. all geometrical characteristics for every fracture. Thus we construct the 3D fracture model via DFN modeling (see Fig. 1). In order to avoid cumbersome computation, when one should generate seismic data and provide seismic migration, we create 3D ideal image for that model via 3D convolutional modeling (see Fig. 2). Thus, the 3D fracture model that we have initially developed is the goal of fracture model reconstruction by the 3D image that is input data in the problem that we solve.

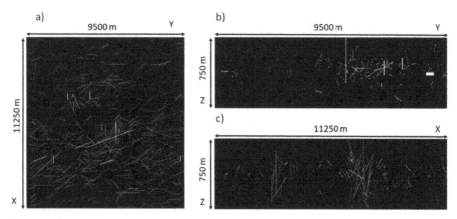

Fig. 1. The 3D fracture model obtained via DFN modeling using geometrical fracture characteristics got from a real reservoir from North of Russia: a) horizontal plane, i.e. x y section; b) vertical plane, i.e. x z section; c) vertical plane, i.e. y z section.

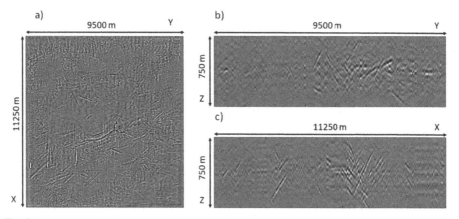

Fig. 2. The 3D diffraction image obtained via 3D convolutional modeling for the 3D realistic fracture model: a) horizontal plane, i.e. x y section; b) vertical plane, i.e. x z section; c) vertical plane, i.e. y z section.

4.1 Simplified Training Dataset

We provide the first series of experiments when we use minimum a-priory information, i.e. average direction and average length of fractures families, for training data set
generation.

We composed the training dataset of 900 samples, i.e. 2D slices of 3D volume, which
is split into train and validation (10%) subsets. For testing purposes we use a true 3D
model and corresponding 3D diffraction image which are not used in training, of course.

We use the diffraction images as an input for the segmentation task. We omit the
choice of model hyper-parameters (e.g., learning rate) because their influence is not significant. Nevertheless, we provide a choice of the most important model parameters, i.e.
we compare the impact of various loss functions on the final model. We provide training
using two different metrics: (a1) with dice loss, and (a2) with an equal combination of
binary cross-entropy, dice and mean square error losses. We set the criterion of early
stopping to 5 epochs of non-decreasing loss (see Fig. 3). Comparison of results for two
different metrics one can find in the Table 2. One can observe that combination of metrics provides better result. One can see on the Fig. 4 that we get appropriate recovered
fracture model in this case.

a)   b)

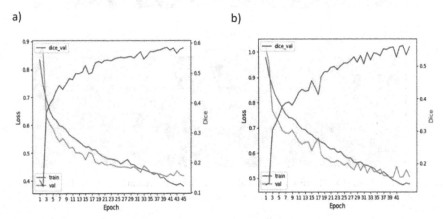

Fig. 3. Training process showing decreasing the training (blue) and validation (orange) losses
along with increasing the quality measure (green): (a1) with dice loss only, and (a2) with three
losses combination.

Table 2. Comparison of recovered models with the true one via the metrics that were used in ML
inversion with a simplified training dataset.

Losses	Dice score	Epochs	Time, h
$\mathcal{L}_{Dice}$ (a1)	0.410	45	2
$\mathcal{L}_{BCE} + \mathcal{L}_{Dice} + \mathcal{L}_{MSE}$ (a2)	0.439	45	2

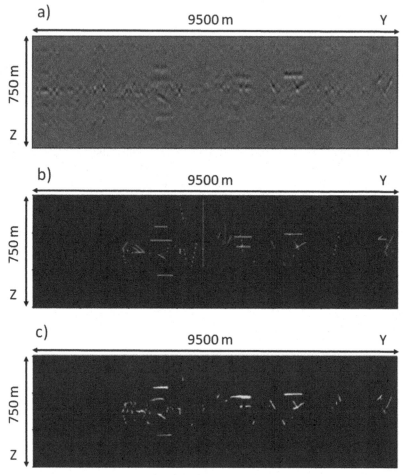

Fig. 4. Vertical slices from the test dataset with Dice equal to the mean Dice score (0.439) over-all test set: (a) diffraction image, (b) true model, (c) recovered model when using simplified dataset.

4.2 Sophisticated Training Dataset

We provide a second series of experiments when we use minimum and additional a-priory information, i.e. average direction and average length of fractures families, and density distribution of fractures, for training data set generation. We composed the training dataset of two subsets – one with 900 samples and the second with 2700. We split the 3600 samples into train and validation (10%) subsets, taking 10% of validation separately from each initial training subset.

Again, for testing purposes we use a true 3D model and corresponding 3D diffraction image which are not used in training, of course.

Also, we use the diffraction images as an input for the segmentation task. We provide training using two different metrics: (b1) with dice loss, and (b2) with an equal combination of binary cross-entropy, dice and mean square error losses. We set the criterion of early stopping to 5 epochs of non-decreasing loss (see Fig. 5). The comparison for different metrics and comparison with simplified task results one can observe in the Table 3 (Fig. 6).

The provided metrics show us that a sophisticated training dataset provides better results in comparison with the simplified case. One can observe visually from Fig. 7 that the reconstructed model using a sophisticated training dataset corresponds better to the true model than the reconstructed model using a simplified training dataset. However, both results provide satisfactory model recovery.

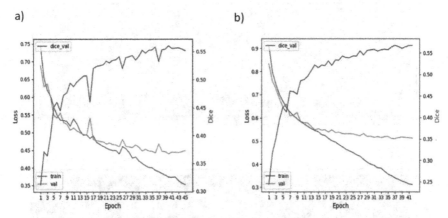

Fig. 5. Training process showing decreasing the training (blue) and validation (orange) losses along with increasing the quality measure (green): (b1) with dice loss only, and (b2) with three losses combination. (Color figure online)

Table 3. Comparison of recovered models with the true one via the metrics that were used in ML inversion with simplified and sophisticated training datasets.

Losses	Dice score	Epochs	Time, h
$\mathcal{L}_{Dice}$ (a1)	0.410	45	2
$\mathcal{L}_{BCE} + \mathcal{L}_{Dice} + \mathcal{L}_{MSE}$ (a2)	0.439	45	2
$\mathcal{L}_{Dice}$ (b1)	0.502	45	7
$\mathcal{L}_{BCE} + \mathcal{L}_{Dice} + \mathcal{L}_{MSE}$ (b2)	0.568	43	7

For the described numerical examples, we use reasonable computational resources. We loaded all training data, including validation subset (1,6 GB) into RAM, so there were no reads from disk during the training process. We used one node with CPU i7-6700K @ 4 GHz, 32 GB RAM and GPU NVidia Titan X (3584 cores @ 1.5 GHz). Each neural network model train process took 2 and 7 h for simplified and sophisticated cases accordingly with the usage of GPU at 100% load and RAM at 9.5 GB (79%).

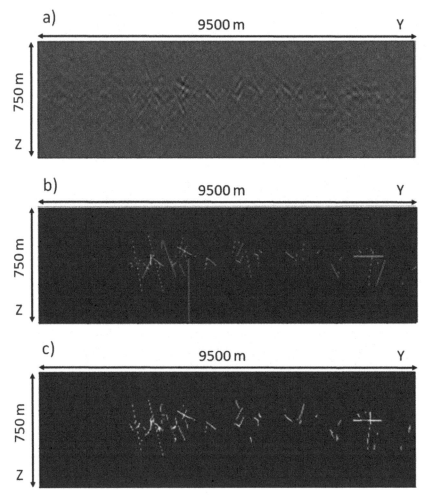

Fig. 6. Vertical slices from the test dataset with Dice equal to mean Dice score (0.509) over all test set: (a) diffraction image, (b) true model, (c) recovered model when using sophisticated dataset.

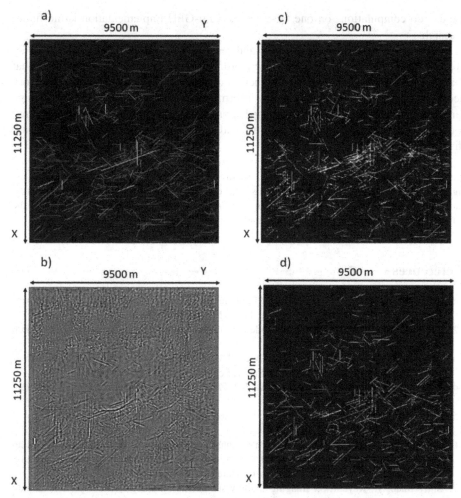

Fig. 7. a) The true 3D fracture model, horizontal x y section; b) the corresponding 3D diffraction image, horizontal x y section; c) the recovered 3D fracture model when using simplified training dataset, horizontal x y section; d) the recovered 3D fracture model when using sophisticated training dataset, horizontal x y section.

5 Conclusions

In the paper, we propose and investigate 3D seismic inversion for fracture model reconstruction based on machine learning. We provide implementation of the machine learning based approach which uses U-net neural network and 3D convolutional model. The suggested solution uses the construction of 3D discrete fracture models and 3D ideal seismic images, which allows a proper description of the fractured model, and it provides computationally cheap procedures for creating a dataset for machine leaning. Thus, the proposed approach based on usage of U-net neural network allows construction of the training data set within a reasonable computational time. Within the presented research we can do computations on one GPU node, multi-GPU implementation is the future research.

We provide numerical experiments and results for a realistic 3D fractured model created using real seismic data from the North of Russia. Numerical results show that the proposed approach allows reconstruction of the fractured model with satisfactory accuracy when using minimum a-priory information, i.e. average direction and average length of fractures families. The proposed approach provides recovery of the fractured model with a better accuracy when we use additional a-priory information, i.e. density distribution of fractures.

Acknowledgments. The presented research is supported and done within the scope of investigations of RSF grant 21-71-20002. We use the computational resources of Peter the Great Saint-Petersburg Polytechnic University Supercomputing Center (scc.spbstu.ru) to provide the numerical experiments and to obtain the numerical results.

References

1. Manzocchi, T., Walsh, J.J., Bailey, W.R.: Population scaling biases in map samples of power-law fault systems. J. Struct. Geol. **31**, 1612–1626 (2009)
2. Xu, C., Dowd, P.: A new computer code for discrete fracture network modelling. Comput. Geosci. **36**, 292–301 (2010)
3. Ampilov, Yu.P., Barkov, A.Yu., Yakovlev, I.V., Filippova, K.E., Priezzhev, I.I.: Almost everything is about seismic inversion. Part 1. Seismic Technol. **4**, 3–16 (2009)
4. Yakovlev, I.V., Ampilov, Yu.P., Filippova, K.E.: Almost everything is about seismic inversion. Part 2. Seismic Technol. **1**, 5–15 (2011)
5. Russell, B. H.: Introduction to Seismic Inversion Methods. Course Notes Series, Society of Exploration Geophysicists, pp. 80–101 (1988)
6. Liu, E., et al.: Fracture characterization by integrating seismic-derived attributes including anisotropy and diffraction imaging with borehole fracture data in an offshore carbonate field. In: International Petroleum Technology Conference, IPTC-18533 (2015)
7. Shtivelman, V., Keydar, S.: Imaging shallow subsurface inhomogeneities by 3D multipath diffraction summation. First Break **23**, 39–42 (2005)
8. De Ribet, B., Yelin, G., Serfaty, Y., Chase, D., Kelvin, R., Koren, Z.: High resolution diffraction imaging for reliable interpretation of fracture systems. First Break **35**(2), 43–47 (2017)
9. Jin, Y., Wu, X., Chen, J., Han, Z., Hu, W.: Seismic data denoising by deep-residual networks. In: SEG Technical Program Expanded Abstracts, pp. 4593–4597 (2018)
10. Jia, Y., Ma, J.: What can machine learning do for seismic data processing? An interpolation application. Geophysics **82**, V163–V177 (2017)
11. Hou, S., Messud, J.: Machine learning for seismic processing: the path to fulfilling promises. In: SEG Technical Program Expanded Abstracts, pp. 3204–3208 (2021)
12. Bagheri, M., Ali Riahi, M.: Modeling the facies of reservoir using seismic data with missing attributes by dissimilarity based classification. J. Earth Sci. **28**(4), 703–708 (2017)
13. Chen, Y., Schuster, G.: Seismic inversion by Newtonian machine learning. Geophysics **85**, WA185-WA200 (2020)
14. Pintea, S.L., Sharma, S., Vossepoel, F.C., Van Gemert, J.C., Loog, M., Verschuur, D.J.: Seismic inversion with deep learning. Comput. Geosci. **26**, 351–364 (2022)
15. Ronneberger, O., Fischer, P., Brox, T.: U-net: convolutional networks for biomedical image segmentation. arXiv:1505.04597v1 (2015)

16. Protasov, M.: High-performance implementation of 3D seismic target-oriented imaging. Commun. Comput. Inf. Sci. **1510**, 125–136 (2021)
17. Protasov, M.I., Reshetova, G.V., Tcheverda, V.A.: Fracture detection by Gaussian beam imaging of seismic data and image spectrum analysis. Geophys. Prospect. **64**(1), 68–82 (2016)
18. Loshchilov, I., Hutter, F.: Decoupled weight decay regularization. arXiv preprint arXiv:1711. 05101 (2017)

A Computational Model for Interactive Visualization of High-Performance Computations

Pavel Vasev$^{(\boxtimes)}$ (iD)

N.N. Krasovskii Institute of Mathematics and Mechanics of the Ural Branch of the Russian Academy of Sciences, Ekaterinburg, Russia
vasev@imm.uran.ru

Abstract. Interactive visualization of high-performance computations is important area in supercomputing. Interactivity assumes that visualization of results of computation is generated during computation process. However there is a problem: due to overwhelming size of data to visualize, a visualization program should be itself parallel and executed on supercomputer. Beside that, such program should allow to be changed dynamically, because visualization pipeline may change due to user steering of interactive visualization. Current mainstream frameworks for interaction with supercomputer programs assume usage of external parallel programming methods. In current paper, an original parallel programming model is suggested that have built-in capabilities for online interactive visualization. At basic level, it is based on messages and reactions. At higher level it uses promises for inter-operation of computation and visualization parts.

Keywords: Computational Model · Parallel Programming · Online Visualization · Insitu Visualization

1 Introduction

Interactive visualization of high-performance computations is covered by online and insitu visualization areas. These are crucial areas in modern supercomputing. In some cases, it is impossible to achieve results of computation without them [1, 3].

Online visualization is a process of interactive visualization of running computation [1]. **Insitu visualization** is a process of generating visual images of results during computation [2]. The difference is that online is considered to be interactive, steered by user or algorithms working on user's behalf. Insitu on other hand underlines the placement of visualization processes closer to a computation. Whereas terms are different, they are interconnected and have common aspect: use of supercomputer not only for computations, but also for visualization purposes.

Due to the fact that supercomputer power is to be used, visualization pipeline algorithms have to be implemented in parallel form. Thus, to achieve online visualization of supercomputing, following tasks have to be solved:

V. Voevodin et al. (Eds.): RuSCDays 2023, LNCS 14389, pp. 118–133, 2023.
https://doi.org/10.1007/978-3-031-49435-2_9

1. Provide a way of interaction of visualization part and computation part.
2. Provide a way of parallel programming of visualization algorithms.

The first task usually is solved using various approaches, for example see [2–4]. A most common approach is to provide some data transmission service, and a library for interacting with it. Computing application is instrumented with calls to such library and thus data is offloaded from application into visualization processing via such transmission service. However, existing approaches doesn't solve the second task – they don't provide any parallel programming models, in particular for implementing visualization algorithms.

On other hand, there are a plenty of technologies for parallel programming. However they are mostly not considering an interaction with existing parallel programs, which are built using other parallel technologies. They are more focused to be self-sufficient. Thus often a some kind of bridge is required.

In the current paper, the author suggest single solution that solves both stated tasks. The solution is proposed in a form of computational model. It may be used for interaction with HPC programs and for programming parallel algorithms of visualization.

The current paper is devoted to the main part of any software technology – the model. It is called main because other parts, e.g. implementation, depends on it. The suggested model, in turn, is not a ready-to-run software. It may be implemented using various programming technologies with some kind of model variations.

We need to note the following. It might be philosophically incorrect that single tool solves two problems, as in our case. In current work, we join those problems into one: construct a way for high-performance online visualization. At least, it is not looking bad to have a parallel computational technology that may interoperate with other computational technologies well.

The structure of this paper is as follows. In Sect. 2, the problem statement is defined. Sections 3, 4 and 5 propose a designed model for parallel programming. Section 6 highlights prototype implementation details. Section 7 suggest an experimental application of the model for parallel rendering task. Section 8 express related works.

2 Problem Statement

To going further, we should define what we consider as a typical parallel computational program. It will give us a picture what kind of software in which environment we should operate with for online visualization.

2.1 Formalization of Online Visualization

Without loss of generality, we fix the scope of the developed online visualization model in the following formulation.

There is a set of information entities $\{D\}$. Each entity D divided into parts in the domain sense (so called domain decomposition), e.g. each $D = \{d_i\}$. For example, one may consider a structured grid D which is decomposed into parts $\{d_i\}$, as on Fig. 1. These parts d_i are such that each part fits into the memory of the computation process that calculates this part (whereas maybe two parts will not fit in its memory).

The scientific simulation is implemented in the form of a set of computation processes (processes of the operating system and processes on accelerators like GPU) located on a set of hardware nodes. These processes interact as necessary with each other and with external sources for the exchange of input, intermediate, boundary, and output values. The set of computation processes and the structure of their interaction can change over time, as well as the set of computed entities *{D}*.

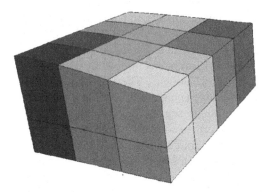

Fig. 1. An example distribution of structured data on computation cores, from [5].

A significant feature of entities D is that their content (e.g. data) changes over time. Thus, entity D is a "living" informational "matter", its life (evolution) is a process of change of it's content in the course of the computational process.

The variability of the content of D is primarily due to the limited memory of the hardware nodes. Usually, only the contents of the previous and current iteration step of the computational process are stored in memory. Of course, in general, computation may store a larger number of steps in nodes memory (for example also using disks). But this does not change the nature of the entities D - they evolve in time, and a limited trace of their states or images of that states from previous iterations follows them.

At the same time, in practice, the structure of the partition of D onto parts d_i does not usually change during the calculation, although this is sometimes used, for example in adaptive mesh refinements.

The **task of online visualization** is to build numerical and visual images of entities D and transfer them to the destination, build visual images of the composition of computational processes, supply control signals to computational processes, and possibly manage their composition (that is, control the calculation process).

Using to this definition, **insitu visualization** may be considered as a specific case or part of online visualization. It doesn't need interactivity and concentrates on generating images using HPC power. Also, **parallel rendering** and **remote visualization** may be considered as areas used by online visualization: they fit naturally in the phenomenon.

Now we are ready to provide problem statement: create a technology (a model, and it's implementation) that solves the stated task of online visualization.

3 Computation Model. Basic Level

The model consists of three levels. This section deals with the first, basic level. Then in ongoing sections two additional levels will be described.

The model starts with the concept of a message. A **message** is a triple *(label,dictionary,payload)*, where

- *label* – is a message label
- *dictionary* – is a key-value dictionary
- *payload* – binary large objects associated with that message.

The message label may be different, which will be discussed later. A dictionary is understood in the usual programmer sense, that is, a set {(key, value)} with unique keys. The payload is the additional binary information associated with the message. Its structure and meaning are determined by the interacting parties. The payload is not placed in the dictionary for technical purposes – so that the dictionary takes up relatively little memory; while a payload can be relatively large.

A **system** is a computation that performs certain actions according to the model. **Acting parties** interacts with each other via the system by the following.

The message can be "sent" to the system. The system processes incoming messages using the so-called reactions. **Reaction** is the pair of *(criteria, action)*, where

- *criteria* – triggering criteria,
- *action* – action to execute when the reaction triggered.

Any party may register reactions within the system. When a new message is sent, actions of all reactions whose criteria matches a message are executed, in order as they were registered.

Actions can do arbitrary processing and, in particular, a) test additional conditions (inexpressible in criteria), b) send new messages to the system, c) register additional reactions. Additionally, an action is able to cancel further processing of other actions.

The list of registered reactions can change dynamically over time.

Reactions are considered to have no shared state between each other. This design decision allows to execute actions without synchronization, in parallel for each arriving message.

A Note About the Reaction Criteria. The criteria used by model might be different. The main demand for criteria is that is should allow to identify reactions matching incoming message with little computational complexity.

Without loss of generality, the current paper uses the following mechanism of criterion: the message label and reaction criterion are strings. If **message label equals to criterion**, then (and only then) we assume that criterion matches that message.

The reaction definition operates criteria, while here we denoted single criterion. It is assumed that criteria is constructed as a list of criterion. When message matches any of criterion from list in reaction, the message is considered matched to that reaction. Thus, we consider logical OR. This design decision is made because it is ergonomic to have single reaction to match different kinds of messages.

4 Computation Model. Service Level

The basic level of the model does not allow solving the entire range of tasks required to solve online visualization problems. However, this level is extensible, it allows to add additional features to it. It is suggested to add these new features using the following concept of services.

A **service** is a set of reactions registered within the system, and possibly additional software processes and other components. Together, they implement the functionality of a service, e.g. some logical process.

Interaction with Services is expected to be done primarily through messages introduced at basic level of the model. This design decision allows other parties to hook into such communications by placing additional reactions, which is considered to add flexibility to the computation. But there is no restriction that interaction is allowed only through messages. One may implement custom API of any service if required.

The list of services can be updated as needed. To date, the practical need for the following services has been identified.

4.1 Service for Managing Reactions via Messages

It was found convenient to manage list of reactions using messages. This allows to use only message sending API to interact with the system. The service adds the reaction to the system that reacts to following message:

- label: "manage_reactions"
- cmd:"add" | "update" | set | "remove"
- reaction_id: string
- criterion: string, a criterion of controlled reaction
- action: string, the action code of the controlled reaction.

When message of such kind arrives, the service manages the list of reactions registered. The service assumes that each reaction must be associated with a globally unique identifier. This is due to the need to distinguish between reactions.

The action code of an action is assumed to be possible to execute in a programming environment that the system supports. It may contain for example source code in interpreted language like Python or IDs of methods to invoke for compiled languages.

4.2 Query Service

A **query** is a special kind of reaction, which differs in that the action of such reaction is executed on the client process that issued the query. As a consequence, an action may directly interact with a client program. Additionally, query may have a counter N which means that action should be executed no more than N times. Queries are useful for detecting messages of interest and implementing various logic. For example, queries are used by following runner service to register tasks to be executed.

Query service might be implemented using ordinal reaction, whose action send signals to the client using some network protocol, when message of interest is detected.

4.3 Task Service

Task service is designed to execute arbitrary tasks using automatic balancing. Clients schedules tasks using messages. Tasks then distributed to dedicated runner nodes, which in turn execute these tasks and respond with results. This allows to program various algorithms using steps (e.g. a task is a such step) that are executed in parallel.

A task in our model is scheduled using message of the following signature:

- label: "exec-request"
- *code*: operation code
- *args*: a list of operands for operations
- *result-label*: the label for message with results of execution.

Here *operation code* defines operation to be performed. *Args* is a list of operands that may contain constants, references to payloads (see payload service), and other values recognized by the system. They will be passed to the operation. After execution of the operation, it's result is sent using message with label specified by *result-label*. This allows client to generate unique label, issue tasks, and catch results of those tasks.

Operation code might specify function in some programming language, or might specify a function defined in operations table. In latter case, such table is configured using messages of the following signature:

- label: "setenv"
- name: string
- value: definition of function to execute.

Here *name* corresponds to operation *code*. *Value* defines a function which will be called when operation is called. For example, it's code in a programming language.

Additionally, it might be useful to consider different values for single operation, corresponding for different execution environments. For example, one may specify operation both for CPU and for GPU. The system then will be able to choose appropriate variant according to actual hardware environment.

A Note on "Needs". During experimentation it was noted that it is inefficient to execute some tasks from scratch. Sometimes, there are repetitive subtasks occurred required by various tasks. An example of such subtask is to load some programming library, configure a kernel for GPU, and so on. It was found efficient to cache results of such subtasks and reuse them between different tasks. Thus a concept of *needs* was appeared.

A **need** is state of memory and hardware that is required by tasks to perform. A same need might be required by different tasks, and might be reused. A runner, before running operation of a tasks, prepares all needs required by that tasks. If some need is already prepared (e.g. its result is in cache), runner just touches it's access timestamp.

Needs should be identifiable, because caching algorithm should be able to distinguish them and associate with incoming tasks. Thus system user have to provide globally unique identifier with each *need*.

As it noted, a *need* corresponds to some state of memory and hardware. This means that *need* is tied to runner, and different runners prepare their own copies of *needs*.

Needs of a task are enlisted in *args* field of task signature (specified in *exec-request* message), together with other arguments. After a *need* is computed, it's value replaces corresponding argument. Thus applicative-order evaluation is performed.

A Note on Resources Limits. Both *operations* and *needs* require computing resources to be available: for example, some amount of memory, hardware, so on. The actual amount of such resources on available nodes is limited. So the implementation of the computational model should consider those limits and and correlate them with task's and need's requirements. This is also important for maintaining cache of prepared needs to keep it within available limits.

4.4 Payload Service

Payloads are binary large byte objects (blobs). Due to the large amount of required memory, they are processed separately from message bodies. It is implemented by a special service that store payloads and present them as needed. This significantly "unloads" the main system. This idea was suggested earlier by M. O. Bakhterev [6].

If one want to send a message with payloads, it should go through following:

1. Upload payloads to the payload service. The service generates unique URL for each stored payload. This URL might be used later by any other parties to download payload from the service.
2. Put the received URLs of payloads into payload field of the message dictionary, and then send the message to the system.

Implementation of payload service should consider the aspect of actually not moving data when payload is "uploaded" or "downloaded". Same should be implemented for memory on accelerators. Thus, any real movement of data should occur only when data is requested by party on remote node. This for example might be implemented by placing service parts directly into client processes.

However, extra "technical" movement of data may occur to offload payloads from RAM to persistent storage when it is still required but not accessed to offload RAM. Thus, service should act like a cache.

Implementation also should cleanup of payloads that are no longer required. It is sophisticated theme and might require additional actions from client to take care of some kind of payload usage counters. In ideal, specific cases, it probably might be done automatically, like some kind of garbage collection. Such automatic cleanup probably will be simplified by tracking promises (see below).

Additionally, payloads service might be better interconnected with task service, in aim to implement interleaving of data movements and task computations.

5 Computation Model. Promise Level

Usage of the model shown above is still not ergonomic for final applications. Additional primitives are required to make application code shorter and clearly to human mind.

One suitable known primitive is a promise (also called a *future*). It was developed by many researchers almost 50 years ago, see for example [7]. A **promise** is an object that corresponds to data that will be calculated sometime.

A promise can be created in one process, *resolved* in another process (also term *fulfilled* is used, e.g. bound with data), and perform reactions to promise resolution in some third processes. Promise objects may be freely copied between parties, for example using messages.

The convenience of promises lies in the fact that they can be operated on at any time, even before they resolved. This makes possible to <u>represent parallel processing algorithms using sequential codes</u>, like in *Example application* section.

Promises can be created explicitly or implicitly. One of the convenient methods of implicitly creating and using promises is linking them with asynchronous task execution, which we employed in *Task service,* Sect. 4.4.

To do this, we extend our model with the following:

- **Each task submission is associated with a promise object**. Thus client scheduling a task gains a promise object of that task.
- Allow to specify promises in arguments of scheduled tasks.

In case if task have one or more promises in arguments, its calculation is started only when all such promises are fulfilled. Corresponding arguments are substituted by values of that promises. Thus task operation works as before, using arguments as values and don't boring that they were generated by other tasks.

Sometimes it is required to pass promises to tasks by reference, without applying synchronization logic. Implementation should consider that case.

Explicit Promises. Another way of creating promises is to create them explicitly. We add following operations into model for that:

- *create_promises: n → list of p* – creates a list of *n* promises,
- *resolve: p,data → void* – resolve promise *p* with *data.*

Promises created this way might also be used in arguments of tasks, same as promises created implicitly. So system will wait their fulfillment before running tasks.

Usage of Promises. Explicit promises trivialize connection of the discussed computation model to scientific simulations. We consider the following scenario. As it stated before, each iteration of simulation computes some entity D that has domain decomposition $\{d_i\}$. Let each iteration of simulation have associated structure $S = \{p_i\}$ of promises corresponding to that domain decomposition. Each computational process of simulation fulfills promises which correspond to parts of D that this process computes. Simulation sends S to the system. Visualization algorithms get S and schedule tasks based on promises from S, required to achieve target visualizations.

This logic is modular. Each visualization algorithm may be expressed then as a sequential **function from S to R**, where S is a structure of promises describing source entity and R is a structure of promises describing result of algorithm application.

Such algorithm implementation considered as following. It gets S in arguments, then schedules a set of tasks to *task service,* passing promises from S as arguments for that tasks. Because the model have feature to get promise for each scheduled task, algorithm may then pass such promises to additional tasks or sub-algorithms, so on. Finally, it achieve promises of R and returns it.

Above-mentioned visualization algorithms are functions, however online visualization is a process (because it visualizes ongoing computations). To create a process of visualization, we consider following: add a reaction for each new incoming S, issued by simulation, and pass execution to visualization function with that S as argument. Thus we will achieve that visualization will be built as simulation goes on.

6 Prototype Implementation

The author develops implementation of the suggested model. It uses Javascript language and works within NodeJs and in browsers, and uses TCP, HTTP and Websocket protocols for inter-node communications (use of OpenUCX is considered). Following some ideas achieved during implementation of the model are highlighted.

Client Library. It was found convenient to use client library to access the system API. The library provides entry points for all services described above:

- **msg**(m) – send message m to the system. The m is considered to be javascript object with *label* field, maybe *payload* and other fields.
- **reaction**(criteria, action) – register a reaction within the system, which will call action for every message that meets criteria. The *action* is encoded as a string with a function in Javascript language.
- **query**(criteria,N,callback) – put a query to the system which will call *callback* for at most N times and then stop reacting to messages.
- **exec**(opcode, args) – schedule task defined by (opcode,args) to the task service and return task's promise.
- **setenv**(name, value) – define operation where name is operation code and value defines body of operation.
- **promise**(N) and **resolve**(p) – explicitly creates N promises and resolves given promise.

Thus all clients load the API library and interacts with the system using calls to it.

Distributing Reactions. First implementations were sending messages to some central master node which role was to execute all registered reactions. It was occurred to be non effective. Then a new approach was developed with idea to distribute reactions to clients. When client "sends" a message to the system, it actually doesn't send it, but executes actions of registered reactions corresponding to that message. To get reactions, clients asks the central node, one time per criterion. Thus actions are executed concurrently, on the client processes. Central node role is to manage list of registered reactions, and to send parts of that list and following updates to active clients.

Query Service. As reactions are executed on clients, query service was implemented by the following. When some client (query owner) issues a query, a local TCP server is started up inside that client's process. It provides endpoint *URL* which is ready to receive incoming messages asynchronously. Then query owner registers new reaction within the system. It's *criteria* is a *criteria* of query, and it's action is to send TCP request with found message to endpoint of query owner. Thus when some party "sends" message to the system that is interesting to the query, it actually sends that message directly to the query owner.

Task Service. Current implementation introduces concept of *runner processes* and *runner-manager process*. The manager queries all upcoming scheduled tasks by placing query to messages with *exec-request* label. Runners advertise them to the manager using special messages with *runner-info* label. The manager continuously executes assignment algorithm to decide which tasks on which runners to perform. It then assigns tasks to runners. When runner achieves a task, it executes it and sends results to the manager and to the client of the task.

When assigning tasks to runners, the manager considers *needs* that already prepared on that runner, solving the assignment problem with some kind of heuristics.

Runners track ready state of tasks assigned to them (e.g. all promises in arguments in task are resolved), and execute them as they become ready.

Payload Service is implemented as a part of client library and additional set of servers, which are started on each hardware node participating in computation. When client submits payload, a pointer to payload in RAM is stored in client state. Then a server is started inside client process. Then client library returns unique URL which may be used to access that payload from outside processes within the system.

Thus, when client sends message with payload, actual payload bytes are not moved. It might be transmitted over network later, if some other client would decide to download that payload.

Connecting to Other Platforms. In spite of current implementation uses Javascript language, it might be used within other platforms. First of all the machine-code platform is considered (C++, Fortran, so on) because it is most often used in scientific computations. Two ideas are considered for connecting to other platforms:

- Middleware nodes.
- Specify reaction's actions in different languages.

Middleware node is a node that on one hand interacts with the system, and on other provides special API for it's clients on other platforms. For example, it might be interesting to provide API based on some kind of FUSE file systems to interact with the model. In that idea, writing to file of some specific path will issue the message, while reading some file leads to performing a query.

Another option is to allow specifying reaction's action in language other than Javascript. Currently we implemented this by creating plugin system for runners, and created a special plugin to execute Python codes.

7   Example Application

We showcase the model with parallel interactive rendering of rectilinear grid of cells. It is not actually an online visualization, but it is very close for it's needs. The application is a simplified version of comparison test of ParaView and ScientificView visualization systems given in [5]. In our case, cells have no associated values, just geometry in form of voxels (Fig. 2).

```
let K = 50
let filenames = ["1.dat","2.dat",…,K+".dat"]`
let blocks = filenames.map( __load )

rapi.query( "render",(m) => {
 let images = blocks.map( b =>
                    __render( b, m.camera_position, m.w, m.h) )
 let final_image = recursive_merge( images )
 rapi.msg( {label:"image", final_image } )
})


function __load( filepath ) {
  return rapi.exec( arg =>
      read_file_as_floats(arg.filepath),{filepath} )
}
function __render( block, camera_position, w, h ) {
  return rapi.exec( arg => arg.render_fn(arg.camera_position),
      {render_fn: {code: "cell_render_func", need: true,
                arg: {block,w,h}}})
}

function recursive_merge( images ) {
  if (images.length <= 1) return images[0]
  let acc = []; for (let i=0; i<images.length; i+=2 )
     acc.push( __merge_2( images[i], images[i+1] ) )
  return recursive_merge( acc )
} // Todo: try converting to async queues as in [12].

function __merge_2( image1, image2 ) {
  return rapi.exec( arg =>
      merge_2_zbuf( arg.image1, arg.image2 ), { image1, image2 })
}
```

Fig. 2. Source code of interactive parallel rendering of cells (javascript). The system's API is provided via *rapi* variable. Only codes important for showcasing main structure are provided. An external visualization frontend is considered: it allows user to control camera in 3D space, tracks it and sends 'render' requests, receives 'image' messages and displays it.

It is considered that cells that we have to render are distributed into K parts and stored in files named $k.dat$. The following is going on in the code:

1. The code starts with scheduling file load task for each block. As a result, an array of promises of loaded blocks is stored in the *blocks* variable.

2. The code queries messages with *render* label. It is assumed that visualization frontend issues such messages.

3. When render message detected, the query callback is called and it starts parallel rendering process by calling *__render* function for each block. The *__render* schedules render task to the system for parallel execution. As a result, an array of promises is achieved and stored into *images* local variable. These promises are considered to be fulfilled to rendered images of blocks in the form *(color-buffer,z-buffer)*, e.g. having both color and depth data.

4. *Images* promises array is passed to *recursive_merge* algorithm which in turn schedules tasks to join images using sort-last method.

5. Final image is sent with message labeled *final_image* which is queried and displayed by visualization frontend.

Figure 3 (left) displays sample output of developed application.

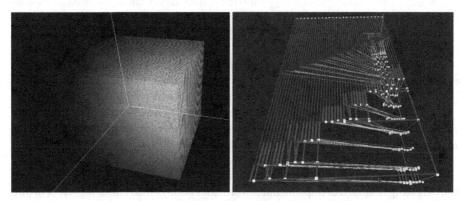

Fig. 3. Left: visual result of interactive parallel rendering of cells. A cube of size 1 is split into 50 parts having 10^9 cells in total. User may rotate view angle and thus change camera position using mouse. After user change camera position, code sends "render" message and the cube gets re-rendered. **Right**: visual debugging of used parallel rendering algorithm. Time goes from up to down. Blue lines are tasks of loading blocks, red lines are tasks of block rendering. White dots are tasks of images merge (actually they are lines too but perform too fast so appear as dots). Task's x location in a view corresponds it's block number. Data dependencies between tasks is shown using cyan lines. There are 8 runners shown on bottom plane, performing tasks. Animation is available: youtu.be/XnV3l8hw8QE.

To debug parallel applications implemented within the suggested model, a task visualization method was created. It queries messages that schedule tasks to the system, and also messages when task is assigned to a runner and when task is completed. Then it visualizes ongoing processes using synthetic view in 3D space. On Fig. 3 (right) an output of such view is presented. The developed debugging method is itself an online visualization of parallel algorithms working within the system.

8 Related Works

According to the aim of our project, we have to consider scientific advances in two areas: online visualization and parallel computation technologies. Former nowadays are mostly introduced by various institu systems. In the latter, our approach is near to task-based parallelism and asynchronous many-task systems (AMT). Also, as we consider visualization of scientific computations, we pay attention to existing parallel visualization areas, including parallel visualization-aimed processing and rendering.

Related AMT systems are: Template Task Graphs [8] and PaRSEC, HPX [11], Charm++, Uintah, Kokkos, Legion, C++ Sender Library, LuNA [13], Dask, and Flyte.

AMT languages: Linda, Pythagoras functional-streaming parallel language [12], Chapel and X10, Cilk, T++, Val, Caper and partially Lingua Franca.

Insitu visualization projects: ADIOS2, Ascent, Sensei, Henson, Damaris, Libsim (Visit institu component), Catalyst (Paraview insitu component).

Parallel visualization processing: Paraview's data-server and Python-based visualization pipeline programming, ScientificView parallel pre-post-processor [5].

Parallel rendering libraries: IceT (used by both Paraview and Visit for rendering), VTK-M (parallel but single node only).

Our project differs from projects stated above in various details. To illustrate this, let's look on two advanced projects – HPX for computations and ADIOS2 for institu.

HPX system has a well-described model named ParalleX (for simplification we refer it here HPX too). HPX is targeted both for single-node and multi-node (e.g. distributed) parallelism. Our model is primarily for multi-node. We rely on existing technologies for single-node parallelism (C++ standard parallelism, SYCL, etc.).

Both HPX and our model work with multi-node parallelism by allowing to run *actions* (HPX term, same as *tasks* in our terms) remotely. In such environment, a question of load balancing occurs. Our implementation provides built-in load balancing. HPX in turn demands user to control that aspect, telling where to run an action – on a specific node (*locality* in HPX terms) or on some HPX component. User may receive performance counters from nodes and so select best ones for ongoing actions.

Sometimes for task to perform, it needs a state existing in memory of a node. In HPX, this accomplished by so called *components*. These are like C++ classes, and even allow migrations of component from node to node. To address components, *active global address space* (AGAS) concept is used. HPX suggests to create components on remote nodes, and call component's actions.

Our model reaches same purposes by means of *needs* (described in Sect. 4.3). A need may be thought as a part of component; each task have a specification of required needs and arguments. This allows our model to distribute tasks easily, because it "migrate" needs automatically by recreating them on any desired nodes. However need's state doesn't considered to be changed, and work with "state" assumes explicit specification of input and output arguments of tasks.

HPX have various advanced features, for example C++ standard-based parallelism implementation, and distributed data containers. Our model doesn't provide such means. It is indeed assumed that these may be implemented by plugins and aside projects, probably inter-operating in different programming languages.

Now we turn to compare with insitu framework ADIOS2. It is based on concept of streams. Streams are established (between producer and consumers) and then running. This provides maximum bandwidth with lowest latencies, but assumes that after establishing the connection a parties are running at fixed OS processes on fixed nodes.

In contrast, our model is designed to send "streams" of meta-data instead of data. The data follows metadata only if required by consumer, and is not sent by default. ADIOS2 users may implement the same by using 2 streams, one for meta-data and one for heavy data. But we found it ergonomic to make this feature present by design.

Our model is not tied to particular OS processes or nodes, because it is task-based (or even reaction-based, at first level). This allows automatic balancing the activities on respond on event occurrences (such as a simulation thread produced new portion of data). This in turn may introduce lags to processing.

But thanks to design of reactions implementation, our system allows to embed algorithms right into event occurrence place. For example, it allows to inject data processing codes right into simulation processes. The same effect is achieved with ADIOS2 operators and plugins. In both our and ADIOS2 cases, this looks like external management of algorithms, performed dynamically.

Despite we look optimistic on our design decisions and their contrasts with presented projects, we think only the practical tasks could highlight best combinations.

9 Conclusion and Future Work

In the paper a specialized model for parallel computations is suggested. It is aimed for online visualization, which assumes that visualization of computation is made during that computation. This demand an ability for inter-operation with working scientific simulation codes. Simulation codes have to pass data to visualization, and to receive commands from it.

The model is based on concept of messages and reactions. Then, a concept of tasks is added, which run concurrently. It was assumed that simulation software sends per-iteration updates on it's data using messages, and reacts to control commands. Then visualization side reacts to data messages and processed it in aims of visualization.

However it was found inconvenient to express parallel algorithms of data processing using reactions on messages. To overcome this, the concept of promises is added.

To pass data from simulation to visualization using promises the following approach is suggested. On each computational iteration, simulation sends message with meta-information about data being computed, represented as structure of promises according to domain decomposition. Such structure or it parts or individual promises then may be easily processed by parallel visualization algorithms. Because with promises parallel algorithms are easily expressed by sequential algorithms.

Future work is currently seen as the following:

- Ability to specify actions of reactions and tasks for various programming platforms. It will allow to achieve inter-operation of system clients programmed in various languages, and easier running tasks on accelerators. We consider SYCL and Kokkos for the latter purpose.

- Suggested model is highly extensible. Provide some kind of plugin concept to involve other people into the project, letting them add more features.

The global aim of the project is to suggest parallel computations methods productive for reasoning, and to separate basics and higher-level. We are inspired for example by models like CSP [9], AST [10], A-system vision [14] and others (like [12]).

Finally, we are going to achieve human-computer interactive supercomputing as described by virtual test stands idea [15].

Author thanks colleagues and reviewers for discussions on the presented work.

References

1. Bennett, J.C., et al.: Combining in-situ and in-transit processing to enable extreme-scale scientific analysis. In: International Conference for High Performance Computing, Networking, Storage and Analysis, SC, vol. 49, pp. 1–49:9 (2012). https://doi.org/10.1109/sc.2012.31
2. Childs, H., Ahern, S.D., Ahrens, J., et al.: A terminology for in situ visualization and analysis systems. Int. J. High Perform. Comput. Appl. **34**(6), 676–691 (2020). https://doi.org/10.1177/1094342020935991
3. Moreland, K., Bauer, A.C., Geveci, B., O'Leary, P., Whitlock, B.: Leveraging production visualization tools in situ. In: Childs, H., Bennett, J.C., Garth, C. (eds.) In Situ Visualization for Computational Science. Mathematics and Visualization, pp. 205–231. Springer, Cham (2022). https://doi.org/10.1007/978-3-030-81627-8_10
4. Vasev, P.: Analyzing an ideas used in modern HPC computation steering. In: 2020 Ural Symposium on Biomedical Engineering, Radioelectronics and Information Technology (USBEREIT), Yekaterinburg, Russia, pp. 1–4 (2020). https://doi.org/10.1109/usbereit48449.2020.9117685
5. Potekhin, A.L.: On one way of organizing data structures in scientific visualization systems. Issues of atomic science and technology. Math. Model. Phys. Process. (4), 64–71 (2022). https://doi.org/10.53403/24140171_2022_4_64 (in Russian)
6. Bakhterev, M., Kazantzev, A., Vasev, P., Albrekht, I., Dataflow-based distributed computing system. In: Grosspietsch, E., Kloeckner, K. (eds.) Proceedings of the Euromicro PDP 2011 Work in Progress Session, pp. 6–7. SEAA-Publications No. SEA-SR-29. Johannes Kepler University Linz (Austria) (2011). ISBN 978-3-902457-29-5
7. Friedman, D.P., Wise, D.S.: Aspects of applicative programming for parallel processing. IEEE Trans. Comput. **C-27**, 289–296 (1978). https://doi.org/10.1109/TC.1978.1675100
8. Schuchart, J., et al.: Generalized flow-graph programming using template task-graphs: initial implementation and assessment. In: 2022 IEEE International Parallel and Distributed Processing Symposium (IPDPS), Lyon, France pp. 839–849 (2022). https://doi.org/10.1109/ipdps53621.2022.00086
9. Hoare, C.A.R.: Communicating Sequential Processes, 4 December 2022
10. Blass, A., Gurevich, Y.: Abstract state machines capture parallel algorithms: correction and extension. ACM Trans. Comput. Log. **9**, 1–32 (2008). https://doi.org/10.1145/1352582.1352587
11. Kaiser, H., et al.: HPX - The C++ standard library for parallelism and concurrency. J. Open Source Softw. **5**(53), 2352 (2020). https://doi.org/10.21105/joss.02352
12. Legalov, A.I., Matkovskii, I.V., Ushakova, M.S., et al.: Dynamically changing parallelism with asynchronous sequential data flows. Aut. Control Comp. Sci. **55**, 636–646 (2021). https://doi.org/10.3103/S0146411621070105

13. Akhmed-Zaki, D., et al.: Automated construction of high performance distributed programs in LuNA system (2019). https://doi.org/10.1007/978-3-030-25636-4_1
14. Kotov, V.E.: Problems of parallel programming development. In: All-Union Symposium on "Problems of System and Theoretical Programming", Novosibirsk, pp. 58–72 (1979). (in Russian)
15. Averbukh, V.L., Averbukh, N.V., Vasev, P., Gajniyarov, I., Starodubtsev, I.: The tasks of designing and developing virtual test stands. In: 2020 Global Smart Industry Conference (GloSIC), Chelyabinsk, Russia, pp. 49-54 (2020). https://doi.org/10.1109/GloSIC50886.2020.9267835

An Algorithm for Mapping of Global Adjacency Lists to Local Numeration in a Distributed Graph in the GridSpiderPar Tool

Evdokia Golovchenko$^{(\boxtimes)}$ (iD)

Keldysh Institute of Applied Mathematics RAS, Moscow, Russia
golovchenko@imamod.ru

Abstract. In parallel programming when a graph is distributed among processors it is useful to introduce consecutive local numeration of vertices for fast access to vertices and their adjacent vertices. The problem of mapping of global adjacency lists to local numeration arises. A graph can be distributed among processors after predecomposition or some vertices can be moved to other processors during partitioning. So vertex global numbers on a processor can be any and in any order. The algorithm devised in the parallel partitioning tool GridSpiderPar works with any local numeration, even with nonoptimal one. It can be applied to a whole graph or to a part of the graph. This algorithm allowed to reduce execution time of mapping of global adjacency lists to local numeration in a distributed graph in 18 times and the time of adding vertices to the graph while redistributing groups of bad subdomains – in 32 times on a tetrahedral mesh with $2 \cdot 10^8$ vertices. All these algorithms are parts of the parallel incremental algorithm for graph partitioning from the GridSpiderPar package. The proposed algorithm can also be used when some information about vertices is received from the other processors. It helps to find these vertices in the local graph faster. In common it replaces a sequence of searches in a large array with one looking through two sorted arrays for coincidences and can be applied in such algorithms.

Keywords: High-performance computing · Distributed graph · Local numeration

1 Introduction

In parallel programming when a graph is distributed among processors it is useful to introduce consecutive local numeration of vertices for fast access to vertices and their adjacent vertices. The problem of mapping of global adjacency lists to local numeration arises.

Distribution of a graph with 6 vertices among 2 processors is presented in Fig. 1. All vertex numbers in the adjacency lists for each processor are global. Adjacency lists after mapping to local numeration are printed in Fig. 2. Figure 2 shows the result obtained by the proposed algorithm on the small graph. First numbers in a row are *local*

V. Voevodin et al. (Eds.): RuSCDays 2023, LNCS 14389, pp. 134–146, 2023.
https://doi.org/10.1007/978-3-031-49435-2_10

number(global number) of the vertex. There are also border vertices in these adjacency lists (border vertices are defined below). The picture of the graph is shown in Fig. 3.

```
Processor 0:
0:        1        2        5
1:        0        2
5:        0        3        4
```

```
Processor 1:
2:        0        1        3
3:        2        4        5
4:        3        5
```

Fig. 1. Distribution of a graph with 6 vertices among 2 processors. Adjacency lists for each processor are shown on the Figure.

```
Processor 0:
0(0):        1        3        2
1(1):        0        3
2(5):        0        4        5
3(2):        0        1
4(3):        2
5(4):        2
```

```
Processor 1:
0(2):        3        4        1
1(3):        0        2        5
2(4):        1        5
3(0):        0
4(1):        0
5(5):        1        2
```

Fig. 2. Adjacency lists for each processor after mapping to local numeration and adding of border vertices.

A graph can be distributed among processors after predecomposition or some vertices can be moved to other processors during partitioning. So vertex global numbers on a processor can be any and in any order. The algorithm proposed in this work deals with any local numeration, even with nonoptimal one. This algorithm is included in the parallel partitioning tool GridSpiderPar for large mesh decomposition [1, 2].

All numbers in all adjacency lists need to be mapped to local numeration. This task may be very time consuming because total number of vertices in adjacent lists is $O(nMy \cdot maxnneigb)$, where nMy is the number of local vertices on a processor and $maxnneigb$ is the maximal number of adjacent vertices. To find local number for each vertex in adjacent lists we need to search in the array $O(n)$, where n is the number of all vertices on the processor (the array with local numbers of the vertices on the processor). So total amount of work is $O(n^2 \cdot maxnneigb)$ for the simple linear search.

In the CSR Format a graph is stored as a set of arrays. Adjacency lists of the vertices are stored consecutively in one array. Such approach is implemented in the ParMETIS package [3]. Nevertheless, the adjacency array needs to be mapped to local numeration and the number of operations in a straightforward algorithm is the same – $O(n^2 \cdot maxnneigb)$.

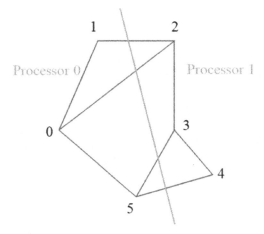

Fig. 3. The graph with 6 vertices.

The total amount of work in the proposed algorithm is $O(n \cdot log(n) + n \cdot maxnneigb)$.

The problem of mapping of global adjacency lists to local numeration isn't described in other papers. It is solved somehow in some parallel applications but it is not mentioned in other works. There are other ways to deal with numeration.

There is no global numeration in some parallel applications. A mesh is constructed for each processor or distributed among them and only local numeration is introduced into each block of the mesh. The blocks are joined by geometric borders not by global numeration of its components [4]. Global numeration can be calculated.

There is no local numeration in other applications for high-performance systems. For example, in the Zoltan package adjacency matrix is divided between $\sqrt{p} \cdot \sqrt{p}$ processors, where p is the total number of the processors. Collective operations by rows or by columns are applied to the whole matrix [5]. In Jostle vertices of a distributed graph are located on a processor using their global numbers, some sophisticated hash table and binary tree searches [6]. GraphA (adaptive scheme for efficient partitioning) operates with the edges of a graph [7, 8]. For each local vertex a linked adjacency list is stored. Adaptive Radix Tree (ART) is used to index the vertices incident to the edges with the hash values of the vertices, owners of adjacency lists. All vertices have global numbers.

Sometimes after predecomposition a mesh is redistributed between processors. A new local numeration is introduced on each processor for elements of the mesh. Then a new local dual graph is constructed using this numeration. There is no redistribution between processors of the old graph with global numeration and mapping of global numeration to local numeration is not needed.

2 The Parallel Incremental Algorithm

The proposed algorithm is a part of the parallel incremental algorithm in the GridSpider-Par tool. The parallel incremental algorithm is developed for graph partitioning. Its main advantage is creation of principally connected subdomains. More detailed description of this algorithm can be found in [1, 2].

The serial incremental algorithm consists of the iterative process:

- incremental growth of subdomains and diffusion of the border vertices between subdomains
- local refinement of the subdomains
- releasing some parts of bad subdomains and repeating the cycle

The process stops when the quality of the subdomains becomes appropriate. Subdomains are considered having layers. The first layer of a subdomain is its border. The second layer contains vertices adjacent to the first layer and not belonging to it. Other layers are defined by analogy. Subdomain quality is considered good if the number of the least noncontinuous layer is greater or equal to a threshold value. The subdomains of poor quality and their neighbours are considered as bad.

The parallel incremental algorithm consists of:

- geometric predecomposition
- local partitioning on each processor using the serial incremental algorithm
- redistribution of the groups of bad subdomains
- local repartitioning of the groups of bad subdomains

Subdomains are formed locally on the processors. It is assumed that there are a great number of subdomains and bad subdomains are formed on the boundaries between the processors. These subdomains are then redistributed between the processors so that each group of bad subdomains is collected on one of the processors and then repartitioned. Additional subdomains are redistributed between the processors to restore initial number of subdomains on the processors.

The proposed algorithm is used after geometric predecomposition to map global adjacency lists to local numeration in the local graph. It is also used when vertices are added to the local graph while redistributing groups of bad subdomains.

3   Graph Storage

In the GridSpiderPar package local graph on each processor is stored as an array of vertex structures. Vertex local number is its index in this array. Vertex structure includes vertex weight, number of adjacent vertices, vertex subdomain, adjacency list (array) and array of edge weights. There are only local vertices and border vertices in the local graph. Images of vertices from the other processors, adjacent to local vertices, are called *border vertices*. There are only local vertices in adjacent lists of border vertices, because only they are used in local computations. Such approach allows to receive only weights, subdomains and flags of belonging to the geometric border of the graph from the processors, owning border vertices. Numbers of adjacent vertices, adjacent lists and arrays of edge weights can be formed locally.

The local array of vertex structures consists of two parts: local vertices and border vertices (see Fig. 4). nMy is the number of local vertices on a processor, n is the number of all vertices on the processor. To delete border vertex with the index i its memory is set free and the last border vertex with the index $n - 1$ is moved to its position with the index i (see Fig. 5). Variable n is decreased by 1. Moving of vertex is simple copying of pointers to arrays with adjacent list and edge weights, and copying of other variables (number of adjacent vertices and etc.). To delete local vertex with the index j its memory is set free and the last local vertex with the index $nMy - 1$ is moved to its place. The last border vertex with the index $n - 1$ is moved to the index $nMy - 1$ (see Fig. 6). The variables nMy and n are decreased by 1.

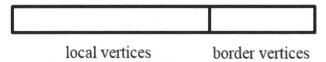

local vertices   **border vertices**

Fig. 4. Graph storage. The local array of vertex structures consists of two parts: local vertices and border vertices. Border vertices are placed in the end of the array.

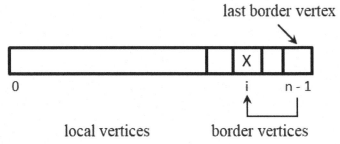

Fig. 5. Border vertex deletion. To delete border vertex with the index i its memory is set free and the last border vertex with the index $n - 1$ is moved to its position with the index i.

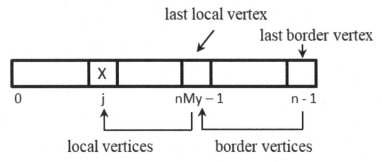

Fig. 6. Local vertex deletion. To delete local vertex with the index j its memory is set free and the last local vertex with the index $nMy - 1$ is moved to its place. The last border vertex with the index $n - 1$ is moved to the index $nMy - 1$.

There are different ways of storage. For example, in the paper [9] vertices on a processor are arranged as follows: own inner vertices, own interface vertices and halo. Own interface vertices are the ones connected with halo vertices. Halo vertices are arranged by processors-owners so that all vertices from every processor are placed together. Physics can be computed on the own inner vertices while the information about own interface vertices is received from the other processors. In the parallel incremental algorithm such complication is not needed.

4 The Algorithm for Mapping of Global Adjacency Lists to Local Numeration in a Distributed Graph

The algorithm for mapping of global adjacency lists to local numeration can be described as follows. A graph is distributed among processors. There is an interval of vertices in the local graph that have global numbers in adjacency lists. It may be the whole local graph. The algorithm maps this global numbers to the indexes of vertices in the local graph and adds missing border vertices to the local graph. The indexes of vertices in the local graph are their local numbers. Records *[vertex global number, vertex index (local number)]* are stored in the array A for all vertices in the local graph. The second array B filled with records *[adjacent vertex global number, vertex index, adjacent vertex index]* for every unknown adjacent vertex of considered vertices. Adjacent vertex index in adjacency list and the vertex index allow to precisely determine the position of the adjacent vertex global number. The array A is sorted by vertex global numbers and the array B is sorted by adjacent vertex global numbers. Serial sorting algorithm from the parallel sorting tool ParSort [10] is used to sort the arrays. Then the algorithm goes through both arrays from the beginnings and looks for coincidences of global numbers. If a coincidence is found the adjacent vertex global number is replaced by the found vertex index. Otherwise, it replaced by the index of the new border vertex.

More detailed description of the algorithm is:

Mapping Algorithm. The algorithm maps global numbers of adjacent vertices to their indexes in the local graph g and adds missing border vertices. *nOld* – initial number of vertices in the graph g.

1. [Fill arrays]. Array $A \leftarrow$ *[vertex global number; vertex index]*. Array $B \leftarrow$ *[adjacent vertex global number; vertex index; adjacent vertex index]*. *nA – number of records in the array A, nB – number of records in the array B.*
2. [Sort]. Sort the arrays A and B.
3. [Initialize]. Set $i \leftarrow 0, j \leftarrow 0$.
4. [Compare]. if $j == nA$ OR $B[3 \cdot i] < A[2 \cdot j]$ go to step 5, otherwise go to step 8. ($B[3 \cdot i]$ – adjacent vertex global number, $A[2 \cdot j]$ – vertex global number. There is no vertex with the global number $B[3 \cdot i]$ in the initial configuration of the graph g).
5. [Compare]. if $g \rightarrow n == nOld$ OR $B[3 \cdot i] >$ *global number of vertex with the index* $(g \rightarrow n - 1)$ then go to step 6, otherwise go to step 7. There $g \rightarrow n$ is the number of vertices in the graph g, $g \rightarrow n \geq nOld$. (If a border vertex with the global number $B[3 \cdot i]$ exists then it is the last vertex in the graph g, because border vertices are added to the end of the graph g and the array B is sorted).
6. [Add]. Add a new border vertex with the index $g \rightarrow n \rightarrow$ graph g. Set global number of this vertex $\leftarrow B[3 \cdot i], (g \rightarrow n) \leftarrow (g \rightarrow n) + 1$.
7. [Map]. Set adjacent vertex with the index $B[3 \cdot i + 2]$ of the vertex with the index $B[3 \cdot i + 1] \leftarrow g \rightarrow n - 1$. Add $B[3 \cdot i + 1]$ to the adjacent list of the vertex with the index $g \rightarrow n - 1$. Set weight of this edge equal to the weight of the edge with the index $B[3 \cdot i + 2]$ of the vertex with the index $B[3 \cdot i + 1]$. Increase i by 1 and go to step 10.
8. [Compare]. If $B[3 \cdot i] > A[2 \cdot j]$ increase j by 1 and go to step 10, otherwise go to step 9.

9. [Map]. In this case $B[3 \cdot i] = A[2 \cdot j]$. Set adjacent vertex with the index $B[3 \cdot i + 2]$ of the vertex with the index $B[3 \cdot i + 1] \leftarrow A[2 \cdot j + 1]$. If the vertex with the index $A[2 \cdot j + 1]$ is boundary then add $B[3 \cdot i + 1]$ to its adjacent list. Set weight of this edge equal to the weight of the edge with the index $B[3 \cdot i + 2]$ of the vertex with the index $B[3 \cdot i + 1]$. Increase i by 1 and go to step 10.
10. If $i < nB$ go to step 4, else finish the algorithm.

The proposed algorithm can be applied to a part of the graph g and the graph g can already contain border vertices.

After this algorithm missing information about the border vertices can be obtained from the processors, owning these vertices.

5 Results

Three tetrahedral meshes with $2 \cdot 10^8$ vertices were partitioned by the parallel incremental algorithm into 25600 subdomains on 512 MPI processes (6 processes per processor, 12 processes per node, 43 compute nodes). Mapping of global adjacency lists to local numeration was done in two ways: first, using the binary search [11] in a sorted array and second, using the algorithm, proposed in this paper. The execution times of mapping of global adjacency lists to local numeration were measured for these meshes. The results are presented in the Table 1. The proposed algorithm outruns in 18 times on the two meshes. The execution times of adding vertices to the graph while redistributing groups of bad subdomains (where the mapping is applied too) are presented in the Table 2. The results show that the proposed algorithm speeded up the adding vertices to the graph in 32 times on the first mesh. The last result depends on the number of vertices added to the graph and indirectly on the number of bad subdomains. There are 51–73 bad subdomains formed on the first mesh and only 1–4 bad subdomains created on the third mesh. The first digits are obtained by the algorithm with the binary search. The last refer to the algorithm where the proposed algorithm is applied. The speed up on the first mesh may increase on the equal number of bad subdomains. The speed up and the execution times obtained on the third mesh are small because of the small number of bad subdomains.

Table 1. Mapping of global adjacency lists to local numeration.

Mesh	Number of vertices in the graph	time of the algorithm with the binary search, sec	time of the algorithm where the proposed algorithm is applied, sec
Mesh1	$2 \cdot 10^8$	97.9	5.4
Mesh2	$2.6 \cdot 10^8$	128	6.7
Mesh3	$1.1 \cdot 10^8$	25.1	2.7

Table 2. Adding vertices to the graph while redistributing groups of bad subdomains.

Mesh	Number of vertices in the graph	Number of bad subdomains (first case, second case)	time of the algorithm with the binary search, sec	time of the algorithm where the proposed algorithm is applied, sec
Mesh1	$2 \cdot 10^8$	51, 73	807.6	24.9
Mesh2	$2.6 \cdot 10^8$	19, 9	17.3	1.3
Mesh3	$1.1 \cdot 10^8$	1, 4	0.17	0.4

The computations were carried out on supercomputer K-100 (Keldysh Institute of Applied Mathematics RAS): 64 compute nodes, processor 2 x Intel Xeon X5670, 12 cores per node. Compute network is Infiniband and Gigabit Ethernet.

Bad subdomains (see the description in the Sect. 2) are usually formed on the boundaries between processors. During redistribution of groups of bad subdomains these groups are distributed between processors so that each group is collected on one of the processors and then repartitioned. Additional subdomains are redistributed between processors to restore initial number of subdomains on the processors. A graph with 9800 vertices was partitioned into 52 subdomains on 4 processors. Distribution of subdomains between processors before collecting of bad subdomain groups is shown in Fig. 7. Borders between processors are colored in red. Picture after redistribution of bad subdomain groups is presented in Fig. 8. Geometric predecomposition is used in the parallel incremental algorithm to distribute vertices between processors. Figure 7 shows that borders between processors look like red vertical lines. One border in Fig. 8 became a polyline because a group of bad subdomains was collected on one of the processors.

Binary search in a sorted array of records can be described as follows. On each step searched element is compared by the key with the median of the array. If it is smaller or equal than the median the left half of the array is selected for the next search. Otherwise the right half of the array is selected. Search is finished when the searched element is found or when the length of the selected array is decreased to 0. During comparison the array with *{vertex global number; vertex index}* was sorted only once. Binary search is used to find global numbers of the adjacent vertices in this array. A new border vertex is added to the local graph if the global number was not found. Its global number and its index are inserted in the sorted array. The end of the array is copied to the buffer then the information is added and the data from the buffer are copied to the end of the array.

The algorithm for mapping of global adjacency lists to local numeration is also used in the parallel incremental algorithm when information about vertices on a processor or about its border vertices is received from the other processors. For example, vertex subdomains are received during uncoarsening of a graph. Then after collecting of information about vertices from all the processors two arrays, one with local vertices global numbers and indexes and the other with received information (including global numbers of vertices which information is received), can be coincided by vertex global numbers.

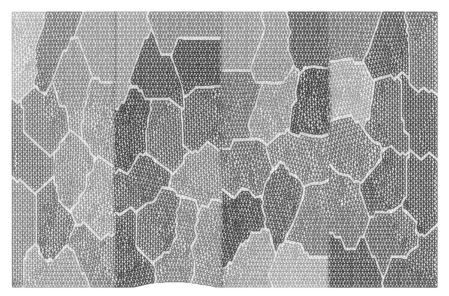

Fig. 7. Subdomains before redistribution of bad subdomain groups. A graph with 9800 vertices was partitioned into 52 subdomains on 4 processors. Borders between the processors look like vertical lines.

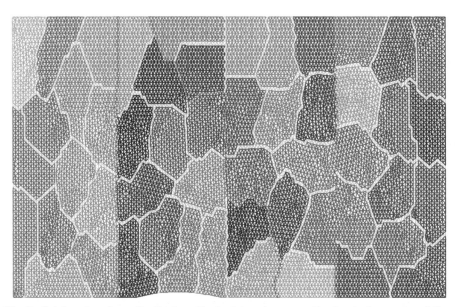

Fig. 8. Subdomains after redistribution of bad subdomain groups. One border became a polyline.

An example of coarsening of a small graph with 5981 vertices is presented in Figs. 9, 10 and 11.

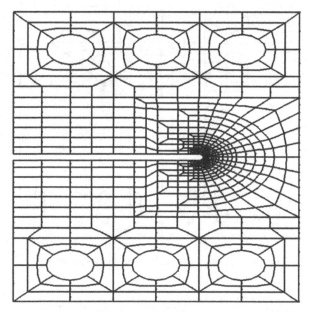

Fig. 9. A small initial graph with 5981 vertices.

In graph coarsening a graph is approximated with a sequence of smaller graphs. The smallest graph is partitioned and the partition is propagated back through the sequence of the graphs with its refining. On each step of coarsening a maximal set of edges is found (maximal matching), such that no two edges in this set are incident on the same vertex. Each edge in this set is contracted and becomes one vertex in the coarse graph. Its weight is the sum of the weights of its constituent vertices. Vertices not included in this set stay untouched. If two vertices incident to a contracted edge have the same adjacent vertex two edges to this vertex are replaced by one and the weights of the edges are summed. In average number of vertices in a graph is decreased by two. Uncoarsening is a reversed process in which the subdomain of a vertex in the coarse graph is chosen as the subdomain of the two vertices incident to the contracted edge in the graph. If the vertex doesn't belong to a contracted edge it is placed in the same subdomain in the graph. Figures 9, 10 and 11 show how the structure of the graph changes during coarsening.

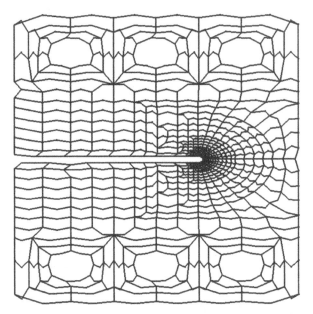

Fig. 10. The small graph after one coarsening phase.

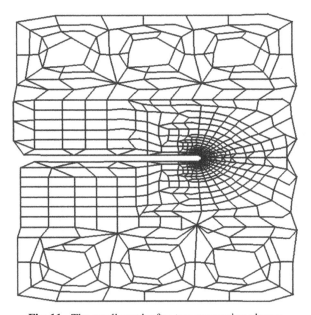

Fig. 11. The small graph after two coarsening phases.

6 Conclusion

An algorithm for mapping of global adjacency lists to local numeration in a distributed graph was devised in the GridSpiderPar tool. This algorithm is applied in the parallel incremental algorithm for graph partitioning. A graph can be distributed among processors after predecomposition or some vertices can be moved to other processors during partitioning. So vertex global numbers on a processor can be any and in any order. The proposed algorithm works with any local numeration, even with nonoptimal one. And it can be applied to a whole graph or to a part of a graph.

Three tetrahedral meshes with $2 \cdot 10^8$ vertices were partitioned by the parallel incremental algorithm into 25600 subdomains on 512 processors. Mapping of global adjacency lists to local numeration was done in two ways: first, using the binary search in a sorted array and second, using the algorithm, proposed in this paper. The execution times of mapping of global adjacency lists to local numeration were measured for these meshes. The proposed algorithm outruns in 18 times on the two meshes. The proposed algorithm also reduced the execution time of adding vertices to the graph while redistributing groups of bad subdomains in 32 times on the first mesh with the large number of bad subdomains.

This algorithm can also be used when local or border vertices data is received from the other processors. It helps to find these vertices in the local graph faster. In common it replaces a sequence of searches in a large array with one looking through two sorted arrays for coincidences and can be applied in such algorithms. In the case of mapping of global adjacency lists to local numeration it reduces the total amount of work from $O(n^2 \cdot maxnneigb)$ to $O(n \cdot log(n) + n \cdot maxnneigb)$, where n is the number of all vertices in the graph and *maxnneigb* is the maximal number of adjacent vertices.

References

1. Golovchenko, E., Dorofeeva, E., Gasilova, I., Boldarev, A.: Numerical experiments with new algorithms for parallel decomposition of large computational meshes. Parallel Computing: Accelerating Computational Science and Engineering (CSE). Advances in Parallel Computing, vol. 25, pp. 441–450. IOS Press (2014)
2. Golovchenko, E.N., Kornilina, M.A., Yakobovskiy, M.V.: Algorithms in the parallel partitioning tool GridSpiderPar for large mesh decomposition. In: Proceedings of the 3rd International Conference on Exascale Applications and Software (EASC 2015), pp. 120–125. University of Edinburgh (2015)
3. Karypis, G., Schloegel, K.: Parmetis. Parallel Graph Partitioning and Sparse Matrix Ordering Library. Version 4.0. University of Minnesota, Department of Computer Science and Engineering. Minneapolis, MN 55455, (2013). karypis@cs.umn.edu
4. Mikhaylov, S.V.: Principles of creating code for solving the aerodynamics and aeroacoustics. Math. Models Comput. Simul. **29**(9), 49–61 (2017)
5. Devine, K.D., Boman, E.G., Heaphy, R.T., Bisseling, R.H., Catalyurek, U.V.: Parallel hypergraph partitioning for scientific computing. In: Proceedings 20th IEEE International Parallel & Distributed Processing Symposium, p. 10 (2010)
6. Walshaw, C., Cross, M., Everett, M.G.: Parallel dynamic graph partitioning for adaptive unstructured meshes. J. Parallel Distrib. Comput. **47**, 102–108 (1997)

7. Zhang, Y., Li, D., Zhang, C., Wang, J., Liu, L.: GraphA: efficient partitioning and storage for distributed graph computation. Trans. Serv. Comput. **14**(8), 155–166 (2016)

8. Leis, V., Kemper, A., Neumann, T.: The adaptive radix tree: artful indexing for main-memory databases. In: European Conference on Computer Systems, pp. 38–49 (2013)

9. Soukov, S.A., Gorobets, A.V., Bogdanov, P.B.: Portable solution for modeling of compressible turbulent flows on whatever hybrid systems. Math. Models Comput. Simul. **10**(2), 135–144 (2018)

10. Golovchenko, E.N.: Computational mesh partitioning in numerical solution of continuum mechanics problems on high-performance computing systems. – Moscow: Keldysh Institute of Applied Mathematics RAS, Ph. D. thesis, Candidate of Science in Physics and Mathematics (2014)

11. Donald, K.: The Art of Computer Programming, v.3. Sorting and Searching 3rd ed., Addison Wesley, Boston, MA (1997)

Construction of Locality-Aware Algorithms to Optimize Performance of Stencil Codes on Heterogeneous Hardware

Vadim Levchenko and Anastasia Perepelkina[(⊠)]

Keldysh Institute of Applied Mathematics RAS, Moscow, Russia
lev@keldysh.ru, mogmi@narod.ru

Abstract. Recently, an increase in code performance has been obtained mainly through parallelism. For codes that implement stencil schemes, parallel processing requires data-intensive exchange. When parallel threads need to communicate, memory bandwidth becomes the bottleneck in performance. To overcome this bottleneck, processors have advanced caches. However, when developing codes for the purposes of scientific modeling, it is still the task of a programmer to make sure that every tool available is used to its highest limit and the best performance is obtained. To simplify this task, we use locally recursive non-locally asynchronous (LRnLA) algorithms. In this work, we develop an algorithm that efficiently localizes data in caches for advanced many-core CPUs with heterogeneous cores. We demonstrate the method by optimizing the performance of a fluid dynamics code on a computer with a many-core CPU with different types of cores.

Keywords: LRnLA algorithms · Stencil · Locality · Data exchange · Roofline · Parallelism · Cache · Many-core

1 Introduction

Many mathematical modeling tasks, such as computational electromagnetics [16], modeling of seismic wave propagation [18], the lattice Boltzmann method [5], and other solvers for fluid dynamics [17], involve updates of data located on a mesh in space and time with a local stencil. A stencil is a pattern of data access represented as a set of mesh nodes. An update of a mesh node in an explicit numerical scheme is written as an arithmetic expression that involves the values located in the neighboring nodes. The set of required neighbors is a stencil.

A typical 3D stencil simulation involves several GB of floating point values updated at least a million times. Thus, high-performance computing is essential for mathematical modeling, and efficient data access is crucial for it.

One of the performance bottlenecks for stencil problems is known as the *memory wall* issue [8]. There are two sources of the memory wall: latency and low memory throughput. Latency is the minimal access time for randomly accessed data. In the development of computer hardware since 1990, latency has mostly

V. Voevodin et al. (Eds.): RuSCDays 2023, LNCS 14389, pp. 147–161, 2023.
https://doi.org/10.1007/978-3-031-49435-2_11

stagnated [15]. On modern computers, the latency is a few orders of magnitude slower than an arithmetic operation. Memory throughput increases in the newer processors, but the growth still falls behind the growth of peak performance. The memory wall issue is solved by increasing the locality of calculations.

As defined by P. Kogge [4], there are two types of locality. In temporal locality, if some memory location is accessed once, there is a high probability that the same location will be accessed again within a short period of time. Temporal locality can be used to overcome the problem of low throughput by using caches to store frequently accessed data. In spatial locality, if one location is accessed, then there is a high probability that nearby locations will be accessed within a short period of time. By storing the subsequently accessed data compactly in the address space, the code can take advantage of such hardware features as wide cache lines and parallel high-frequency buses with deep buffering of requests. Additionally, in parallel systems, the memory wall issue of latency is solved by pipelining the data access requests of the asynchronous threads. In this case, physical locality [4], that is, whether or not the data are in a locally accessible memory of the processing unit, is required. The issue of low throughput is solved through the coalescing of the data requests of the synchronous parallel threads.

As for the trends of modern supercomputing, it is more relevant to talk about the *locality wall* [3]. The locality wall, as defined in Reference [4], is felt from the two viewpoints: the low arithmetic intensity (AI) within a single (perhaps multi-threaded) node and access issues whenever accessing data on remote nodes becomes dominant. AI [21] is defined as the number of floating point operations per byte of data throughput.

Recent advances in supercomputer hardware development have increased computer performance by increasing parallelism on several levels [15]. For CPU simulation, the relevant parallelism options are AVX vectorization, multicore parallelism, and multinode parallelism. The increase in the number of cores per node is an important source of performance, and it has to be used efficiently in code. For efficient many-core parallelism, the issue of the locality wall in both senses has to be solved, and this is the main topic of our research.

In a many-core CPU, cores share the hardware resources, such as the RAM, the communication bus, and the shared L3/LLC cache. Each core has one or several local L1/L2 caches. The data in the local caches has the property of physical locality. The local caches are often coherent, but accessing the cache of another core introduces significant overhead. The scaling of processor hardware in terms of the number of cores leads to a hierarchy of access to the shared resources, including the caches. As a rule, some of the resources, such as L3 cache, become local to some of the cores and non-local to others.

Thereby, the cores have unequal access to the shared caches, and the resources can be distributed unevenly between the cores. The cores in most recent processors are of different types, so that the CPU is heterogeneous by itself. It is a challenge to build a locality-aware algorithm in such an environment.

As the main tool for overcoming the locality wall issue, we use one of the approaches to temporal blocking. By temporal blocking, we mean a wide class of algorithms, in which there is no synchronization after each node in the domain is processed once. Some nodes and their neighbors may progress several time steps into the future, while the nodes far from them can still be in the initial state. Such approaches include techniques such as loop-skewing [24], wavefront method [23], temporal blocking [1], polyhedral decomposition [20].

Specifically, as the main tool in our study, we chose the theory of locally recursive non-locally asynchronous (LRnLA) algorithms [7,10–13] because it is a convenient method of algorithm construction with tools for quantitative assessment of performance bottlenecks. Equipped with the tools provided by LRnLA theory, we aim to solve the following task: For stencil codes on many-core CPUs (including heterogeneous architectures), we aim to develop a method to build algorithms that (1) efficiently localize the data in higher levels of cache in single-core execution; (2) use all available parallelism, including AVX vectorization; and (3) show close to linear parallel scaling up to the total number of CPU cores. Here, (1) and (2) are efficiently solved in previous LRnLA codes [12], and the performance of traditional, stepwise solutions is surpassed. As long as (3) is not solved, some of the processing power of CPUs is wasted, and the code can't be called efficient.

In this text, in Sect. 2, we describe the starting conditions under which we work on the described issue: both the sample stencil and the available hardware; in Sect. 3, we remind the readers of the well-known LRnLA algorithm that is used for the task; in Sect. 4, we construct the locality-aware algorithm; and in Sect. 5, we verify if the outlined goals have been achieved.

2   Problem Statement

We aim to solve the fundamental task of finding the optimal algorithm for parallelism that is not limited by memory throughput bottlenecks. In the current paper, we focus on a specific task on a specific CPU architecture. In this section, we introduce the environment in which we construct the method.

2.1   Lattice Boltzmann Method

As a stencil problem, we chose the Lattice Boltzmann Method (LBM) [5]. It is a method for computational fluid dynamics that is based on the kinetical Boltzmann equation and provides adequate results in many fields of science and engineering. At the same time, it is conveniently parallelizable, and both the stencil size and the number of floating point operations for an update are flexible. Therefore, it is an excellent testbed for algorithm development.

There are Q scalar values f_q (populations) associated with a node on a lattice (mesh). A 3D LBM with $Q = q$ is often denoted as D3Qq. The mesh step is equal to 1 in non-dimensional units. The lattice is a set of nodes $\mathcal{M} = \{\mathbf{r}_i = (x_i, y_i, z_i) : x_i \in \mathbb{N}; y_i \in \mathbb{N}; z_i \in \mathbb{N}; \}$ Here, the index i, $0 \leq i$ enumerates the nodes in $\mathcal{M}$ according to some space filling curve. The numerical scheme has two

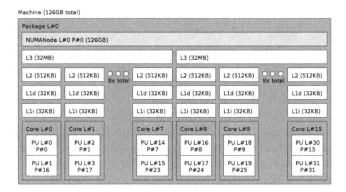

Fig. 1. AMD Ryzen R9 5950 (Zen3) architecture as shown with the `hwloc` program

steps: collision and streaming. The collision operation at node $\mathbf{r}_i$ at the discrete time instant t^k is local and can be written as:

$$f_q(\mathbf{r}_i, t^k) = \Omega_q(f_1^*(\mathbf{r}_i, t^k), ..., f_Q^*(\mathbf{r}_i, t^k)), \quad q = 1..Q. \tag{1}$$

Here, Ω_q is a collision operator, f_q^* is found in (2) later. We use the basic BGK collision operator and the second-order expression for the equilibrium distribution [5].

The second step of LBM is the streaming step, which consists of Q separate transfers of f_q values in the $\mathbf{c}_q$ direction from each node to its neighbors

$$f_q^*(\mathbf{r}_i + \mathbf{c}_q, t^k + 1) = f_q(\mathbf{r}_i, t^k), \quad q = 1..Q. \tag{2}$$

D3Q19 and D3Q27 (cube stencil) are often relevant for fluid dynamics, and D3Q7 (cross) is often used for the solution of the advection-diffusion equation.

2.2 Manycore CPU

Let us take two specific modern CPUs into consideration: the AMD R9 5950X (Zen3) and the Intel Core-i i5-1240P (ADL) (Figs. 1 and 2).

The MD R9 5950X (Zen3) processor has 32 processing units (PU) in 16 CPU cores. A pair of PUs in a core share the L1 cache and the L2 cache. There are two groups of eight CPU cores, and each group has access to the L3 cache.

The Intel Core-i i5-1240P (ADL) processor has two types of cores: 4 P-cores (P for performance) and 8 E-cores (E for efficiency). P-cores contain two PUs each, and have access to individual L2 caches. E-cores have one PU, and there are two groups of E-cores; each group has a shared L2 cache.

In Zen3 and in ADL P-cores, there are 2 PUs per common L2 cache, and in ADL E-cores, 4 PUs share the L2 cache. In both of these cases, it is a challenge to develop a parallel algorithm that can adapt to these different data localization environments.

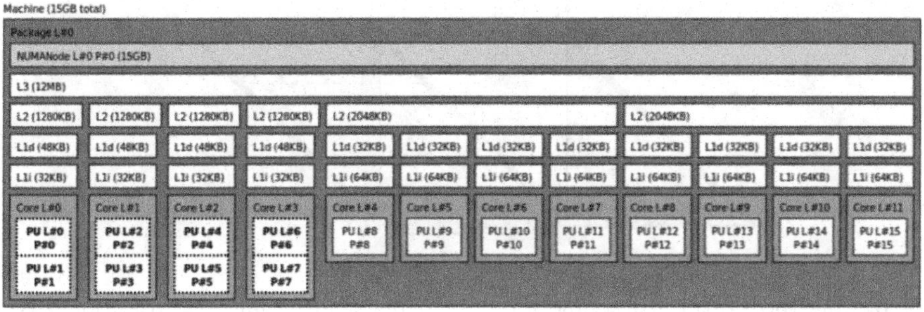

Fig. 2. Intel Core-i i5-1240P (ADL) architecture as shown with the `hwloc` program

3   LRnLA Methods

3.1   ConeTorre LRnLA Algorithm

In the LRnLA method [7], the simulation task is decomposed into subtasks that are local not only in space but also in time. Let us repeat the construction of a general case of ConeTorre (CT) decomposition, and, after that, discuss the optimal CT parameters and the ways of distributing the tasks among CPU cores.

Let us consider a dependency graph. Let a node at $\mathbf{r}_i, t^k$, $\mathbf{r}_i = (x_i, y_i, z_i)$ in 3D1T spacetime denote a scheme update (here, LBM collision (1)).

ReFold. First, let us fold the dependency graph. After folding a graph with $2N$ nodes along the x axis once, a node at $\mathbf{r}_i, t^k$ denotes the operations both at $(\mathbf{r} = (x_i, y_i, z_i), t = t^k)$ and at $(\mathbf{r} = (2N - 1 - x_i, y_i, z_i), t = t^k)$. This means that the operations are performed synchronously at the same time. This is a method to use AVX vectorization. At the same time, the nodes at $(x_i = 0, y_i, z_i)$ and at $(x_i = 2N - 1, y_i, z_i)$ are at the same place, and the stencil dependency for the periodic boundary is local. This is the ReFold method introduced in Reference [10] and used in Reference [13]. For vectors of 8 scalars, we fold the 3D domain once along each of the three axes.

ConeTorre Construction. Second, let us decompose the folded domain into CTs. A 3D CT is a subtask of performing the update in a cube of nodes $C_n(\mathbf{r}_i, t^k) = \{(x, y, z, t) \in \mathcal{M} : x_i \leq x < x_i + n, y_i \leq y < y_i + n, z_i \leq z < z_i + n, t = t^k\}$, then in $C_n(\mathbf{r}_i + \mathbf{c}, t^k + 1)$ ($\mathbf{c} = (1, 1, 1)$), and so on in $C_n(\mathbf{r}_i + i_t \mathbf{c}, t^k + i_t)$, where $0 \leq i_t < N_T$. Let us denote such a CT as a set of operations necessary for performing the scheme updates in nodes $CT_{n,N_T}(\mathbf{r}_i, t^k) = \bigcup_{i_t=0}^{N_T - 1} C_n(\mathbf{r}_i + i_t \mathbf{c}, t^k + i_t)$ performed in a correct order.

A projection to 1D is illustrated in Fig. 3. If a part of the C_n nodes is outside the domain $0 < x < N$, their operations are empty.

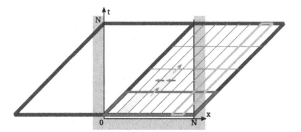

Fig. 3. ConeTorre LRnLA decomposition of a dependency graph. 1D projection. Red: $CT_{N,N}(Color figure online)$. It can be decomposed into subtasks: orange: $CT_{N/8,N}$, blue $CT_{N,N/4}$, or green $CT_{N/8,N/4}$. Horizontal and vertical dependencies for one of the $CT_{N/8,N/4}$ are shown. The two highlighted $CT_{N/8,N/4}$ are asynchronous.

ConeTorre Asynchrony. The dependencies between the nodes inside the CTs determine their correct order of execution. There is a unilateral vertical dependency from $C_n(\mathbf{r}_i, t^k)$ to $C_n(\mathbf{r}_i + N_T\mathbf{c}, t^k + N_T)$ and a unilateral horizontal dependencies from $CT_{n,N_T}(\mathbf{r}_i, t^k)$ to $CT_{n,N_T}(\mathbf{r}_i - n\mathbf{e}_x, t^k)$, to $CT_{n,N_T}(\mathbf{r}_i - n\mathbf{e}_y, t^k)$ and to $CT_{n,N_T}(\mathbf{r}_i - n\mathbf{e}_z, t^k)$, where $\mathbf{e}_x = (1, 0, 0)$, $\mathbf{e}_y = (0, 1, 0)$, and $\mathbf{e}_z = (0, 0, 1)$ are the Cartesian basis vectors. At the same time, there is no dependency between, i.e., $CT_{n,N_T}(\mathbf{r}_i - n\mathbf{e}_y, t^k)$ and $C_n(\mathbf{r}_i + N_T\mathbf{c}, t^k + N_T)$, and *no dependency* between $CT_{n,N_T}(\mathbf{r}_i - n\mathbf{e}_y, t^k)$ and $CT_{n,N_T}(\mathbf{r}_i - n\mathbf{e}_z, t^k)$. Such CTs can be processed in parallel. In the same manner, many asynchronous CTs can be found across different layers in time and space.

ConeTorre Decomposition. A CT task can be further decomposed into subtasks, each of which is also a CT. For example, $CT_{n,N_T}(\mathbf{r}_i, t^k)$ can be decomposed into N_T subtasks $CT_{n,1}(\mathbf{r}_i + i_t\mathbf{c}, t^k + i_t)$, which have to be performed one after another. Alternatively, the base cube $C_n(\mathbf{r}_i, t^k)$ can be divided into smaller cubes that are the start of other CTs. In a special case, $CT_{n,n}$ can be decomposed into 16 similar shapes $CT_{n/2,n/2}$.

Another special case is $CT_{N,1}$. If a $N \times N \times N \times N_T$ dependency graph is decomposed into N_T subtasks $CT_{N,1}$. This corresponds to a traditional, stepwise execution of the simulation task.

ConeTorre Enumeration. Let us decompose CT_{N,N_T} into m^3 subtasks $CT_{N/m,N_T}$. In Sect. 2, we introduced the index i that enumerates the lattice nodes according to some space filling curve. For a simulation domain with $N \times N \times N$ nodes, $0 \leq i < N^3$. The most natural enumeration for CTs is the Z-order. Thus, we usually take $N = 2^R$ for some $R \in \mathbb{N}$. Moreover, if $N/m = 2^r$, $r \in \mathbb{N}$, all $CT_{N/m,N_T}$ can be enumerated in the Z-order as well, where the CT index $i_{CT} = i/(N/m)^3$, $0 \leq i_{CT} < m^3$.

The order of CT execution in the reverse Z-order, that is, from $i_{CT} = m^3 - 1$ down to $i_{CT} = 0$, is the correct dependency preserving order.

3.2 Special Features

There are two special additions to the CT LRnLA algorithm for LBM. The first is the compact streaming update [12]. With it, a CT uses only the data located in the nodes inside it, with no halo. For this purpose, the nodes are assigned into groups, where a group is a cube of $2 \times 2 \times 2$ nodes. The assignment alternates between even and odd time steps. This way, the compact streaming pattern is an advanced version of a swap-shift procedure. The compact update takes exactly Q values to load, update, and save per one full LBM update.

The second is the use of the FArSh (Functionally Arranged Shadow) data structure [11]. For wavefront-type loop tiling, FArSh data provides aligned access for data loaded in an CT in a sequence.

3.3 Localization Properties

When the CT execution advances onto the next time layer, the data in the nodes in the cube gnomon $C_n(\mathbf{r}_i + \mathbf{c}, t^k + 1) - C_n(\mathbf{r}_i, t^k)$ are loaded. Let us denote the number of nodes in this set as $\Gamma_n = n^3 - (n-1)^3 \approx 3n^2$. The data in the cube gnomon $C_n(\mathbf{r}_i, t^k) - C_n(\mathbf{r}_i + \mathbf{c}, t^k + 1)$ is not to be updated any further in this CT task and can be saved into the main memory storage and deleted from the higher memory levels. Let us illustrate how this can be used to improve performance.

Let us consider a hypothetical one core CPU with RAM and three levels of cache. Let Π_{CPU} be its performance in FlOp/s, Θ_{RAM}, Θ_{L3}, Θ_{L2}, Θ_{L1} be the memory throughput of the cache levels (in B/s), and S_{RAM}, S_{L3}, S_{L2}, S_{L1} be the sizes of the memory levels, where $\Theta_{RAM} < \Theta_{L3} < \Theta_{L2} < \Theta_{L1}$ and $S_{RAM} > S_{L3} > S_{L2} > S_{L1}$.

Stepwise Locality Wall. Let us take a simulation task where data fits in the CPU RAM. Let a node update take $\mathcal{O}$ floating point operations. After ReFold folding, a node takes $V\mathcal{O}$ floating point operations, where $V = 8$ if the 3D domain is folded once along each of the three axes, and $V = 1$ if folding is not applied. In the case of stepwise execution, all data has to be updated before the simulation progresses to the next time layer. The calculation rate, measured in lattice nodes updated per second, is limited by $\min\left[\Pi_{CPU}/V\mathcal{O}, \Theta_{RAM}/2VS\right]$, where $S = Q \cdot \texttt{sizeof(float)}$, and $2VS$ is the minimal data throughput per node update: VQ values saved and VQ values loaded. In FlOp/s, the performance limit is obtained by multiplying the value by $V\mathcal{O}$:

$$\Pi \leq \min\left[\Pi_{CPU}, \Theta_{RAM}\mathcal{I}\right], \tag{3}$$

where $\mathcal{I} = \mathcal{O}/2S$ is the arithmetic intensity. This expression is the Roofline model [21].

ConeTorre Localization. Recursive localization is one of the advantages of LRnLA algorithms; the details can be found in Reference [7]. Let us take the same simulation task and perform a recursive CT decomposition. The largest CT covers the whole dependency graph, and it is decomposed into smaller CTs one way or another. Let us decompose it into smaller CTs (denoted by CT_{L3}), such that they access only the data that fits in the S_{L3}. In that case, with a few additional prepositions [7], the performance of the subtasks of such a CT is limited not by Θ_{RAM} but by Θ_{L3}. To describe the limit, we use the arithmetic intensity of CT_{n,n_t}, that is, the number of floating point operations performed in a CT_{n,n_t} divided by the amount of data throughput required for it. A CT_{n,n_t} subtask performs n^3 (in 3D) node updates ($\mathcal{O}$ operations) on each of the n_t time layers. Thus, the number of operations is $n_t n^3 \mathcal{O}$. The base cube (n^d nodes) and n_t gnomons are loaded, and the same number of values are saved. Therefore, the amount of data throughput is $2\left(n^3 + n_t \Gamma_n\right)\mathcal{S}$. The arithmetic intensity is

$$\mathcal{I}_{CT} \equiv \frac{\mathcal{O}_{CT}}{2\mathcal{S}_{CT}} = \frac{n_t n^3 \mathcal{O}}{2\left(n^3 + n_t \Gamma_n\right)\mathcal{S}}. \tag{4}$$

After decomposing CT_{L3}, we can get CT_{L2}, the subtasks of which are limited by Θ_{L2}, and, after that, the similar procedure is repeated for the L1 cache.

The limit that is reached in the case of ideal cache use is

$$\Pi \leq \min\left[\Pi_{CPU}, \Theta_{L1}\mathcal{I}_{CT_{L1}}, \Theta_{L2}\mathcal{I}_{CT_{L2}}, \Theta_{L3}\mathcal{I}_{CT_{L3}}, \Theta_{RAM}\mathcal{I}_{CT_{N,N}}\right]. \tag{5}$$

$\mathcal{I}_{CT_{n,n_t}}$ increases with n. In general,

$$\mathcal{I}_{CT_{N,N}} > \mathcal{I}_{CT_{L3}} > \mathcal{I}_{CT_{L2}} > \mathcal{I}_{CT_{L1}} > \mathcal{I}.$$

Therefore, the limit in (5) is higher than the one in (3), and higher performance can be reached with the use of the CT decomposition than the stepwise one.

4   Construction of an Algorithm for Locality-Aware Parallelism

The ability to decompose a CT into smaller CTs makes CT decomposition versatile enough to adapt to different parallelization strategies.

As an example, we can decompose our task into such CTs, so that a CT fits in the cache of each core, and distribute asynchronous tasks between available PUs. Unfortunately, in doing so, we confront the locality wall problem that is specific to parallel scaling.

This problem became evident in one of our previous works. In the benchmarks on the 12-core AMD Zen2 [12], parallel scaling was close to linear only up to four cores. AMD Zen2 has four core complexes (CCX) with up to four active cores each. In a CCX, the cores share common 16 MBs of LLC cache space. The scaling is good as long as no more than one CT is localized per CCX. When more than one CT is launched in one CCX, less cache is available for each one. Thus, while the degree of parallelism increases, the performance of each CT is limited by slower bandwidth.

In this section, we describe the solution that we developed to overcome this problem.

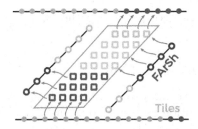

Fig. 4. FArSh data. In the illustration, $CT_{4,7}$ uses data from the main storage in RAM (Tiles) and a FArSh Array. The FArSh array is overwritten in place during the CT execution. In the Tiles array, before the execution of the CT, blue dots correspond to $t = 0$ and green dots correspond to $t = 7$. After the CT is complete, 4 more dots are updated to $t = 7$. In 1D, $\Gamma_N = 1$.

4.1 Data Structure

To take control over localization, it is important to introduce the FArSh data structure [11]. Let the cells in the cube gnomon $C_N(\mathbf{r}_i + \mathbf{c}, t^k + 1) - C_N(\mathbf{r}_i, t^k)$ be enumerated with the index i_g, $0 < i_g \leq \Gamma_N$. Then, for a $CT_{n,N_T}(\mathbf{r}_i, t^k) = \bigcup_{i_t=0}^{N_T-1} C_n(\mathbf{r}_i + i_t \mathbf{c}, t^k + i_t)$, the two types of data are loaded: Tiles and FArSh. Tiles is the data in the base cube. It is stored in the order of increasing index i according to the global space filling curve of the whole simulation domain. The second sort here is FArSh, and it is stored in a separate data array(Figure 4). The data in FArSh is read in the order of increasing i_t. A set of cell data with the same i_g and increasing i_t is a FArSh line, a small continuous array in memory.

The two types of data that are saved are the same two types. The upper cube of a CT is saved into the main data storage in the corresponding position. The FArSh array is overwritten in place. The data that comes into a CT through a horizontal dependency is not used anymore and can be overwritten. The data that is output from a CT through a horizontal dependency is written in its place.

This way, FArSh stores data in a layer of N_T cells on N_T time layers and dynamically progresses through the domain.

The FArSh data, which is output from one CT is further processed by the three CTs that it influences with the horizontal dependency.

4.2 Data Exchange

When a PU finishes one CT_{m,n_t} subtask, it can take another such subtask for execution. If it is a CT that is directly influenced by a CT that was just executed by it, some data that was recently processed by PU can be retained in its cache, and some data should be sent to another PU.

For the data to remain in a higher cache level during the parallel execution of a CT, we require the following. First, the base cube of a CT should fit in the fastest (L1) cache. In the case of LBM, this makes the cube size rather small: $2 \times 2 \times 2$ nodes. Second, the FArSh for CT should fit in the L2 cache. In this

case, all the data that are accessed during the CT execution is in the highest
cache levels.

4.3   Time-Domain Decomposition

After a CT is executed, we can choose which CT should be started after it by
the same PU. If the execution continues to the next time layer, i.e., $CT_{n,n_t}(\mathbf{r}_i + n_t\mathbf{c}, t^k + n_t)$ is performed after $CT_{n,n_t}(\mathbf{r}_i, t^k)$, the data of the base cube remains
in its higher cache, and FArSh is sent to another process. Alternatively, if the
execution continues in the order of horizontal dependency, that is, $CT_{n,n_t}(\mathbf{r}_i - n\mathbf{e}_x, t^k)$, $CT_{n,n_t}(\mathbf{r}_i - n\mathbf{e}_x, t^k)$, or $CT_{n,n_t}(\mathbf{r}_i - n\mathbf{e}_x, t^k)$, FArSh stays in the L2
cache, and the base cube is sent to the other core through (hopefully) L3.

In our construction, the base cube is smaller than FArSh. Therefore, *one
thread should perform CTs of the same time layer*. Hence, the parallelism is in
the time domain: a parallel process performs all calculations in a layer $t_k \leq i_t < t_k + n_t$.

4.4   FArShFold Algorithm

In total, the algorithm is built as follows: Let us start with a domain decomposed
into $CT_{N,N}$. A 3D domain with N^3 nodes is completely covered by eight $CT_{N,N}$,
where each CT intersects a boundary. If we take a larger domain that consists of
several such cubes, there are CTs (inner CTs) that do not intersect a boundary
and contain a full set of non-empty operations. Let us decompose each such CT
into N_C flat layers CT_{N,N_L}, which are processed one by one. The N_L parameter
is chosen so that FArSh data for the CT can be localized in the on-chip cache.

The CT_{N,N_L} is further decomposed into slices $CT_{N,N_L/N_C}$, and parallelism
is applied. A thread executes $CT_{2,N_L/N_C}$ in one slice, one by one, in the reverse
Z-order.

The execution of one CT_{2,N_L} is executed as a pipeline. It is decomposed into
N_C subtasks $CT_{2,N_L/N_C}$. The first thread executes the lowest part, sends the
data of the top cube to the next thread, and so on.

4.5   Heterogeneous Cores

In the algorithm construction, one of the goals is good parallel scaling up to the
total number of PUs. However, if two PUs share one L2 cache (Zen3, Fig. 1 and
P-cores in ADL, Fig. 2), or if four PUs share one L2 cache (E-cores in ADL,
Fig. 2) some of the localization ability is lost. Thus, we make a pair (or four) of
PUs that share the same L2 cache share the same FArSh array. In this case, the
task decomposition begins with the distribution of FArSh for CT_{N,N_L} (data of
$\Gamma_N N_L$ nodes) between L2 caches, and N_C is chosen to be equal to the number of
L2 caches. In each layer $i_C, 0 \leq i_C < N_C$, FArSh spans the nodes in $0 < i_g < \Gamma_N$,
$i_C N_L/N_C < i_t < (i_C + 1)N_L/N_C)$.

After that, the processing of $CT_{2,N_L/N_C}$ in the layer is distributed between
two or four threads, depending on the number of PUs that share the L2 cache.

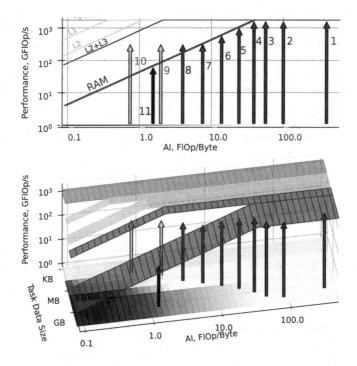

Fig. 5. Roofline analysis. Same figure from two viewpoints.

4.6 L3 Localization

For the most part, due to the Z-order execution, FArSh is expected to stay in the L2 cache. L3 cache accesses happen in FArSh access, but this does not impair the performance since the L3 throughput is high enough.

It is more important to make sure that the threads send data to each other through L3 and that accesses to RAM are infrequent.

To achieve this goal, we make sure that all subtasks CT_{2,N_L} that are processed at some point in time are not too far away from each other, so that their combined data can fit in the L3.

Access to RAM is inevitable only at the very start and the very end of CT_{2,N_L}. Two threads are allocated solely for the costly operations of saving and loading to and from RAM, respectively.

4.7 Roofline Analysis for Zen3

In Fig. 5, we illustrate the cache aware Roofline analysis with a graph. With a 3D depiction, it is shown how the Roofline limit depends on the memory size of the task.

The constructed algorithms can be analyzed with the tools introduced in Sect. 3.3. The parameters are $N = 256$, $N_L = 256$, $N_C = 16$. The rightmost arrow (1) corresponds to a whole dependency graph, with 512^3 nodes updated 256 times. Arrow (2) corresponds to a $CT_{256,256}$ after the domain is folded with ReFold. Arrow (3) is $CT_{256,64}$, one layer of FArShFold.

With the reverse Z-order execution of $CT_{2,4}$ subtasks in a slice, we can treat the algorithm subdivision as $CT_{256,4} \rightarrow CT_{128,4} \rightarrow CT_{64,4} \rightarrow CT_{32,4} \rightarrow CT_{16,4} \rightarrow CT_{8,4} \rightarrow CT_{4,4} \rightarrow CT_{2,4}$. In Fig. 5, arrows (4–7) correspond to CTs from $CT_{256,4}$ to $CT_{32,4}$. $CT_{16,4}$ (arrow 8) fits in the combined L2+L3 cache and is limited by a higher RoofLine. $CT_{8,4}$, $CT_{4,4}$ (arrows 9, 10) fit in the L2 cache, and the limit is higher.

Finally, the performance peak of the constructed algorithms with these parameters is found as the minimal height of the arrows (1–10), and is equal to 345 GFlop/s. Accordingly, the RAM bandwidth was found to be the bottleneck.

In stepwise execution, i.e., when the code is implemented with a time loop, and in each loop iteration all 512^3 nodes are updated once, the data is pulled from RAM each time. Arrow (11) illustrates the stepwise peak (67 GFlop/s).

5   Benchmarks

5.1   Code Implementation

The described algorithm is implemented for $Q = 19$ LBM in C++. Parallelism is implemented with standard threads and synchronization primitives in C++20. The main synchronization tool is a semaphore that is implemented with atomic variables. In the case of a prolonged wait, control is handed over to the OS. Thread binding to cores is implemented with the HWloc API. AVX vectorization is implemented manually with intrinsic instructions.

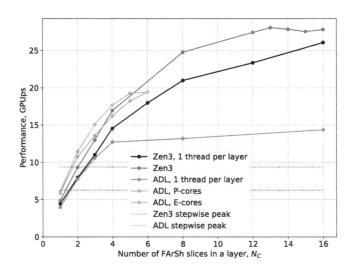

Fig. 6. Benchmark scaling results

5.2   Performance Tests

We tested the performance of one full $CT_{N,N}$ task, $N = 256$. With ReFold, this is a total of $N(2N)^3$ node updates on $8N^3$`sizeof(float)` bytes of data. Single precision is used.

In Fig. 6, we plotted the performance scaling result for the two hardware choices. The performance is measured in GPUps, that is, billions of population (f_q) updates per second. The PUps measure is obtained by multiplying the performance measured in lattice site updates per second (LUps) multiplied by Q. The theoretical stepwise peak is ≈ 6 and ≈ 10 GPUps in the case of ideal memory throughput and ideal many-core scaling for Zen3 and ADL, respectively.

With FArShFold, we obtain higher results. First, when we run FArShFold without taking into account the heterogeneity of CPU cores (one thread per FArSh layer), we get the two lower lines. Evidently, the scaling is only up to 4 threads in ADL and 8 threads in Zen3. This is because two layers of FArSh try to fit in one L2 cache in some cases, and the CT performance bottleneck that is determined by localization (Sect. 3.3) decreases.

When several threads are assigned to one layer, the performance obtained is higher. In ADL benchmarks, we approach the scaling test in two ways. We start increasing the number of threads and bind the first threads either to E-cores or to P-cores. This way, two scaling patterns are obtained, but the final point corresponds to exactly the same setup. Both variations are more efficient than the one-thread-per-layer setup.

5.3   Related Works

LBM is a benchmark for many performance tests [2,22]. All recent results that were published without spacetime decomposition of the tasks [2,6,14,22] were obtained without data reuse in higher caches and can not exceed the stepwise peak outlined in Fig. 6.

LBM was a testbed used in some temporal blocking codes for the CPU before [1,9,19]. Evidently, such algorithms are underdeveloped, and do not take account of cache localization and parallelism at the same time.

In comparison to our previous works with the LRnLA method [10,12,13], Sects. 4.5 and 4.6 explain the novelty. Most importantly, as illustrated in Fig. 6, the performance of more than 25 GPUps, which is $\sim 1.5 \cdot 10^9$ lattice site updates per second for D3Q19 BGK LBM, is obtained on a single CPU for the first time. This is in the range of high performance implementations on GPU [6]. Previously, we used ConeTorre in the LBM code [13], and the performance close to 25 GPUps was obtained with the use of GPU. CT was also used in the CPU part, but the parallelization method did not allow localizing the CT data in the local caches of the cores, thus, the CPU portion of the computation was significantly slower.

6   Conclusion

We constructed the algorithm FArShFold for the LBM, which is efficient enough to obtain GPU-level performance on a single CPU. This was made possible with the use of LRnLA algorithms and the introduction of time-domain parallelism, which starts by creating a separate array for data exchange in horizontal dependencies (FArSh) and distributing FArSh between cores in a way that localizes FArSh in L2 caches.

One impact of this development is that it shows that CPU performance can still be on par with GPU performance of LBM codes, while this idea was doubted (i.e., in Reference [6]).

While the construction was made with specific hardware in mind, the tools for algorithm construction, such as CT decomposition, parameter adjustment, and performance peak analysis, are stated in a general form and can be applied to different environments in the future.

Therefore, for any other memory-bound stencil codes where high many-core CPU performance is important, it is recommended to build a code on the basis of the introduced solution.

References

1. Endo, T.: Applying recursive temporal blocking for stencil computations to deeper memory hierarchy. In: 2018 IEEE 7th Non-Volatile Memory Systems and Applications Symposium (NVMSA), pp. 19–24. IEEE (2018)
2. Ho, M.Q.: Optimization of data transfer on many-core processors, applied to dense linear algebra and stencil computations, Ph. D. thesis, Université Grenoble Alpes (2018)
3. Kogge, P., Bergman, K., et al.: Exascale computing study: Technology challenges in achieving exascale systems, Tech. Rep 15, Defense Advanced Research Projects Agency Information Processing Techniques Office (DARPA IPTO) (2008)
4. Kogge, P.M., Page, B.A.: Locality: the 3rd wall and the need for innovation in parallel architectures. In: Hochberger, C., Bauer, L., Pionteck, T. (eds.) ARCS 2021. LNCS, vol. 12800, pp. 3–18. Springer, Cham (2021). https://doi.org/10.1007/978-3-030-81682-7_1
5. Krüger, T., Kusumaatmaja, H., Kuzmin, A., Shardt, O., Silva, G., Viggen, E.M.: The Lattice Boltzmann Method. GTP, Springer, Cham (2017). https://doi.org/10.1007/978-3-319-44649-3
6. Lehmann, M., Krause, M.J., Amati, G., Sega, M., Harting, J., Gekle, S.: Accuracy and performance of the lattice Boltzmann method with 64-bit, 32-bit, and customized 16-bit number formats. Phys. Rev. E **106**(1), 015308 (2022)
7. Levchenko, V., Perepelkina, A.: Locally recursive non-locally asynchronous algorithms for stencil computation. Lobachevskii J. Math. **39**(4), 552–561 (2018)
8. McCalpin, J.D.: Memory bandwidth and machine balance in current high performance computers. IEEE Comput. Soc. Tech. Committee Comput. Architect. Newsl. **2**, 19–25 (1995)
9. Nguyen, A., Satish, N., Chhugani, J., Kim, C., Dubey, P.: 3.5-D blocking optimization for stencil computations on modern CPUs and GPUs. In: SC 2010: Proceedings of the 2010 ACM/IEEE International Conference for High Performance Computing, Networking, Storage and Analysis, pp. 1–13. IEEE (2010)

10. Perepelkina, A., Levchenko, V.: LRnLA algorithm ConeFold with non-local vectorization for LBM implementation. In: Voevodin, V., Sobolev, S. (eds.) RuSCDays 2018. CCIS, vol. 965, pp. 101–113. Springer, Cham (2019). https://doi.org/10.1007/978-3-030-05807-4_9

11. Perepelkina, A., Levchenko, V.D.: Functionally arranged data for algorithms with space-time Wavefront. In: Sokolinsky, L., Zymbler, M. (eds.) PCT 2021. CCIS, vol. 1437, pp. 134–148. Springer, Cham (2021). https://doi.org/10.1007/978-3-030-81691-9_10

12. Perepelkina, A., Levchenko, V., Zakirov, A.: New compact streaming in LBM with ConeFold LRnLA algorithms. In: Voevodin, V., Sobolev, S. (eds.) Supercomputing. RuSCDays 2020. Communications in Computer and Information Science, vol. 1331, pp. 50–62 (2020)

13. Perepelkina, A., et al.: Heterogeneous LBM simulation code with LRnLA algorithms. Commun. Comput. Phys. **33**(1), 214–244 (2023)

14. Riesinger, C., Bakhtiari, A., Schreiber, M., Neumann, P., Bungartz, H.J.: A holistic scalable implementation approach of the lattice Boltzmann method for CPU/GPU heterogeneous clusters. Computation **5**(4), 48 (2017)

15. Rupp, K.: Microprocessor trend data. https://github.com/karlrupp/microprocessor-trend-data. Accessed 11 Apr 2023

16. Taflove, A., Hagness, S.C., Piket-May, M.: Computational electromagnetics: the finite-difference time-domain method. Electr. Eng. Handb. **3**, 629–670 (2005)

17. Toro, E.F.: Riemann Solvers and Numerical Methods for Fluid Dynamics: A Practical Introduction. Springer Science & Business Media (2013). https://doi.org/10.1007/978-3-662-03915-1

18. Virieux, J., et al.: Modelling seismic wave propagation for geophysical imaging. In: Kanao, M. (ed.) Seismic Waves, chap. 13. IntechOpen, Rijeka (2012). https://doi.org/10.5772/30219

19. Wellein, G., Hager, G., Zeiser, T., Wittmann, M., Fehske, H.: Efficient temporal blocking for stencil computations by multicore-aware WaveFront parallelization. In: 2009 33rd Annual IEEE International Computer Software and Applications Conference, vol. 1, pp. 579–586. IEEE (2009)

20. Wilde, D.K.: A library for doing polyhedral operations, Tech. Rep. 785, IRISA (1993)

21. Williams, S., Waterman, A., Patterson, D.: Roofline: an insightful visual performance model for multicore architectures. Commun. ACM **52**(4), 65–76 (2009)

22. Wittmann, M., Haag, V., Zeiser, T., Köstler, H., Wellein, G.: Lattice Boltzmann benchmark kernels as a testbed for performance analysis. Comput. Fluids **172**, 582–592 (2018)

23. Wolfe, M.: Loops skewing: the wavefront method revisited. Int. J. Parallel Prog. **15**, 279–293 (1986)

24. Wonnacott, D.G., Strout, M.M.: On the scalability of loop tiling techniques. Impact **2013**, 3 (2013)

Development of Components for Monitoring and Control Intelligent Information System

Dmitry Balandin$^{(\boxtimes)}$, Oleg Kuzenkov , and Albert Egamov

Lobachevsky University, Nizhny Novgorod, Russia
{dmitriy.balandin,oleg.kuzenkov,albert.egamov}@itmm.unn.ru

Abstract. Development of digital economy requires improving of IT personnel training to ensure a more complete interaction of education and industry. In particular, it is necessary to develop the students' ability to design industrial intellectual information systems. The article analyzes the experience of Lobachevsky State University of Nizhny Novgorod in organizing a series of educational projects for the information support of Sergach Sugar Plant. These projects were aimed at the development of components of an intellectual and information system for monitoring and controlling sugar production. The purpose of the research was to create educational and methodological support of these projects. Such educational support includes the definition of objectives, plans and schedules, the creation of educational resources. The most important educational objective of the projects was the practical learning of the methodology of intellectual information system creating. The project approach was used as the main method of organizing the educational and research work. The considered training experience is of a great importance not only for solving the partial production problem. It can be useful in a general case when students study the methodology of intellectual information system creating. This approach is the important form in the training of IT personnel for the digital economy.

Keywords: Digital economy · Information technology · Project training · Educational and research project · Sugar Plant · Sugar beet processing

1 Introduction

One of the most important factors of economic development at present is the digitalization of economy [1–4]. The implementation of intelligent information monitoring and management systems plays a leading role in increasing competitiveness of industrial enterprises [5–9]. The needs of the modern digital economy dictate new tasks for the education system [6,7,10]. Now education should provide conscious knowledge of information technologies, understanding of their theoretical foundations, the ability to use them in real conditions to solve economic problems. The tasks of training personnel for the digital economy are relevant, first of all, for educational areas of information technology, since their graduates form the main human resource for the digitalization of economy [11]. Here, the study of digital technologies is the main goal of the curricula. However, such a study is often abstracted from the practical problems of specific industrial enterprises. In this regard, it is necessary to improve the educational process in order to ensure a more complete interaction of education and industry [12]. This improvement concerns the formation of students' ability to design and develop intellectual and information systems to support specific productions. Here it is impossible to form the skills of the competent use of digital technologies without a deep knowledge of the subject area, the specifics of an individual enterprise, understanding the needs of the manufacturer, without agreeing with him development plans and their results. Thus, the modernization of the educational process should provide for the possibility of students to participate in the development of such systems for economic enterprises [13].

The understanding of the methodological principles and concepts of digitalization is possible only in the case of practical activity. Students can take an active part in the development of separate components of the intelligent information system during a series of educational, research and laboratory work [13,14]. The most productive way to achieve educational goals is to combine this series into a single interconnected complex, thanks to which students will be able to study partial aspects of design, while obtaining a holistic view of the global task. Within the framework of this study, the experience of improving the educational process Lobachevsky State University of Nizhny Novgorod is analyzed. This experience is based of interaction with the Sergach Sugar Plant of the Nizhny Novgorod region [13,14]. Currently, the modernization of the Sergach Sugar Plant is being carried out according to the decree of the Government of the Russian Federation. Automated monitoring, control and management systems have long been used in sugar production, in particular, there is the system "Technohimuchet" [9,15–17]. But the capabilities of such systems are quite limited, their functions are far from comprehensive. These systems do not provide a complete solution of all tasks of managing sugar production. Most of these systems solve only the most elementary tasks of tracking and displaying the state of the production system, some of them allow one the possibility of automated adjustment. Thus, the task of creating an intelligent information system for monitoring and controlling sugar beet production remains relevant. The staff and students of Lobachevsky University take an active part in the development of such a system for the Sergach Sugar Factory. In full, the creation of such a system cannot be the content of student practices. However, it is possible to select partial components of the system. Their development can become the subject of educational research and laboratory work. Such works will be of practical importance only if they are coordinated with each other, when continuity in their implementation is ensured. That is, they should all form a single educational complex with common goals, a single subject area, a single customer. The implementation of such a complex requires general educational and methodological support [13]. The purpose of the research is to create educational and methodological support for an educational complex to develop components of an intellectual and information system for monitoring the technological process of sugar beet processing, forecasting the production of finished products and implementing optimal settings of technological parameters.

2   Materials and Methods

The project approach is used as the main method of organizing educational and research work. The methodology of the project approach has been the subject of many years of research and is now well known [11, 13]. The use of this method makes it possible to teach students in conditions corresponding to real production. At the same time, successful and effective implementation of project-based learning from the point of view of achieving educational goals requires deep educational and methodological support [14]. The most important component of the educational materials of the educational complex is the presence of a common system project, the creation of which precedes the educational and research work. When carrying out research work, the decomposition method is used. It allows us to present a common task as a sequence of relatively autonomous interconnected partial tasks; to transit from a general project to partial components [14]. The methodology of the educational complex involves a consistent movement from theoretical acquaintance with these concepts to understanding their essence and significance in the course of practical creation of a specific system. One of the most important concepts is the concept of information [18]. Existing textbooks and manuals do not help in solving the problem at all. They very often try to explain information as messages, data or signals [19, 20]. However, this approach does not allow us to understand the essence, meaning and role of information in the intellectual information system. When revealing the meaning of the concept of information, first of all, it is necessary to proceed from the fact that information is always the result of mapping a certain set of elements (alternatives, outcomes, states, etc.) into another set, which can be both natural and symbolic (virtual). For example, such a set can be alphabetic characters or binary numbers. In this case, the selection of some element from the first set (the realization of the outcome or state) leads to the selection of the corresponding element from the second set, which represents information about this state. That is, information is not just some numbers, it is values (possibly numeric) associated with the states of the primary object, reflecting them. Such an understanding of the information concept is necessary to build a model of the objects and processes under study. A model of an object, process, or system is considered to be another object similar to the original one in the most important features, preserving its essential properties. The modeling method is the most important in the development of intellectual and information systems [15, 21]. The basis of such systems is an information model. Here the information is usually presented in digital format (digital model), but in this case it is not an arbitrary set of numbers. This set is strictly structured, each number (indicator) displays the state of individual fragments of the original object; these numbers are related to each other. Thus, one of the main methods of solving research problems within the framework of the implemented educational complex is the method of creating an information model. To create an information model, it is necessary to collect and structure the relevant indicators, as well as to ensure their further continuous receipt in order to ensure the adequate functioning of the information model. To ensure the proper level of efficiency of the created model, the method of intelligent data processing is used. An intelligent information system is usually understood as a data processing system capable of summarizing the accumulated experience, analyzing the current state and predicting its change, forming behavior goals, building the best solutions to achieve the goals based on flexible adaptation [9,22,23]. Such data processing uses methods of machine learning, neural networks, evolutionary computing, global optimization, etc. [24]. At the primary level, the intellectual capabilities of the system are expressed in its ability to predict [25,26]. The method of mathematical modeling is widely used for forecasting within the information system [27]. This creates the means to ensure the possibility of predicting the further development of the situation, future changes in characteristic indicators. In information systems for the sugar production support, simplified models are more often used then detailed models. They describe the production process in an enlarged way through a sequence of transfer functions based on balanced equations for substances and energy more than the features of the ongoing physico-chemical processes. Also simulation models are widely used; they are constructed in the form of regression dependencies based on the processing of available empirical data. To obtain a model corresponding to a specific production, as a rule, additional calibration of coefficients is required based on the analysis of data from this particular enterprise. At the same time, methods of intelligent data processing, methods of regression analysis are used. The next level of the intellectual abilities of the system involves the construction of control for a predetermined goal with known limitations, ensuring decision-making on the choice of the best impact on the system, in particular, the adjustment and regulation of control parameters. Here, optimization methods are used, both exact and heuristic, in particular, methods of discrete optimization, global optimization, optimal control [28–33]. Finally, the most advanced systems are such intelligent systems that can, within certain limits, independently form management goals, or make adjustments to the original goal systems taking into account incoming information [34]. Intelligent data processing allows you to formalize the target functions, a set of criteria for the quality of the production process. The principles, concepts and methods listed above form the basis of the educational complex being created.

3   Results

3.1   General Educational and Methodological Support

As a result of the research, educational and methodological support for the educational complex was created. This ensures the implementation of educational and research projects on the development of components of an intelligent information system for monitoring and controlling sugar production. The educational and methodological support of the educational complex includes the formulation of goals and objectives, the definition of the plan and schedule, their correlation with the current curriculum, the creation of educational resources. The most important educational goal is the practical studying of the basic principles and methodology of creating intellectual information systems. The main purpose of the intellectual information system is to ensure maximum sugar yield by monitoring the plant's technological processes in real time, operational analysis and transmission of information for making management decisions to optimize production processes. The practical objectives of the projects are to create the components of an intellectual information system. The cycle of projects was carried out by bachelors of 3 years of study in the area of "Fundamental Informatics and Information Technologies" through practical and independent work provided for in the curriculum of the disciplines "Mathematical modeling of selection processes" and "Computational Methods". The subject of projects work is closely related to the content of these disciplines. Within the framework of lectures on the discipline "Mathematical modeling of selection processes", students get acquainted with the concept of information related to the reflection of selecting an element from a certain set, with the concepts of information and mathematical models, methods of mathematical modeling and global optimization necessary for the implementation of the project. To support studying intellectual information systems methodology, a synchronous electronic resource on this discipline was developed in MOODLE. Within the framework of the discipline "Computational Methods", the methods of discrete optimization necessary for the projects ("Hungarian algorithm", etc.) are considered. This material was prepared for the laboratory work "Solving applied problems of discrete optimization" (http://e-lib.unn.ru/MegaPro/UserEntry? Action=FindDocs&ids=850257&idb=0). A series of projects were carried out during the academic year. They were also carried out during the students' practical training at the UNN Department of Differential Equations, Mathematical and Numerical Analysis. To implement educational and research projects it is necessary to present a general structure of the intellectual and information system for monitoring and controlling sugar beet processing. As a basis for their implementation, a scheme of an information model of this processing was developed. It was then the subject to detail within the framework of individual studies. Sugar beet production is characterized by complexity and multi-stage [35]. Currently, sugar production technologies comprise up to eleven separate technological procedures. Their sequence is reflected in the corresponding information model. The information system has a multi-level structure. The lower level of monitoring involves the collection of operational empirical data at all stages of the production process through the use of continuous laboratory analysis and the installation of monitoring sensors. Such data, in particular, include the main indicators of the chemical composition of raw materials, intermediate products of sugar beet production and sugar-containing solutions: diffusion juice, purified juice, sugar syrup, molasses, pulp, filtration sludge (defecate), etc. The indicators of dry matter content, sucrose content, quality factor (purity) are determined [15, 16]. In addition to these indicators, data on the content of ash, potassium, sodium, alpha-amine nitrogen, invert sugar (reducing substances) in raw materials and purified juice have a significant impact on the production process [36]. Obtaining these data is not the subject of the educational and research projects. It is believed that this data has been collected and is available for further processing. Based on the collected data, using mathematical models, it is possible to build an operational forecast of sugar production, which is the main task of the second level of the information and intellectual system. At the upper level of the information system, the problem of optimizing the production process is solved. A prerequisite for the implementation of each project work was the creation of software for solving the corresponding problem in the Python language. The choice of this language is due to the fact that it is convenient when working with matrices and easy to learn [37]. In addition, there is an extensive library of routines in this language (in particular, the Munkres library, where there is software for solving the optimization assignment problem).

Thus, an educational complex was formed, including the implementation of two main educational and research projects dedicated to the development of two modules of an intelligent information system for monitoring and controlling sugar production: a sugar yield assessment module and a sugar yield optimization module. The educational complex is coordinated with the curriculum for the training of bachelors of information technology. A methodology for the implementation of the envisaged projects was developed. The methodology provides for the use of project-based learning. Each project is carried out by a group of students of 3–5 people. The goal and objectives of each project, the plan and schedule for its implementation, the distribution of responsibilities between the project participants are determined. For theoretical support of the implementation of projects, orientation lectures are provided within the framework of individual disciplines of the curriculum. They discuss the general principles of building intelligent information systems, methods of machine learning and optimization. To study the necessary material, the recommended educational literature was selected and a teaching aid was published. Regular consultations are held in accordance with the schedule. The passage of each stage of the project is accompanied by an intermediate delivery, during which the degree of formation of the provided competencies is checked. To test practical skills, a fund of evaluation tools has been created, which includes the solution of practical problems on project topics. Based on the results of the implementation, projects are defended and final reports are prepared.

3.2 Development of the Sugar Yield Assessment Module

The purpose of the first project was to create a module for estimating sugar yield based on the processing of current data and technological parameters of sugar beet production. For this purpose, monitoring results are used at the main stages of sugar production—diffusion extraction of beet juice from raw materials, purification, evaporation and crystallization. The input data for the module was the content of sucrose and solids in raw materials and intermediate products of production, the content of potassium, sodium, alpha-amine nitrogen, invert substances. There are various calculation formulas that are used to predict the sugar yield [36,38]. The main step in predicting the yield is the use of sucrose balance models, the general equation of which has the form [15,16].

$$CX = V + CX_M + P_0.$$

Here CX_M, (%)—the content of sucrose in the molasses, P_0, (%) is the total loss of sucrose (sugar) before receiving molasses, $P_0 = 1.1$. To calculate the loss of sucrose in the molasses was established relationships appropriate to domestic conditions [35]:

$$CX_M = 0.1541 \times (K + Na) + 0.2159 \times N + 0.9989 \times I + 0.1967.$$

Here K, Na, N have the value of the content of potassium, sodium, α-amine nitrogen in beets, measured in mmol per 100 g of beet; I, (%) is the content of reducing substances.

The sucrose losses in molasses can be also fairly accurately estimated taking into account the data on the purity of beet syrup Ψ_S and the purity of factory molasses Ψ_M as follows [36]

$$CX_M = \frac{1.07 \times (CX - 0.9) \times K_C}{K_M}, \tag{1}$$

where K_M and K_C are the molasses-forming coefficients of molasses and syrup calculated by the formulas

$$K_M = \frac{\Psi_M}{100 - \Psi_M}, \quad K_C = \frac{\Psi_C}{100 - \Psi_C}.$$

A number of other more complex formulas are also used, which make it possible to predict the sugar yield by analyzing purified juice, by the purity of beet juice, by the purity of diffusion juice and factory molasses, etc. These formulas use dependencies that allow us, in particular, to calculate the efficiency of purification by the efficiency of diffusion extraction of beet juice, predict sugar yield by the Silin method, etc.

It should be noted that all equations use coefficients that were determined approximately by processing observational data using regression analysis methods. As it is rightly noted in the manuals on the use of such formulas, a positive effect from them for assessing the yield of sugar in a separate production can be obtained by adjusting the values of these coefficients corresponding to the characteristics of a particular plant. For example, formula (1) can be used only when the average purity of factory molasses is known, as well as the average purity of beet syrup for a given plant for a given beet variety. Thus, it is necessary to ensure the calculation of the required values based on the available production data. Figure 1 shows data on the purity of factory molasses for the month of October 2021, when the same beet variety was processed.

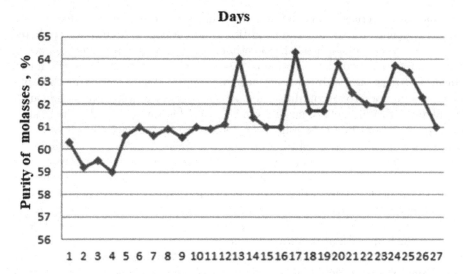

Fig. 1. Data on the purity of factory molasses for October 2021 of the Sergach Sugar Plant

From the data provided, it can be seen that the value we are interested in allows for significant fluctuations. It leads to an inadequate estimate of sugar yield if this estimate is based on one of the selected values. To eliminate this difficulty, averaging of the desired value is used. The average value of molasses purity for October is 61.5%. Similarly, the average purity of the syrup is calculated, which is 92.08%. Hence the molasses-forming coefficient of molasses $K_M = 1.6$; molasses-forming coefficient of juice $K_C = 11.63$. If we consider a batch of beets with an initial sugar content of 17.5%, then the loss of sucrose in molasses according to Formula (1) will amount to 2.44%. Taking the value of losses before molasses formation for 0.9%, we get that the sugar yield will be 14.16% of the mass of processed raw materials. As a result of the design work carried out, a software module was created that allows calculating the predicted sugar yield according to known sucrose balance formulas. At the same time, it is possible to refine the parameters used in these formulas according to the plant data.

3.3   Development of a Sugar Yield Optimization Module

The obtained estimations of the sugar yield is being used for the development of the third level module to optimize the beet processing schedule. One of the tasks that require the use of software in the production of sugar is to optimize the schedule of processing of raw materials [38]. Beetroot for sugar production is harvested during a short ripening period and stored until processing. The production value of raw materials depends on the chemical composition of root crops and varies for different varieties. During storage, the production value of raw materials decreases, and the rate of decline is also different for different varieties. It depends on the storage conditions and cannot be accurately predicted for the entire processing period. Sometimes there is a ripening effect. It lies in the fact that the production value of raw materials can increase at the initial stage of storage and only then its decrease begins. The selection of the optimal schedule for processing different batches of raw materials can significantly increase the overall yield of sugar from the available raw materials. The task of drawing up an optimal processing schedule can be mathematically posed as the assignment problem. The solution of such a problem allows us to calculate the absolute maximum sugar yield with the available raw materials. However, for such a solution, it is necessary to know in advance all changes in the production value of all beet batches during the entire processing (storage) season, which is impossible in practice. In conditions of beet degradation uncertainty, easily implemented, simple and reliable heuristic quasi-optimal algorithms are of great interest. Such algorithms require only information about the production value of raw materials at the current moment of processing and do not require exhaustive knowledge of all the details of the degradation of raw materials in the future. Two simplest heuristic algorithms are quite well known—"greedy" and "thrifty" [14,37]. The "greedy" algorithm consists of priority processing the beet batch that can give the greatest output of products at the moment. The "thrifty" algorithm consists of primary processing the batch with the lowest production value. Taking into account the effect of ripening, it is possible to propose additional heuristic processing algorithms—various combinations of greedy and "thrifty" algorithms. The "thrifty/greedy" algorithm consists of the fact that during the stages of ripening, the "thrifty" algorithm is implemented, and then the "greedy" algorithm is used during the process of withering root crops. When implementing a "greedy/thrifty" algorithm, a "greedy" algorithm is used during the ripening period, and a "thrifty" algorithm is used during the withering period.

In addition, various combinations of such algorithms are possible. As such, a group of algorithms called "T(k)G" is considered. Here k is a parameter of each algorithm, a natural number. The essence of the T(k)G algorithm is as follows. At each step during the ripening process, the current production value of all remaining unprocessed batches of raw materials is calculated. These batches are then ordered and numbered in ascending order of production value. From this ordered set, the k-th batch is selected and processed at this stage. At the next stage, the ordering and selection procedure is repeated. At the end of the ripening process, the usual greedy algorithm is used during the withering process of raw materials. For example, when $k = 1$, the algorithm "T(1)G" is a "thrifty/greedy" algorithm.

The purpose of the project was to assess the loss of sugar yield (relative to the absolute maximum) when implementing different heuristic processing algorithms. To assess the possibilities of heuristic algorithms in increasing sugar production, computer simulations of the process of degradation of raw materials were used, taking into account the long-term data of the Sergach Sugar Plant. Software has been created that allows such imitations. The total number of days of sugar beet processing for the Sergach Sugar Plant is approximately 100 day, the daily processing is 3000 tons of sugar beet. On average, for a week, as the data of a real plant show, changes in the amount of processed raw materials (which is determined by the production capacity of the enterprise) are insignificant. Changes in the characteristics of raw materials on certain days of the week have almost negligible effect on the sugar yield, so you can take their average values for weeks for estimates. Hence, the number of processing stages was chosen equal to 15. It is assumed that there are raw materials (beets) of different varieties, and at each stage a batch of raw materials of only one variety is processed. Then the number of batches of beets that the plant processes per season is equal to the number of processing stages. The following designations are used: a_i, $i = \overline{1,n}$, are the initial production value of the i-th batch of raw materials (beets), i.e. the amount of sugar that can be produced from a unit of this raw material; b_{ij}, $i = \overline{1,n}$, $j = \overline{1,n-1}$, are the coefficient of change in the production value of the i-th batch of raw materials at the j-th storage stage compared to the previous one.

Then the production value of the i-th batch of raw materials will change as follows: in the beginning $p_{i1} = a_i$, $p_{i2} = a_i b_{i1}$—after the first period, $p_{i3} = a_i b_{i1} b_{i2}$—after the second period, $p_{in} = a_i b_{i1} b_{i2}, \cdots, b_{in-1}$—just before the last period. Let ν be the stage number of the stage when the ripening process ends. The process of withering of all batches of raw materials began simultaneously. At $j \leq \nu - 1$ the degradation coefficients will be $b_{ij} > 1$, at $j \geq \nu$, they can also be called ripening coefficients. the degradation coefficients are less than one: $b_{ij} < 1$, they can also be called withering coefficients In this article, it is implied that the ripening takes place after the harvest of sugar beet, and all the beets included in the batch are harvested before the beginning of the first period.

Two cases with different duration of the ripening process were considered. In the first case, it was believed that the ripening process ends at the sixth stage ($\nu = 5$), and in the second case—at the fourth stage ($\nu = 5$).

Taking into account the data of the Sergach Sugar Plant, the following constants were set for each series of experiments: a_{min}, a_{max}, b_{min}, b_{max}, $\widetilde{b}_{min}$, $\widetilde{b}_{max}$. They are the boundaries of values for the permissible ranges of the initial production value of raw materials of all batches $[a_{min}, a_{max}]$, and ranges of values of degradation coefficients: for the stages of ripening $[b_{min}, b_{max}]$, for the stages of withering $[\widetilde{b}_{min}, \widetilde{b}_{max}]$. Parametrs a_i, b_{ij}, $i = \overline{1,n}$, $j = \overline{1,n-1}$, were generated for each experiment of series.

Then 20 numerical experiments were carried out in each series. The initial parameters a_{min}, a_{max}, b_{min}, b_{max}, $[\widetilde{b}_{min}, \widetilde{b}_{max}]$ were varied and were different for each series. The length of the permissible segments changed in turn. In some series, the initial sugar content and degradation coefficients of each batch were distributed uniformly over an acceptable segment, while in others they were close to each other in the δ-neighborhood of randomly selected points, where δ is a small positive number, selected for this series of experiments, etc.

During each experiment, the value of the absolute maximum sugar yield S^* was calculated for these raw material parameters, as an exact solution

to the assignment problem. Then the sugar yield was experimentally calculated by implementing the following heuristic algorithms: "greedy", "thrifty",
"greedy/thrifty", "thrifty/greedy" and algorithms "T(k)G", $k = \overline{1, n - \nu + 1}$, too.

After calculating the sugar yield obtained as a result of applying each algorithm, this result was compared with the absolute maximum S^* and losses were
calculated in comparison with the maximum possible sugar yield $S^* - S$.

Based on the results of each series of experiments, the following values were
calculated for each al gorithm: the average sugar yield value is the arithmetic
mean of the 20 yield values obtained in each of 20 experiments; $\langle \Delta S_0 \rangle = \langle S^* - S \rangle$
is the average absolute loss value is the average difference value S^* and S; $\mu =$
$\langle \Delta S_0 \rangle / \langle S^* \rangle$—average relative losses. Among the "T(k)G" algorithms, algorithms
were calculated for all permissible k, but only the results and nunber k of the
best of them in each experiment were remembered and taken into account in the
table.

The experimental results are shown in Tables 1 and 2. Table 1 shows the
results of a series of 20 experiments for the first case of ripening ($\nu = 5$), Table 2
shows the results of a series of 20 experiments for the second case of ripening
($\nu = 5$).

Table 1. Experimental results for the first case of ripening ($\nu = 5$)

№	the best T(k)G-algorithm	relative losses of the best T(k)G-algorithm	relative losses of the greedy algorithm	relative losses of the thrifty algorithm
1	T(11)G	1.62	1.73	4.72
2	T(11)G	1.54	1.70	4.42
3	T(11)G	1.71	1.68	4.24
4	T(10)G	2.70	3.14	10.93
5	T(11)G	2.33	2.51	3,54
6	T(9)G	1.07	1.67	4.68
7	T(9)G	0.73	1.26	2.69
8	T(11)G	1.87	2.05	2.69
9	T(10)G	1.84	1.94	2.97
10	T(10)G	3.94	4.05	6.13

The study shows a significant impact of the choice of beet processing schedule on the amount of sugar produced. An unsuccessful choice of this schedule
can lead to significant losses. At the same time, from the analysis of numerical
experiments, it follows that in the presence of a ripening process, the algorithm
T(k)G represents, on average, a very good result in sugar yield, slightly inferior
to the absolute maximum. In this case, the best value of k is determined by the
duration of the ripening process. The longer this process takes, the smaller the
value of k should be selected for optimal algorithm tuning. The algorithm can be

Table 2. Experimental results for the second case of ripening ($\nu = 7$)

№	the best T(k)G-algorithm	relative losses of the T(k)G-algorithm	relative losses of the greedy algorithm	relative losses of the thrifty algorithm
1	T(8)G	0.63	1.54	3.57
2	T(8)G	0.78	1.69	3.65
3	T(7)G	1.65	1.94	2.70
4	T(7)G	0.94	3.20	8.32
5	T(9)G	1.34	2.07	3.53
6	T(6)G	0.47	1.23	3.30
7	T(6)G	0.18	1.10	3.37
8	T(8)G	2.27	2.17	3.69
9	T(7)G	2.00	2.30	2.86
10	T(5)G	4.44	6.15	5.94

used as quasi-optimal, since it is among the top three algorithms in both series of experiments.

In 90% of experiments, algorithm T(k)G for different k under different conditions on the batch parameters is the best heuristic algorithm. Tables 1 and 2 contain averaged relative losses when using the best of the T(k)G algorithms and pure strategies—greedy and thrifty algorithms. It can be seen from them that the loss of the thrifty is quite large relative to the algorithm T(k)G, but the greedy algorithm as a whole is not much worse than the algorithm T(k)G, except, perhaps, in the case when $\nu \approx n/2$ and the withering coefficients of the batches are close to one. In this case, the losses of the greedy algorithm are traditionally high. In this case, even the losses of the thrifty algorithm become less than the losses of the greedy algorithm.

In the course of the project work, a software module was created that allows you to evaluate the capabilities of various heuristic algorithms for beet processing. This module can be used not only for the raw material parameters considered during the experiments, but also for other possible cases.

The work was carried out to create a version of this module using parallel programming ideas. The need to use such technologies appears with a significant increase in the number of processing stages under consideration. If the duration of one stage is one day (which may well be of interest to the manufacturer), then the number of stages reaches 150. In this case, a significant calculation time is required to conduct an experiment to evaluate different algorithms. Thus, it is advisable to use approaches that significantly accelerate the work of the module. To implement algorithms that require a significant amount of operations on vectors or matrices, the most convenient is the Python algorithmic language with the numpy plug-in, which adds support for multidimensional arrays and matrices in combination with an extensive library of high-performance mathematical functions. Parallelism in this case provides simultaneous independent calculations for all the algorithms under study. Thread-level parallelism is implemented using the built-in threading module.

4 Conclusion

The article analyzes the experience of Lobachevsky State University of Nizhny Novgorod in organizing a series of educational project works in the interests of the Sergach sugar factory. The conducted research was aimed at creating educational and methodological support for the implementation of a set of educational and research projects for the development of components of an intellectual and information system for monitoring and controlling sugar production. Such educational and methodological support includes the formulation of goals and objectives, the definition of the plan and schedule of work carried out, their correlation with the current curriculum, the creation of educational resources. The most important educational purpose of conducting educational and research work was the practical development of the basic principles and methodology of creating intellectual information systems. The considered training experience is important not only for solving a private production task. It can be useful in general when teaching students the methodology of creating intellectual information systems. The implemented approach seems to be an important form in the training of IT personnel for the digital economy.

The created educational and methodological support has been introduced into the educational process of the Lobachevsky State University of Nizhny Novgorod. The authors express their gratitude to the 3rd year student A. Churkin for technical assistance in the preparation of the article.

Acknowledgments. The article was carried out under the contract No. SSZ-1771 dated 22.04.2021 on the implementation of R&D on the topic: "Creation of high-tech sugar production on the basis of JSC "Sergach Sugar Plant", within the framework of the Agreement on the provision of subsidies from the federal budget for the development of cooperation between the Russian educational organization of higher education and the organization of the real sector of the economy in order to implement a comprehensive project to create high-tech production No. 075-11-2021-038 of 24.06.2021. (IGC 000000S407521QLA0002).

References

1. Arias-Pérez, J., Velez-Ocampo, J., Cepeda-Cardona, J.: Strategic orientation toward digitalization to improve innovation capability: why knowledge acquisition and exploitation through external embeddedness matter. J. Knowl. Manag. **25**(5), 1319–1335 (2021). https://doi.org/10.1108/JKM-03-2020-0231
2. Li, L., Ye, F., Zhan, Y., et al.: Unraveling the performance puzzle of digitalization: evidence from manufacturing firms. J. Bus. Res. **149**, 54–64 (2021). https://doi.org/10.1016/j.jbusres.2022.04.071

3. Petrikova, E.M.: Digital transformation of the economy and financing of the national project "Digital Economy of the Russian Federation." Financ. Manag. **2**, 94–105 (2021)

4. Zaikina, L.V.: Introduction and development of digital technologies in Russia. Rossijskij ekonomicheskij vestnik (Russ. Econ. Bull.) **4**(6), 100–108 (2021). (In Russian)

5. Glinkina, O.V., Ganina, S.A., Maslennikova, A.V., et al.: Digital changes in the economy: advanced opportunities for digital innovation. Int. J. Manag. **11**(3), 457–466 (2020). https://doi.org/10.34218/IJM.11.3.2020.049

6. Rastorguev, S.V., Tjan, Y.S.: Digitalization of the Russian economy: trends, personnel, platforms, challenges to the state. Monitoring obshchestvennogo mneniya: ekonomicheskie i social'nye peremeny. (Public opinion monitoring: economic and social changes). **153**(5), 136–161 (2019). https://doi.org/10.14515/monitoring. 2019.5.08. (In Russia)

7. Rajkov, A.N., et al.: The concept of an information system to support the interaction of enterprises of the agro-industrial complex, science and education. Cifrovaya ekonomika. (Digit. Econ.) **3**(19), 45–51 (2022). (In Russian)

8. Shen, L., Zhang, X., Liu, H.: Digital technology adoption, digital dynamic capability, and digital transformation performance of textile industry: moderating ole of digital innovation orientation. Manager. Decision Econ. **43**(6), 2038–2054 (2021). https://doi.org/10.1002/mde.3507

9. Kharchenko, S.V.: Formation of an automated information system at the enterprises of sugar companies as the main element of the internal control system. Successes Mod. Sci. **4**, 29–33 (2015)

10. Tishchenko, I.A.: Digital economy as a contour of the study of digital transformation of the economy. Econ. Humanitarian Sci. **3**(362), 3–15 (2022). https://doi. org/10.33979/2073-7424-2022-362-3-3-15

11. Soldatenko, I.S., et al.: Modernization of math-related courses in engineering education in Russia based on best practices in European and Russian universities. In: 44th Annual Conference of the European Society for Engineering Education - Engineering Education on Top of the World: Industry-University Cooperation, SEFI, p. 131 (2016)

12. Snegurenko, A.P., et al.: Using E-learning tools to enhance students-mathematicians' competences in the context of international academic mobility programmes. Integraciya obrazovaniya. (Integrat. Educ.) **23**(1), 8–22 (2019). https://doi.org/10.15507/1991-9468.094.023.201901.008-022. (In Russian)

13. Balandin, D.V., Kuzenkov, O.A., Egamov, A.I.: Project-based learning in training IT-personnel for the digital economy. E3S Web Conf. **380**, 01035 (2023). https:// doi.org/10.1051/e3sconf/202338001035

14. Balandin, D.V., et al.: Educational and research project "Optimization of the sugar beet processing schedule". In: Voevodin V., Sobolev S., Yakobovsky M., Shagaliev R. (eds). Supercomputing. LNCS, vol. 13708, pp. 409–422. Springer, Cham (2022). https://doi.org/10.1007/978-3-031-22941-1_30

15. Tuzhilkin, V.I., et al.: Mathematical model of operational accounting and control of sugar beet production. Izvestiya vuzov. Pishchevaya tekhnologiya. (News Uiversit. Food Technol.) **2–3**, 117–121 (2018). (In Russian)

16. Tuzhilkin, V.I., et al.: Operational accounting and control of sugar beet production. Theor. Aspects Storage Process. Agricult. Prod. **1**, 20–34 (2019)

17. Kharchenko, S.V.: Formation of primary accounting and analytical information for accounting and control during sugar beet processing at sugar industry enterprises.

Ekonomika: vchera, segodnya, zavtra. (Econ. Yesterday, Today, Tomorrow) **10**(2–1), 407–419 (2020). (In Russian)

18. Saprykin, M.Yu., Saprykina, N.A.: Analysis of the concept of "information" from the standpoint of an object-oriented approach. Sci. Sci. **8**(2), 1–10 (2016). (In Russian). https://doi.org/10.15862/36TVN216

19. Simonovich, S.V.: Computer Science. Basic course: Textbook for Universities, 3rd edn. The Third Generation Standard, 640p. Peter, St. Petersburg (2011). (In Russian)

20. Makarova, N.V., Volkov, V.B.: Informatics: Textbook for Universities, 576p. St. Petersburg, St. Petersburg (2011). (In Russian)

21. Junqueira, R., Morabito, R.: Modeling and solving a sugarcane harvest front scheduling problem. Int. J. Prod. Econ. **231**(1), 150–160 (2019)

22. Kaplan, A., Haenlein, M.: Siri, Siri, in my hand: who's the fairest in the land? On the interpretations, illustrations, and implications of artificial intelligence. Bus. Horiz. **62**(1), 15–25 (2019)

23. Gorbachenko, V.I., Akhmetov, B.S., Kuznetsova, O.Yu.: Intelligent systems: fuzzy systems and networks. In: Textbook for Universities, 2nd edn., Corr. and Add, 105p. Yurayt Publishing House, Moscow (2019)

24. Flach, P.: Machine learning. In: The Science and Art of Building Algorithms that Extract Knowledge from Data, 400p. DMK Press Publishing House (2015)

25. Gruzdev, A.V.: Predictive Modeling in IBM SPSS Statistics, R and Python: The Method of Decision Trees and a Random Forest. DMK Press Publishing House, 642p. (2018). ISBN: 978-5-97060-539-4

26. Shah, S.N.R., Siddiqui, G.R., Pathan, N.: Predicting the behaviour of self-compacting concrete incorporating agro-industrial waste using experimental investigations and comparative machine learning modelling. Structures **52**, 536–548 (2023). https://doi.org/10.1016/j.istruc.2023.04.009

27. Taskiner, T., Bilgen, B.: Optimization models for harvest and production planning in agri-food supply chain: a systematic review. Logistics **5**(3), 52 (2021). https://doi.org/10.3390/logistics5030052

28. Li, J., et al.: Production plan for perishable agricultural products with two types of harvesting. Inf. Process. Agricult. **7**(1), 83–92 (2020). https://doi.org/10.1016/j.inpa.2019.05.001

29. Varasa, M., Bassob, F., Maturana, S., Osorio, D., Pezoa, R.: A multi-objective approach for supporting wine grape harvest operations. Comput. Indust. Eng. **145**, 106497 (2020). https://doi.org/10.1016/j.cie.2020.106497

30. Armin, C.A., Emad, R.: Review of optimization researches in the field of agricultural supply chain. Mod. Concep. Dev. Agrono. **5**(4), 556–560 (2020). https://doi.org/10.31031/MCDA.2020.05.000619

31. Morozov, A.Y., Sandhu, S.K., Kuzenkov, O.A.: Global optimization in Hilbert spaces using the survival of the fittest algorithm. Commun. Nonl. Sci. Numer. Simul. **103**, 106007 (2021)

32. Grishagin, V.A., Barkalov, K.A., Kozinov, E.A.: ML-based approach for accelerating global search algorithm for solving multicriteria problems. In: Learning and Intelligent Optimization (LION 2022). LNCS, vol. 13621, pp. 123–129. Springer, Cham (2023). https://doi.org/10.1007/978-3-031-24866-5_9

33. Nguyen, T.-D., et al.: Mathematical programming models for fresh fruit supply chain optimization: a review of the literature and emerging trends. AgriEngineering **3**, 519–541 (2021). https://doi.org/10.3390/agriengineering3030034

34. Kuzenkov, O.A., Kuzenkova, G.V. Identification of the fitness function using neural networks. Procedia Comput. Sci. **169**, 692–697 (2020). https://doi.org/10.1016/j.procs.2020.02.179

35. Anichin, V.L.: Theory and Practice of Production Resources Management in the Beet Sugar Subcomplex of the Agro-industrial Complex. Publication House of the BelGSHA, Belgorod (2005). (In Russian)

36. Kukhar, V.N., Chernyavsky, A.P., Chernyavskaya, L.I., Mokanyuk, Y.A.: Methods for assessing the technological properties of sugar beet using indicators of the content of potassium, sodium and α-amine nitrogen determined in beetroot and its processing products. Sugar **1**, 18–36 (2019). (In Russian)

37. Rafgarden, T.: Perfect algorithm. In: Greedy Algorithms and Dynamic Programming, 256p. St. Petersburg (2020) (In Russian)

38. Chernyavskaya, L.I., Mokanyuk, Yu.A., Kuhar, V.N., Chernyavsky, A.P.: The efficiency of sugar beet processing depends on the loss of sugar during the storage of root crops. Part 3. Chemical and phytopathological indicators of sugar beet mechanized harvesting after storage in kagats. Sugar **1**, 36–45 (2021). https://doi.org/10.24411/2413-5518-2021-10103. (In Russian)

Image Segmentation Algorithms Composition for Obtaining Accurate Masks of Tomato Leaf Instances

Ivan Zhuravlev$^{(\boxtimes)}$ and Andrey Makarenko

V.A. Trapeznikov Institute of Control Sciences of Russian Academy of Sciences, Moscow, Russia
zhursvlevy@mail.ru

Abstract. Large agro-industrial complexes are interested in deep automation of the yields control processes to reduce costs caused by errors or a shortage of qualified personnel. Existing approaches solve problems such as yield assessment or plant pathologies detection, but they cannot properly quantify the volume of plant biomass or the diseased area. One of the reasons for this limitation is the poor quality of masks of object instances formed in machine vision systems. This occurs because of Mask R-CNN architecture, which is usually used in the computer vision. In this paper, we propose an algorithms composition for obtaining accurate masks of objects in task of segmentation of tomato leaf instances in images collected in difficult conditions of industrial greenhouses. The use of Mask R-CNN combined with CascadePSP neural network algorithm increased the average IoU by 1.194% compared to "pure" Mask R-CNN on images with complex object-like background.

Keywords: Machine Vision · Video Analytics · Instance Segmentation · Deep Learning · Crop Production

1 Introduction

Agriculture is an important part of the economy of any country. According to statistics, 55% of the percent of food consumed by humans is vegetables [5]. To provide the population with plant products, industrial greenhouses are being created for growing various types of vegetables and fruits. However, like any living organism, plants need regular care: watering, fertilizers, treatment of diseases. Basically, the analysis of the yield assessment is provided by people manually, and therefore takes a lot of time due to the scale of industrial greenhouses and does not allow timely obtaining complete information about the health of plants, and the identification of plant growth abnormalities and their classification is often carried out by non-specialists, which usually leads to incorrect conclusions about the plant health. Due to these factors, according to the UN [2], about 50% of the crop is lost annually.

V. Voevodin et al. (Eds.): RuSCDays 2023, LNCS 14389, pp. 178–194, 2023.
https://doi.org/10.1007/978-3-031-49435-2_13

Since the process of analyzing the state of crops is monotonous human labor, there is a need to automate this process. Agro-industrial companies are interested in automatic plant development control systems, as this will help to increase the speed of the crops condition analysis and at the same time reduce the level of errors made in the process of manual analysis. There are various approaches to automating plant health monitoring, in particular, algorithms based on computer vision have been widely used to detect and classify plant pathologies. Intelligent recognition systems are an advantageous solution, since these systems allow visual analysis without the direct involvement of specialists in this process. Thus, machine vision systems not only reduce the time and financial costs of companies, but also reduce the number of errors that are made in the process of manual analysis.

At the moment, computer vision algorithms allow solving problems of detection or classification plant pathologies or calculating yields [11], however, these methods only establish the presence of pathologies, and fruit counting does not provide information about the state of the crops themselves, namely, there is no way to quantify the increase in plant biomass or the relative area of the diseased regions. For visual plant analysis, it is necessary to obtain images of instances of its components. Instance segmentation algorithms, in particular solutions based on Mask R-CNN [8], solve with this task nicely.

However, the instance masks of objects that generate these algorithms have a low resolution. This is critical in tasks such as assessing plant biomass growth and estimating the diseased area, where it is extremely important to obtain accurate information about the shape of objects. This is critical in the agricultural industry. In particular, tomato leaves have a complex shape and the use of Mask R-CNN without additional post-processing introduces a bias in the measurement of the total area of plant leaves or the proportion of diseased regions. In addition to the complex border of the leaf, in real shooting conditions, the leaves are arranged very tightly, the instances overlap each other, and the shooting scene has a uniform color palette, which is why at the moment there are no approaches that solve the problem of assessing plant biomass growth and assessing the affected area.

In this paper, we propose a image segmentation algorithms composition that allows us to obtain accurate instance masks of objects of complex shape, allowing us to solve the problem described above. For this study, images of tomato leaves were collected in difficult conditions of industrial greenhouses. We compared the quality of segmentation with "pure" Mask R - CNN, Mask R - CNN with increased resolution of the mask decoder output and Mask R-CNN with subsequent processing of the model outputs using CascadePSP [6], as well as an algorithm for false positives suppression of the model. Studies have shown that the use of this composition of algorithms gave an increase in the quality of object masks by 1.194% according to the IoU metric averaged over all instances of tomato leaves. Such an improvement characterizes a significant increase in the accuracy of segmentation masks at the border of object instances both in area and shape, which makes it possible to use the proposed method as a basic element in solving problems of assessing the increase in plant biomass and the diseased plant area.

2   Related Work

2.1   Instance Segmentation

At the moment, there are many algorithms of instance segmentation [7]. These ones are divided into two groups: one-stage and two-stage. Among the one-stage methods, the most popular are: YOLACT [4], which generates masks of object instances from a linear combination of mask "prototypes" and is able to work in real-time mode; SOLO [15] use "instance categories" assigning labels to pixels based on the position and size of the object instance; YOLO, which is a SOTA in real-time detection, the latest implementation of which received a branch for instance segmentation. However, one-stage methods are inferior in segmentation quality to two-stage methods.

Among the two-stage ones, one can single out the most popular Mask R-CNN [8], using the so-called region proposal network (RPN), which predicts the objectness score in a specific area of the image which are named region of interest (RoI). The vast majority of modern approaches are based on this architecture. PointRend [9] generates masks of higher resolution than Mask R-CNN (224×224), but requires more data to obtain high-quality masks. Our work does not require real-time processing, so we will give preference to two-stage methods. We choose Mask R-CNN as the basic instance segmentation model.

2.2   High-Resolution Segmentation

Most of the existing high-quality segmentation algorithms were created for the task of semantic segmentation. The main works in this field are [10,14,17]. Separately, we highlight the work [6], which offers the CascadePSP algorithm. The authors use a specific approach to model training: the model is trained using an input image and a coarse semantic mask to obtain a mask of increased quality. At the same time, the authors claim that the model does not need additional training and works on any data "out of the box". In our work, we adapt this model to the task of instance segmentation.

2.3   Agricultural Industry

Most of the solutions that exist today are aimed at detecting and classifying plant diseases based on photodata [11]. Thus, in the works [1,2], the possibility of disease classification based on convolutional networks is investigated. The proposed approaches show high classification accuracy (more than 90% of correct answers), however, these experiments were carried out on datasets containing laboratory data: the leaves are in one copy on a clean background under good lighting. In real shooting conditions, such algorithms degrade greatly due to changing lighting, complexity and diversity of perspectives, the presence of a dense cluster of instances, occlusions. There are also more complex methods for solving the problem of plant disease detection that are tested in real conditions. In the work [13], Faster-RCNN is used as a detector of diseased areas with subsequent classification of pathologies in bananas. The authors of the article [12] use Mask-RCNN to segment instances of grape fruits to determine the degree of maturity of berries. [3] also uses Mask-RCNN to segment broccoli inflorescence and determine the presence and type of pathology.

These methods make it possible to establish the presence of pathologies or to calculate yields but some of them have been studied to work in favorable simple conditions and are not suitable for use in production, while others, more "advanced" methods based on detection and segmentation algorithms are not able to quantify the proportion of affected plant diseases or biomass growth. The disadvantage of the "advanced" methods is due to the fact that the authors use Mask R-CNN, which generates low-resolution masks (28×28 pixels). This is critical in the task of estimating the growth of biomass or the affected area, since the constituent plants often have a complex shape. In particular, tomato leaves have a complex border relief, so masks of such leaves are of very poor quality. In this paper, we propose a method for obtaining masks of high-quality object instances based on improving the masks generated by Mask R-CNN using CasadePSP and an additional false positive suppression algorithm applied to the problem of segmentation of tomato leaf instances.

3 Dataset

3.1 Agricultural Industry

We have a database of more than 100 thousand images of more than 2,400 high-resolution tomato plants captured in difficult conditions of industrial greenhouses. Data collection took place between October 2020 and January 2022, which corresponds to several cycles of plant development. The process and shooting conditions correspond to the conditions of application of the developed algorithms for wearable cameras, stationary and mobile, installed on a greenhouse robot. Thus, the shooting distance varied from 15 cm to 60 cm. The database contains a description of each image, which includes information about more than 40 pathologies discernible in this image, part of the tomato and the address of the plant. This dataset is designed to build a complex of algorithms for automating the analysis of the state of tomato crops, including for assessing the increase in plant biomass, as well as assessing the area of damage to branches, leaves, petioles, stems and fruits. But, as it was said in the introduction, the main problem of solving such a problem is the very low quality of masks generated by Mask R-CNN-like algorithms. This problem is most pronounced on objects with a very relief contour. Such objects are tomato leaves. In addition to the complex border of the sheet (Fig. 1) the task is also complicated by the uniform green color palette of the entire image (the most striking examples are (a), (b));

an object-like background (b); a large cluster of leaves and branches (d); heavily overlapped or blurred objects (d), different times of day, in in particular, night shooting under artificial lighting (c). This variability and complexity of the data characterizes the actual shooting conditions and distinguishes this dataset from others used in the works [1,2]. As a rule, it is not possible to create more favorable angles or conditions for shooting plants, therefore, the assembled dataset most accurately reflects the process of conditions under which the assessment of the state of plants by machine vision methods takes place.

(a)   (b)   (c)   (d)

Fig. 1. Data examples.

3.2   Data Markup Methodology

Before the direct construction of the algorithms composition, there was a problem of the data markup methodology. How can the annotator determine which objects are the background of the image, and which are subject to markup. A variant was considered in which all the leaves that are in focus and do not overlap with other objects are marked, but in this case problems may arise in the convergence of segmentation algorithms, since semantically the same object is considered as a target object in one case, and as a background in the other. The second option was to mark up all the non-blurred leaves, but there was a problem in formalizing this process: the degree of blurring varies greatly on the collected data, as a result of which the annotator will not be able to objectively evaluate this parameter. It was decided to mark leaves whose borders do not merge with the background and a person is able to "mentally" mark the boundaries of the leaf. The "labelme" program was used as a tool, which provides the ability to save the markup of objects in the form of coordinates of a polygon bounding a leaf. This program supports the ability to create multiple polygons per instance and combine them into groups, which makes the markup more flexible.

3.3   Data Sampling

A total of 2000 images of leaves were posted. It is worth noting that on different parts of the tomato, the leaves have different shapes, sizes and growth densities.

So, in the images where the subject of the shooting were branches, the leaves are much smaller and more densely arranged than in the images where there was a large leaf in the center of the frame. At the same time, different parts of the plant may have different pathologies. On the branches, the disease "leaf proliferation" is more pronounced, while on the lower level of the plant, large old leaves are susceptible to diseases that manifest themselves in the form of dry leaves. To avoid biases in the data, we made a uniform selection of branches and leaves from several levels of the plant with a volume of 1000 images for manual annotation.

3.4 Semi-automatic Annotation

After marking up 1000 images, it turned out that on average a person spent about 7 min on a photo. In the case of images with a large density of leaves (about 20 items), it could take up to 15–20 minutes for the annotator to process a photo. In this regard, a way to simplify data annotation was proposed. It consisted in pre-learning the composition of algorithms and obtaining rough masks of leaf instances. Preliminary results showed that there is a significant acceleration of marking in semi-automatic mode, especially if there are many small leaves in the image. The quantitative study of the increase in the speed and quality of markup is the subject of the following studies for us, and a more detailed annotation process is described in the Sect. 6. In semi-automatic mode, the remaining part of the images (1000 photos) was marked up, while the sampling was carried out in such a way that more large dry leaves of complex shape were present in the images, since in the first sample, after analyzing the area of the marked objects, a strong imbalance towards small young leaves with a convex smooth border was shown, as indicated by the median area value of 32500 and the value of the 75th quantile (Fig. 2).

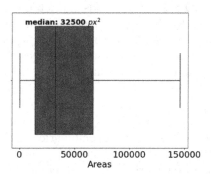

Fig. 2. Distribution of leaves over the bounding box areas.

3.5   Preprocessing

Images are reduced to a single size of 1024×1024 pixels while maintaining the aspect ratio. This image resolution was chosen because we were looking for a trade-off between the computational resources expended and the image detail. To speed up the mini-batch loading, polygonal annotation is converted into binary masks. In addition to masks, the coordinates of the bounding boxes are also calculated. At the time of the mini-batch formation, the pixels of the image are normalized to the segment $[0; 1]$. Additionally, standard augmentation is applied in the form of random rotations and mirror reflections to ensure the invariance of the algorithm to the rotation of objects.

4   Method

As mentioned earlier, Mask R-CNN produces low-resolution masks (28×28 or 14×14 pixels). With an increase in resolution, the quality of masks does not lead to a significant improvement, while the time for calculating the outputs of the mask decoder increases. In our work, we also conducted experiments with increasing the size of feature maps at the output of the mask decoder and did not get a significant improvement in quality. In some tasks, high-quality masks are not required, but in the case of segmentation of objects of complex shape, where the area of the object plays a key role in the subsequent stages of solving the problem, this is a serious limitation of the algorithm. In the problem of tomato leafs segmentation under consideration, with subsequent assessment of biomass growth and diseased area, much higher accuracy is required than that which can be obtained using a "pure" Mask R-CNN.

However, we note the advantage of this architecture. Mask R-CNN is an extension of Faster-CNN, a two-stage detector that uses the region proposal network (RPN) to generate regions of interest, which provides high quality object detection in the image. One-stage methods do not use RPN, so they lose in quality. In addition, Mask R-CNN has a "modular" architecture and can easily adapt to a specific task. Therefore, the choice of most researchers falls on this neural network. The listed properties inspired us to keep this architecture in use, but to introduce additional post-processing.

4.1   Mask R-CNN Settings

The convolutional network ResNet-50 in combination with the feature pyramid network (FPN) was chosen as the backbone. It is known that the deep layers of the convolutional neural network (CNN) contain semantic features, but lose information about the details of the object, for example, about the boundaries. In contrast, the upper layers of CNN contain more general features, such as lines or angles. FPN allows you to take into account both the detailed characteristics of the object, as well as semantic, which is important when segmenting instances of objects. Anchors were generated at the following scales: $[64, 128, 256, 512, 1024]$

with aspect ratio $[1:2, 1:1, 2:1]$. Such variability of scales is necessary due to the large dispersion of leaf areas. The configuration of the heads of the regions of interest was chosen the same as described in the original article, except for the number of classes, since there is only one class in our problem. To experiment with increasing the output resolution of the mask decoder, we used 4 deconvolution layers [16] with ReLU activations. The use of more layers did not lead to quality increase. The predicted masks of objects are interpolated to the size of the original image 1024×1024 pixels.

4.2   Masks Refinement

Our goal is to perform a transformation that would receive coarse masks of the object in the image as input and give out an improved quality mask at the output. CascadePSP [6] implements such a transformation. Initially, this algorithm was developed to improve masks in the semantic segmentation problem for subtask named scene parsing. This means that the single mask contains all objects that belong to the same class, both during model training and inference.

We assumed that this model can be adapted to the instance segmentation problem. We trained the model on semantic masks of objects, but during the inference, we submitted masks of instances to the input. Experiments have shown that this approach is working and object masks are significantly improved, in particular, on large objects of complex shape. The network architecture and loss functions are taken the same as in the original article. During the output of the model, two steps are performed to improve the mask: global and local. The first step takes the mask and the image as an input in its entirety and produces an initial improvement of the mask. During the second step, the image is fed in parts: regions of 224×224 pixels are cut out on the image and the mask obtained in the first step, then the resulting improved masks are concatenated into the final version, which is the output of the model. Note that the authors of the article claimed that this algorithm does not need to be retrained on new data, but early experiments demonstrated degradation of the quality of masks on our specific task. More specifically, the improved mask captured the petiole, which is unacceptable.

4.3   Suppression of False Positive Hypotheses

During the testing of the algorithm composition, a visual analysis was made and a problem was found related to the filtering of hypotheses (network outputs) by the non maximum suppression (NMS) algorithm. Tomato leaves have a complex shape, part of the leaf is similar to the whole leaf, twisting forms fictitious boundaries, as a result of which the segmentation algorithm recognizes part of the leaf as a separate instance (false positive hypothesis). An original algorithm "false positive suppression" (FPS) is proposed.

Let $S_i = (B_i, M_i), i = \overline{1, N}$, where N is the number of hypotheses, B_i, M_i is the bounding box and the instance mask. Let a hypothesis with a larger and smaller area of bounding box be found among a pair of hypotheses S_i and S_j, then we denote the corresponding bounding box and masks as $B_{\min}$, $B_{\max}$, $M_{\min}$, $M_{\max}$. Checking whether the smaller hypothesis is a false positive is performed as follows. The metric $IoU(S_1, S_2) is calculated$:

$$IoU(S_1, S_2) = IoU(M_{\max}^{crop}, M_{\min}), \tag{1}$$

where $M_{\max}^{crop}$ is calculated as follows:

$$M_{\max}^{crop} = crop\_mask(M_{\max}, B_{\min}). \tag{2}$$

If the metric (1) exceeds the specified threshold, then the smaller hypothesis is considered a false positive and is removed from the list of hypotheses. In our problem, we took a threshold of 0.5. The function (2) cuts out on the mask of the larger hypothesis the area occupied by the bounding box of the smaller hypothesis.

4.4   Algorithms Composition Inference

Schematically, the sequence of obtaining accurate masks is shown in Fig. 3. The part that is used to obtain the final results in plant condition monitoring tasks is highlighted in blue, and the proposed modification for solving the problem of segmentation of objects of complex shape is highlighted in red. An image is fed to the Mask R-CNN input, the output of the model contains an bounding boxes, classes of object instances and instance masks filtered by a given threshold of objectness score in the region of interest and the NMS algorithm. The resulting masks, together with the original image, are alternately passed through CascadePSP, then hypotheses with improved masks are processed by the FPS algorithm and at the output we get a set of bounding boxes, classes, as well as masks of high-resolution instances.

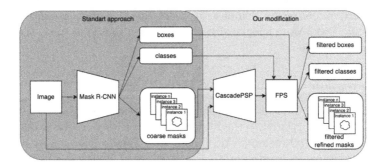

Fig. 3. A scheme for obtaining improved masks of object instances.

4.5   Training Parameters

Mask R-CNN. Due to the small size of the training sample, the R-CNN pre-trained on MS COCO Mask was used. The weights on the first two residual resnet-50 blocks of Mask R-CNN were frozen, since these layers contain the most common features. SGD with an initial learning rate of $5 \cdot 10^{-4}$ with a 10-fold decrease in speed after the 70th epoch was chosen as the optimization method. The total number of epochs is 100. The warmup technique was also used in the first epoch of training. A linear increase in speed was performed over two hundred iterations to the initial learning rate. L_2 regularization with a coefficient of $5 \cdot 10^{-4}$ was also applied. The size of the mini-batch is 8 examples. The volume of the training and validation samples was 80% and 20%, respectively.

CascadePSP. The BIG dataset [6] weights pre-trained on the were used. The configuration of the optimizer and the learning rates are the same as described in the original article. The size of the mini-batch is 8 examples. Before submitting images and semantic coarse masks to the input, a random cutout was made on the image and masks with a size of 224×224 pixels.

5   Experiments

The training results are presented in the Table 1. Precision was used as a metric to estimate the proportion of false positives, recall to estimate the proportion of false omissions, and F1-measure, since it is important for us that Mask R-CNN detects all instances of tomato leaves. 4 models were compared: basic Mask R-CNN and one with increased mask resolution up to 112×112; Mask R-CNN + CascadePSP and with a FPS filter. To evaluate the quality of masks, the IoU metric was used, averaged over all detected leaf instances. The results show an improvement in the average IoU by 1.194% with the best confidence threshold of the network $t_{objectness} = 0.8$ for the latest model in the table compared to the basic one.

Table 1. Models comparison

Model	precision	recall	F1	average IoU	ms/image
Mask R-CNN	0.8656	0.8349	0.8500	0.8896	**202**
Mask R-CNN 112 × 112	0.8541	0.8563	0.8552	0.8912	211
Mask R-CNN + CacadePSP	0.8675	0.8367	0.8518	**0.9018**	5540
Mask R-CNN + CascadePSP + FPS	**0.8737**	0.8342	0.8535	**0.9016**	5663

Training and inference of both Mask R-CNN and cascadePSP is carried out by parallelizing calculations on a single Nvidia Titan RTX 24GB GPU using NVIDIA CUDA. The inference time of the model is greatly increased when Mask R-CNN followed by cascadePSP is used (the last column of the Table 1). This is due to the repeated passing of a single instance mask through CascadePSP, while the output of each iteration of the improvement produces caching, which affects the amount of video memory used ≈3GB per instance. At the moment, Cascade PSP does not support mini-batch calculations during model inference, however, parallelization of the algorithm by object instances or video streams is possible, which will reduce the total inference time. In addition, a real-time algorithm is not required for this range of tasks, so when developing an approach, we give preference primarily to the quality of the model. Our experiments demonstrate that the task is solvable, so optimizing the algorithm in terms of inference time and memory usage will be the next step.

In order to verify the results obtained, a Student's t-test was conducted on a sample of the average IoU calculated from the outputs of the basic model and improved one. The null hypothesis was that there are no differences in the average values of IoU, the alternative is that there are. The significance level was chosen 10^{-4}. The Table 2 shows the p-value obtained during the comparison of models. At the selected significance level, simply adding mask decoder layers does not give statistically significant results (first line), however, an improvement in the model is observed when comparing Mask R-CNN in conjunction with CascadePSP.

Table 2. t-test for average IoU

Base model	Improved model	p-value
Mask R-CNN	Mask R-CNN 112 × 112	0.543
Mask R-CNN	Mask R-CNN + CascadePSP	10^{-6}

A visual comparative analysis is shown in Fig. 4. Columns (a), (b), (c), (d) – the original image, markup, Mask R-CNN, outputs of the algorithms composition respectively. The top two rows demonstrate how the quality of the mask changes in large leaves with a complex border, almost pixel-by-pixel accuracy is observed. Note that the difference in the quality of small masks is poorly traced (third row), which is logical, since small leaves have a convex shape and a fairly simple border, which potentially makes it possible to use Mask R-CNN for objects of this size without additional processing using CascadePSP, however, the research data relate to the optimization of the model in this work are not carried out. In the last row, you can see how the FPS algorithm works (columns (c) and (d)). Part of the leaf was recognized as a separate instance and was filtered. There are also some inaccuracies of the mask in the last row, which are associated with a difference in the brightness of the areas of the sheet. With the help of additional augmentation by varying brightness, as well as the expansion of the dataset, such side effects will disappear.

The question may arise whether the improvement of masks is significant from the point of view of application to the task of determining the increase in plant biomass and assessing the diseased area. The answer is yes, because often dangerous pathologies, such as cancer in the early stages, manifest themselves at the borders of the leaf. These areas are cut off during rough segmentation,

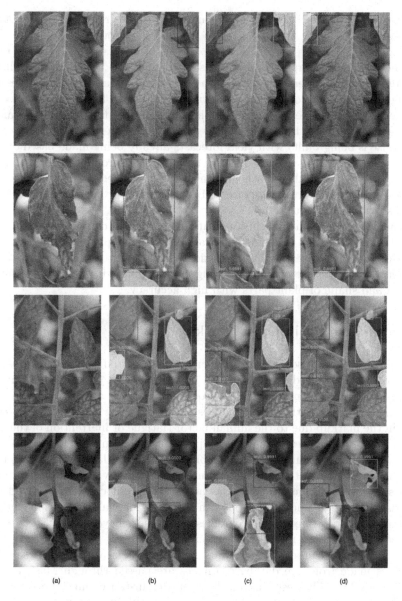

Fig. 4. Model inference examples. (a) – image, (b) – markup, (c) – Mask R-CNN, (d) – Mask R-CNN + CascadePSP + FPS.

so there is a risk of detecting pathologies only at the moment when the area of lesions acquires a large scale. This problem is most clearly demonstrated in the second row in Fig. 4. "Clean" Mask R-CNN captures the border along with the background, or, conversely, does not cover the affected area. The algorithms composition segments with high accuracy.

It should be noticed that at first glance there is a problem: for both tasks it is necessary to know the distances to the objects in order to calculate their actual dimensions, but the distance to the shooting plane is unknown to us with the required accuracy. In many cases, it is not the actual volume that is important, but its increase relative to the previous biomass assessment session. It is the dynamics of growth that often turns out to be a key factor in assessing the intensity of plant development. At the same time, if the shooting is carried out by a mobile robot then each plant is evaluated (i.e. a digital 4D map of the greenhouse is being built) with yield forecasts already being made based on this data. If the shooting is carried out "by hand, by an agronomist" or by means of stationary cameras, then mathematical statistical criteria are applied: for the observed plants, an average estimate and confidence intervals for the greenhouse block as a whole are output.

Thus, we come to the conclusion that this algorithm can be used as a basic element of systems for assessing yield and diagnosing plant pathologies. Our algorithm has been investigated in relation to tomatoes but can be transferred to other plants. The use of the improving module makes it possible to estimate the area and shape of plant parts with high accuracy.

6   Semi-automatic Data Markup

Since the deadlines for solving the problem were short and the financial possibilities were small, we needed optimization in data markup. 7 min to mark up one image is a lot. The monotony of the process of marking complex objects for a long time, as shown by the visual analysis of the first 1000 marked photos, led to errors in the markup due to the human factor (fatigue or inattention of the marketer). After 1000 images were marked up completely manually, it was proposed to train the composition of algorithms on the available data. Our assumptions were that even poorly trained algorithms would simplify the markup process. The resulting rough masks at the Cascade PSP output can be converted to a data markup format and corrections can be made manually. Intuition suggests that it is easier to correct the inaccuracies of masks, remove noise or add missing instances than to make markup "from scratch".

Fig. 5 shows the process of obtaining preliminary data markup. A selection of data is made from the database. Images are passed through Mask R-CNN and CascadePSP. The resulting masks of object instances must be translated into markup format. It implies storing masks in the form of coordinates of polygon faces. If we use the transformation of the mask into an array of coordinates directly, we will get a huge number of points, which on the contrary will complicate the process of additional markup. Therefore, it is necessary to reduce the number of coordinates in such a way that the markup is comfortable, but at the same time not to lose the quality of the preliminary markup.

We analyzed the distribution of the number of polygon points set during manual marking and the area of instances (Fig. 6). Our assumption was that the best number of points should correspond to the average number of points that

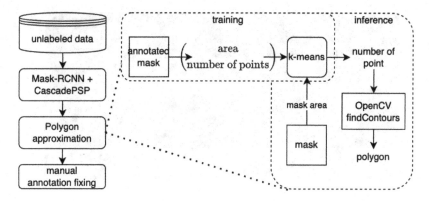

Fig. 5. Scheme for obtaining preliminary data markup.

falls on an instance of a particular area. We used the k-means method to cluster instances by the number of coordinates and areas.

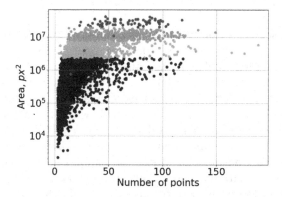

Fig. 6. Joint distribution of the instance mask areas and the number of polygon points during marking.

Thus, the process of approximation of polygons do in the following way. The area of the instance mask is calculated, the nearest cluster center of the distribution of areas and the number of points is located, and the average number of points for this cluster is matched to this instance mask. Then, by means of OpenCV, the mask is converted into a polygon. We chose to split the distribution into 4 clusters, and also tripled the number of points when converting the mask into a polygon, since already at this stage the outputs of CascadePSP turned out to be quite accurate. Examples of the obtained preliminary markup are shown in Fig. 7.

To quantify the effectiveness of markup by the time of its execution, it is necessary to conduct testing with measuring the time spent by the markup

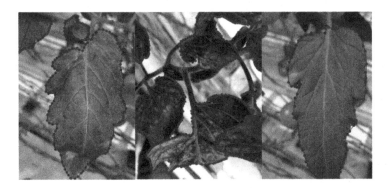

Fig. 7. Examples of the received preliminary markup.

without using this approach and using one. These studies will be carried out in subsequent works.

7 Conclusion

In this paper, a segmentation algorithms composition was proposed to obtain accurate instance masks of complex objects in relation to the problem of segmentation of tomato leaves. The main feature of the method was the use of the CascadePSP neural network algorithm as a postprocessing of the Mask R-CNN segmenter output. A statistically significant increase in the quality of masks of tomato leaf instances by 1.194% was obtained, while the algorithm achieved such an increase in quality on a small dataset with a volume of 2000 images. In addition, an algorithm for suppressing false positive hypotheses was proposed to filter Mask R-CNN outputs for objects of complex shape. An algorithm for obtaining preliminary data markup was also proposed and tested using the composition of mask improvement algorithms proposed in this paper, trained on a small dataset.

The results of this work demonstrated that the solution of the problem of assessing the increase in biomass and the area affected by pathologies is possible and this approach can be used as a basic part of the plant development monitoring system. Our algorithm can be adapted to different types of plants. The use of the mask refinement module makes it possible to estimate the area and shape of plant parts with high accuracy, and the shooting conditions in which the data were collected make it possible to apply this method using both wearable cameras and stationary ones. In addition, mobile cameras installed on the greenhouse robot are also supported. In the future, it is planned to optimize the output time of the model, the efficiency and speed of marking, as well as the introduction the algorithms composition into the systems for monitoring the condition of crops of agro-industrial companies.

The authors thank the anonymous referees for their helpful comments.

References

1. Veluswami, J.R.S.: Plant disease detection using transfer learning in precision agriculture. Ambient Sci. **9**(3), 34–39 (2022). https://doi.org/10.21276/ambi.2022.09.3.ta02
2. Arunnehru, J., Vidhyasagar, B.S., Anwar Basha, H.: Plant leaf diseases recognition using convolutional neural network and transfer learning. In: Bindhu, V., Chen, J., Tavares, J.M.R.S. (eds.) International Conference on Communication, Computing and Electronics Systems. LNEE, vol. 637, pp. 221–229. Springer, Singapore (2020). https://doi.org/10.1007/978-981-15-2612-1_21
3. Blok, P.M., Kootstra, G., Elghor, H.E., Diallo, B., van Evert, F.K., van Henten, E.J.: Active learning with MaskAL reduces annotation effort for training mask r-CNN on a broccoli dataset with visually similar classes. Comput. Electron. Agricult. **197**, 106917 (2022). https://doi.org/10.1016/j.compag.2022.106917
4. Bolya, D., Zhou, C., Xiao, F., Lee, Y.J.: YOLACT: real-time instance segmentation. In: 2019 IEEE/CVF International Conference on Computer Vision (ICCV), IEEE (2019). https://doi.org/10.1109/iccv.2019.00925
5. Cassidy, E.S., West, P.C., Gerber, J.S., Foley, J.A.: Redefining agricultural yields: from tonnes to people nourished per hectare. Environm. Res. Lett. **8**(3), 034015 (2013). https://doi.org/10.1088/1748-9326/8/3/034015
6. Cheng, H.K., Chung, J., Tai, Y.W., Tang, C.K.: CascadePSP: toward class-agnostic and very high-resolution segmentation via global and local refinement. In: 2020 IEEE/CVF Conference on Computer Vision and Pattern Recognition (CVPR), IEEE (Jun 2020). https://doi.org/10.1109/cvpr42600.2020.00891
7. Hafiz, A.M., Bhat, G.M.: A survey on instance segmentation: state of the art. Inter. J. Multimedia Inform. Retrieval **9**(3), 171–189 (2020). https://doi.org/10.1007/s13735-020-00195-x
8. He, K., Gkioxari, G., Dollár, P., Girshick, R.B.: Mask R-CNN. CoRR abs/arXiv: 1703.06870 (2017)
9. Kirillov, A., Wu, Y., He, K., Girshick, R.: PointRend: image segmentation as rendering. In: 2020 IEEE/CVF Conference on Computer Vision and Pattern Recognition (CVPR). IEEE (June 2020). https://doi.org/10.1109/cvpr42600.2020.00982
10. Lin, G., Milan, A., Shen, C., Reid, I.: RefineNet: multi-path refinement networks for high-resolution semantic segmentation. In: 2017 IEEE Conference on Computer Vision and Pattern Recognition (CVPR). IEEE (July 2017). https://doi.org/10.1109/cvpr.2017.549
11. Rakhmatulin, I., Kamilaris, A., Andreasen, C.: Deep neural networks to detect weeds from crops in agricultural environments in real-time: a review. Rem. Sens. **13**(21), 4486 (2021). https://doi.org/10.3390/rs13214486
12. Santos, T.T., de Souza, L.L., dos Santos, A.A., Avila, S.: Grape detection, segmentation, and tracking using deep neural networks and three-dimensional association. Comput. Electron. Agricul. **170**, 105247 (2020). https://doi.org/10.1016/j.compag.2020.105247
13. Selvaraj, M.G., et al.: AI-powered banana diseases and pest detection. Plant Methods **15**(1) (2019). https://doi.org/10.1186/s13007-019-0475-z
14. Shen, T., et al.: High quality segmentation for ultra high-resolution images. In: 2022 IEEE/CVF Conference on Computer Vision and Pattern Recognition (CVPR), IEEE (June 2022). https://doi.org/10.1109/cvpr52688.2022.00137
15. Wang, X., Kong, T., Shen, C., Jiang, Y., Li, L.: SOLO: segmenting objects by locations. In: Vedaldi, A., Bischof, H., Brox, T., Frahm, J.-M. (eds.) ECCV 2020.

LNCS, vol. 12363, pp. 649–665. Springer, Cham (2020). https://doi.org/10.1007/978-3-030-58523-5_38

16. Zeiler, M.D., Krishnan, D., Taylor, G.W., Fergus, R.: Deconvolutional networks. In: 2010 IEEE Computer Society Conference on Computer Vision and Pattern Recognition. IEEE (June 2010). https://doi.org/10.1109/cvpr.2010.5539957

17. Zhao, H., Qi, X., Shen, X., Shi, J., Jia, J.: ICNet for real-time semantic segmentation on high-resolution images. In: Ferrari, V., Hebert, M., Sminchisescu, C., Weiss, Y. (eds.) ECCV 2018. LNCS, vol. 11207, pp. 418–434. Springer, Cham (2018). https://doi.org/10.1007/978-3-030-01219-9_25

Implementation of Dusty Gas Model Based on Fast and Implicit Particle-Mesh Approach SPH-IDIC in Open-Source Astrophysical Code GADGET-2

Tatiana Demidova[1(✉)], Tatiana Savvateeva[2,3], Sergey Anoshin[3], Vitaliy Grigoryev[1,2], and Olga Stoyanovskaya[2]

[1] Crimean Astrophysical Observatory, p. Nauchny, Crimea, Russia
proxima1@list.ru
[2] Lavrentyev Institute of Hydrodynamics SB RAS, Novosibirsk, Russia
{ta-savvateeva,vitaliygrigoryev}@yandex.ru
[3] Novosibirsk State University, Novosibirsk, Russia

Abstract. Particle approaches considered to study the interaction of dust grains of the same size and a gas medium based on Smoothed Particle Hydrodynamics method. The paper compares two algorithms for solving this problem, described in [1,2]. Both algorithms were implemented by in a modified version of the GADGET-2 program code. One-dimensional and three-dimensional tests were carried out in order to confirm the properties of the algorithms and to make performance measurements of the code.

Keywords: Computational Physics · Hydrodynamics · Epstein drag simulation

1 Introduction

The interaction of dust and gas plays an important role in studies of the dynamics of matter in space objects. Despite the fact that the amount of fine dust in the interstellar medium is only 1% of the total mass of matter, it plays an important role in the heat balance of the system. Moreover, understanding the mechanisms of dust growth and concentration in circumstellar disks (astrophysical precursors of planetary systems) is necessary in developing theory of planet formation and organic matter evolution. Coupled dynamics of gas and dust in such disks is often described on microscale level as two-fluid mixture model (see e.g. [1] for survey of different approaches to gas-dust media modelling).

A number of algorithms have been described for including dust particles into astrophysical simulation of gas dynamic. This algorithms are formulated using grid-based [6,7,9] or particle-based [4,5,8,10–16] approach. An important feature of considered mixture model is the presence of the time scale t_{stop} (stopping time). This is the time of the velocity relaxation, during which the velocity of a dust particle decreases by a factor of e as a result of drag forces. For explicit time integrators this stopping time imposes a restriction on the time step $\tau < 2t_{stop}$ [14] besides Courant-Fridrichs-Levy condition. For small dust grains ~ 1 microns in size, $t_{stop} \approx 100$ seconds, while the typical calculation times are hundreds and thousands of years in astronomy. Therefore, the problem of calculating the dynamics of dust in a gaseous media is an extremely actual problem of computational physics.

In [1,3], fast and accurate method for the numerical simulation of gas and dust media based on Lagrangian Smoothed Particle Hydrodynamics (SPH) method is proposed. This method is called SPH-IDIC (Implicit Drag in Cell). This paper describes the implementation of SPH-IDIC in the cosmological open-source parallel code Gadget-2 [17,18], modified for simulation of circumstellar disk [19]. However, the code can be used for gas dynamic calculations of different classes of problems. One-dimensional and three-dimensional tests of this implementation are introduced in the paper. The results of calculations performed using the SPH-IDIC are compared with the classical approach from [2].

2   Numerical Methods

The basic gas dynamic equations implemented in Gadget-2 is describe in [17,18]. The dusty component is modelled as inviscid pressureless fluid with velocity different from velocity of the gas as described in [15]. The system of partial differential equation (PDE) includes the equation of continuity and the equation of motion for dust and gas, as well as the equation for the internal energy of the gas.

The paper considers the approximation of this PDE system with two interacting sets of particles (gas particles and dust particles). Using the SPH method [20,21] this PDE system is rewritten for numerical solution. Physical quantities related to gas particles have subscripts a, b, c, and to dust ones are i, j, k. If the equation is the same for both types of particles, then a mixed subscript is used, for example a, i. Current and next time steps are indicated by superscript $n, n + 1$. Thus, the density of each kind of particles (ρ_a and ρ_i) can be determined as follows:

$$\rho_a^n = \sum_b m_b W(r_{ab}^n, h_a^n); \qquad \rho_i^n = \sum_j m_j W(r_{ij}^n, h_i^n), \qquad (1)$$

where m_b and m_j are the masses of gas and dust particles, respectively, and $W(h)$ is the interpolation kernel. It determines the degree of influence of a neighboring particle on the physical value of the particle under consideration, depending on the distance between them $r_{ab} = |r_a - r_b|$. In the calculations, particles of the same type have the same masses, and the interpolation kernel is specified as a spline $W_4(r, h)$ [22]. The summation is performed over particles inside the volume with a radius h, the so-called smoothing length.

The program code implements two options for determining the smoothing length. In the first case, it is set constant and is a parameter of the problem.

In the second it is variable and depends on the density of the substance. The parameter of the problem is the number of particles that must fall into the volume over which smoothing is performed. Since the density ρ and the smoothing length h depend on each other, an iterative approach is used. The criterion for stopping the iterations is the required number of particles in the volume h^3. In this case, the spatial derivatives of h do not vanish. Therefore, as a coefficient, the equations include the factor $\Omega_{a,i}^n$ [18]. In the case of constant smoothing length $\Omega_{a,i}^n = 1$.

The continuity equation has the form:

$$\frac{d\rho_{a,i}^n}{dt} = -\frac{m_{a,i}}{\Omega_{a,i}^n} \sum_{b,j} (\mathbf{v}_{a,i}^n - \mathbf{v}_{b,j}^n) \nabla_{a,i} W^n (r_{ab,ij}^n, h_{a,i}^n), \tag{2}$$

where $\mathbf{v}^n$ is the particle velocity.

In the problem under consideration, the equation of motion for gas includes hydrodynamic acceleration (Ψ), viscous acceleration (ν), gravitational (G) and drag acceleration (D):

$$\frac{dv_a^n}{dt} = \Psi_a^n + \nu_a^n + G_a^n + D_a^n, \tag{3}$$

and the last two remain in the case of dust particles:

$$\frac{dv_i^n}{dt} = G_i^n + D_i^n. \tag{4}$$

The hydrodynamic acceleration is determined by the pressure gradient and, in the SPH formalism, is written as:

$$\Psi_a^n = -m_a \sum_b \left(\frac{P_a^n}{\Omega_a^n (\rho_a^n)^2} \nabla_a W(r_{ab}^n, h_a^n) + \frac{P_b^n}{\Omega_b^n (\rho_b^n)^2} \nabla_a W(r_{ab}^n, h_b^n) \right). \tag{5}$$

Viscous forces characterize dissipative processes and are usually determined by the numerical viscosity tensor Π_{ab} [23, 24]:

$$\nu_a^n = -m_a \sum_b \Pi_{ab}^n [\nabla_a W(r_{ab}^n, h_a^n) + \nabla_a W(r_{ab}^n, h_b^n)]. \tag{6}$$

The gravitational acceleration is determined by the gravitational potential of the system. In the paper $G_{a,i}^n = 0$.

2.1 Monaghan and Kocharyan Scheme (MK)

To calculate the acceleration of friction, which describes the interaction of gas and dust particles, in the SPH formalism, the classical approach from [2] was used:

$$D_a^n = -\lambda \sum_j m_j \frac{K_{aj}^n}{\rho_a^n \rho_j^n} \frac{(\mathbf{v}_a^n - \mathbf{v}_j^n) \cdot (\mathbf{r}_j^n - \mathbf{r}_a^n)}{|\mathbf{r}_j^n - \mathbf{r}_a^n|^2 + \eta \overline{h}_{aj}^{n\,2}} |\mathbf{r}_j^n - \mathbf{r}_a^n| W(r_{ja}^n, h_a^n), \tag{7}$$

$$D_i^n = \lambda \sum_b m_b \frac{K_{bi}^n}{\rho_b^n \rho_i^n} \frac{(\mathbf{v}_b^n - \mathbf{v}_i^n) \cdot (\mathbf{r}_i^n - \mathbf{r}_b^n)}{|\mathbf{r}_i^n - \mathbf{r}_b^n|^2 + \eta \overline{h}_{bi}^{n^2}} |\mathbf{r}_i^n - \mathbf{r}_b^n| W(r_{ib}^n, h_i^n). \qquad (8)$$

Coefficient $\lambda = 1$ and $\lambda = 1/3$ for one-dimensional and three-dimensional cases, respectively.

$$K_{aj}^n = \frac{\rho_j^n \rho_a^n c^n}{s \rho_s}, \qquad (9)$$

where s is the size of the dust grain, and ρ_s is the density of the substance of the dust grain.

2.2   SPH-IDIC Algorithm

When modifying the GADGET-2 code, the possibility of using the SPH-IDIC scheme for calculating the interaction of the dust and gas components of a substance was added [3]. The gas-dust medium in the considered approach is divided into non-intersecting cells, and the acceleration of drag forces is written as follows:

$$D_a^n = -\frac{K^n}{\overline{\rho_g}^n}(v_a^{n+1} - \overline{v_d}^{n+1}), \qquad (10)$$

$$D_i^n = \frac{K^n}{\overline{\rho_d}^n}(\overline{v_g}^{n+1} - v_i^{n+1}). \qquad (11)$$

The coefficient K is determined through the average density of dust grains in the cell $\overline{\rho_d}^n = \frac{\sum_{j=0}^{L^n} \rho_j^n}{L^n}$ (L^n is the number of dust particles in a cell) and the stopping time t_{stop}. It was accepted:

$$K^n = \frac{\overline{\rho_d}^n}{t_{stop}^n}, \qquad (12)$$

$$t_{stop}^n = \frac{s \rho_s}{\overline{\rho_g}^n c^n}, \qquad (13)$$

where $\overline{\rho_g}^n = \frac{\sum_{b=0}^{N^n} \rho_b^n}{N^n}$ is the average density of gas particles, and N^n is the number of gas particles in the cell. A semi-implicit scheme for calculating the velocities $v_a^{n+1}, v_i^{n+1}, \overline{v_d}^{n+1}, \overline{v_g}^{n+1}$ at the next integration step is given in [3].

2.3   Energy Equation

The program code provides three modes for changing the internal energy of the gas. First, the isothermal case, in which the system of equations is closed by the equation of state for an ideal gas: $P_a^n = c^2 \rho_a^n$, where $c = $ const is the speed of sound in the substance, which characterizes the temperature and effective viscosity of the disk.

Second, in the non-isothermal version, the system of equations includes the energy equation:

$$\frac{du_a^n}{dt} = \frac{P_a^n}{\Omega_a^n(\rho_a^n)^2}m_a\sum_b(\mathbf{v}_a^n - \mathbf{v}_b^n)\nabla_a W(r_{ab}^n, h_a) + U_D^n. \tag{14}$$

The equation of state for an ideal gas can be specified in the adiabatic form: $P_a^n = u_a^n(\gamma - 1)\cdot\rho_a^n$, where u is specific internal energy of gas. The change in energy due to the drag forces between the gas and the dusty media has the form:

$$U_D^n = \lambda\sum_j m_j \frac{K_{aj}^n}{\rho_a^n\rho_j^n} \frac{[(\mathbf{v}_a^n - \mathbf{v}_j^n)\cdot(\mathbf{r}_j^n - \mathbf{r}_a^n)]^2}{|\mathbf{r}_j^n - \mathbf{r}_a^n|^2 + \eta\overline{h_{aj}^n}^2}|\mathbf{r}_j^n - \mathbf{r}_a^n|W(r_{ja}^n, h_a^n), \tag{15}$$

for MK scheme and

$$U_D^n = \frac{K^n}{\overline{\rho_g}^n}(v_a^{n+1} - \overline{v_d}^{n+1})^2 \tag{16}$$

for SPH-IDIC algorithm.

The third option is to set the temperature profile in the approximation of local thermodynamic equilibrium.

3   Results

3.1   One-Dimensional Tests

As a one-dimensional test, the Riemann problem is considered, the solution of which is a classical test for methods of numerical integration of the equations of dynamics of continuous media [25–28]. In the case of a gaseous medium, the analytical solution to this problem is known. In the case of a gas-dust media, the analytical solution can be obtained at time $t > t_{stop}$ provided that $t_{stop}max(c, v_a, v_i) \ll l$, where l is linear the size of the computational domain.

At the initial moment of time $t = 0$, the following values of the system macro parameters were set for the left and right parts with respect to the discontinuity:

$$[\rho_l, P_l, v_l, u_l] = [1, 1, 0, 2.5], \tag{17}$$

$$[\rho_r, P_r, v_r, u_r] = [0.125, 0.1, 0, 2], \tag{18}$$

$$\gamma = 1.4. \tag{19}$$

The masses of dust and gas particles are equal to each other. The density and velocity of dust coincide with those for gas. The solution uses a non-isothermal energy equation. The particles were distributed in the interval $[-0.5 : 0.5]$, outside this segment, stationary particles were added. It provide a pressure gradient close to zero and the absence of density drops at the ends of the segment under consideration. The density of matter of dust particles in all models was set equal to $\rho_s = 1$ g cm^{-3}.

There are two options for specifying a medium of different density outside the discontinuity at the initial moment of time. In the first case, a different number of particles is used on the left (N) and on the right $(N/8)$ parts with the same masses of all particles. In the second case, the number of particles was the same, but the masses of particles on the left (m) and on the right $(m/8)$ parts differed. The calculations showed that the differences in the calculation results of both approaches are insignificant (Fig. 1), therefore, in what follows, all tests are given for the second case.

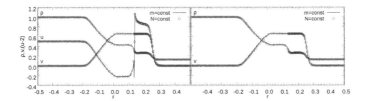

Fig. 1. The density, velocity, and internal energy of the gas are shown on the left, and of the dust are on the right at the moment of time $t = 0.2$. The solid line corresponds to the model in which the mass of particles is constant, but their number changes to the right and to the left parts of the discontinuity. The empty circles for model in which the number of particles is constant, but their mass is not the same. The size of the dust grains is $s = 1$ microns, and the density is $\rho_s = 1$ g cm^{-3}. The smoothing length and time step are constant $h = 0.02$ and $\tau = 0.001$, the SPH-IDIC schema was used.

A comparison was made of the numerical results obtained using the SPH-IDIC and MK scheme. It should be noted that the MK scheme failed to obtain a numerical solution converging to the analytical one for dust grains $s = 1$ μm in size and a time step $\tau > 0.00001$. In the case of dust grains with a larger size $s = 10$ μm, it can be seen that the SPH-IDIC scheme shows a solution that is closer to analytical calculations (Fig. 2). In addition, for the convergence of the MK scheme, it is necessary to specify a 10 times smaller time step, than for SPH-IDIC. It was shown in [3] that the better convergence of the solution obtained using the MK scheme to the analytical one can be achieved by decreasing the smoothing length. In this implementation, to match the results of calculations using the SPH-IDIC and MK scheme, it is sufficient to reduce the smoothing length for the latter by 4 times. In the case of large particles $s = 100$ μm and $s = 1$ mm, both schemes show similar calculation results (Fig. 3).

Code tests were performed using constant and variable smoothing length. The constant smoothing length was set equal to $h = 0.02$, the variable was calculated from the condition that the number of particles inside a segment of length h^n is equal to $N_{nb} = 50 \pm 2$. The calculations did not show significant differences between the two approaches. Figure 4 shows the deviations of the values of physical quantities in the numerical solution and analytical ones. It can be seen that noticeable deviations appear near the discontinuities, and their amplitude is the same for both approaches. Root-mean-square deviations from

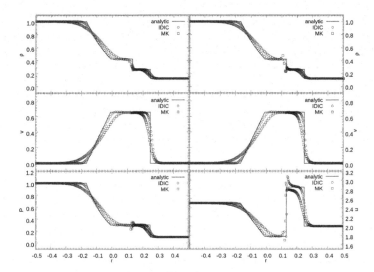

Fig. 2. The top and middle panels on the left show the density and velocity of the gas and on the right, the density and velocity of the dust the bottom panel shows the gas pressure (left) and internal energy of the gas (right) at time $t = 0.2$. The solid line corresponds to the analytical solution of the problem, the empty circles correspond to the numerical calculations using the SPH-IDIC scheme, and the empty squares correspond to the MK scheme. The size of the dust grains is $s = 10$ μm. The smoothing length and time step are constant $h = 0.02$, and $\tau = 0.001$ for the SPH-IDIC and $\tau = 0.0001$ for the MK scheme.

the analytical solution for constant smoothing length are $\Delta V = 0.057$, $\Delta \rho = 0.016$, $\Delta u = 0.087$ for gas and $\Delta V = 0.048$, $\Delta \rho = 0.018$ for dust, and for the variable one are $\Delta V = 0.054$, $\Delta \rho = 0.015$, $\Delta u = 0.073$ for gas and $\Delta V = 0.04$, $\Delta \rho = 0.020$ for dust. However, with an increase in the number of particles, calculations with a variable smoothing length are performed more slowly than in the case of a constant one. The calculations also showed that the variable time step also does not significantly affect the calculation results if it is bounded from above by the value $\tau = 0.01$.

3.2   Three-Dimensional Tests

In the three-dimensional case, the method was tested on the problem of the expansion of a gas and dust ball into vacuum under the action of its own pressure. A similar problem that considers a pure gas is the classical problem of fluids mechanics. Its extension to the case of a gas-dust media was obtained by authors of [29].

The problem statement is as follows. Let a gas-dust medium of mass $M = M_g + M_d$, where M_g is the mass of gas, M_d is the mass of particles, represents two nested concentric balls centered at the origin and of radii $R_{g,0}$ and $R_{d,0}$ respectively, $R_{g,0} \geq R_{d,0}$. We assume that the gas ball is inviscid and non-heat-

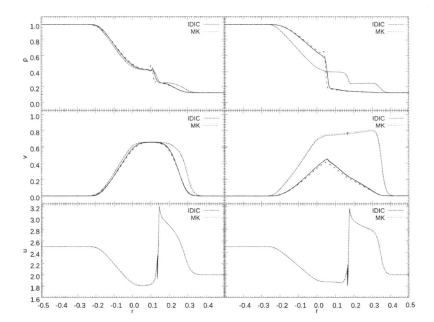

Fig. 3. The densities, velocities of dust (bold lines) and gas (thin lines) and the internal energy of the gas in the case of dust grains $s = 100 \ \mu$m are shown on the left. The same in the case of $s = 1$ mm at time $t = 0.2$ are on the right. The solid line corresponds to the numerical calculations using the SPH-IDIC scheme, the dashed line corresponds to the MK one. Smoothing length and time step are constant $h = 0.02, \tau = 0.001$.

conducting. We will assume that for dust particles the averaged local values of density and velocity in the entire ball are determined. Let us also assume that the gas and dust particles exchange momentum, but not mass and energy. Let us assume that at the initial moment of time there is a spherically symmetric distribution of pressure in the gas, as well as velocities in the gas and particles. This means that at subsequent moments of time, the distribution of macroparameters in the medium will also retain spherical symmetry. At the initial moment of time, a uniform velocity gradient and a uniform density are set in the gas and dust balls, that is, the velocity distribution along the radius is linear (velocity is zero in the center of the ball, and the maximum speed is at the ball boundary). In this case, the energy of the gas has a quadratic distribution along the radius, the energy is maximum at the center of the ball and vanishes at the boundary of the ball.

Calculations were carried out using the SPH-IDIC method with a constant smoothing radius $h = 0.15$, $\tau = 0.005$, with the total number of gas and dust particles $N_{\mathrm{g}} = N_{\mathrm{d}} = 65752$, respectively, and the following dimensionless initial parameters:

$$R_{0,\mathrm{g}} = R_{0,\mathrm{d}} = 1, \ \ v_{0,\mathrm{g}} = v_{0,\mathrm{d}} = 1, \ \ M_{\mathrm{g}} = 1000, M_{\mathrm{d}} = 800, \gamma = \frac{4}{3}, \qquad (20)$$

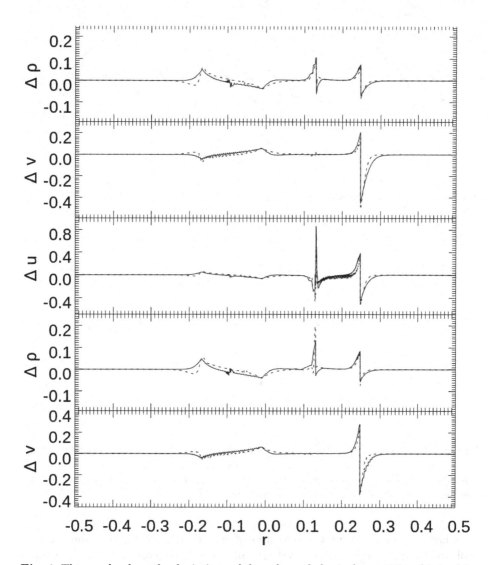

Fig. 4. The graphs show the deviations of the values of physical quantities obtained in numerical calculations using the SPH-IDIC scheme and an analytical solution at the time $t = 0.2$. The solid line shows the deviations for the case of constant smoothing length, and the dashed line is for the variable one. The three top graphs show the deviations of the density, velocity, and internal energy of the gas, and the two bottom graphs show the deviations of density and velocity of the dust. The size of the dust grains is $s = 10$ μm, and the time step is constant $\tau = 0.001$.

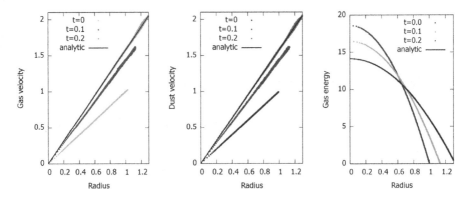

Fig. 5. 3D test with $t_{\text{stop}} = 10^{-3}$. Gas velocity (left panel), dust velocity (middle panel) and gas energy (right panel). The x-axis marks the radius of the particles. The black line denotes the analytical solution at time $t = 0.2$ and colored lines present numerical solutions at $t = 0.2, t = 0.1$ and initial moment $t = 0$.

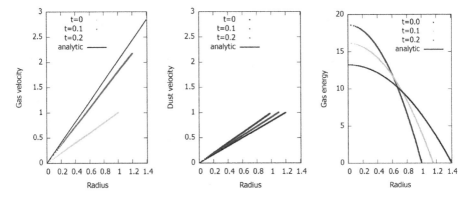

Fig. 6. 3D test with $t_{\text{stop}} = 10^3$. Gas velocity (left panel), dust velocity (middle panel) and gas energy (right panel). The x-axis marks the radius of the particles. The black line denotes the analytical solution at time $t = 0.2$ and colored lines present numerical solutions at $t = 0.2, t = 0.1$ and initial moment $t = 0$.

where $v_{0,\text{g}}$ and $v_{0,\text{d}}$ are the velocities of gas and dust at the boundary of the ball, respectively. In the article, we present two calculations with fixed parameters $t_{\text{stop}} = 10^{-3}$ and $t_{\text{stop}} = 10^3$. The former value corresponds to the particle size $s \approx 1$ mm the latter $s \approx 1$ km.

Boundary particles were used in the calculation to fulfill the boundary conditions. These particles were placed around the ball in the same way as inside the area, expanding it by a radius of $2h$. The main difference between boundary and inner particles is the way in which the velocity is calculated. For internal particles, the velocity was calculated using the formulas (3)-(4), then for external particles, the velocity was found by linear extrapolation from internal ones.

Figure 5 shows the calculation results for $t_{stop} = 10^{-3}$. On the panels of the figure the gas velocity (left panel), dust velocity (middle panel) and gas energy (right panel) are given. The x-axis marks the radius on which the particles are located. The black line denotes the analytical solution at time $t = 0.2$ and colored lines present numerical solutions at $t = 0.2, t = 0.1$ and initial moment $t = 0$. It can be seen that at the time point $t = 0.2$, the numerical values coincide with the analytical solutions for all parameters of the gas and dust medium. In this case, the dust velocity coincides with the gas velocity, due to the strong drag force between the phases.

Figure 6 shows the calculation results for $t_{stop} = 10^3$. Gas velocity (left panel), dust velocity (middle panel) and gas energy (right panel) are given. The black line denotes the analytical solution at time $t = 0.2$ and colored lines present numerical solutions at $t = 0.2, t = 0.1$ and initial moment $t = 0$. In this case, we also see a correspondence between the numerical solution and the analytical one. Moreover, the drag between dust and gas is weak, so the velocities of gas and dust are different.

3.3 Parallelization Efficiency

Parallelization efficiency of the 3D test (ball expansion problem, see Subsect. 3.2) was performed on 12th Gen Intel© Core™i9-12900K × 16 processor. This processor has 8 Performance-cores (with Intel ® Hyper-Treading Technology, up to 5.20 GHz frequency) and 8 Efficient-cores (no Hyper-Threading, up to 3.90 GHz frequency)[1], so it has 16 physical cores, but 24 threads. The distribution of SPH-particles in the computational domain between MPI-threads during runs was automatic, not manual.

Figure 7 shows the calculation time of the runs with different number of used MPI-threads. In fact of high performance of the Processor and moderate number of SPH particles ($\sim 130 \times 10^3$), calculations don't last long: even 1 thread successfully handles the test in two minutes. But it is enough to show sub-linear speedup (see Fig. 8) with growing of number of computational threads. Indeed, when using up to 8 computational threads, we get an acceleration of more than 6 times. The same speedup could be seen in intervals 10–14 and 16–22 threads. Unfortunately, in case of 10 MPI-threads there were used one or two Efficient cores (slow), what negatively affected the performance growth. The same effect is observed in intervals 14–16 and 22–24 of MPI-threads. Overall, we get speedup ~ 10 with using all 24 threads.

---

[1] https://www.intel.co.uk/content/www/uk/en/products/sku/134599/intel-core-i912900k-processor-30m-cache-up-to-5-20-ghz/specifications.html.

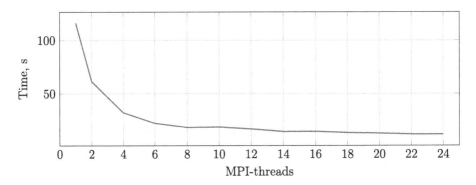

Fig. 7. Calculation time vs. number of MPI-threads with 3D test of ball expansion problem.

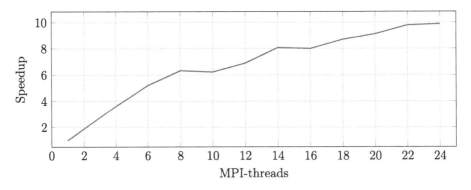

Fig. 8. Speedup of calculations vs. number of MPI-threads with 3D test of ball expansion problem.

4   Conclusions

In the work, the SPH-IDIC algorithm [3] was implemented in the Gadget-2 cosmological code. This algorithm makes it possible to economically calculate the dynamics of gas and dust media, which take into account the momentum exchange between the gas and dust. In addition, the code also implements the classical algorithm MK [2] for simulation of dusty gas dynamics.

To demonstrate the properties of the algorithm, test problems were solved in one-dimensional and three-dimensional cases for different sizes of dust particles. In the one-dimensional case, the Sod problem was solved by two implemented methods. For small grain sizes ($s = 1$ μm), the SPH-IDIC scheme showed a significant advantage over the MK scheme. In the case of large particles ($s = 100$ μm and $s = 1$ mm), both schemes show similar calculation results. This confirms the previously obtained results in [3]. For the three-dimensional case, the problem of the expansion of a gas-dust ball into vacuum was solved using the SPH-IDIC method. A good agreement with the analytical solution is obtained for both small and large particle sizes at low computational costs.

The efficiency of parallelization on 12th Gen Intel© Core ^{TM}i9-12900K $\times$ 16 processor was also investigated. It is shown that when using 24 threads, we get a speedup ~ 10.

Acknowledgements. The study was founded by the Russian Science Foundation grant number 23-11-00142.

References

1. Stoyanovskaya, O., Davydov, M., Arendarenko, M., Isaenko, E., Markelova, T., Snytnikov, V.: Fast method to simulate dynamics of two-phase medium with intense interaction between phases by smoothed particle hydrodynamics: gas-dust mixture with polydisperse particles, linear drag, one-dimensional tests. J. Comput. Phys. **430** (2021). https://doi.org/10.1016/j.jcp.2020.110035
2. Monaghan, J.J., Kocharyan, A.: SPH simulation of multi-phase flow. Comput. Phys. Commun. **87**(1–2), 225–235 (1995). https://doi.org/10.1016/0010-4655(94)00174-Z
3. Stoyanovskaya, O.P., Glushko, T.A., Snytnikov, N.V., Snytnikov, V.N.: Two-fluid dusty gas in smoothed particle hydrodynamics: fast and implicit algorithm for stiff linear drag. Astronomy Comput. **25**, 25–37 (2018). https://doi.org/10.1016/j.ascom.2018.08.004
4. Monaghan, J.J.: Implicit SPH drag and dusty gas dynamics. J. Comput. Phys. **138**(2), 801–820 (1997). https://doi.org/10.1006/jcph.1997.5846
5. Barrière-Fouchet, L., Gonzalez, J.F., Murray, J.R., Humble, R.J., Maddison, S.T.: Dust distribution in protoplanetary disks. Vertical settling and radial migration. Astronomy Astrophys. **443**(1), 185–194 (2005). https://doi.org/10.1051/0004-6361:20042249
6. Bai, X.N., Stone, J.M.: Particle-gas dynamics with Athena: method and convergence. Astrophys. J. Suppl. **190**, 297–310 (2010). https://doi.org/10.1088/0067-0049/190/2/297
7. Kulikov, I., Chernykh, I., Sapetina, A., Vorobyov, E., Elbakyan, V.: On a godunov-type numerical scheme for describing gas and dust components in star formation problems. J. Appl. Ind. Math. **17**, 110–119 (2023). https://doi.org/10.1134/S199047892301012X
8. Cha, S.H., Nayakshin, S.: A numerical simulation of a "Super-Earth" core delivery from $\sim$100 to $\sim$8 au. MNRAS **415**(4), 3319–3334 (2011). https://doi.org/10.1111/j.1365-2966.2011.18953.x
9. Zhu, Z., Nelson, R. P., Dong, R., Espaillat, C., Hartmann, L.: Dust filtration by planet-induced gap edges: implications for transitional disks. Astrophysical J. **755**(1), 6 (2012). https://doi.org/10.1088/0004-637X/755/1/6
10. Lorén-Aguilar, P., Bate, M.R.: Two-fluid dust and gas mixtures in smoothed particle hydrodynamics: a semi-implicit approach. MNRAS **443**(1), 927–945 (2014). https://doi.org/10.1093/mnras/stu1173
11. Lorén-Aguilar, P., Bate, M.R.: Two-fluid dust and gas mixtures in smoothed particle hydrodynamics II: an improved semi-implicit approach. MNRAS **454**(4), 4114–4119 (2015). https://doi.org/10.1093/mnras/stv2262
12. Booth, R.A., Sijacki, D., Clarke, C.J.: Smoothed particle hydrodynamics simulations of gas and dust mixtures. MNRAS **452**(4), 3932–3947 (2015). https://doi.org/10.1093/mnras/stv1486

13. Cuello, N., Gonzalez, J.F., Pignatale, F.C.: Effects of photophoresis on the dust distribution in a 3D protoplanetary disc. MNRAS **458**(2), 2140–2149 (2016). https://doi.org/10.1093/mnras/stw396
14. Stoyanovskaya, O.P., Snytnikov, V.N., Vorobyov, E.I.: Analysis of methods for computing the trajectories of dust particles in a gas-dust circumstellar disk. Astron. Rep. **61**(12), 1044–1060 (2017). https://doi.org/10.1134/S1063772917120071
15. Stoyanovskaya, O.P., Vorobyov, E.I., Snytnikov, V.N.: Analysis of numerical algorithms for computing rapid momentum transfers between the gas and dust in simulations of circumstellar disks. Astron. Rep. **62**, 455–468 (2018). https://doi.org/10.1134/S1063772918060069
16. Vorobyov, E.I., Akimkin, V., Stoyanovskaya, O., Pavlyuchenkov, Y., Liu, H.B.: Early evolution of viscous and self-gravitating circumstellar disks with a dust component. Astron. Astrophys. **614**, A98 (2018). https://doi.org/10.1051/0004-6361/201731690
17. Springel, V., Yoshida, N., White, S.D.M.: GADGET: a code for collisionless and gasdynamical cosmological simulations. New Astron. **6**(2), 79–117 (2001). https://doi.org/10.1016/S1384-1076(01)00042-2
18. Springel, V.: The cosmological simulation code GADGET-2. MNRAS **364**(4), 1105–1134 (2005). https://doi.org/10.1111/j.1365-2966.2005.09655.x
19. Demidova, T.V.: Modelling the gas dynamics of protoplanetary disks by the SPH method. Astrophysics **59**, 449–460 (2016). https://doi.org/10.1007/s10511-016-9448-3
20. Lucy, L.B.: A numerical approach to the testing of the fission hypothesis. Astron. J. **82**, 1013–1024 (1977). https://doi.org/10.1086/112164
21. Gingold, R.A., Monaghan, J.J.: Smoothed particle hydrodynamics: theory and application to non-spherical stars. MNRAS **181**, 375–389 (1977). https://doi.org/10.1093/mnras/181.3.375
22. Monaghan, J.J., Lattanzio, J.C.: A refined particle method for astrophysical problems. Astron. Astrophys. **149**, 135–143 (1985)
23. Monaghan, J.J., Gingold, R.A.: Shock simulation by the particle method SPH. J. Comput. Phys. **52**, 374–389 (1983). https://doi.org/10.1016/0021-9991(83)90036-0
24. Balsara, D.S.: von Neumann stability analysis of smooth particle hydrodynamics-suggestions for optimal algorithms. J. Comput. Phys. **121**, 357–372 (1995). https://doi.org/10.1016/S0021-9991(95)90221-X
25. Chertok, A., Cui, S., Kurganov, A.: Hybrid finite-volume-particle method for dusty gas flows. SMAI JCM **3**, 139–180 (2017). https://doi.org/10.5802/smai-jcm.23
26. Laibe, G., Price, D.J.: Dusty gas with smoothed particle hydrodynamics - I Algorithm and test suite. MNRAS **420**(3), 2345–2364 (2012). https://doi.org/10.1111/j.1365-2966.2011.20202.x
27. Saito, T., Marumoto, M., Takayama, K.: Numerical investigations of shock waves in gas-particle mixtures. evaluation of numerical methods for dusty-gas shock wave phenomena. Shock Waves **13**(4), 299–322 (2003). https://doi.org/10.1007/s00193-003-0217-y
28. Sod, G. A.: Review, a survey of several finite difference methods for systems of nonlinear hyperbolic conservation laws. J. Comput. Phys. **27**(1), 1–31 (1978). https://doi.org/10.1016/0021-9991(78)90023-2
29. Stoyanovskaya, O.P., Grigoryev, V.V., Suslenkova, A.N., Davydov, M.N., Snytnikov, N.V.: Two-phase gas and dust free expansion: three-dimensional benchmark problem for CFD codes. Fluids **7**(2), 51 (2022). https://doi.org/10.3390/fluids7020051

MDProcessing.jl: Julia Programming Language Application for Molecular Dynamics Trajectory Processing

Vasily Pisarev[1,2][✉] [iD] and Mikhail Panov[1]

[1] HSE University, Moscow, Russia
{vpisarev,mfpanov}@hse.ru
[2] Joint Institute for High Temperatures of RAS, Moscow, Russia

Abstract. Molecular simulations and molecular dynamics in particular are among the most performance-demanding computational methods. As the scale of simulations increases, the task of processing the simulation results becomes a computationally-hungry problem as well. The usual approach to build easy-to-use post-processing tools is based on providing an interface to a high-performance library called from a scripting language such as Python. We overview the advantages of using Julia programming language for building such tools, due to its easy surface syntax close to that of scripting languages and JIT compilation enabling high runtime performance. Then, we overview the package MDProcessing.jl written in Julia, regarding its customizability, abstractions for common processing workflows and performance characteristics.

Keywords: Molecular Dynamics · Julia Language · Trajectory Processing · Neighbor Search

1 Introduction

The task of molecular simulations is among the most demanding HPC applications. Getting the mesoscale properties from the molecular simulations requires analysis of the atomic structure, typically computing spatial and temporal correlations between atomic positions or other properties along simulation trajectories. Such an analysis may be done on-the-fly or in post-processing. The on-the-fly processing might seem promising, however, it is limited to what is implemented in the simulation package, whilst post-processing is more flexible because the analysis methods are only limited by what a scientist can implement.

Given that the standards for molecular simulation accuracy and reproducibility become higher, the interesting properties require averaging over long time windows and/or tens or even hundreds of individual simulations. That means that even post-processing becomes a demanding task which benefits from high performance. On the other hand, it is also beneficial to implement novel analysis techniques in a scripting programming language because of ease of the initial

V. Voevodin et al. (Eds.): RuSCDays 2023, LNCS 14389, pp. 209–222, 2023.
https://doi.org/10.1007/978-3-031-49435-2_15

implementation compared to statically-typed compiled languages. That means, the analysis tools developed by HPC experts in statically-compiled languages are extremely important for getting accurate results in shortest time, whilst the tools made in scripting languages are popular as well because users can more easily modify and extend them.

As a result, we can formulate the following requirements that analysis tools ideally should have:

- high serial performance
- parallelization
- ease of use
- extensibility
- focus on trajectory processing
- open-source software

The existing tools include the analysis shipped with the simulation packages (LAMMPS [1], Gromacs [2]), which focus on high performance. The downside is that such packages implement a fixed number of analysis algorithms, and extension requires a user to modify the simulation package source code. Another choice is third-party tools such as OVITO [3], Atomic Simulation Environment [4], MDAnalysis [5,6], PyLAT [7], VMD [8] and many others, which provide an iterface for scripting programming languages (Python or Tcl). That means, some common analysis algorithms are implemented in a high-performance language, but users can write their own extensions in a "slower" language. Such extensions may be later reimplemented in the library core for increased performance. The approach of initial prototyping in a slow scripting language with the following rewrite of critical parts in a fast statically-compiled language, although quite common in scientific computing (i.e., interface to access optimized BLAS procedures from Python through Numpy, to mathematical operations through SciPy etc.), manifests the so-called "two-language problem".

Julia [9] is a relatively new programming language striving to overcome that two-language problem. It combines dynamic typing with optional type annotations, user control over data structure memory layout and type deduction. All that allows a user to easily prototype algorithms and then optimize them without leaving the single language ecosystem.

In the rest of the paper, we analyze which potential advantages the Julia programming language may have over Python for the molecular simulation post-processing tools and demonstrate some of the features on the example of the MDProcessing.jl package [10].

2   Julia Programming Language for Simulation Processing

The approach to a convenient and high-performance simulation processing tool taken by the packages with Python interface works well enough for most users, as long as the analysis procedures they typically need are implemented and have sufficient performance. Examples of packages with extensive sets of analysis procedures are OVITO [3] focused at the simulations of solid state and having lots of built-in tools for analyzing crystal structure, coordination, atomic volume etc., and MDAnalysis [5] focused at the simulations of soft matter and molecular systems. Both packages provide users with means to write custom analysis procedures in Python and incorporate them in the processing pipelines. A downside is that such customized analysis functions suffer from the performance bottlenecks inherent to Python language:

- low performance unless operations are not dominated by linear algebra
- inherent single-threaded execution of pure-Python code due to GIL
- overhead for passing data objects between Python interpreter and the core library

One of the ways to overcome those limitations is to extend the core package directly, however, that is less convenient and more error-prone for users whose background is primarily scientific, and not programming.

In our work, we try to overcome those limitations by implementing the MD analysis package in Julia language, which has fewer inherent performance bottlenecks than Python or Python/C++ binding if the extensibility is considered. In the following subsections, we review some favorable features of the Julia language for scientific computing in general which are also used in our package.

2.1   Optional Typing and Multiple Dispatch

Julia language has semantically dynamic typing, meaning that functions can be defined without specifying the types of arguments, the return value and intermediate variables. For example, the code for computing the running integral using the trapezoid rule looks as follows:

Listing 1. Computing running integral by the trapezoid rule using an array of function values assuming a constant spacing between argument values.

```
1  function integrate_trap(fvalues, dx)
2      runsum = zeros(length(fvalues)) # allocate
           output
3      for n in 2:length(fvalues)
4          next_term = fvalues[n-1] + fvalues[n]
5          runsum[n] = runsum[n-1] + next_term * dx
6      end
7      return runsum / 2
8  end
```

Here, we assume that `input` is a 1-based array of values of function that needs to be integrated, and `dx` is the separation between the x-points for the function values. However, any data structure that "looks like" an array from outside can be used as input, as the `integrate_trap` function only requires that `input` can be indexed by consecutive integers and produce numbers.

This "duck typing" approach facilitates the prototyping phase because the user does not have to know in advance which types exactly will be passed to their functions.

However, an important feature of the Julia language is the ability to add function definitions ("methods") specific to the argument data types. For example, another use case for numerical integration is when the values of x_i and $f(x_i)$ are passed separately as arrays. To reflect that a certain function definition applies only for arguments of specific types, Julia allows the programmer to optionally specify the argument types.

Listing 2. Computing running integral by the trapezoid rule using arrays of function values and argument values.

```
 1  function integrate_trap(
 2      fvalues,
 3      xvalues::AbstractVector
 4  )
 5      runsum = zeros(length(xvalues))
 6      for n in 2:length(xvalues)
 7          x = xvalues[n]
 8          xpre = xvalues[n-1]
 9          dx = x - xpre
10          f = fvalues[n]
11          fpre = fvalues[n-1]
12          next_term = dx * (f + fpre)
13          runsum[n] = runsum[n-1] + next_term
14      end
15      return runsum / 2
16  end
```

Unlike purely duck-typed languages, the definitions in Listing 2 and Listing 1 may co-exist in the same program without overriding each other. Listings 1 and 2 demonstrate a case of so-called single dispatch: the interpreter chooses the method of the function `integrate_trap` to call based on the type of `xvalues` argument. However, Julia supports multiple dispatch, i.e., the specific method is chosen based on types of all arguments. As an example, the programmer may want to define an integration procedure for a function, given an array of arguments where it has to be evaluated.

Listing 3. Computing running integral of a given function by the trapezoid rule using an array of argument values.

```
 1  function integrate_trap(
 2      f::Function,
 3      xvalues::AbstractVector
 4  )
 5      runsum = zeros(length(xvalues))
 6      if length(xvalues) > 0
 7          fprev = f(xvalues[1])
 8          for n in 2:length(fvalues)
 9              fx = f(xvalues[n])
```

```
10                    dx = xvalues[n] - xvalues[n-1]
11                    next_term = (fprev + fx) * dx
12                    runsum[n] = runsum[n-1] + next_term
13                    fprev = fx
14                end
15            end
16        return runsum / 2
17    end
```

This mechanism allows a user to add methods to extend any function, including the functions from the standard library, for use with custom data types. That, on one hand, allows one to write code which works for multiple representation of abstract data (e.g., a programmer writing a Newton solver does not need to know if the jacobian of a problem is represented as a dense or sparse matrix, provided that it can be used as a matrix for a linear system). On the other hand, programmers can easily write optimized methods for their specific data types (e.g., efficient solvers for specific matrix types).

An important application of the multiple dispatch is the extension of certain "magic" functions of the Julia standard library to user types. In that way, users may define the behavior of arithmetic operations, indexing or iteration for new types, similar to operator overloading in C++.

2.2   Code Compilation

To provide high runtime performance of programs, Julia uses JIT compilation and extensive type inference. The type system of Julia language is designed with performance considerations in mind, so that it is more restrictive than in popular dynamically-typed languages yet quite powerful in terms of abstraction. In addition, the compiler uses the binding strategy that may be described as "bind as soon as possible" to generate performant native code from duck typed source code. These features will be discussed in more details in the following two subsections.

Type System. Julia programmers can define custom datatypes ("structs"). Unlike class-based object-oriented languages, structs contain only data, while methods belong to functions. To facilitate compilation, programmers are encouraged to specify the types of struct fields. For example, a type to hold a complex number can be defined as follows:

```
struct ComplexNumber
    re::Float64
    im::Float64
end
```

As the number and types of the datatype attributes are fixed after the type definition, the compiler can generate a fixed memory layout for the instances of the datatype, and can also infer the types of all operations with its fields.

Type Inference and Variable Binding. Although Julia is semantically a late-binding language, it leverages the fact that the high-performance code is written statically, which means types of all inputs are known and types of the intermediate variables can be inferred even without explicit specification (so-called "type-stable" code). In that case, the Julia compiler can bind the intermediate variables early and use stack or registers to store simple datatypes such as integers, floating-point numbers, short tuples etc. That brings the performance of type-stable code close to what statically-compiled languages achieve. The semantic difference from the early-binding languages is that in cases when Julia compiler cannot infer variable types, it falls back to late binding strategy, instead of producing a compile-time error. As an example, Listing 4 shows the results for calling the function `integrate_trap` in two cases: one is when `fvalues` is an array of double precision floating-point numbers (`Vector{Float64}` in Julia notation), and another when it is an array that may hold arbitrary Julia objects (`Vector{Any}`).

Listing 4. Runtimes of the same function in the type-stable and type-unstable cases.

```
1  xvalues = collect(Float64, 0:9_999)
2  arr_float = rand(10_000)
3  # an array with the same contents but element type '
     Any'
4  arr_any = collect(Any, arr_float)
5
6  julia> @time integrate_trap(arr_float, xvalues);
7    0.000045 seconds (2 allocations: 78.172 KiB)
8
9  julia> @time integrate_trap(arr_any, xvalues);
10    0.002852 seconds (59.49 k allocations: 1007.609
       KiB)
```

The difference in runtime comes from the fact that the compiler cannot infer the concrete types of the elements of `arr_any` based solely on the array type (its element type is the abstract type `Any`). In the call `integrate_trap(arr_any, xvalues)`, the objects coming from accessing `fvalues` have to be unboxed to determine their types. However, if a vector `fvalues` contains only numbers, the function produces the same result as if it was specifically a `Vector{Float64}` object, although the runtime becomes much higher.

We can see that the type-stable code has only two heap allocations (allocation and resizing of the output array) and runs much faster than the type-unstable call, which also produces multiple heap allocations due to unboxing values from an abstractly-typed array. This example demonstrates that Julia programs typically achieve high runtime performance, if the programmer pays attention to the type stability.

2.3 Library Tools

In addition to basic operations, Julia has an extensive standard library to use it as a general-purpose programming language, and the ecosystem has a large number of third-party packages for various scientific computing tasks, as well as for program analysis and programmer productivity.

Data Storage. Out of the box, Julia has various data structures for data storage. Arrays with an arbitrary number of axes are fully supported in the standard library, The language manual specifies the interface for custom array styles, so that there are community packages for more specific array types. To name some:

- OffsetArrays.jl implements arrays which can be indexed using arbitrary axes offsets, in contrast to the standard 1-based indexing
- StaticArrays.jl implements fixed-size mutable and immutable array types which can be allocated more efficiently than the standard arrays with dynamic size

For small collections of fixed length, programmers may use tuples or named tuples which may be more efficient than arrays. Dynamic maps are implemented on the base of hash tables as the `Dict` type in the standard library. The `Set` type implements the unordered set data structure.

Vectorization, Broadcasts and Loop Fusion. Unlike Numpy for Python or Matlab, Julia does not extend certain mathematical operations (e.g., square root, trigonometric functions, exponentiation etc.) to be applied elementwise for arrays. Instead, it provides a generic mechanism for "broadcasting" any function, either from the standard library or a user-defined one, over arrays and tuples via "dot syntax" `f.(x)`. The broadcast mechanism allows the programmer to choose whether to write explicit loops to iterate over arrays or to use the short "vectorized" notation.

One of the advantages of the more explicit dot syntax is that operations like exp, sin etc. can be defined for matrices in the sense of power series.

A distinguishing feature of Julia broadcast syntax is that it performs syntactic loop fusion. That means that broadcasted operations can be applied in-place without allocating new arrays for intermediate results, which is crucial for reaching peak performance. Consider the expression $a. = x.\hat{}2. + \cos.(y).\hat{}3$. Without loop fusion, the compiler would allocate intermediate arrays $a1 = x.\hat{}2$, $a2 = \cos.(y)$, $a3 = a2.\hat{}3$, $a4 = a1 .+ a3$. The Julia compiler instead expands that expression into a code equivalent to Listing 5.

Listing 5. Expansion of a broadcast expression with loop fusion.

```
for i in eachindex(a, x, y)
    a[i] = x[i]^2 + cos(y[i])^3
end
```

Linear Algebra. Julia ships with a version of OpenBLAS and LAPACK for efficient linear algebra operations on arrays of machine number types. If needed, users may switch to another BLAS and LAPACK implementations [11]. Bindings are available for common operations, as well as for matrix factorization procedures and linear solvers. The operations on sparse matrices are supported via the bindings to the SuiteSparce library.

Parallel and Distributed Computing. Julia supports multi-threading in the standard library. The module `Threads` includes tools for parallel execution. The basic tool is the `@threads` macro which can be applied to a for-loop to distribute the iterations over the working threads. The module also contains helper macros to use atomic operations and the `@spawn` macro for creating a task and scheduling it to run on the next available thread.

The distributed computing may be done natively using the tools provided by the module `Distributed`. For high-performance numerical applications, bindings-passing library [12].

3   MDProcessing.jl Package

In this section, we describe features and analyze performance of the pure-Julia module for analysis of molecular dynamics (MD) trajectories [10]. The tool is currently designed to work with LAMMPS output files.

3.1   Data Types

MDProcessing.jl internal representation of an atomic system snapshot is the `MDState` structure. It includes box basic vectors, atomic coordinates, velocities, atom IDs and assigned molecule IDs. The performant use of these attributes is ensured by the static typing of the corresponding fields: a static 3×3 matrix for box vectors, arrays of static length-3 vectors for coordinates and velocities, arrays of integers for atom and molecule IDs.

However, that basic structure is not sufficient for full support of LAMMPS dumps, as they can contain any number of per-particle properties. To support that, the structure can optionally hold any number of per-atom scalar and vector properties (such as mass, charge, force or dipole vectors etc.) which are stored in an associative array. The main data constructor is the `read_dump` function which reads a LAMMPS dump file into memory.

For convenience, the `MDState` data objects are iterable. The iteration produces the objects of the type `MDParticle`. A particle holds a reference to its parent state, so that any per-particle property stored in `MDState` can be accessed from `MDParticle`. As shown in the following subsection, that is convenient for filtering particles satisfying some criterion based on their properties.

3.2   Customization

MDProcessing.jl package is designed with support of user-defined processing functions. As the user-defined functions are implemented in Julia, the same as core package, the user functions don't have an inherent performance penalty. That is an advantage over the case with e.g. Python processing libraries, where the core methods may be optimized in C, so that even the most carefully written user processing function cannot reach the same performance as built-in functions.

The standard library function `Base.filter` is extended by the method `Base.filter(prefix, state::MDState)`, which allows the user to remove particles that do not satisfy the condition `prefix`. An example of usage is shown in Listing 6.

Listing 6. Application of filter over particles in MDProcessing.jl.

```
1   original_state = read_dump("./input.dump")
2
3   # remove all particles left from the plane x = 5
4   sliced_state = filter(
5       part -> part.coord[1] > 5,
6       original_state
7   )
```

To make it easier to cache user-computed particle characteristics (e.g., coordination numbers, symmetry parameters etc.) in the `MDState` data structure, the function `addproperty!(state, propertyname, datavector)` allows the user to add a new per-atom property stored as elements of `datavector`.

One of the common tasks for processing is computing a certain parameter for a number of configurations along a simulation trajectory and averaging that parameter. This workflow is implemented as the function `traj_average`, which takes the parameters `func` for a function that computes the needed property for a single configuration via a call `func(state::MDState)`, `dir` for the directory of the stored trajectory, `fmask` for filename mask, and `timesteps` which specifies which timesteps to use for the averaging. As an example, Listing 7 shows the computation of the trajectory-averaged kinetic temperature.

Listing 7. Computing the kinetic temperature in MDProcessing.jl.

```
1   temperature = traj_average(
2       "./",
3       "conf.*.dump",
4       0:1000:100_000
5   ) do state
6       ke = 0.0
7       for particle in state
8           vel = particle.vel
9           ke += particle.mass / 2 * (vel' * vel)
10      end
11      return ke / (natoms(state) * 3 / 2 * kboltz)
12  end
```

Another common trajectory processing task is computing of correlation between two consecutive states along the simulation trajectory separated by time Δt, i.e.

$$C(\Delta t) = \langle f(\mathbf{r}_i(t), \mathbf{r}_i(t + \Delta t)) \rangle, \tag{1}$$

where C is the correlation function, f is a function that computes a property based on simulation states at times t and $t + \Delta t$, angle brackets denote the averaging over the trajectory (i.e., over the initial moments t). This concept is implemented in the function `traj_correlate(func, dir, fmask, delta_steps)`. Here, `func` is a function that computes the needed correlation function for a pair of configurations via a call `func(state::MDState, ref_state::MDState)`. `dir` and `fmask` specify the directory and filename mask for the stored trajectory, and `delta_steps` specifies the desired delay between two configurations in MD time steps. The function then finds all pairs of configurations separated by that delay, computes the correlation function for them and averages the result over the pairs. As an example, Listing 8 shows how one might compute the average number of particle neighbors within a certain radius that remain in the neighborhood after time Δt, assuming that there is a function `neighbors(particle, r0)` which returns indices of particles which are within a given radius from the central particle.

Listing 8. Computing a trajectory correlation in MDProcessing.jl.

```
1   coord_number = traj_correlate(
2       "./",
3       "conf.*.dump",
4       1000
5   ) do state, ref_state
6       corr = 0.0
7       npart = 0
8       for (particle, particle0) in zip(state,
                ref_state)
9           neigh1 = neighbors(particle, r_cut)
10          neigh0 = neighbors(particle, r_cut)
11          n_retain = length(intersect(neigh1, neigh0))
12          corr += n_retain
13          npart += 1
14      end
15      return corr / npart
16  end
```

Thus, arbitrary nonlinear correlation functions may be computed for a given time delay.

3.3 Performance

Most MD configuration analysis procedures involve the analysis of the short-range arrangement of particles. As such, efficient and scalable algorithms for fixed-radius nearest-neighbor search are necessary. This section presents the performance results for computing the radial distribution function (RDF) for a Lennard-Jones system at the density $\rho^* = 0.75$. The systems of different size are obtained by replicating a 1000-particle system in all direction. The timings are measured using the BenchmarkTools.jl package [13] on a laptop with Intel Core i7-1165G7 CPU and on a cHARISMa supercomputer cluster at the

HSE [14]. All the computations are implemented in pure Julia. The function that computes RDF is implemented with the support of multi-threading. For the reference, the times are compared with the times of RDF computation in OVITO 3.0.0-dev362 measured via the Python interface.

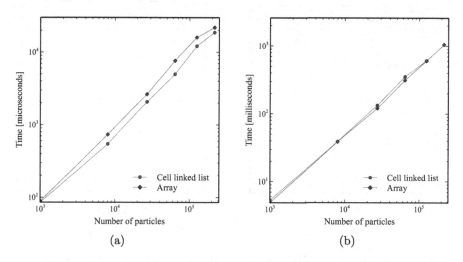

Fig. 1. Time to build the cell list for radius $r^*_{cut} = 2.5$ (a) and time to compute the RDF within radius $r^*_{cut} = 2.5$ (b) depending on the number of particles in the system in the single-threaded environment.

The fixed-radius neighbor search is implemented using a cell list data structure [15]. In such structure, the simulation box is subdivided into cells of size $r_{cut} \times r_{cut} \times r_{cut}$, so that the neighbor search within r_{cut} for a particle belonging to a particular cell requires only to search over the neighboring cells, reducing the neighbor search complexity from $O(N^2)$ to $O(N)$, where N is the number of particles in the system. The cell list is implemented in two variants: as a 3D array of vectors and as a linked-list structure. In the array implementation, element $a_{i,j,k}$ of the array holds the indices of particles belonging to cell (i, j, k). The linked-list implementation follows the textbook approach [15], where the indices of particles belonging to each cell are stored in linked-list structures. Figure 1(a) shows the time needed to construct the cell list for both implementations. From that, we can see that building a linked-list structure is slightly faster, because the data for all cells are stored in a single array. For the array-of-arrays storage, a fresh array for each cell has to be allocated, which brings some overhead. Both implementations, however, show a linear scaling with the number of particles in the system, in agreement with the theoretical expectation.

Figure 1(b) shows the time to compute the RDFs in the systems of different sizes using the pre-computed cell lists. First, one can see that the time to build the cell list is negligible compared to the time of neighbor search for both array and linked-list implementations. Second, the neighbor search times are virtually the same for both cell list representations. Third, the time for neighbor search also scales linearly with the number of particles, in agreement with the theoretical expectation.

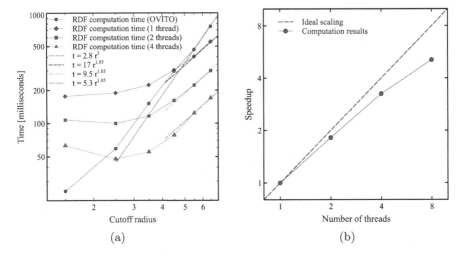

Fig. 2. (a) Time to compute RDF in the 27000-particle Lennard-Jones system at the reduced density $\rho^* = 0.75$ as a function of the cutoff radius. (b) Speedup for the computation of the RDF for the radius $r^*_{cut} = 5.5$.

To show the strong scaling of the problem, the parallel version of the RDF calculation was benchmarked on the Type-D nodes of the HSE cHARISMa HPC cluster with 24-core Intel Xeon Gold 6248R CPUs. Figure 2 shows the times to compute the RDF in the system with 27000 particles, depending on the cutoff radius, depending on the number of threads used for computation. The time to compute RDF using OVITO package on a single thread is shown as a reference. Theoretically, the expected time is proportional to the number of particle neighbors within the given radius, i.e. the time must scale as r^3_{cut}. In practice, the results obtained in OVITO follow that expectation, while the results obtained in MDProcessing.jl show a weaker scaling. That means that the time is not dominated by iteration over the possible neighbors. In fact, the neighbor search consists of iteration over the cells of the cell list and iteration over the particles in the neighboring cells for each cell in the list. The presented scaling shows that iteration over the particles in the cells does not dominate the neighbor search time, so that a significant contribution is likely due to the starting of the cell iteration. That is supported by the fact that the neighbor search with cut-off radius $r^*_{cut} = 2.5$ is faster than with $r^*_{cut} = 1.5$, due to the larger number of cells in the latter case. Overall, the single-thread performance of the neighbor search implemented in pure Julia is competitive with the C++ implementation in OVITO. For the large cutoff radii, the Julia implementation is faster, while the OVITO implementation is faster for small cutoff radii, likely due to the possibility of more fine-grained control over memory allocation in C++.

The approximations shown in Fig. 2(a) show that the scaling with the cut-off radius is nearly the same ($t \approx Ar_{cut}^{1.85}$) in single-threaded and multi-threaded implementation of the RDF computation. Figure 2(b) shows the speedup for the task of computing the RDF for cutoff radius $r_{cut}^* = 5.5$. As we see, there is a fairly good strong scaling up to 4 threads.

4   Conclusions

In this paper, we present a review of the Julia programming language in context of tasks related to the analysis of the molecular simulation trajectories. Compared to the non-compiled languages which rely on optimized C/C++/Fortran libraries for performance, Julia has advantage of JIT compilation to native code, which lets the programs achieve high runtime performance, while still having a dynamically-typed language semantics, which lowers the entry barrier for new programmers. Additionally, garbage collection makes it easier to use dynamic memory.

The tools provided by the Julia standard library and open-source community libraries allow us to write concise and idiomatic, yet high-performance programs.

The package MDProcessing.jl has been developed for the post-processing of the molecular dynamics (MD) trajectories. Implementing the package in Julia eliminates one of the problems of tools implemented as Python wrappers over C libraries, namely that the package users and developers work in different languages, so that the user extensions have lower performance than the built-in functions. With a Julia package, the user-written processing functions may be as performant as the developer-written. We present the MDProcessing API functions designed to capture typical tasks of simulation processing: averaging properties over a trajectory and computing correlation functions. The comparison of the neighbor search performance with the OVITO library shows that the Julia implementation is competitive with the C++ implementation, especially for large neighbor search radii. The native Julia multithreading provides a fairly good strong scaling of the neighbor search problem (about 3x speedup on 4 threads and 4x speedup on 8 threads).

Acknowledgements. The article was prepared within the framework of the HSE University Basic Research Program. The research was supported in part through computational resources of HPC facilities at HSE University

References

1. Thompson, A.P., Aktulga, H.M., Berger, R., et al.: LAMMPS – a flexible simulation tool for particle-based materials modeling at the atomic, meso, and continuum scales. Comp. Phys. Comm. **271**, 108171 (2022). https://doi.org/10.1016/j.cpc.2021.108171

2. Abraham, M.J., Murtola, T., Schulz, R., et al.: GROMACS: high performance molecular simulations through multi-level parallelism from laptops to supercomputers. SoftwareX **1**, 19–25 (2015). https://doi.org/10.1016/j.softx.2015.06.001

3. Stukowski, A.: Visualization and analysis of atomistic simulation data with OVITO - the Open Visualization Tool. Modelling Simul. Mater. Sci. Eng. **18**(1), 015012 (2009). https://doi.org/10.1088/0965-0393/18/1/015012

4. Larsen, A.H., Mortensen, J.J., Blomqvist, J., et al.: The atomic simulation environment - a Python library for working with atoms. J. Phys. Condens. Matter **29**(27), 273002 (2017). https://doi.org/10.1088/1361-648X/aa680e

5. Michaud-Agrawal, N., Denning, E.J., Woolf, T.B., Beckstein, O.: MDAnalysis: a toolkit for the analysis of molecular dynamics simulations. J. Comput. Chem. **32**(10), 2319–2327 (2011). https://doi.org/10.1002/jcc.21787

6. Gowers, R.J., et al.: MDAnalysis: a Python package for the rapid analysis of molecular dynamics simulations. In: Proceedings of the 15th Python in Science Conference. SciPy Austin, TX, vol. 98, p. 105 (2016). https://doi.org/10.25080/Majora-629e541a-00e

7. Humbert, M.T., Zhang, Y., Maginn, E.J.: PyLAT: Python LAMMPS analysis tools. J. Chem. Inf. Model. **59**(4), 1301–1305 (2019). https://doi.org/10.1021/acs.jcim.9b00066

8. Humphrey, W., Dalke, A., Schulten, K.: VMD: visual molecular dynamics. J. Molec. Graphics **14**(1), 33–38 (1996). https://doi.org/10.1016/0263-7855(96)00018-5

9. Bezanson, J., Edelman, A., Karpinski, S., Shah, V.B.: Julia: a fresh approach to numerical computing. SIAM Rev. **59**(1), 65–98 (2017). https://doi.org/10.1137/141000671

10. MDProcessing.jl package. https://gitlab.com/pisarevvv/mdprocessing.jl

11. Intel MKL linear algebra backend for Julia. https://github.com/JuliaLinearAlgebra/MKL.jl

12. Byrne, S., Wilcox, L.C., Churavy, V.: MPI.jl: Julia bindings for the message passing interface. In: JuliaCon Proceedings, vol. 1, p. 68 (2021). https://doi.org/10.21105/jcon.00068, https://github.com/JuliaParallel/MPI.jl

13. Chen, J., Revels, J.: Robust benchmarking in noisy environments. arXiv e-prints arXiv:1608.04295 (2016)

14. Kostenetskiy, P.S., Chulkevich, R.A., Kozyrev, V.I.: HPC resources of the higher school of economics. J. Phys. Conf. Series **1740**(1), 012050 (2021). https://doi.org/10.1088/1742-6596/1740/1/012050

15. Allen, M.P., Tildesley, D.J.: Computer Simulation of Liquids. Oxford University Press, Oxford (2017)

Methods and Algorithms for Intelligent Video Analytics in the Context of Solving Problems of Precision Pig Farming

Vsevolod Galkin$^{(\boxtimes)}$ and Andrey Makarenko

Institute of Control Sciences, Russian Academy of Sciences, ul. Profsoyuznaya 65, Moscow 117977, Russia
galckin.vsevolod@gmail.com

Abstract. The paper proposes an approach to developing a video data pipeline that addresses the basic tasks of precision pig farming. The pipeline performs both low-level tasks, such as data pre-processing, object detection, instance segmentation, tracking, object density estimation, etc., and high-level tasks, e.g. livestock counting, feeders and drinkers condition assessment, behavioral patterns analysis, estimation of livestock activity and weight, etc. The proposed solution is based on neural network algorithms and can be flexibly adjusted to specific conditions and tasks, including while sending emergency notifications. Furthermore, the system is architecturally capable of integrating additional sensor and input data. The approach is demonstrated by solving several problems in the fattening phase. The system has proven to have a number of competitive advantages, including stable operation in a high animal density environment.

Keywords: Precision livestock farming · Video monitoring · Deep learning · Instance segmentation · Object density · Animal weight estimation · Animal activity analysis

1 Introduction

Over the past three decades, the agribusiness industry has undergone two inter-related trends [31]: business consolidation and labor shortages. These trends also extend to livestock farming, and specifically pig farming, which is the focal point of this paper. Consolidation means mergers of huge corporations and/or takeover of small farms by larger companies. On the one hand, large-scale production reduces the costs of per-head technological processes, resulting in lower production costs. On the other hand, the combination of these two trends decreases the potential efficiency of production systems. Thus, streamlining and improving the efficiency of technological processes in agriculture, particularly in livestock and pig farming, appear to be urgent and relevant issues.

One possible approach to streamlining livestock farming is the use of precision livestock farming, or PLF [7]. PLF scales and adapts the advantages of

V. Voevodin et al. (Eds.): RuSCDays 2023, LNCS 14389, pp. 223–238, 2023.
https://doi.org/10.1007/978-3-031-49435-2_16

small farms to large producers, allowing them to individualize their technological processes. PLF relies on a combination of various sensors (e.g. cameras, microphones and other sensors) and algorithms for automated monitoring of the livestock physical environment, as well as of each individual animal in order to improve their performance and detect physical and behavioral changes in real time.

This paper advances the PLF approach by presenting a video data pipeline that solves the basic tasks of precision pig farming during pigs' fattening phase in the pen. Raw video data is recorded in the visible wavelength range by an engineered machine vision system which is installed above the pen to monitor animal activity 24/7. Video data from the cameras are then transmitted to the computing device where they are further recorded and processed by the data processing pipeline. The results of such calculations are subsequently used to generate analytical reports for the farm's staff.

The video monitoring tasks can be divided into two groups: (a) low-level data processing, (b) analytical/high-level report generation. The low-level tasks include localization and/or object segmentation, tracking, density estimation. High-level tasks are aimed at generating relevant information for the farm's staff based on the obtained low-level data. High-level reports may include such information as the number of animals in the pen, feeding/drinking behavior analysis, estimation of the livestock activity and weight, etc.

The paper is structured as follows: Section 2 provides an overview of related studies, Sect. 3 describes the dataset and the data labeling approach. Section 4 offers a detailed insight into the low-level data pipeline. Section 5 demonstrates how the technology in question can be used in pig farming. The concluding paragraph, Sect. 6, summarizes the key takeaways of the paper.

2   Related Works

Precision pig farming has been the subject of numerous scientific and technical studies, as well as commercial solutions. A recent review [10] examined the available technologies: as of 2021, there had been about 2 500 relevant research articles, with only 111 of them validating the potential application of PLF technologies to practice (45 pieces of such technologies were vision-based solutions). However, only 5% of the available PLF technologies had passed the external validation procedure [10]. This paper deals with machine vision solutions, so further discussion will be carried out in the context of computer vision-based technologies. The reasons behind such a low ratio of the technologies used in practice to the total number of studies are the absence of an integrated approach, simplification of the problem statement (e.g. artificially setting animal density too low), and the lack of relevant analytical tools.

As noted above, the predominant majority of scientific articles focused on individual, often low-level tasks. The basic task of a video monitoring system is to localize and/or segment objects. Deep convolutional neural networks are often used as the algorithmic kernel of the solution to this task [13,25,34]. The central flaw of most solutions is the simplification of the problem statement or the failure to take into account the actual conditions of animal husbandry. For instance, in article [26], as well as in some others, only the foreground data are segmented, while the background data are ignored. Such simplifications are further discussed in Sect. 3.

The second basic low-level task is object tracking in the video stream, more specifically simultaneous multi-object tracking. The PLF approach implies the tracking of each individual animal. Thus, two mutually exclusive problems arise: identification of animals in the pen vs. long-term object tracking. On the one hand, identifying animals in the pen by using scalable solutions in a full-scale production environment appears to be impossible; on the other hand, long-term tracking in a high animal density environment is just as impossible. Thus, the PLF approach that uses only video surveillance is currently not applicable in practice. However, a constructive assumption can be made that (1) estimating animals' characteristics in terms of average values per pen may be relevant and (2) that short-term tracking may be sufficient for some tasks. The solution described in this paper is designed for robotic sensor platforms. In such platforms, video cameras move between the pens, which automatically limits the time of tracking. Such algorithms as SORT [32], DeepSort [30], ByteTrack [35], and others have proven to be successful for short-term tracking.

This overview will now proceed to focus on complex data pipeline processes, rather than individual tasks. A number of selected articles [1,4,18,22] were aimed at recognizing animal postures (standing, sitting, kneeling, lying) and identifying the simplest actions, such as eating, drinking, moving. It should be noted that these are the tasks that most research papers seek to solve. On the one hand, the obtained results demonstrate that such a solution is feasible; on the other, the information about each animal's posture behavior may be redundant in large-scale production.

Several studies and technologies only focus on counting pigs in the pens [15, 29] or during their crossings of the counting zone [24]. It should be pointed out that the latter is a less complex task which does not require major changes in the structures and technological processes of the farm. For this reason, the technology presented in [24] has been implemented in practice.

In pig farming, one of the key and most relevant indicators is animals' weight and its dynamic. Lack of weight gain can be a sign of poor husbandry conditions and/or diseases. The traditional, direct method of weight estimation is "contact" measurement, the one that uses mechanical and/or electronic scales. This method is accurate and reliable. However, the use of scales is not always feasible on account of high labor intensity or the physical impossibility to perform contact weighing. Therefore, the need for an automated non-contact method of weighing objects based on their visual characteristics has gained increasing relevance. The vision-based solutions can be split into two groups: (a) weighing animals individually within a designated platform/area [23,27,33]; and (b) weighing pigs in their pens [16]. The literature overview has revealed that most studies focus on weighing each animal individually, outside their pigpen. This, in turn, requires additional movement of pigs, offsetting the advantages of camera-based solutions and making this approach similar to contact weight measurement. Moreover, since weight is regarded as one of the vital indicators in monitoring animals' growth dynamic, this approach would mean that pigs must be moved regularly. On the other hand, without individual identification, the weight of each animal in the pen can only be measured as "the-average-per-pen" value, which runs counter to the concept of precision livestock farming but is sufficient in practice.

The next task is temperature measurement. To estimate environmental temperatures, as well as the temperature of each individual animal [28,36], thermal imaging approaches have been used. However, due to the expensiveness of thermal imagers, a set of methods has been developed to indirectly measure environmental temperatures inside the pen, based on the analysis of pig group lying patterns [20,21].

The last task under consideration is the recognition of behavioral patterns, such as aggression [3,17] and tail biting [6]. These patterns are undoubtedly important for the farm's staff to be able to take prompt action and reduce animal mortality during the fattening phase.

A number of conclusions follow from this literature overview. The vast majority of the articles describe simplified machine vision systems (using only one camera) which lead to low-quality raw data, e.g. due to low-resolution images or a poor camera angle. Furthermore, the results of solved subtasks are often presented in an uninformative, often redundant form. Lastly, no integrated approach is proposed. On the one hand, the absence of an integrated approach narrows the focus to a more specific task, suggesting a more targeted solution. On the other hand, the large amount of funds and resources required for the implementation of the technology prevents it from going beyond scientific research towards being used in practice to solve relevant subtasks.

3 Dataset

The dataset consists of a series of multiple pigpen videos captured with 2 cameras. Each pen is a 3.8 m × 5.5 m rectangle that contains two drinkers and a wide feeder with 4 feeding spaces. Four pens were used for data collection that involved the monitoring of pigs during their fattening phase, from the moment they had been brought to the pen up to their slaughter. The weight of the pigs under monitoring varied from 17.5 to 125.5 kg. The recorded number of pigs ranged from 0, when the animals were moved between the pens, to 45, when they were moved from the nursery, with the number of large animals in the pen decreasing to 38 by the end of the fattening.

Wide-angle cameras with a 4000 × 3000 resolution and a 10 fps frame rate were used to collect the data. One pigpen used 2 cameras with overlapping fields of view. The cameras were positioned at a height of 2.8 m above the center of the pen, each monitoring a half of it. The video data from the cameras were then processed, synchronized and stitched into a single image.

Video streams are not stitched at the data collection stage; instead, it is done during pre-processing, meaning that raw data are extracted from the cameras independently. The recorded videos are three-channel images (RGB), have a fixed duration (600 frames), and are stored in a compressed format using the H.264 codec. The size of the collected data exceeds 11 TB, and the total length is 810 h.

See [1] for a comparison table of datasets on precision pig farming. The collected data show animal densities that are at least 1.5 times higher, compared with the prevailing majority of datasets. High livestock density significantly complicates data processing due to the high degree of occlusions and "clumping" of objects.

Low-level tasks required manual data labeling, which involved identifying each pig in the pen with a segmentation mask. Labeling video data to segment objects in high-density scenes is a highly labor-intensive process. To reduce the complexity of labeling, at the pre-processing stage we used an original approach which includes the thinning of the raw data, "rough" frame-by-frame annotation by means of hexagons in Inkscape, interpolation of annotation between frames, and mask refinement using CascadePSP [5] in order to compensate for low light and noise. This approach helped to speed up the data labeling process from 45 to 9 min per frame. A total of 16 one-minute videos were annotated; an example of the labeled data is given in Fig. 1.

Fig. 1. Labeled data example.

Following [9], to augment the labeled dataset, a synthetic training dataset was generated, which was used to improve the quality and stability of the solutions under development.

4 Pipeline

This section describes the operating principles of the raw data pipeline and demonstrates the results of solving several tasks that involve the extraction of low-level information from the raw data. The section also considers such issues as data pre-processing, instance segmentation in dense scenes, short-term object tracking in the video stream, estimation of total mass and density of animals.

4.1 Data Pre-preprocessing

As noted in Sect. 3, two independent wide-angle cameras are used to monitor the pigpen. Data pre-processing includes merging/stitching images from the wide-angle cameras into a single picture. This is done in two steps: (1) distortion correction; (2) stitching of the corrected images.

The use of wide-angle cameras makes it possible to capture large scenes at close distances, but due to optical lens aberration it fails to preserve the geometric similarity of objects, resulting in image distortion. This, in turn, acts as a hindrance towards solving the problems that involve metric and/or geometric characteristics of objects.

Distortion correction requires finding coefficients in a given parametric distortion model to subsequently recalculate pixel coordinates without distortion. To address this problem, an original method was developed, based on the classical chessboard approach to video data. However, several modifications were designed and implemented which included the creation and analysis of "a point cloud" within the camera field of view, as well as the generation of a set of hypotheses with subsequent selection of the optimal one in terms of the functionality of the resulting vector of the distortion model parameters.

On the one hand, the use of two wide-angle cameras complicates data processing, entailing the problem of a very time-consuming stitching. On the other hand, it has a number of advantages, such as a full capture of the scene where camera mounting height possibilities are limited, and increased detail of the resulting data. This work adopts a standard homography-based approach to image stitching, known as global deformation, where one of the images is selected as the base image and remains unaltered, while the second image is deformed and merged with the first one along the seam-line. It should be noted that our approach relies on an original method of keypoint selection. Since homography fails to preserve the original proportions of the image, the stitching process must be followed by perspective transformation according to the pre-set metric characteristics of the scene. The data pipeline with the examples of such transformations is illustrated in Fig. 2.

4.2 Instance Segmentation

An essential task in a video monitoring system is instance segmentation, which is a combination of localization and semantic segmentation. It suggests assigning each pixel of the image to a certain class, while also performing intra-class segmentation of objects. Therefore, instance segmentation requires that segmentation masks distinguish each object separately. The main challenge in instance segmentation is overcoming intra-class similarities of overlapping or occluded objects. According to some studies [8,12,14], deep neural networks are biased

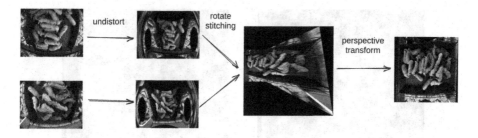

Fig. 2. Stitching pipeline.

in favor of the texture of an object rather than its shape. For these reasons, intra-class separation of visually hard-to-distinguish objects is a difficult task.

The Mask R-CNN framework is one of the most general, effective and widely-used neural networks for instance segmentation [11]. It should be pointed out that although approaches for instance segmentation based on video data exist, so far they have not been widely used in practice due to their complexity and the incompleteness of the technology.

In this work, we used the Mask R-CNN architecture, with the number of classes reduced to 2 (pig/background). The input data for the network comprise three-channel images of a pigpen with a 512×512 resolution. Before feeding the input data into the network, the CLAHE algorithm was used for low-light image enhancement. The network's output was also processed. To adapt the network to occlusions, the classical NMS algorithm was replaced by soft-NMS. To avoid capturing pigs from neighboring pens, the network's output applied detection rules according to the predetermined mask of the pigpen.

Mask R-CNN contains approximately 45 million weights. With a limited dataset, training the network "from scratch" will lead to overtraining. To avoid this, we used weights that had been pre-trained on MS COCO. The strategy for fine-training the network is illustrated in Table 1. To expand the dataset, in addition to the annotated and synthetic datasets, we used an augmentation strategy which included rotations, reflections, various noises, image quality reduction, etc.

Table 1. Mask-RCNN training parameters.

	optimizer	epoch	batch size	learning rate	weight decay	scheduler
Training	AdamW	75	16	$2\,e^{-4}$	0.05	StepLR
Fine-tune	AdamW	50	16	$5\,e^{-5}$	$1\,e^{-8}$	StepLR

The results of the segmentation model are presented in Fig. 3.

It is important to note that while the trained network has a high accuracy, it is not free from shortcomings, such as failing to count an animal even when it is visually observed, eliciting false-positive responses, and merging two objects

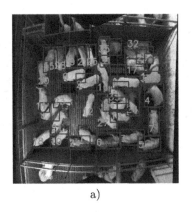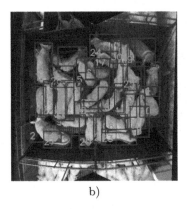

a)   b)

Fig. 3. Inference of Mask R-CNN trained on unlabeled data.

into one mask ("clumping" of objects). However, when network inferences that have been performed over a long time interval (e.g. one minute) are integrated, the median value of the number of objects coincides with the true value.

4.3   Tracking

As noted in Subsect. 4.2, the segmentation algorithm runs on a frame-by-frame basis. To track each object in the video stream, an appropriate solution should be found. Since the analysis tools that we have developed are aimed at calculating average values per pen, tracking may be largely considered as a secondary task intended for short-term monitoring of animals.

To track objects in the video stream, we used an approach based on examining a weighted undirected bipartite graph and finding the maximum matching in the graph through the use of the Hungarian algorithm. IoU values are used as weights in the graph. To evaluate the quality of the tracking algorithm, the basic MOTA and MOTP metrics were employed [2]. Three test videos with different numbers of objects were used for evaluation. The results of the experiments are shown in Table 2.

Table 2. Tracking accuracy on test set.

No.	number of objects	MOTA	MOTP
experiment No. 1	16	0.989	0.035
experiment No. 2	10	0.961	0.032
experiment No. 3	6	0.994	0.007
Result		0.981	0.024

4.4   Weight Estimation

To address this task, additional data collection and labeling were carried out by using the original methodology. Pigs were taken out of their pen one by one at [0.5, 4] min intervals and sent to the scales for weight measurement. Once the pen was empty, the animals were made to pass through it one at a time, staying inside for [0.5, 2] min. The total duration of the annotated data exceeds 12 h of video records; the number of the videos where the total weight of animals is constant is $N = 349$.

This work relies on a two-step approach: (1) automatic evaluation of pigs' morphological traits, and (2) approximating empirical relationship between weight and morphology through the use of regression models. In terms of animal morphology, only one trait was used - body area in the top view. As a result of segmentation, time series are obtained, each of which contains the total area of the observable objects' masks per each frame. The monitored scene is dynamic, so mask areas may vary from frame to frame while the total weight of the objects remains unchanged. For a more accurate estimation, the time series were aggregated into the median area value.

To approximate the unknown functional dependency between the median area and total weight, we compared three models: RANSAC, 2nd-order polynomial regression, and 3rd-order polynomial regression. The use of simple regression models is motivated by the high degree of correlation between the median area and weight, with the correlation coefficient being 0.98. However, the high degree of correlation does not fully reflect the relationship between area and weight.

A visual analysis (see Fig. 4) indicates data heterogeneity with respect to various hyperparameters of the experiment, such as pigpen video data (resolution discrepancies as a result of image stitching) and weight of the observed animals. Data heterogeneity reduces the potential accuracy of the solution, so homogenization of the dataset must be performed. In this paper, the normalizing function was found empirically.

To assess the quality of the trained models, the following classical regression quality estimates were used: the mean absolute percentage error (MAPE), the median absolute percentage error (median APE) and the coefficient of determination (R^2). The training and testing of the models was carried out on a complete set of data, without splitting into training and testing parts. Due to the simplicity of the data and models, a small number of training parameters, in comparison with the data size, the estimates obtained will be objective. In order to increase the stability of the obtained results, 500 of repeated runs are made for each model, from which one, the most accurate (top-1) model in terms of the median absolute percentage error, will be selected.

To assess the quality of the trained models, we used the following standard metrics of regression performance: mean absolute percentage error (MAPE), median absolute percentage error (median APE), and coefficient of determination (R^2). The models were trained and tested on the full dataset, i.e. no divisions were made between training and test parts. The simplicity of the data and mod-

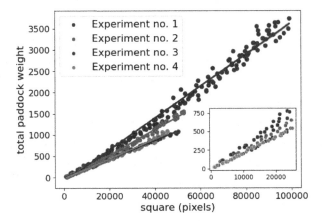

Fig. 4. Animal weight vs. median area of masks in different experiments.

els, as well as the small number of training parameters compared to the dataset size, ensure the objectivity of resulting estimates. To increase the stability of the results, each model is rerun 500 times. Subsequently, the model which has proven the most accurate (top-1), according to the median APE metric, is selected.

The resulting accuracy of the models after data conversion is shown in Table 3. The resulting error, according to the median APE metric, is no more than 4.2% of the actual weight of the animal.

Table 3. Accuracy of models.

	MAPE	median APE	R^2
RANSAC	0.243	0.091	0.991
polynomial regression (1st order)	0.061	0.042	0.991
polynomial regression (2st order)	0.892	0.132	0.983

4.5   Density Maps

A trending and promising avenue in pig farming is the analysis of animal crowding, more specifically estimating animal density in the pen, because the distribution of objects in the pen and the dynamic of such distribution shed light on a number of relevant macro characteristics.

Currently, the main tool for generating density maps has been deep neural networks. They approximate the unknown mapping between the image and the density map. Our work is no exception.

The annotated dataset described in Sect. 3 was used to solve the problem. The network training requires creating a true density map. In addressing this task, the vast majority of works on density map estimation rely on a pointwise labeling, followed by blurring of the Gaussian kernel normalized to unity 1.

$$F(\boldsymbol{x}) = \sum_{i=1}^{N} \delta\left(\boldsymbol{x} - \boldsymbol{x}_i\right) \times G_{\sigma_i}(\boldsymbol{x}). \tag{1}$$

Density map generation may vary, depending on the type of the function σ_i. To solve this problem, we used a function to estimate the average distance in pixels $\overline{d}$ to k nearest objects with a coefficient β:

$$\sigma = \beta\overline{d},$$

with parameters: $k = 3$, $\beta = 0.3$. The segmentation mask's center of mass acts as the keypoint detecting the object (Fig. 5).

a)   b)

Fig. 5. Density map generation: a) original image; b) density map.

The CSRNet neural network [19] is used to solve the problem. The network is fed with a 512×512 input image, with the CLAHE algorithm applied in advance. Architecturally, the output resolution is 8 times smaller than the input, i.e. 64×64. The resolution of the input image and the resulting density map must correspond, so the output is bilinearly interpolated back to the input.

To expand the training dataset and improve network convergence, a strong augmentation strategy involving the Albumentations library was used. It included random rotations, mirror reflections, Gaussian noise, blur, random scaling, perspective transformation, distortion, and RGB channel shuffling. The AdamW optimizer was used to train the neural network. The training procedure can be divided into 2 parts: training the network and fine-tuning the weights. The configuration of training parameters is shown in Table 4. Density estimation lies within the category of regression tasks, that is why the MSE function was used as a loss function.

The presented architecture is a composition of convolutional and pooling layers. Generally, architectures of such topology are known to be difficult to train for a number of reasons, such as data erasure, gradient attenuation, etc. To facilitate the training, we used ImageNet pre-trained VGG-16 weights with frozen layers.

Table 4. Model training parameters.

	optimizer	epoch	batch size	learning rate	weight decay	scheduler
Training	AdamW	35	32	$7\,e^{-4}$	$5\,e^{-4}$	StepLR
Fine-tuning	AdamW	150	32	$5\,e^{-5}$	$1\,e^{-8}$	CosineAnnealingLR

To assess the quality of the model, three appropriate metrics are used, namely: MSE, structural similarity (SSIM) coefficient to estimate the accuracy of the density map, and MAPE with regard to the number of objects. Since the number of observed objects can be calculated directly from the density map through integration, an error in the count of animals is a good indicator of accuracy. A comparison of the test set training results is presented in Table 5. For accuracy estimation, we calculated the median of all frames from 3 test videos.

Table 5. Quality of the model evaluation on the test sample.

$MSE_{density}$	$SSIM_{density}$	$MAPE_{obj}$
$1.707\,e^{-9}$	0.999	0.035

The findings reveal that even when highly accurate density maps (MAE $=$ 10^{-9}) are generated, the count of the number of animals remains less accurate and stable.

5 Tools of Analysis

This section presents tools of analysis that generate relevant high-level information. Due to space limitations, this paper will only focus on some of them.

Figure 6a shows the relative loading time of the feeders, depending on the number of animals feeding at the same time; Fig. 6a illustrates the distribution of the relative loading time for each drinker. A value of 0 corresponds to zero loading (animals not feeding). These distributions not only demonstrate feeding or drinking behavior of the animals, but also indicate technical malfunctions of the equipment.

Figure 6b represents the distribution of animal activity in the pen. A permanently low degree of activity at certain time intervals can potentially signal a health status of the animals in the pen. Conversely, bursts of activity demonstrate abnormal behavior.

Figure 6c shows the animal weight dynamic. We used data gathered over 8 days, with the weight of the animals measured over a two-hour time interval. It can be noticed that the daily weight gain of the pig fluctuates in a larger range than the real weight gain. This effect is caused by high animal density, overlaps, and, consequently, partial unobservability of the animals. It is worth noting that

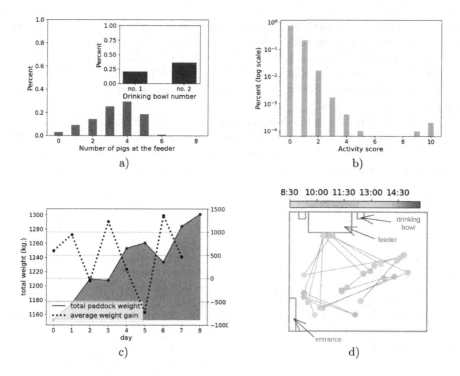

Fig. 6. Tools of analysis. a) distribution of relative loading time of feeders and drinkers; b) distribution of degrees of activity; c) dynamic of changes in total weight of animals and average weight gain, d) dynamics of the density of the accumulation of animals in the pen.

when averaging the weight gain over a weekly period, the daily weight gain amounts to an average of 600 g, which matches the true values.

Fig. 6d shows the patterns of animal crowding between 8:30 and 16:30. This tool not only sheds light on the routine of the animals (sleeping/feeding), but also provides information about hierarchical patterns, indirectly indicates thermal comfort, signals jostling, etc.

6   Conclusion

This work has proposed a video data processing pipeline that solves the basic tasks of precision pig farming. It demonstrates solutions for basic low-level tasks, such as instance segmentation, tracking, estimation of object density distribution, weight measurement. The Mask-R CNN neural network has been adapted to high-density scenes and trained to solve the problem of instance segmentation. The pre-trained network demonstrates high accuracy and stability of segmentation. For tracking, we have employed an approach based on the segmentation model, weighted bipartite graph, and the Hungarian algorithm. The resulting tracker accuracy has proven sufficient for short-term tracking. A solution to the problem of measuring the total weight of animals has been found based on the area of the segmentation mask and the 2nd-order polynomial regression model. The resulting error of the algorithm does not exceed 4.3% of the real weight of the animals. For object density estimation, the high-accuracy CSRNet neural network has been trained.

Based on the resulting low-level video data pipeline, several tools of analysis have been developed to generate relevant high-level information for the farm's staff. The performance of some of these tools is outlined in the paper. Finally, a prototype of the software package has been developed and tested at the Agro-Belogorye facilities.

The authors express their gratitude to the anonymous reviewers for their helpful comments and suggestions.

References

1. Bergamini, L., et al.: Extracting accurate long-term behavior changes from a large pig dataset. In: 16th International Joint Conference on Computer Vision, Imaging and Computer Graphics Theory and Applications, VISIGRAPP 2021, pp. 524–533. SciTePress (2021)
2. Bernardin, K., Elbs, A., Stiefelhagen, R.: Multiple object tracking performance metrics and evaluation in a smart room environment. In: Sixth IEEE International Workshop on Visual Surveillance, in conjunction with ECCV, vol. 90. Citeseer (2006)
3. Chen, C., et al.: Detection of aggressive behaviours in pigs using a RealSence depth sensor. Comput. Electron. Agric. **166**, 105003 (2019)
4. Chen, C., Zhu, W., Steibel, J., Siegford, J., Han, J., Norton, T.: Recognition of feeding behaviour of pigs and determination of feeding time of each pig by a video-based deep learning method. Comput. Electron. Agric. **176**, 105642 (2020)
5. Cheng, H.K., Chung, J., Tai, Y.W., Tang, C.K.: CascadePSP: toward class-agnostic and very high-resolution segmentation via global and local refinement. In: Proceedings of the IEEE/CVF Conference on Computer Vision and Pattern Recognition, pp. 8890–8899 (2020)
6. D'Eath, R.B., et al.: Automatic early warning of tail biting in pigs: 3D cameras can detect lowered tail posture before an outbreak. PLoS ONE **13**(4), e0194524 (2018)
7. Garcia, R., Aguilar, J., Toro, M., Pinto, A., Rodriguez, P.: A systematic literature review on the use of machine learning in precision livestock farming. Comput. Electron. Agric. **179**, 105826 (2020)
8. Geirhos, R., Rubisch, P., Michaelis, C., Bethge, M., Wichmann, F.A., Brendel, W.: Imagenet-trained cnns are biased towards texture; increasing shape bias improves accuracy and robustness. arXiv preprint arXiv:1811.12231 (2018)
9. Ghiasi, G., et al.: Simple copy-paste is a strong data augmentation method for instance segmentation. In: Proceedings of the IEEE/CVF Conference on Computer Vision and Pattern Recognition, pp. 2918–2928 (2021)
10. Gómez, Y., et al.: A systematic review on validated precision livestock farming technologies for pig production and its potential to assess animal welfare. Front. Vet. Sci. **8**, 660565 (2021)

11. He, K., Gkioxari, G., Dollár, P., Girshick, R.: Mask R-CNN. In: Proceedings of the IEEE International Conference on Computer Vision, pp. 2961–2969 (2017)
12. Hermann, K., Chen, T., Kornblith, S.: The origins and prevalence of texture bias in convolutional neural networks. Adv. Neural. Inf. Process. Syst. **33**, 19000–19015 (2020)
13. Hu, Z., Yang, H., Lou, T.: Dual attention-guided feature pyramid network for instance segmentation of group pigs. Comput. Electron. Agric. **186**, 106140 (2021)
14. Islam, M.A., et al.: Shape or texture: understanding discriminative features in CNNs. arXiv preprint arXiv:2101.11604 (2021)
15. Jensen, D.B., Pedersen, L.J.: Automatic counting and positioning of slaughter pigs within the pen using a convolutional neural network and video images. Comput. Electron. Agric. **188**, 106296 (2021)
16. Kashiha, M., et al.: Automatic weight estimation of individual pigs using image analysis. Comput. Electron. Agric. **107**, 38–44 (2014)
17. Lee, J., Jin, L., Park, D., Chung, Y.: Automatic recognition of aggressive behavior in pigs using a kinect depth sensor. Sensors **16**(5), 631 (2016)
18. Leonard, S.M., Xin, H., Brown-Brandl, T.M., Ramirez, B.C.: Development and application of an image acquisition system for characterizing sow behaviors in farrowing stalls. Comput. Electron. Agric. **163**, 104866 (2019)
19. Li, Y., Zhang, X., Chen, D.: CSRNet: dilated convolutional neural networks for understanding the highly congested scenes. In: Proceedings of the IEEE Conference on Computer Vision and Pattern Recognition, pp. 1091–1100 (2018)
20. Nasirahmadi, A., Hensel, O., Edwards, S., Sturm, B.: A new approach for categorizing pig lying behaviour based on a delaunay triangulation method. Animal **11**(1), 131–139 (2017)
21. Nasirahmadi, A., Richter, U., Hensel, O., Edwards, S., Sturm, B.: Using machine vision for investigation of changes in pig group lying patterns. Comput. Electron. Agric. **119**, 184–190 (2015)
22. Nasirahmadi, A., et al.: Deep learning and machine vision approaches for posture detection of individual pigs. Sensors **19**(17), 3738 (2019)
23. Pezzuolo, A., Guarino, M., Sartori, L., González, L.A., Marinello, F.: On-barn pig weight estimation based on body measurements by a kinect v1 depth camera. Comput. Electron. Agric. **148**, 29–36 (2018)
24. Ro-Main: automatic pig counter (2023). https://ro-main.com/our-products/smart-counting-for-farms/. Accessed 06 May 2023
25. Seo, J., Ahn, H., Kim, D., Lee, S., Chung, Y., Park, D.: EmbeddedPigDet–fast and accurate pig detection for embedded board implementations. Appl. Sci. **10**(8), 2878 (2020)
26. Shao, H., Pu, J., Mu, J.: Pig-posture recognition based on computer vision: dataset and exploration. Animals **11**(5), 1295 (2021)
27. Shi, C., Teng, G., Li, Z.: An approach of pig weight estimation using binocular stereo system based on LabVIEW. Comput. Electron. Agric. **129**, 37–43 (2016)
28. Stukelj, M., Hajdinjak, M., Pusnik, I.: Stress-free measurement of body temperature of pigs by using thermal imaging-useful fact or wishful thinking. Comput. Electron. Agric. **193**, 106656 (2022)
29. Tian, M., Guo, H., Chen, H., Wang, Q., Long, C., Ma, Y.: Automated pig counting using deep learning. Comput. Electron. Agric. **163**, 104840 (2019)
30. Tu, S., et al.: Automated behavior recognition and tracking of group-housed pigs with an improved DeepSORT method. Agriculture **12**(11), 1907 (2022)
31. Walter, P., Herther, M.: Nine trends transforming the agribusiness industry. Executive Insights **19**, 62 (2017)

32. van der Zande, L.E., Guzhva, O., Rodenburg, T.B.: Individual detection and tracking of group housed pigs in their home pen using computer vision. Front. Anim. Sci. **2**, 669312 (2021)
33. Zhang, J., Zhuang, Y., Ji, H., Teng, G.: Pig weight and body size estimation using a multiple output regression convolutional neural network: a fast and fully automatic method. Sensors **21**(9), 3218 (2021)
34. Zhang, L., Gray, H., Ye, X., Collins, L., Allinson, N.: Automatic individual pig detection and tracking in pig farms. Sensors **19**(5), 1188 (2019)
35. Zhang, Y., et al.: ByteTrack: multi-object tracking by associating every detection box. In: Avidan, S., Brostow, G., Cissé, M., Farinella, G.M., Hassner, T. (eds.) ECCV 2022. LNCS, vol. 13682, pp. 1–21. Springer, Cham (2022). https://doi.org/10.1007/978-3-031-20047-2_1
36. Zhang, Z., Zhang, H., Liu, T.: Study on body temperature detection of pig based on infrared technology: a review. Artif. Intell. Agric. **1**, 14–26 (2019)

Nucleic Acid-Protein Interaction Prediction Using Geometric Deep Learning

Elizaveta Geraseva$^{(\boxtimes)}$ [ID] and Andrey Golovin [ID]

Bioengineering and Bioinformatics Department, M. V. Lomonosov Moscow State University, Moscow, Russia
{geraseva,golovin}@fbb.msu.ru

Abstract. In biology, it remains challenging to predict interactions between proteins and DNA or RNA. When it comes to nucleic acids, existing methods of binding site identification or interaction prediction are inefficient, especially in minor cases, such as aptamer binding. In order to predict NA-protein interactions, we use a deep-learning framework called dMaSIF. Therefore, we modified the atom encoding module to reflect atom positions and relationships more precisely and used parallel calculation to optimize training process. The framework showed effectiveness on two tasks: identifying NA binding sites and predicting NA-protein interactions. This approach can thereby be used to find potential NA binding sites, to perform NA-protein docking and virtual screening, etc.

Keywords: DNA-protein interaction · RNA-protein interaction

1 Introduction

Protein characterization through its surface is actively used in the analysis of protein interactions with other proteins and low molecular weight ligands since it can be said that the protein surface determines the interaction. The protein surface is characterized by curvature and physicochemical properties, such as electrostatic potential, hydrophobicity, etc.

Most methods based on protein surface analysis exploit so-called surface complementarity [1,2], as interacting surfaces tend to have opposite curvature and electrostatics. This feature is used in protein-protein docking [3], protein design [4] and so on.

Protein surfaces can also be processed using deep learning approaches to generate more general features. The masif approach is one of them [5]. In this approach, the surface is divided into radial patches of a fixed geodesic radius, onto which the surface characteristics are projected, and the patches are then processed by convolutional layers. Thus the surface enhanced new features representing not only local surface properties but its fingerprints.

V. Voevodin et al. (Eds.): RuSCDays 2023, LNCS 14389, pp. 239–251, 2023.
https://doi.org/10.1007/978-3-031-49435-2_17

The main disadvantage of methods based on surface analysis is the duration of both the calculation of the coordinates of the surface points and the calculation of its physicochemical and geometric characteristics. To overcome this disadvantage, there is a dmasif approach that allows calculating and sampling the molecular surface on-the-fly from a cloud of atomic points [6]. The calculation of chemical characteristics in this approach has been replaced by the calculation of quasi-chemical features using a multi layer perceptrone, which receives protein atoms as input. As a result, this approach makes it possible to process large collections of proteins in an end-to-end way, taking raw three-dimensional coordinates and chemical types of their atoms as input, eliminating the need for pre-calculated functions or tools.

The effectiveness of the approach was shown on two tasks in the field of structural bioinformatics of proteins: identification of interaction sites and prediction of protein-protein interactions (PPI). High performance has been achieved in both tasks.

The work aims to adapt the dmasif framework to predict the interaction of nucleic acids (NA) with the protein surface.

There are several NA binding site identification methods. Most of them are sequence-based [7–10], while those using 3D structure information are usually knowledge-centered [11–14], i.e. use evolutionary or motif information obtained from well-characterized NA binding proteins. This makes all these methods inefficient when applied to non-standard NA-binding proteins, such as aptamer targets, or minor NA-binding families. Pure surface-based methods also exist [15], but are time-consuming and efficient only for regular structures such as dsDNA. So, surface-based deep learning approach, such as dmasif, might be more efficient for identification of NA binding sites.

This approach can also be useful for NA-protein interaction prediction. There are a lot of structure-based methods aimed at ligand-protein and protein-protein interaction prediction, including classical surface-based methods [16–19] and deep learning methods on 3D structural data [20–24]. However, NA-protein interaction (NPI) prediction faces some problems that are difficult to solve using existing approaches. The dynamic nature of NA 3D structures or the large size of interaction surfaces are examples of such problems. These specifics limit the efficacy of methods, useful either for ligand-protein interaction or for PPI, when applied to NPI. This problem may be solved using surface fingerprints, which consider both local surface properties, independent of chain flexibility, and global context capturing a significant part of an interaction site.

Another potential application of the framework is NA-binding protein design. For example, we can use the framework to predict the probability of interaction of a certain type of nucleotide at each point on the surface. We can obtain a scoring function that estimates the binding of all possible NA sequences, thus dealing with an off-target effect.

2   Method

2.1   Architecture

Here we used a modified dmasif framework. Its detailed description can be found in the original paper [6]. In short, it consists of the following stages:

1. Sampling of surface points and normals (random sampling points in the neighborhood of protein atoms, optimizing their position using gradient descent on logsumexp distance function, subsampling and filtering).
2. Computation of mean and Gaussian curvatures at 5 scales.
3. Computation of quasi-chemical features of the protein surface using deep learning on protein atoms.
4. Using quasi-geodesic convolutions on surface points to calculate embeddings for each point.

Initially, the module for computation of quasi-chemical features works as follows. For each surface point, it takes 16 nearest atom centres encoded as one-hot vectors in $\mathbb{R}^6$ stacked with reversed distances to the surface point. These vectors in $\mathbb{R}^7$ are transformed using one three-layer FCNN (fully connected neural network), then summarized over the indices k = 1, ..., 16 and then applying a second FCNN to the result. This module is further called Atomnet.

To take into account atom-atomic interactions, atoms are encoded using not a simple FCNN, but a way similar to those described above, taking atoms instead of surface points, and finding nearest atoms for them. The resulting atom embeddings are further used to process surface points in the same way. This module is further called Atomnet_MP.

These two original modules were modified to take into account not only the distances to the nearest atoms but also the directions.

Thus, the first FCNN gets 16 nearest atom centres as one-hot encoded vectors x_k in $\mathbb{R}^6$. The outputs from the first FCNN are multiplied with natural vectors from surface points to atoms $\vec{r_k}$, divided by square lengths of the vectors, then summarized over the indices k = 1, ..., 16 with trainable coefficients A_k and scalarized by calculating a Euclidean distance over the 3 natural dimensions. The result is transformed with a second FCNN (Eq. 1). This module is further called Atomnet_V:

$$Y_i = FCNN_2(||\sum_{k=1}^{16} A_k FCNN_1(x_k)\frac{\vec{r_{ik}}}{r_{ik}^2}||) \tag{1}$$

This module was also upgraded to take into account atom-atomic interactions. For each atom embeddings are calculated using a module similar to described above, for atoms instead of surface points (Eq. 2). These embeddings are added to the encoded atoms and processed as that described above (Eq. 3). This module is further called Atomnet_V_MP:

$$E_k = FCNN_2(\|\sum_{m=1}^{16} A_m FCNN_1(x_m) \frac{\overrightarrow{r_{km}}}{r_{km}^2}\|) \tag{2}$$

$$Y_i = FCNN_4(\|\sum_{k=1}^{16} B_k(FCNN_3(x_k) + E_k) \frac{\overrightarrow{r_{ik}}}{r_{ik}^2}\|) \tag{3}$$

2.2 Dataset

Structures of DNA-protein complexes were taken from the NPIDB database [26]. The files of the structures in the biological assembly were downloaded, and only those protein chains that interact with DNA were selected (the interaction was determined from NPIDB contact data). Not chains, but proteins as a whole were taken as separate objects for training. This is because it was assumed that subunit interaction sites could also form DNA-protein contacts. Also, there was no cutoff for sequence identity, since the dataset is not very large; also, small differences in the sequence, in our opinion, are quite enough to ensure significant structural and functional differences.

The structures were stored as numpy arrays of coordinates, types of atoms and types of residues.

Structures with atoms less than 250 (it is assumed that such short peptides are unrepresentative) and greater than 30 000 (these structures greatly increase the calculation time) were discarded.

For each structure in the dataset, surface points were calculated once using the dmasif functional. For each point, the interaction label was determined (the type of nucleotide to which the atom closest to the point belongs, if it is closer than 5 angstroms). Thus, 5 labels were obtained: A, G, C, T and 0. Non-standard nucleotides were ignored. Proteins, in which the area of contact with DNA did not exceed 30 points or exceeded 75% of the surface, were discarded.

A list of representative structures for all pfam families found in NPIDB was added to the test dataset as well as structures with the aptamers, and the remaining structures were randomly divided into training and validation datasets (9:1). The final proportion of train:val:test was 4981:554:542.

The same procedure was done for RNA-protein complexes (the number of atoms was set between 1000 and 40 000, and labels were A, G, C, U and 0), obtaining the proportion 1932:215:287.

The protein-protein interaction (PPI) dataset from the masif paper was used for comparison [5].

2.3 Training

The framework was tested on the following tasks:

Identification of NA Binding Sites. To predict NA binding for each surface point, the described above framework was followed by a three-layer FCNN with one output channel (the same as in the original framework). The radius of a patch in the convolution module was set to 9 angstroms, and the number of convolution layers was set to 3. During training, BCELoss was used along with the Adam optimizer. Models were trained independently on DNA-protein and RNA-protein datasets, as well as on PPI dataset for comparison. All four modules described above for the computation of chemical features were tested. Since zero-class labels prevail, in each sample a random part of zero-class points equal to the number of points of a non-zero class was taken into account during loss computation. Random rotation augmentations were used for surface point sampling and training.

Identification of Nucleotide Specificity. To predict a particular nucleotide binding for each surface point, the framework was followed by a three-layer FCNN with five output channels. During training, FocalLoss was used. In each sample, a random part of zero-class points equal to the mean number of points of a non-zero class was taken into account during loss computation. Other parameters were the same as in the previous task.

Interaction Prediction. The framework is trained to achieve embeddings for protein and NA surface patches. This is so that by having two embeddings we can predict whether they are likely to interact in a complex. The framework includes two geodesic convolution modules (one for a straight surface, one for a complementary surface), and the dot product of two embeddings is taken as an output, which is to be maximized if the patches interact. Each partner of a protein-NA binding pair passes through both convolution modules, achieving two (straight and complementary) embeddings for each surface point. All interacting pairs of surface points as well as the corresponding number of random pairs were used for loss computation. During training BCELoss was used along with Lion [25] optimizer. The model was trained on the NA-protein dataset, as well as on the PPI dataset for comparison.

2.4   Implementation

The architectures are implemented using PyTorch [28] and KeOps [29] for fast geometric computations. PyTorch Geometric [30] is used for data processing and batching.

All models are trained on a single NVIDIA A100 SXM4 40 GB or NVIDIA GeForce RTX 3080. Also, parallel training on multiple GPUs is implemented using the Distributed Data Parallel module of PyTorch with NCCL backend [31]. Run times are measured on multiple NVIDIA A100 SXM4.

As every 3D structure constitutes a single data item, which consumes a significant amount of memory during computation, it is impossible to create large batches, so parallel training may be ineffective. So, two strategies were tested: to use the maximum possible batch size (e.g. 8) or to use a batch size equal to the number of GPUs. Testing was performed on a single epoch of PPI interaction task training.

3   Results

3.1   Identification of NA Binding Sites

Dmasif site prediction on the PPI dataset achieved 0.87 mean AUC on the test set. Models that include atom-atomic interactions information performed a subtle improvement (0.5%) compared with models that do not.

Table 1. AUC metrics for the binary model.

PPI site AUC	Atomnet	Atomnet_V	Atomnet_MP	Atomnet_V_MP
train	0.85097	0.84291	0.84885	0.85131
val	0.82853	0.84950	0.84844	0.84451
test	0.85479	0.86116	0.87042	0.86882
DNA site AUC	Atomnet	Atomnet_V	Atomnet_MP	Atomnet_V_MP
train	0.93929	0.93478	0.94281	0.94697
val	0.92086	0.92422	0.94349	0.94461
test	0.89681	0.90204	0.91618	0.92115
RNA site AUC	Atomnet	Atomnet_V	Atomnet_MP	Atomnet_V_MP
train	0.90825	0.90908	0.90456	0.91008
val	0.87347	0.90373	0.91391	0.91127
test	0.86878	0.87851	0.87936	0.88144

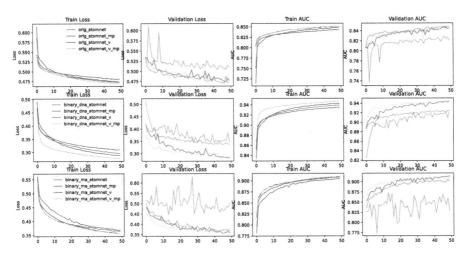

Fig. 1. Learning curves for prediction of interaction sites. Top - protein-protein interaction, middle - DNA-protein interaction, bottom - RNA-protein interaction.

Binary prediction of DNA-protein interaction achieved 0.92 AUC on the test set, while prediction of RNA-protein interaction achieved 0.88. Models that use atom-atomic distances perform better than modules that do not, and the model using both vector representations of distances and atom-atomic distances performs the best (Table 1). Learning curves of models with vector representation are more smooth (Fig. 1).

It can be considered that the models using vector representations and atom-atomic interactions reflect surface chemical features more precisely, resulting in more accurate prediction, so further calculations were made for Atomnet_V_MP only.

Models trained on DNA and RNA datasets can be used to predict RNA and DNA binding sites respectively (Fig. 2).

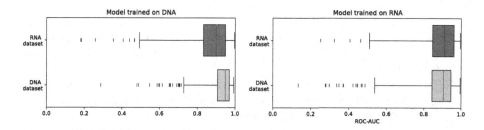

Fig. 2. Performance of models on different testing datasets.

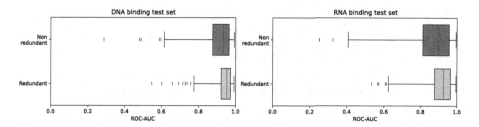

Fig. 3. Comparison of AUC scores in redundant and non-redundant proteins for DNA binding (left) and RNA binding (right).

The model trained on DNA shows higher performance on the DNA-binding dataset than on the other combinations, which could be the consequence of model overfitting on dsDNA binding sites, which form the majority of the DNA-binding dataset. But generally, the models do not distinguish between DNA and RNA interacting surfaces.

As mentioned above, the datasets were formed without any sequence identity cutoff due to the small number of structures in the training set. To check for overfitting on similar sequences, the testing datasets were divided into redundant and non-redundant proteins (by 90% sequence identity, using cd-hit-2d [27]).

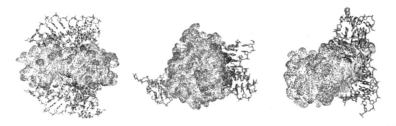

Fig. 4. NA binding prediction for proteins complexed with aptamers. Left - 5hru (LDH), center - 5ew1 (thrombin), right - 4ni7 (interleukin 6). Surface points colored from red to blue, corresponding to predicted binding probability from 0 to 1. (Color figure online)

As we can see in Fig. 3, prediction works better on redundant proteins, showing overfitting (Mann-Whitney test p-value 9.59e–07 for DNA binding and 1.64e–02 for RNA binding).

Nevertheless, the average performance on both redundant and non-redundant proteins is good enough to consider that the model catches some general regularities instead of memorizing common patterns.

The models show superior performance for families excluded from the training set and having no natural binding with NA, such as aptamer targets (Fig. 4).

3.2 Identification of Nucleotide Specificity

Multiclass prediction of DNA-protein interaction achieved 0.7 AUC (ovo) on the test set, while prediction of RNA-protein interaction achieved 0.72 AUC on the test set. Both cases show the same behaviour between different atom representations as in binary prediction (Table 2).

Table 2. AUC metrics for the multiclass model.

DNA npi AUC	Atomnet	Atomnet_V	Atomnet_MP	Atomnet_V_MP
train	0.70905	0.69914	0.70493	0.70185
val	0.69905	0.69762	0.70068	0.70296
test	0.68501	0.69148	0.69650	0.70123
RNA npi AUC	Atomnet	Atomnet_V	Atomnet_MP	Atomnet_V_MP
train	0.71098	0.70648	0.70544	0.71226
val	0.68984	0.70060	0.70239	0.71493
test	0.71108	0.71532	0.71818	0.72097

None of these models, anyway, have reliable predictive power.

The first potential reason for failure is that the backbone atoms of nucleic acids play the most significant role in NA-protein binding, while nucleobases are almost hidden from the protein surface and participate mainly in secondary structure formation.

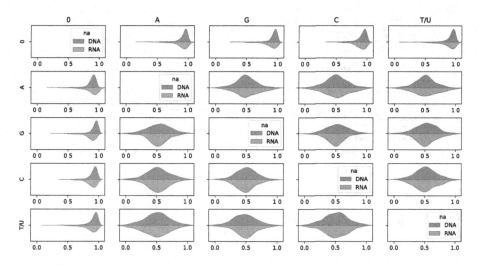

Fig. 5. Distribution of AUC ovo scores for all combinations of labels.

The second reason is that the complexes used for training are not exact matches between a protein and a particular sequence. Some proteins have no sequence specificity, others are complexed with non-optimal NA sequences.

The third reason is that the multiclass prediction scheme includes a label for non-binding surfaces, which is much easier to predict than positive nucleotide labels (as we can see from the previous task). So the model prefers to predict binding in general, ignoring the nucleotide prediction task (see Fig. 5).

3.3 Interaction Prediction

The PPI interaction prediction model achieved 0.88 mean AUC on the test set, as well as the NPI interaction model (Table 3). As we can see, atom-atomic interaction information improves scores (Fig. 6). Vectoric representations of atoms perform better in the case of NPI, preventing overfitting.

Table 3. AUC metrics for the interaction prediction model.

PPI AUC	Atomnet	Atomnet_V	Atomnet_MP	Atomnet_V_MP
train	0.89893	0.89127	0.90127	0.90448
val	0.89391	0.88808	0.89761	0.90305
test	0.87362	0.86474	0.87541	0.87767
NPI AUC	Atomnet	Atomnet_V	Atomnet_MP	Atomnet_V_MP
train	0.89722	0.89526	0.90900	0.91111
val	0.86739	0.89419	0.90696	0.91060
test	0.84242	0.85625	0.87837	0.87845

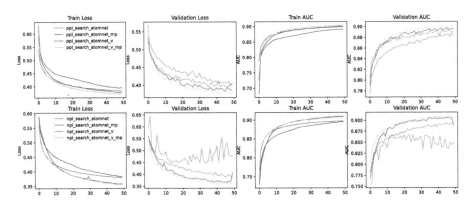

Fig. 6. Learning curves of interaction prediction models (top - PPI, bottom - NPI).

The higher performance of PPI interaction prediction comparing to the original paper [6] (0.87 vs 0.81), even despite using smaller patch radius (9 angstrom instead of 12), might be the result of the Lion optimizer application.

3.4 Parallel Training

Parallel training experiments are shown in Fig. 7. They show significant time savings when using a small number of GPUs in parallel (up to 3). As we can see, proportional batching does not offer benefits over maximum batch size. This is even when the maximum batch size is not divisible by the count of GPUs.

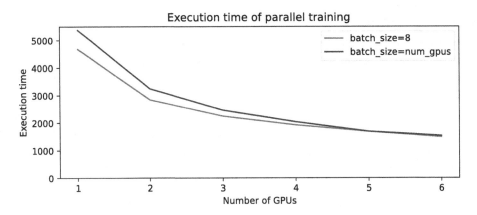

Fig. 7. Execution times for one epoch of PPI prediction training.

4   Conclusion

The nature of nucleic acids makes the surfaces of nucleic acids generally more uniform and less complex compared to the scale of protein surfaces in PPI. While proteins exhibit sidechain atoms, which possess highly diversified chemical features, nucleic acid surfaces are mainly formed of backbone atoms and a small range of similar nucleobases. Sometimes the simplicity of nucleic acid surfaces can be an advantage, as it allows for easier interpretation. But in machine learning approaches it may lead to overfitting, or lower performance.

The modules for quasi-chemical feature generation developed here may help overcome this problem. It has been shown that though they did not improve the result on PPI tasks, there was a quality gain on NPI tasks.

Previously it was shown that dmasif is effective for PPI prediction. Now we can assume that this approach can also be useful for NA-protein interaction analysis. NPI detection is solved well, providing opportunities for the identification of novel NA binding sites in known proteins, either responsible for previously unknown protein functions, or potential targets for aptamers.

Despite heterogeneous data, the dmasif approach also successfully solves NA-protein interaction prediction. Thus, we can assume that the model can be trained not only on proteins but also on other macromolecular compounds. This could lead to the creation of a universal molecular surface analysis tool.

In this particular case the framework may be used to generate embeddings for surface points. These embeddings can further be used to find potential nucleic acid binders of a protein and vice versa. It can be taken as a basis for the development of a new effective tool for NA-protein virtual screening, as contemporary virtual screening instruments are not quite suitable for NA-protein screening.

5   Code Availability

Both the code and scripts to reproduce the experiments of this paper are available at https://github.com/geraseva/masif_npi.

Acknowledgements. This research was done with the support of MSU Program of Development, Project No 23-SCH03-05. The research was carried out using the equipment of the shared research facilities of HPC computing resources at Lomonosov Moscow State University.

References

1. Lawrence, M.C., Colman, P.M.: Shape complementarity at protein/protein interfaces. J. Mol. Biol. **234**(4), 946–950 (1993)
2. McCoy, A.J., Epa, V.C., Colman, P.M.: Electrostatic complementarity at protein/protein interfaces. J. Mol. Biol. **268**(2), 570–584 (1997)
3. Chen, R., Weng, Z.: Docking unbound proteins using shape complementarity, desolvation, and electrostatics. Proteins: Struct. Function Bioinform. **47**(3), 281–294 (2002)

4. Scheck, A., et al.: RosettaSurfA surface-centric computational design approach. PLoS Comput. Biol. **18**(3), e1009178 (2022)
5. Gainza, P., Sverrisson, F., Monti, F., Rodola, E., Boscaini, D., Bronstein, M.M., Correia, B.E.: Deciphering interaction fingerprints from protein molecular surfaces using geometric deep learning. Nat. Methods **17**(2), 184–192 (2020)
6. Sverrisson, F., Feydy, J., Correia, B.E., Bronstein, M.M.: Fast end-to-end learning on protein surfaces. In Proceedings of the IEEE/CVF Conference on Computer Vision and Pattern Recognition, pp. 15272–15281 (2021)
7. Ozbek, P., Soner, S., Erman, B., Haliloglu, T.: DNABINDPROT: fluctuation-based predictor of DNA-binding residues within a network of interacting residues. Nucleic Acids Res. **38**(suppl_2), W417–W423 (2010)
8. Qiu, J., et al.: ProNA2020 predicts proteinDNA, proteinRNA, and protein protein binding proteins and residues from sequence. J. Mol. Biol. **432**(7), 2428–2443 (2020)
9. Zhang, F., Zhao, B., Shi, W., Li, M., Kurgan, L.: DeepDISOBind: accurate prediction of RNA-, DNA-and protein-binding intrinsically disordered residues with deep multi-task learning. Briefings Bioinform. **23**(1), bbab521 (2022)
10. Wang, N., Zhang, J., Liu, B.: IDRBP-PPCT: identifying nucleic acid-binding proteins based on position-specific score matrix and position-specific frequency matrix cross transformation. IEEE/ACM Trans. Comput. Biol. Bioinf. **19**(4), 2284–2293 (2021)
11. Nimrod, G., Schushan, M., Szilágyi, A., Leslie, C., Ben-Tal, N.: iDBPs: a web server for the identification of DNA binding proteins. Bioinformatics **26**(5), 692–693 (2010)
12. Chen, Y.C., Wright, J.D., Lim, C.: DR_bind: a web server for predicting DNA-binding residues from the protein structure based on electrostatics, evolution and geometry. Nucleic Acids Res. **40**(W1), W249–W256 (2012)
13. Gao, M., Skolnick, J.: DBD-Hunter: a knowledge-based method for the prediction of DNAprotein interactions. Nucleic Acids Res. **36**(12), 3978–3992 (2008)
14. Nagarajan, R., Ahmad, S., Michael Gromiha, M.: Novel approach for selecting the best predictor for identifying the binding sites in DNA binding proteins. Nucleic Acids Res. **41**(16), 7606–7614 (2013)
15. Tsuchiya, Y., Kinoshita, K., Nakamura, H.: PreDs: a server for predicting dsDNA-binding site on protein molecular surfaces. Bioinformatics **21**(8), 1721–1723 (2005)
16. Chen, R., Li, L., Weng, Z.: ZDOCK: an initial stage protein docking algorithm. Proteins Struct. Funct. Bioinform. **52**(1), 80–87 (2003)
17. Dominguez, C., Boelens, R., Bonvin, A.M.: HADDOCK: a protein protein docking approach based on biochemical or biophysical information. J. Am. Chem. Soc. **125**(7), 1731–1737 (2003)
18. Pierce, B., & Weng, Z. (2007). ZRANK: reranking protein docking predictions with an optimized energy function. Proteins: Structure, Function, and Bioinformatics, 67(4), 1078-1086
19. Keskin, O., Nussinov, R., Gursoy, A.: PRISM: protein-protein interaction prediction by structural matching, pp. 505–521. Methods and Protocols, Functional Proteomics (2008)
20. Wang, X., Terashi, G., Christoffer, C.W., Zhu, M., Kihara, D.: Protein docking model evaluation by 3D deep convolutional neural networks. Bioinformatics **36**(7), 2113–2118 (2020)
21. Jiang, M., et al.: Drugtarget affinity prediction using graph neural network and contact maps. RSC Adv. **10**(35), 20701–20712 (2020)

22. Wallach, I., Dzamba, M., Heifets, A.: AtomNet: a deep convolutional neural network for bioactivity prediction in structure-based drug discovery. arXiv preprint arXiv:1510.02855 (2015)
23. Fout, A., Byrd, J., Shariat, B., Ben-Hur, A.: Protein interface prediction using graph convolutional networks. In: Advances in Neural Information Processing Systems, 30 (2017)
24. Jiménez, J., Doerr, S., Martínez-Rosell, G., Rose, A.S., De Fabritiis, G.: DeepSite: protein-binding site predictor using 3D-convolutional neural networks. Bioinformatics 33(19), 3036–3042 (2017)
25. Chen, X., et al.: Symbolic discovery of optimization algorithms. arXiv preprint arXiv:2302.06675 (2023)
26. Kirsanov, D.D., Zanegina, O.N., Aksianov, E.A., Spirin, S.A., Karyagina, A.S., Alexeevski, A.V.: NPIDB: nucleic acidprotein interaction database. Nucleic Acids Res. 41(D1), D517–D523 (2012)
27. Li, W., Godzik, A.: Cd-hit: a fast program for clustering and comparing large sets of protein or nucleotide sequences. Bioinformatics 22(13), 1658–1659 (2006)
28. Paszke, A., et al.: Pytorch: an imperative style, high-performance deep learning library. In: Advances in Neural Information Processing Systems, 32 (2019)
29. Feydy, J., Glaunès, A., Charlier, B., Bronstein, M.: Fast geometric learning with symbolic matrices. Adv. Neural. Inf. Process. Syst. 33, 14448–14462 (2020)
30. Fey, M., Lenssen, J.E.: Fast graph representation learning with PyTorch Geometric. arXiv preprint arXiv:1903.02428 (2019)
31. Jeaugey, S.: Nccl 2.0. In: GPU Technology Conference (GTC), vol. 2 (2017)

Parallel Algorithm for Incompressible Flow Simulation Based on the LS-STAG and Domain Decomposition Methods

Valeria Puzikova[1(✉)] and Ilia Marchevsky[2]

[1] YADRO, HPC Libraries Department, Moscow, Russia
v.puzikova@yadro.com
[2] Bauman Moscow State Technical University, Applied Mathematics Department,
Moscow, Russia
iliamarchevsky@mail.ru

Abstract. The problem of incompressible flow simulation around rigid bodies of arbitrary shape is considered. The LS-STAG immersed boundary method is used for its numerical solving. This method is based on the accurate discretization of the governing equations in cells that are cut by the boundary. The aim of the research is to develop parallel algorithm for incompressible flow simulation based on the LS-STAG and the Schur complement methods to accelerate the most time-consuming parts of the LS-STAG algorithm connected with solving of the Poisson equation for the pressure function and the Helmholtz equation for velocities prediction. The developed algorithm is implemented in a software package on C++ using OpenMP technology for parallelization. The problem of two-dimensional flow simulation around a fixed circular airfoil was considered to validate the developed parallel algorithm.

Keywords: LS-STAG method · Domain decomposition method · Incompressible viscous flows · Parallel computations · Immersed boundary method · FGMRES method · Large sparse system

1 Introduction

The immersed boundary methods [1] are quite popular in numerical flow simulation around bodies of arbitrary shape. In such methods, the computational grid is not connected with the immersed boundary, as a result there is no need to rebuild it even if the bodies are movable. One of these methods is the LS-STAG method [2], which uses the level-set function [3,4] to represent the complex shape of the immersed boundary. Its main advantages are the preservation of the five-point structure of a stencil, which allows using efficient solvers for systems of linear equations, as well as good conservation properties due to discretization and solution of the governing equations at all cut-cells. At the moment, a number of modifications of the LS-STAG method have been developed, which

© The Author(s), under exclusive license to Springer Nature Switzerland AG 2023
V. Voevodin et al. (Eds.): RuSCDays 2023, LNCS 14389, pp. 252–266, 2023.
https://doi.org/10.1007/978-3-031-49435-2_18

make it possible to solve coupled hydroelastic problems [5–7], as well as to simulate the flows of non-Newtonian fluids [8,9]. Some modifications are adapted for simulation of high-Reynolds flows using well-known approaches and turbulence models [10,11].

The most time-consuming parts in numerical flow simulation using the LS-STAG method are solving of the Poisson equation for the pressure function and the Helmholtz equation for velocities prediction. Various domain decomposition methods can be used   [12]. This method allows to solve a series of problems in non-overlapping subdomains instead of the problem in the original computational domain. In this approach the boundary conditions at the boundaries between subdomains, called as interface ones, are taken into account implicitly. At each outer iteration two problems are solved for each subdomain and one system is solved for interface. The problems can be solved using efficient Krylov subspace methods [13,14] with various preconditioners [13,15–17]. In this research the original implementation of these methods is used, but the corresponding sparse problems can also be solved by using HPC libraries developed by such companies as Intel, YADRO, etc.

The aim of the research is to develop parallel algorithm for incompressible flow simulation based on the LS-STAG and the Schur complement methods. Although the LS-STAG method allows to simulate three-dimensional flows [18, 19], as well as to solve coupled hydroelastic problems taking into account airfoils motion, we consider one of the simplest two-dimensional test cases to validate the developed parallel algorithm.

2   The Test Problem Statement

Let us consider a flow around a fixed circular airfoil in the rectangular computational domain (Fig. 1). The problem is well investigated both numerically [20–22] and experimentally [23], thus it can be considered as a test for validation of a new computational algorithms.

A two-dimensional viscous incompressible flow with constant density in a domain Ω with a boundary Γ is described by the Navier – Stokes equations:

$$\nabla \cdot \boldsymbol{v} = 0, \qquad \frac{\partial \boldsymbol{v}}{\partial t} + (\boldsymbol{v} \cdot \nabla)\boldsymbol{v} = -\nabla p + \frac{1}{\mathrm{Re}}\Delta \boldsymbol{v}, \qquad \boldsymbol{r} \in \Omega. \qquad (1)$$

Here t is the time, $\boldsymbol{r} = (x,y)$ is the radius vector, p is the pressure, $\boldsymbol{v} = (u,v)$ is the velocity, Re is the Reynolds number (all variables are dimensionless). The boundary conditions are the following:

$$\begin{cases} \dfrac{\partial u}{\partial \boldsymbol{n}}\bigg|_{\Gamma^n} = \dfrac{\partial u}{\partial \boldsymbol{n}}\bigg|_{\Gamma^s} = 0, \quad v\big|_{\Gamma^n} = v\big|_{\Gamma^s} = 0, \\[3mm] u\big|_{\Gamma^w} = V_\infty, \; v\big|_{\Gamma^w} = 0, \quad \dfrac{\partial \boldsymbol{v}}{\partial \boldsymbol{n}}\bigg|_{\Gamma^e} = \mathbf{0}, \; \boldsymbol{v}\big|_K = \mathbf{0}. \end{cases}$$

Here Γ^e, Γ^n, Γ^w and Γ^s are east, north, west and south boundaries of the computational domain, respectively, K is the immersed boundary, corresponding to the airfoil, n is the outward-pointing normal to the boundary. To simulate the flow around the airfoil in an unbounded domain, it is necessary to choose a sufficiently large computational domain. Numerical experiments show that the domain parameters (Fig. 1) can be chosen as follows: $Y_l = Y_u = 12D$, $X_f = 8D$, $X_b = 15D$, where D is the airfoil diameter. Such computational domain is large enough for obtaining results that are practically independent on the domain size.

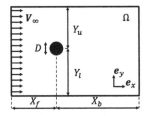

Fig. 1. Computational domain

3   Main Ideas of the LS-STAG Method

In the LS-STAG method [2] the Cartesian grid with $\Omega_{i,j} = (x_{i-1}, x_i) \times (y_{j-1}, y_j)$ cells is introduced in the rectangular computational domain. These cells are considered as control volumes for discretization of the continuity equation. The discrete pressure is assumed to be piecewise constant over cells, therefore values $p_{i,j}$ can be referred to the centers $r_{i,j}^c = (x_i^c, y_j^c)$ of cells $\Omega_{i,j}$. This location is used only for visualization purpose and will never be used explicitly for the discretization. Unknown components $u_{i,j}$ and $v_{i,j}$ of velocity field v are computed in the middle of the cell fluid faces (Fig. 2). So, the so-called x-grid and y-grid with cells $\Omega_{i,j}^u = (x_i^c, x_{i+1}^c) \times (y_{j-1}, y_j)$ and $\Omega_{i,j}^v = (x_{i-1}, x_i) \times (y_j^c, y_{j+1}^c)$, respectively, are also introduced in addition to the main grid. These cells are considered as control volumes for the momentum equation. Thus, if $G = N \cdot M$ is the number of the main grid cells, then the x-grid and the y-grid consist of $G_x = (N-1) \cdot M$ and $G_y = N \cdot (M-1)$ cells, respectively.

In order to describe the immersed boundary position a signed level-set function $\varphi(r)$ is used in the LS-STAG method. Its absolute value is equal to the distance between the point and the immersed boundary and its values are negative in the fluid region and positive in the solid one. The immersed boundary is represented by a line segment on the cell $\Omega_{i,j}$. Its endpoints are defined by linear interpolation between two values of the level-set function in adjacent corners of the main grid cell. Such cell is called as cut-cell. In two-dimensional case there are three basic types of cut-cells: trapezoidal, triangular and pentagonal cells (Fig. 2). The common compass notation is used for cut-cells.

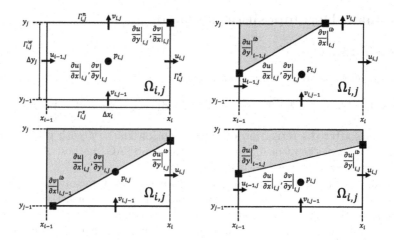

Fig. 2. Location of the variables discretization points on the LS-STAG mesh: fluid, N-W pentagonal, N-W triangular, and N trapezoidal cells

The governing equations are discretized in space and solved for all types of cells. As a result, the Eqs. (1) are replaced by the following:

$$\begin{cases} \mathcal{D}U + \overline{U}^{ib} = 0, \\ \dfrac{d}{dt}(\mathcal{M}U) + (\mathcal{C}[\overline{U}]U + \mathcal{S}^{ib,c}) + \mathcal{G}P - \nu(\mathcal{K}U + \mathcal{S}^{ib,\nu}) = 0. \end{cases} \quad (2)$$

Here U and P are the vectors that contain the unknown velocity components and the pressure values, the diagonal mass matrix $\mathcal{M}$ holds areas of cells, matrix $\mathcal{C}$ represents the skew-symmetric discretization of the convective fluxes, $\mathcal{G} = (-\mathcal{D})^T$ is the discrete pressure gradient, $\mathcal{K}$ represents the diffusive, $\mathcal{D}$ is the matrix that corresponds to the divergence operator, $\overline{U}$ and $\overline{U}^{ib}$ denote vectors of mass flux values through the fluid and solid part of the cell boundary, resprectively. Since we consider a fixed airfoil, the term $\overline{U}^{ib}$ vanishes.

The time integration of the system (2) is performed using a method based on the first-order predictor-corrector scheme. The predictor step leads to discrete analogue of the Helmholtz equation for velocities prediction $\tilde{U}$ at time step $t_{n+1} = (n+1)\Delta t$ and the corrector step leads to the discrete analogue of the Poisson equation for pressure function $\Phi = \Delta t(P^{n+1} - P^n)$:

$$\frac{\mathcal{M}(\tilde{U} - U^n)}{\Delta t} + \mathcal{C}[\overline{U}^n]U^n + \mathcal{S}^{ib,c,n} - \mathcal{D}^T P^n - \nu(\mathcal{K}\tilde{U} + \mathcal{S}^{ib,\nu,n}) = 0; \quad (3)$$

$$A\Phi = \mathcal{D}\tilde{U} + \overline{U}^{ib,n+1}, \quad A = -\mathcal{D}\mathcal{M}^{-1}\mathcal{D}^T. \quad (4)$$

Then velocity and pressure values at the next time step can be computed:

$$U^{n+1} = \tilde{U} + \mathcal{M}^{-1}\mathcal{D}^T\Phi, \quad P^{n+1} = P^n + \frac{\Phi}{\Delta t}. \quad (5)$$

4   Domain Decomposition Method

4.1   Main Ideas

Let us consider a system of linear equations

$$Ax = b, \qquad x, b \in \mathbb{R}^{N_d}, \qquad A \in M(\mathbb{R})_{N_d \times N_d}, \qquad \det A \neq 0, \qquad (6)$$

that appears after discretization of some equation $Lu = f$ with differential or integro-differential operator L. In case of the LS-STAG method A is a sparse matrix with nonzero entries on five diagonals.

Our aim is to develop a parallel algorithm for iterative solving of the system (6). Let us assume that the computational system consists of P nodes. According to the Schur complement method, the whole computational domain is divided into nonoverlapping subdomains such that there is only one cell layer between each pair of neighboring subdomains. These cells are called as 'interface' ones. The unknown vector x is partitioned into P nonoverlapping subvectors $x_p \in \mathbb{R}^{N_p}$ ($p = \overline{0, P - 1}$), which correspond to the subdomains cells. The unknowns corresponding to interface cells are denoted as $x_s \in \mathbb{R}^{N_s}$, ($N_s + \sum\limits_{p=0}^{P-1} N_p = N_d$). It should be noted that these unknowns don't belong to any of subdomain cells. It is necessary to reorder the unknowns within subdomains and within the interface, and to define the relationships between these local numeration and the original global one. For the LS-STAG method the simplest way of transfer between the local numeration and global one is shown in Fig. 3.

Let the main grid contains N cells along the Ox and M ones along the Oy. It is supposed that the subdomain Ω_p contains N cells along the Ox and M_p ones along the Oy ($p = \overline{0, P - 1}$). Since $(P - 1)$ interface rows Γ_i ($i = \overline{0, P - 2}$) are placed between P subdomains, so that $\Omega = \bigcup\limits_{p=0}^{P-1} \Omega_p \cup \left(\bigcup\limits_{i=0}^{P-2} \Gamma_i \right)$, $\sum\limits_{p=0}^{P-1} M_p = M - (P - 1)$,

$$M_p = m = \left[\frac{M}{P} \right] - 1, \quad p = \overline{0, P - 2}, \quad M_{P-1} = M - (P - 1)(m + 1). \qquad (7)$$

Here $[z]$ is a floor of z. Thus,

$$N_p = N \cdot M_p, \qquad N_s = N(P - 1). \qquad (8)$$

To implement the Schur complement method, we also introduce the following reordering of unknowns in the global computational domain. Control volumes are numerated from left to right across all subdomains from bottom to up, and then similarly all control volumes on the interface rows are numerated (Fig. 4). So, vector of unknowns from (6) can be represented as follows:

$$x = [x_0, x_1, \ldots, x_{P-1}, x_s]^T. \qquad (9)$$

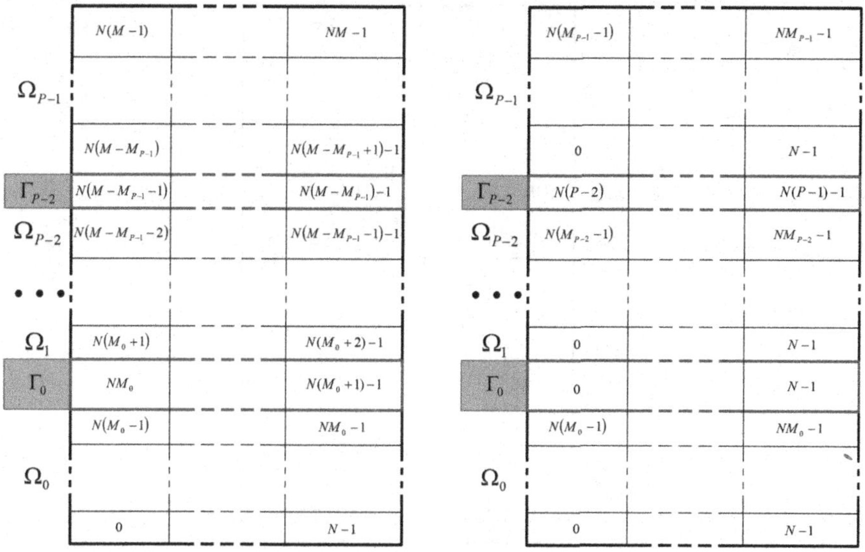

Left grid (global numeration):

Ω_{P-1}	$N(M-1)$			$NM-1$
	$N(M-M_{P-1})$			$N(M-M_{P-1}+1)-1$
Γ_{P-2}	$N(M-M_{P-1}-1)$			$N(M-M_{P-1})-1$
Ω_{P-2}	$N(M-M_{P-1}-2)$			$N(M-M_{P-1}-1)-1$
$\cdots$				
Ω_1	$N(M_0+1)$			$N(M_0+2)-1$
Γ_0	NM_0			$N(M_0+1)-1$
	$N(M_0-1)$			NM_0-1
Ω_0	0			$N-1$

Right grid (local numeration):

Ω_{P-1}	$N(M_{P-1}-1)$			$NM_{P-1}-1$
	0			$N-1$
Γ_{P-2}	$N(P-2)$			$N(P-1)-1$
Ω_{P-2}	$N(M_{P-2}-1)$			$NM_{P-2}-1$
$\cdots$				
Ω_1	0			$N-1$
Γ_0	0			$N-1$
	$N(M_0-1)$			NM_0-1
Ω_0	0			$N-1$

Fig. 3. Dividing of the computational domain into subdomains with global (left) and local (right) numeration of control volumes

By consistent reordering the matrix A and the right-hand side b vector, we obtain that (6) takes the following form:

$$\begin{bmatrix} A_{0,0} & \Theta & \cdots & \Theta & A_{0,s} \\ \Theta & A_{1,1} & \cdots & \Theta & A_{1,s} \\ \vdots & \vdots & \ddots & \vdots & \vdots \\ \Theta & \Theta & \cdots & A_{P-1,P-1} & A_{P-1,s} \\ A_{s,0} & A_{s,1} & \cdots & A_{s,P-1} & A_{s,s} \end{bmatrix} \cdot \begin{bmatrix} x_0 \\ x_1 \\ \vdots \\ x_{P-1} \\ x_s \end{bmatrix} = \begin{bmatrix} b_0 \\ b_1 \\ \vdots \\ b_{P-1} \\ b_s \end{bmatrix} \qquad (10)$$

Here $b_p \in \mathbb{R}^{N_p}$ $(p = \overline{0,P-1})$; $b_s \in \mathbb{R}^{N_s}$; $\Theta \in M(\mathbb{R})_{N_p \times N_p}$ is a zero matrix; $A_{p,p} \in M(\mathbb{R})_{N_p \times N_p}$, $A_{p,s} \in M(\mathbb{R})_{N_p \times N_s}$, $A_{s,p} \in M(\mathbb{R})_{N_s \times N_p}$ $(p = \overline{0,P-1})$ and $A_{s,s} \in M(\mathbb{R})_{N_s \times N_s}$ are sparse matrices for which the portrait and relation to the LS-STAG matrix A will be described below.

We apply the Gaussian elimination method to the system (10), formally treating the block matrices as ordinary scalars, i.e. the block Gaussian method is applied. As a result, the last block equation of (10),

$$[A_{s,0}, A_{s,1}, \ldots, A_{s,P-1}, A_{s,s}] \cdot [x_0, x_1, \ldots, x_{P-1}, x_s]^T = b_s, \qquad (11)$$

takes the following form:

$$[\Theta_s, \Theta_s, \ldots, \Theta_s, \tilde{A}_{s,s}] \cdot [x_0, x_1, \ldots, x_{P-1}, x_s]^T = \tilde{b}_s. \qquad (12)$$

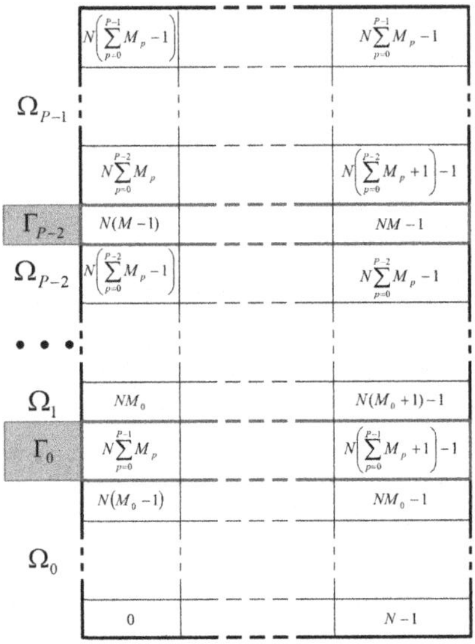

Fig. 4. Splitting of the computational domain and reodering of global numeration

Here $\Theta_s \in M(\mathbb{R})_{N_s \times N_p}$ is the zero matrix;

$$\tilde{A}_{s,s} = A_{s,s} - \sum_{p=0}^{P-1} A_{s,p} A_{p,p}^{-1} A_{p,s}, \quad \tilde{A}_{s,s} \in M(\mathbb{R})_{N_s \times N_s}; \tag{13}$$

$$\tilde{b}_s = b_s - \sum_{p=0}^{P-1} A_{s,p} A_{p,p}^{-1} b_p, \quad \tilde{b}_s \in \mathbb{R}^{N_s}. \tag{14}$$

So, we have the following linear system for interface unknowns:

$$\tilde{A}_{s,s} x_s = \tilde{b}_s. \tag{15}$$

It means that the interface unknowns can be defined as the solution of system (15) before computing of unknowns in subdomains. After the components of the vector x_s are computed, each of vectors x_p $(p = \overline{0, P-1})$ can be found as a solution of the following system of linear algebraic equations:

$$A_{p,p} x_p = b_p - A_{p,s} x_s. \tag{16}$$

This system is obtained by substitution of the x_s into the p-th block equation from the system (10).

The computation of the matrix $\tilde{A}_{s,s}$ is performed once at the stage of data preparing for the simulation according to (13). It is denoted that $\tilde{A}_{s,s}^p = A_{s,p} A_{p,p}^{-1} A_{p,s}$ $(p = \overline{0, P-1})$. Then, (13) takes the following form:

$$\tilde{A}_{s,s} = A_{s,s} - \sum_{p=0}^{P-1} \tilde{A}_{s,s}^p. \tag{17}$$

In the computational algorithm, all elements of the matrix $\tilde{A}^p_{s,s}$ are initialized with zeros. We denote the c-th column of the matrix $A_{p,s}$ as $[A_{p,s}]_c$. If $[A_{p,s}]_c$ contains at least one nonzero element, then the following system should be solved:

$$A_{p,p}t = [A_{p,s}]_c. \tag{18}$$

Then the c-th column of $\tilde{A}^p_{s,s}$ matrix can be computed as follows:

$$[\tilde{A}^p_{s,s}]_c = A_{s,p}t. \tag{19}$$

Some features of the LS-STAG matrix $\tilde{A}^p_{s,s}$ computation are described below.

The same approach is used to construct the right-hand side $\tilde{b}_s$ for the interface system (10) at each time step: we denote $\tilde{b}^p_s = A_{s,p}A^{-1}_{p,p}b_p$ $(p = \overline{0, P-1})$, so (14) takes the following form:

$$\tilde{b}_s = b_s - \sum_{p=0}^{P-1} \tilde{b}^p_s. \tag{20}$$

In this case, it is necessary to solve a system of linear algebraic equations in the corresponding subdomain to compute $\tilde{b}^p_s$:

$$A_{p,p}t = b_p \tag{21}$$

and then we multiply the obtained solution by the sparse matrix:

$$\tilde{b}^p_s = A_{s,p}t. \tag{22}$$

So, the algorithm of the Schur complement method takes the following form:

Algorithm 1. DDM algorithm

1: ...
2: **for** $p = \overline{0, P-1}$ **do**
3:     **for** $c = \overline{0, N-1}$ **do**
4:         $A_{p,p}t = [A_{p,s}]_c$
5:         $\left[\tilde{A}^p_{s,s}\right]_c = A_{s,p}t$
6:     **end for**
7: **end for**
8: $\tilde{A}_{s,s} = A_{s,s} - \sum_{p=0}^{P-1} \tilde{A}^p_{s,s}$
9: ...
10: **while** (time steps) **do**
11:     ...

12:     **for** $p = \overline{0, P-1}$ **do**
13:         $A_{p,p}t = b_p$
14:         $\tilde{b}^p_s = A_{s,p}t;$
15:     **end for**
16:     $\tilde{b}_s = b_s - \sum_{p=0}^{P-1} \tilde{b}^p_s$
17:     $\tilde{A}_{s,s}x_s = \tilde{b}_s$
18:     **for** $p = \overline{0, P-1}$ **do**
19:         $A_{p,p}x_p = b_p - A_{p,s}x_s;$
20:     **end for**
21:     ...
22: **end while**

4.2 Computing LS-STAG Matrices for Subdomains and Interface Problems

Now let us take into account specific features of the matrix portrait for systems of linear algebraic equations, arising in the LS-STAG-discretization in case of two-dimensional problems. It is necessary to describe sparse matrices' $A_{p,p}$, $A_{p,p}$, $A_{p,s}$, $A_{p,s}$, $\tilde{A}_{s,s}$ portraits and to obtain computational formulae for their elements.

The following notations are used to describe the coefficients of matrices for systems of linear algebraic equations arising from the LS-STAG method. Coefficients of the linear equation for the control volume $\Omega_{i,j}$ are stored in the matrix row with the number $i + N \cdot j$. Here i and j are indices of the cell in horizontal and vertical directions. We denote the diagonal element as $A_P(i,j)$, the element $A_W(i,j)$ is placed in the column which number is equal to the index of the control volume neighboring with the $\Omega_{i,j}$ from the west, the element $A_S(i,j)$ is placed in the column that corresponds to the south neighbouring cell, etc. In the two-dimensional case the LS-STAG-discretization provides a five-point stencil, so the matrix A contains diagonals A_P, A_S, A_N, A_W, A_E. Since subdomains are horizontal bands of the computational domain (Fig. 3, left), to determine the local number for the control volume in the subdomain (Fig. 3, right), we need to calculate only the local number of the row at the Oy direction while i remains the same for the whole grid.

First, it is required to determine the relationship between the $A_{p,p}$ ($p = \overline{0, P-1}$) and A matrices. Taking into account expressions (7) for M_p, we obtaine that the p-th subdomain corresponds to the values $j = \overline{j_{s,p}, j_{s,p} + M_p - 1}$ in the global numeration. Here $j_{s,p} = p(m+1)$. It means that the matrix $A_{p,p}$ must coincide with the block of the matrix A consisting of rows and columns, which numbers belong to $[N \cdot j_{s,p}, N(j_{s,p} + M_p) - 1] \times [N \cdot j_{s,p}, N(j_{s,p} + M_p) - 1]$ excluding the rows which correspond to the cells located in the first and last row of the subdomain: $A_{p,p}$ doesn't contain $A_S(i,j)$ for $j = j_{s,p}$ and $A_N(i,j)$ for $j = j_{s,p} + M_p - 1$. Thus, the matrix $A_{p,p}$ ($p = \overline{0, P-1}$) can be constructed as follows:

$$A_{p,p}|_P(i,j) = A_P(i, j + j_{s,p}), \qquad i = \overline{0, N-1}, \quad j = \overline{0, M_p - 1}, \qquad (23)$$

$$A_{p,p}|_S(i,j) = A_S(i, j + j_{s,p}), \qquad i = \overline{0, N-1}, \quad j = \overline{1, M_p - 1}, \qquad (24)$$

$$A_{p,p}|_N(i,j) = A_N(i, j + j_{s,p}), \qquad i = \overline{0, N-1}, \quad j = \overline{0, M_p - 2}, \qquad (25)$$

$$A_{p,p}|_W(i,j) = A_W(i, j + j_{s,p}), \qquad i = \overline{1, N-1}, \quad j = \overline{0, M_p - 1}, \qquad (26)$$

$$A_{p,p}|_E(i,j) = A_E(i, j + j_{s,p}), \qquad i = \overline{0, N-2}, \quad j = \overline{0, M_p - 1}. \qquad (27)$$

The matrix $A_{s,s}$ contains coefficients of the equations written for the control volumes, which belong to interface rows Γ_k ($k = \overline{0, P-2}$), Fig. 3. Since the interface rows are always not neighboring in the global computational domain, $A_{s,s}$ has a block-diagonal structure:

$$
A_{s,s} = \begin{bmatrix} A_{s,s}^0 & \Theta & \dots & \Theta \\ \Theta & A_{s,s}^0 & \dots & \Theta \\ \vdots & \vdots & \ddots & \vdots \\ \Theta & \Theta & \dots & A_{s,s}^{P-2} \end{bmatrix}. \tag{28}
$$

Here $\Theta \in M(\mathbb{R})_{N \times N}$ is a zero matrix; $A_{s,s}^k \in M(\mathbb{R})_{N \times N}$ $(k = \overline{0, P-2})$ is a tridiagonal matrix associated with the A matrix as follows:

$$
A_{s,s}^k|_P(i) = A_{s,s}|_P(i,k) = A_P(i, (k+1)(m+1) - 1), \qquad i = \overline{0, N-1}, \quad (29)
$$

$$
A_{s,s}^k|_W(i) = A_{s,s}|_W(i,k) = A_W(i, (k+1)(m+1) - 1), \qquad i = \overline{1, N-1}, \quad (30)
$$

$$
A_{s,s}^k|_E(i) = A_{s,s}|_E(i,k) = A_E(i, (k+1)(m+1) - 1), \qquad i = \overline{0, N-2}. \quad (31)
$$

The coefficients $A_N(i,j)$ and $A_S(i,j)$ from the rows corresponding to the interface control volumes and their southern and northern neighbors are not included in the matrices $A_{p,p}$ and $A_{s,s}$, so they should be taken into account in the $A_{p,s}$ and $A_{s,p}$ $(p = \overline{0, P-1})$. In a block form, these matrices can be written as follows:

$$
A_{0,s} = \begin{bmatrix} \Theta_x & \Theta_{x,P-2} \\ A_{0,s}^N & \Theta_{d,P-2} \end{bmatrix}, \quad A_{p,s} = \begin{bmatrix} \Theta_{d,p-1} & A_{p,s}^S & \Theta_d & \Theta_{d,P-2-p} \\ \Theta_{z,p-1} & \Theta_z & \Theta_z & \Theta_{z,P-2-p} \\ \Theta_{d,p-1} & \Theta_d & A_{p,s}^N & \Theta_{d,P-2-p} \end{bmatrix}_{N_p \times N_s},
$$

$$
A_{P-1,s} = \begin{bmatrix} \Theta_{d,P-2} & A_{P-1,s}^S \\ \Theta_{x,P-2} & \Theta_x \end{bmatrix}; \quad A_{s,0} = \begin{bmatrix} \Theta_x^T & A_{s,0}^S \\ \Theta_{x,P-2}^T & \Theta_{d,P-2}^T \end{bmatrix}, \tag{32}
$$

$$
A_{s,p} = \begin{bmatrix} \Theta_{d,p-1}^T & \Theta_{z,p-1}^T & \Theta_{d,p-1}^T \\ A_{s,p}^N & \Theta_z & \Theta_d \\ \Theta_d & \Theta_z & A_{s,p}^S \\ \Theta_{d,P-2-p}^T & \Theta_{z,P-2-p}^T & \Theta_{d,P-2-p}^T \end{bmatrix}_{N_s \times N_p}, \quad A_{s,P-1} = \begin{bmatrix} \Theta_{d,P-2}^T & \Theta_{x,P-2}^T \\ A_{s,P-1}^N & \Theta_x^T \end{bmatrix}.
$$

Here $\Theta_{d,q} \in M(\mathbb{R})_{N \times (N \cdot q)}$, $\Theta_z \in M(\mathbb{R})_{(N_p - 2N) \times N}$, $\Theta_{z,q} \in M(\mathbb{R})_{(N_p - 2N) \times (N \cdot q)}$, $\Theta_x \in M(\mathbb{R})_{(N_p - N) \times N}$, $\Theta_{x,q} \in M(\mathbb{R})_{(N_p - N) \times (N \cdot q)}$ are zero matrices; $A_{p,s}^S$, $A_{p,s}^N$, $A_{s,p}^S$, $A_{s,p}^N \in M(\mathbb{R})_{N \times N}$ $(p = \overline{0, P-1})$ are diagonal matrices associated with the A matrix as follows:

$$
A_{p,s}^S|_P(i) = A_S(i, j_{s,p}), \quad A_{s,p}^N|_P(i) = A_N(i, j_{s,p} - 1), \quad p = \overline{1, P-1}; \tag{33}
$$

$$
A_{p,s}^N|_P(i) = A_N(i, j_{s,p} + M_p), \quad A_{s,p}^S|_P(i) = A_S(i, j_{s,p} + M_p + 1), \quad p = \overline{0, P-2}. \tag{34}
$$

Here $i = \overline{0, N-1}$ and, as noted above, $j_{s,p} = p(m+1)$.

It should be emphasized that the diagonal of the matrix $A_{p,s}^S$ is formed from the coefficients of equations for the cells from the first row of the p-th subdomain, similarly the $A_{p,s}^N$ matrix coefficients correspond to the cells from the last row of the p-th subdomain, the diagonal of the matrix $A_{s,p}^S$ is formed from the coefficients of the equations for the cells from the interface row after the p-th subdomain, similarly the $A_{s,p}^N$ matrix coefficients correspond to the cells from the interface row before the p-th subdomain.

Since LS-STAG matrices $A_{p,s}$ and $A_{s,p}$ contain large number of zero elements and can be represented in a block form (32), it is possible to rewrite the algorithm of the Schur complement method. To do this, we represent the vector x_s as follows:

$$x_s = [x^0, x^1, \ldots, x^{P-2}]^T. \tag{35}$$

Here $x^k \in \mathbb{R}^N$ ($k = \overline{0, P-2}$) are the vectors of unknowns for the k-th interface row. Besides of that, vector $t \in \mathbb{R}^{N_p}$ in (21) can be represented as follows:

$$t = [t^0, t^1, \ldots, t^{M_p-1}]^T. \tag{36}$$

Here $t^k \in \mathbb{R}^N$ ($k = \overline{0, M_p - 1}$) are the vectors of unknowns for the k-th row of the p-th subdomain for the linear system (21). For unification, we assume that

$$A_{s,0}^N = A_{s,P-1}^S = A_{0,s}^S = A_{P-1,s}^N = x_s^{-1} = x_s^{P-1} = \tilde{b}_s^{-1} = \tilde{b}_s^{P-1} = 0. \tag{37}$$

Algorithm 2 takes into account (32)–(37).

Algorithm 2. DDM algorithm taking into account the LS-STAG structure of matrices

1: ...	8: $\tilde{b}_s^p = \tilde{b}_s^p - A_{s,p}^S t^{M_p-1}$
2: **while** (time steps) **do**	9: **end for**
3: ...	10: $\tilde{A}_{s,s} x_s = \tilde{b}_s$
4: $\tilde{b}_s = b_s$	11: **for** $p = \overline{0, P-1}$ **do**
5: **for** $p = \overline{0, P-1}$ **do**	12: $A_{p,p} x_p = b_p - A_{p,s}^S x_s^{p-1} - A_{p,s}^N x_s^p;$
6: $A_{p,p} t = b_p$	13: **end for**
7: $\tilde{b}_s^{p-1} = \tilde{b}_s^{p-1} - A_{s,p}^N t^0$	14: ...
	15: **end while**

Finally, let us describe the algorithm for computation of the matrix $\tilde{A}_{s,s}$ that is described by the formulae (13), (17)–(19) in case of the LS-STAG method. It should be recalled that in case of fixed immersed boundaries this computation is performed once on the stage of data preparation for the simulation. The matrix $\tilde{A}_{s,s}$ has the following tridiagonal block structure:

$$\tilde{A}_{s,s} = \begin{bmatrix} \tilde{A}_{s,s}^{0,0} & \tilde{A}_{s,s}^{0,1} & \Theta_d & \Theta_d & \cdots & \Theta_d & \Theta_d & \Theta_d & \Theta_d \\ \tilde{A}_{s,s}^{1,0} & \tilde{A}_{s,s}^{1,1} & \tilde{A}_{s,s}^{1,2} & \Theta_d & \cdots & \Theta_d & \Theta_d & \Theta_d & \Theta_d \\ \Theta_d & \tilde{A}_{s,s}^{2,1} & \tilde{A}_{s,s}^{2,2} & \tilde{A}_{s,s}^{2,3} & \cdots & \Theta_d & \Theta_d & \Theta_d & \Theta_d \\ \vdots & \vdots & \vdots & \vdots & \ddots & \vdots & \vdots & \vdots & \vdots \\ \Theta_d & \Theta_d & \Theta_d & \Theta_d & \cdots & \tilde{A}_{s,s}^{P-4,P-5} & \tilde{A}_{s,s}^{P-4,P-4} & \tilde{A}_{s,s}^{P-4,P-3} & \Theta_d \\ \Theta_d & \Theta_d & \Theta_d & \Theta_d & \cdots & \Theta_d & \tilde{A}_{s,s}^{P-3,P-4} & \tilde{A}_{s,s}^{P-3,P-3} & \tilde{A}_{s,s}^{P-3,P-2} \\ \Theta_d & \Theta_d & \Theta_d & \Theta_d & \cdots & \Theta_d & \Theta_d & \tilde{A}_{s,s}^{P-2,P-3} & \tilde{A}_{s,s}^{P-2,P-2} \end{bmatrix}. \tag{38}$$

Here $\tilde{A}_{s,s}^{k,q} \in M(\mathbb{R})_{N \times N}$ are dense matrices. As at the construction of the algorithm for $\tilde{b}_s$ computation, we take into account (32), (35)–(37) and assume that

$$\tilde{A}_{s,s}^{-1,k} = \tilde{A}_{s,s}^{P-1,k} = 0, \quad k = \overline{0, P-2}. \tag{39}$$

Then, formulae (13), (17)–(19) are converted to the following algorithm for the matrix $\tilde{A}_{s,s}$ computation:

Algorithm 3. Algorithm for interface matrix computation at the LS-STAG and DDM methods usage

---

1: ...

2: $\tilde{A}_{s,s} = A_{s,s}$

3: **for** $p = \overline{1, P-1}$ **do**

4:     **for** $c = \overline{0, N-1}$ **do**

5:         $A_{p,p}t = [A_{p,s}]_c$

6:         $\left[\tilde{A}_{s,s}^{p-1,p-1}\right]_c - = A_{s,p}^N t^0$

7:         $\left[\tilde{A}_{s,s}^{p,p-1}\right]_c - = A_{s,p}^S t^{M_p - 1}$

8:     **end for**

9: **end for**

10: **for** $p = \overline{0, P-2}$ **do**

11:     **for** $c = \overline{0, N-1}$ **do**

12:         $A_{p,p}t = [A_{p,s}]_{N_d - N + c}$

13:         $\left[\tilde{A}_{s,s}^{p-1,p}\right]_c - = A_{s,p}^N t^0$

14:         $\left[\tilde{A}_{s,s}^{p,p}\right]_c - = A_{s,p}^S t^{M_p - 1}$

15:     **end for**

16: **end for**

It should be recalled that the matrix $A_{s,s}$ has a block form (28) and it is related to the matrix A by the formulae (29).

5   Numerical Experiments

In the framework of this research a software package was developed for two-dimensional incompressible flow simulation by the LS-STAG method using the domain decomposition method for the Poisson equation numerical solving. The software package is developed on C++ in an object-oriented style using OpenMP.

To solve linear systems in subdomains, the FGMRES [13] iterative method is used with incomplete LU-factorization [16] as a preconditioner for the Helmholtz equation and with multigrid [17] preconditioner for the Poisson equations. The Schur complement method assumes direct solution of the linear system for the interface unknowns, therefore, the Gaussian elimination method was used to solve the Eq. (15).

Let us estimate the efficiency of the developed implementation on the problem of two-dimensional flow simulation around a fixed circular airfoil at Reynolds number Re = 200 during 100 dimensionless time units. The problem were solved using two non-uniform spatial grids with uniform block near the airfoil. The grids main properties are summarized in Table 1. In the table ND is the number of grid cells (in the mentioned uniform grid block) per airfoil diameter.

Computations were performed on a PC with the AMD Ryzen 7 5800H 8-core (Zen 3 with SMT, 16 threads) processor (3.2 GHz, L3 cach 16 Mb). The PC is

Table 1. Main properties of the used grids.

Grid	ND	$N \times M$	Δt
G_1	16	120×148	1×10^{-2}
G_2	32	240×296	2.5×10^{-3}

equipped with 16 GB of DDR4-3200 RAM and 512 Gb SSD NVMe PCIe. This PC is running with Windows 11 operating system.

At $ND = 16$, the task is not large enough to effectively use a large number of nodes with 1 subdomain per node (Fig. 5). It should be noted that the developed algorithm with domain decomposition allows to speed-up simulation even on 1 node because number of iterations is decreased. In case of the Helmholtz equation, the problem in a whole computational domain is solved in 1 iteration for any number of subdomains greater than 1 while 2 iterations are required for problem solving without subdomains. The Poisson equation solving without subdomains requires about 8–12 iterations. These numbers can be reduced to 1–2 iterations with the optimal choice of the subdomains number. As our numerical experiments have shown, in case of 1 node the best acceleration is reached when number of equations for subdomain problems is 2 times more than number of equations for the interface system. So, it would be better to use 8 subdomains on 1 node for G_1 grid (acceleration by 1.55 times) and 16 subdomains for G_2 grid (acceleration by 2.32 times).

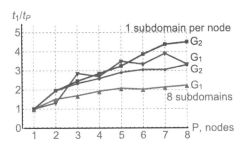

Fig. 5. Acceleration of the computations obtained by different number of nodes for problems with different parameters

There is a mention of the LS-STAG method parallelization in [18], but without details and without studying the efficiency of parallelization: only the solution accuracy was considered for 2 and 4 nodes. We could not find other works on parallelization of cut-cells methods, in which discretization and solution of equations take place on the immersed boundary. However, for the classical immersed boundary methods, in which the solution is only interpolated on the immersed boundary, there is the algorithm [24] based on splitting the system in directions, reducing to tridiagonal systems and their parallel solution using the Schur complement, in addition, algorithm [25] based on the Aitken-Schwarz algorithm is used. On a problem of similar size (400×100 cells, 1..8 nodes), a comparable acceleration was obtained in [25] as for G_2 on Fig. 5.

6 Conclusions

The parallel algorithm for incompressible flow simulation based on the LS-STAG and the Schur complement methods is developed. The developed algorithm is used to accelerate the most time-consuming parts of the LS-STAG algorithm that are solving of the Poisson equation for the pressure function and the Helmholtz equation for velocities prediction. The developed algorithm is implemented in a software package on C++ using OpenMP technology for parallelization.

The two-dimensional flow around a fixed circular airfoil was simulated to validate the developed parallel algorithm. It should be noted that the domain decomposition usage accelerates simulation even on 1 node due to decreasing number of iterations. In the future, it is planned to implement distributed storage for LS-STAG matrices in the developed software package and to use MPI instead of OpenMP to parallelize computations.

References

1. Mittal, R., Iaccarino, G. Immersed boundary methods. Annu. Rev. Fluid Mech. **37**, 239–261 (2005)
2. Cheny, Y., Botella, O. The LS-STAG method: a new immersed boundary/level-set method for the computation of incompressible viscous flows in complex moving geometries with good conservation properties. J. Comput. Phys. **229**, 1043–1076 (2010)
3. Osher, S., Fedkiw, R.P.: Level set methods: an overview and some recent results. J. Comp. Phys. **169**(2), 463–502 (2001)
4. Osher, S.J., Fedkiw, R.: Level set methods and dynamic implicit surfaces. Springer, New York (2003)
5. Marchevsky, I.K., Puzikova, V.V.: Numerical simulation in coupled aeroelastic problems by using the LS-STAG method. In: Joint EUROMECH/ERCOFTAC Colloquium, pp. 45–47. Leiden, The Netherlands (2013)
6. Puzikova, V. V., Marchevsky, I. K.: Application of the LS-STAG immersed boundary method for numerical simulation in coupled aeroelastic problems. In: 11th World Congress on Computational Mechanics, 5th European Conference on Computational Mechanics, 6th European Conference on Computational Fluid Dynamics, pp. 1995–2006. Barcelona, Spain (2014)
7. Marchevsky, I.K., Moreva, V.S., Puzikova, V.V.: The efficiency comparison of the vortex element method and the immersed boundary method for numerical simulation of airfoil's hydroelastic oscillations. In: VI International Conference on Computational Methods for Coupled Problems in Science and Engineering, pp. 800–811. CIMNE, Venice (2015)

8. Botella, O., Ait-Messaoud, M., Pertat, A., Cheny, Y., Rigal, C. The LS-STAG immersed boundary method for non-Newtonian flows in irregular geometries: flow of shear-thinning liquids between eccentric rotating cylinders. Theor. and Comp. Fluid Dyn. **29**(1), 93–110 (2015)
9. Botella, O., Cheny, Y.: The LS-STAG method for viscous incompressible flows in irregular geometries: basics of the discretization and application to viscoelastic flows. In: Fluids Engineering Division Summer Meeting, pp. 2441–2451. Montreal, Canada (2010)
10. Puzikova, V.V.: Extension of the LS-STAG cutcell immersed boundary method for RANS-based turbulence models, pp. 411–417. St.-Petersburg, Russia (2014)
11. Puzikova, V. V., Marchevsky, I. K.: Extension of the LS-STAG immersed boundary method for RANS-based turbulence models and its application for numerical simulation in coupled hydroelasctic problems. In: VI International Conference on Computational Methods for Coupled Problems in Science and Engineering, pp. 532–543. CIMNE, Venice (2015)
12. Quarteroni, A., Valli, A.: Domain Decomposition Methods for Partial Differential Equations. Oxford University Press, Oxford (1999). http://infoscience.epfl.ch/record/140704
13. Saad, Y.: Iterative Methods for Sparse Linear Systems. SIAM, New York (2003)
14. Van der Vorst, H. A. Bi-CGSTAB: A fast and smoothly converging variant of Bi-CG for the solution of nonsymmetric linear systems. SIAM J. Sci. and Stat. Comp. **13**(2), 631–644 (1992)
15. Van der Vorst, H.A.: High performance preconditioning. SIAM J. Sci. and Stat. Comp. **10**(6), 1174–1185 (1989)
16. Van Kan, J., Vuik, C., Wesseling, P.: Fast pressure calculation for 2D and 3D time dependent incompressible flow. Num. Lin. Alg. with App. **7**(6), 429–447 (2000)
17. Wesseling, P.: An introduction to multigrid methods. John Willey & Sons Ltd., Chichester (1991)
18. Nikfarjam, F., Cheny, Y., Botella, O. The LS-STAG immersed boundary/cut-cell method for non-Newtonian flows in 3D extruded geometries. Comp. Phys. Comm. **226**, 67–80 (2018)
19. Cheny, Y., Nikfarjam, F., Botella, O.: Towards a fully 3D version of the LS-STAG immersed boundary/cut-cell method. In: Eighth International Conference on Computational Fluid Dynamics, pp. 1–10. St.-Petersburg, Russia (2014)
20. Park, J., Kwon, K., Choi, H.: Numerical solutions of flow past a circular cylinder at Reynolds numbers up to 160. KSME Int. J. **12**(6), 1200–1205 (1998). https://doi.org/10.1007/bf02942594
21. Kuzmina, K., Marchevsky, I.: Flow simulation around circular cylinder at low Reynolds numbers using vortex particle method. J. Phys. Conf. Series. **1715**, 1–7 (2021). https://doi.org/10.1088/1742-6596/1715/1/012067
22. Schäfer, M., Turek S., Durst, F., Krause, E., Rannacher, R.: Benchmark Computations of Laminar Flow Around a Cylinder. In: Notes on Numerical Fluid Mechanics, pp. 547–566. Vieweg und Teubner Verlag, Leipzig (1996). https://doi.org/10.1007/978-3-322-89849-4_39
23. Zdravkovich, M.M.: Flow around circular cylinders. OUP, Oxford (1997)
24. Pacull, F., Garbey, M. A parallel immersed boundary method for blood-like suspension flow simulations. Lect. Notes in Comp. Sci. and Eng. **74**, 1–8 (2010). https://doi.org/10.1007/978-3-642-14438-7_16
25. Wiens, J.K., Stockie, J.M.: An efficient parallel immersed boundary algorithm using a pseudo-compressible fluid solver. J. Comp. Phys. **281**, 917–941 (2015). https://doi.org/10.1016/j.jcp.2014.10.058

Parallel Algorithm for Source Type Recovering by the Time Reversal Mirror

Anastasia Galaktionova and Galina Reshetova[✉]

The Institute of Computational Mathematics and Mathematical,
Geophysics SB RAS, Novosibirsk, Russia
`kgv@nmsf.sscc.ru`

Abstract. The problem of reconstructing the location and type of a seismic source in a three-dimensional medium based on seismic observations is considered. The Time Reverse Mirror (TRM) method is used to solve this problem. Recently, the TRM method has been used in seismology to detect earthquake sources, in industry to detect defects in structures, in medicine to detect masses in human tissues, and in other fields. We were the first in the seismic industry to use TRM to simultaneously identify the type and location of the seismic source. Numerical modelling was carried out on three-dimensional synthetic models using finite difference techniques, which allowed us to develop an algorithm for reconstructing the seismic source type from observational data recorded on a free surface. Solution of this problem is impossible without using parallel architecture computing systems. Several parallelization techniques have been used to achieve high efficiency of the parallel program. In particular, we use non-blocking MPI library functions and the domain decomposition technique to optimise the exchange of data between processes.

Keywords: Seismic sources · Seismic wave propagation · Time Reversal Mirror · Parallel techniques · Finite difference schemes · Domain decomposition · MPI

1 Introduction

Geophysical methods are one of the most important tools for studying the deep structure of the Earth. Geophysical studies are used to solve many important practical problems, such as the identification of mineral deposits (including oil and gas), the solution of hydrogeological and engineering geological problems, the assessment of seismic hazards, the prediction of earthquakes and many others. The methods for solving such problems are based on the study of wave processes, since waves passing through the medium indirectly carry the information about the interior property of the medium.

Waves in the medium are excited by seismic sources of either artificial or natural origin. For example, an earthquake is a naturally occurring source, while quarrying, seismic surveys or detection of structural defects are carried out using artificial wave sources.

V. Voevodin et al. (Eds.): RuSCDays 2023, LNCS 14389, pp. 267–281, 2023.
https://doi.org/10.1007/978-3-031-49435-2_19

A wave field propagates in an inhomogeneous medium and interacts with various inhomogeneities of the medium by reflecting, refracting or scattering. In order to obtain the necessary information about the medium under investigation, this wave field is registered by receivers on a free surface and subjected to special processing. One of the important tasks of a seismic survey is to locate a seismic source, such as the location of an earthquake or the origin of a structural failure.

The greater the volume of data recorded, the more accurately the task of determining the position and nature of the seismic source can be solved. The mathematical algorithms used to solve this problem must be designed to handle large amounts of data, and therefore must be based on the use of high performance computing systems with parallel architecture.

The solution of the seismic source reconstruction problem can be categorised as the solution of inverse problems. Approaches such as emission tomography in microseismic source reconstruction [1], earthquake source waveform inversion [2,3] and others are now well recognized and used. The inversion method [2] uses the minimisation of the differences between recorded and obtained data by finite difference mathematical modelling in the time domain for a set of test sources.

Unfortunately, since the structure of the algorithm requires an a priori determination of one of the pre-selected source types (vertical dipole, horizontal dipole or monopole) [4], this method is not suitable for determining the source type.

In this paper we are trying to solve a much more complicated problem than just locating a source. In addition to finding the location of the source, we also try to determine its type. The type of source is a very important characteristic of a source. For example, in an earthquake source determination task, knowledge of the source type helps to understand the shear processes at the epicentre of the event.

We propose an approach to the problem of seismic source type reconstruction in a three-dimensional medium applying the Time Reversal Mirror (TRM) method. The TRM method is based on the theoretical fact of reversible wave processes for unattenuated media and has a number of applications. For example, it is used in engineering to find defects in materials [5,6] and in seismic exploration to study the subsurface structure of the Earth [7–11].

The TRM method has already been used for source localisation and has been the subject of a number of articles. We can refer to an article on the location of seismic sources [12] and our work on the location of acoustic emission sources in core samples [13]. However, the question of whether this method can be used to identify source type remains of great interest.

2   Mathematical Statement

To describe the seismic wave propagation in an elastic medium, the first-order velocity-stress formulation with the following equations is used:

$$
\begin{aligned}
\rho \frac{\partial v_x}{\partial t} &= \frac{\partial \tau_{xx}}{\partial x} + \frac{\partial \tau_{xy}}{\partial y} + \frac{\partial \tau_{xz}}{\partial z} \\
\rho \frac{\partial v_y}{\partial t} &= \frac{\partial \tau_{xy}}{\partial x} + \frac{\partial \tau_{yy}}{\partial y} + \frac{\partial \tau_{yz}}{\partial z} \\
\rho \frac{\partial v_z}{\partial t} &= \frac{\partial \tau_{xz}}{\partial x} + \frac{\partial \tau_{yz}}{\partial y} + \frac{\partial \tau_{zz}}{\partial z} \\
\frac{\partial \tau_{xx}}{\partial t} &= (\lambda + 2\mu) \frac{\partial v_x}{\partial x} + \lambda(\frac{\partial v_y}{\partial y} + \frac{\partial v_z}{\partial z}) + F_{xx} \\
\frac{\partial \tau_{yy}}{\partial t} &= (\lambda + 2\mu) \frac{\partial v_y}{\partial y} + \lambda(\frac{\partial v_x}{\partial x} + \frac{\partial v_z}{\partial z}) + F_{yy} \\
\frac{\partial \tau_{zz}}{\partial t} &= (\lambda + 2\mu) \frac{\partial v_z}{\partial z} + \lambda(\frac{\partial v_x}{\partial x} + \frac{\partial v_y}{\partial y}) + F_{zz} \\
\frac{\partial \tau_{xy}}{\partial t} &= \mu \left(\frac{\partial v_x}{\partial y} + \frac{\partial v_y}{\partial x} \right) + F_{xy} \\
\frac{\partial \tau_{xz}}{\partial t} &= \mu \left(\frac{\partial v_x}{\partial z} + \frac{\partial v_z}{\partial x} \right) + F_{xz} \\
\frac{\partial \tau_{yz}}{\partial t} &= \mu \left(\frac{\partial v_y}{\partial z} + \frac{\partial v_z}{\partial y} \right) + F_{xz},
\end{aligned}
\tag{1}
$$

where $v = (v_x, v_y, v_z)$ is the displacement velocity vector and $(\tau_{xx}, \tau_{yy}, \tau_{zz}, \tau_{xy}, \tau_{xz}, \tau_{yz})$ is the stress tensor in the Cartesian system of coordinates. The Lamé modules λ, μ describe the media and can be obtained from the density ρ and the velocities of the P-wave and the S-wave according to the following formula:

$$
\lambda = \rho \left(V_p^2 - 2V_s^2 \right), \qquad \mu = \rho V_s^2.
$$

Since we are interested in source type recovery, we need to be able to simulate different types of seismic sources. This can be done by using the functions $F_{xx}, F_{yy}, F_{zz}, F_{xy}, F_{xz}, F_{yz}$ on the right side of the Eqs. 1, which allow us to specify a generalised source moment-tensor. In particular, in the case $F_{xx} = F_{yy} = F_{zz} = f(t) \cdot \delta(x - x_0, y - y_0, z - z_0)$ we define a volumetric source. The delta function of Dirac $\delta(x - x_0, y - y_0, z - z_0)$ defines the source location (x_0, y_0, z_0) and $f(t)$ defines the wavelet of the source in time (e.g. Ricker wavelet). A more general definition of sources is given in [14] . We assume that the stress tensor components, including the normal $(\tau_{xx}, \tau_{yy}, \tau_{zz})$ and shear $(\tau_{xy}, \tau_{xz}, \tau_{yz})$ components, are zero at the free surface, which simulates real wave propagation near the Earth's free surface.

3   Numerical Simulation

To solve the system of differential equations (1), we implemented an explicit finite difference method with second order accuracy both in time and space, as described in [15]. The article also includes information on stability conditions and dispersion properties. By employing this finite difference method, we approximate all the equations in the system using central differences, which leads to a second-order increase in the system's order. Therefore, fewer computational resources are necessary. Furthermore, this finite-difference scheme incorporates efficient absorbing boundary conditions that hold great importance for numerical experiments.

Using this technique, we introduced both integer nodes, where $x_i = i\Delta x$, $y_j = j\Delta y$, $t^n = n\Delta t$ and $z_k = k\Delta z$, and half-integer nodes, where $x_{i+1/2} = (i + 1/2)\Delta x$, $y_{j+1/2} = (j + 1/2)\Delta y$, $t^n = n\Delta t$ and $z_{k+1/2} = (k + 1/2)\Delta z$. Here, Δx, Δy, Δt and Δz denote the sampling intervals for the space and time variables (x, y, z, t) on the grid.

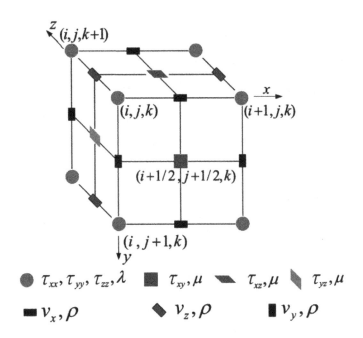

Fig. 1. Finite difference staggered grid.

The wave field components and medium parameters are defined at separate nodes of the temporal and spatial grid (Fig. 1). Within each grid cell $[x_{i-1/2}, x_{i+1/2}] \times [y_{j-1/2}, y_{j+1/2}] \times [z_{k-1/2}, z_{k+1/2}]$, the medium parameters are considered constant, with potential discontinuities aligned with the grid lines. The velocity components for displacement are defined as $(v_x)_{i+1/2,j,k}^{n-1/2}$, $(v_y)_{i,j+1/2,k}^{n-1/2}$, and $(v_z)_{i,j,k+1/2}^{n-1/2}$. The normal stress tensor components are $(\tau_{xx})_{i,j,k}^n$, $(\tau_{yy})_{i,jk}^n$, and $(\tau_{zz})_{i,j,k}^n$. Moreover, the shear stress tensor components are $(\tau_{xy})_{i+1/2,j+1/2,k}^n$, $(\tau_{xz})_{i+1/2,j,k+1/2}^n$, and $(\tau_{yz})_{i,j+1/2,k+1/2}^n$.

For the discrete function $f_{i,j}^n$, which corresponds to $f(t^n, x_i, y_j, z_k)$, we will implement a second-order centred finite difference time operator

$$D_t[f]_{i,j,k}^n = (\ (f)_{i,j,k}^{n+1/2} - (f)_{i,j,k}^{n-1/2}\ )/\Delta t \tag{2}$$

and finite difference second-order centred spatial operators

$$D_x[f]_{i,j,k}^n = (\ (f)_{i+1/2,j,k}^n - (f)_{i-1/2,j,k}^n\ )/\Delta x, \tag{3}$$

$$D_y[f]_{i,j,k}^n = (\ (f)_{i,j+1/2,k}^n - (f)_{i,j-1/2,k}^n\ )/\Delta y, \tag{4}$$

$$D_z[f]_{i,j,k}^n = (\ (f)_{i,j,k+1/2}^n - (f)_{i,j,k-1/2}^n\ )/\Delta z. \tag{5}$$

A staggered grid's finite difference scheme is obtained through the balance law in the finite volume method [17] and takes the form

$$D_t[v_x]_{i+1/2,j,k}^{n-1/2} = \langle 1/\rho_0 \rangle_{i+1/2,j,k} \left(D_x[\tau_{xx}]_{i+1/2,j,k}^{n-1/2} + D_y[\tau_{xy}]_{i,j+1/2,k}^{n-1/2} + D_z[\tau_{xz}]_{i,j,k+1/2}^{n-1/2} \right) \tag{6a}$$

$$D_t[v_y]_{i,j+1/2,k}^{n-1/2} = \langle 1/\rho_0 \rangle_{i,j+1/2,k} \left(D_x[\tau_{xy}]_{i,j+1/2,k}^{n-1/2} + D_y[\tau_{yy}]_{i,j+1/2,k}^{n-1/2} + D_z[\tau_{yz}]_{i,j+1/2,k}^{n-1/2} \right), \tag{6b}$$

$$D_t[v_z]_{i,j,k+1/2}^{n-1/2} = \langle 1/\rho_0 \rangle_{i,j,k+1/2} \left(D_x[\tau_{xz}]_{i,j,k+1/2}^{n-1/2} + D_y[\tau_{yz}]_{i,j,k+1/2}^{n-1/2} + D_z[\tau_{zz}]_{i,j,k+1/2}^{n-1/2} \right), \tag{6c}$$

$$D_t[\tau_{xx}]_{i,j,k}^n = (\lambda + 2\mu)_{i,j,k} D_x[v_x]_{i,j,k}^n + \lambda(D_y[v_y]_{i,j,k}^n + D_z[v_z]_{i,j,k}^n) + (F_{xx})_{i,j,k}^n \tag{6d}$$

$$D_t[\tau_{yy}]_{i,j,k}^n = (\lambda + 2\mu)_{i,j,k} D_y[v_y]_{i,j,k}^n + \lambda(D_x[v_x]_{i,j,k}^n + D_z[v_z]_{i,j,k}^n) + (F_{yy})_{i,j,k}^n \tag{6e}$$

$$D_t[\tau_{zz}]_{i,j,k}^n = (\lambda + 2\mu)_{i,j,k} D_z[v_z]_{i,j,k}^n + \lambda(D_x[v_x]_{i,j,k}^n + D_y[v_y]_{i,j,k}^n) + (F_{zz})_{i,j,k}^n \tag{6f}$$

$$D_t[\tau_{xy}]_{i+1/2,j+1/2,k}^n = \{\mu\}_{i+1/2,j+1/2,k} \left(D_y[v_x]_{i+1/2,j+1/2,k}^n + D_x[v_y]_{i+1/2,j+1/2,k}^n \right) + (F_{xy})_{i+1/2,j+1/2,k}^n \tag{6g}$$

$$D_t[\tau_{xz}]_{i+1/2,j,k+1/2}^n = \{\mu\}_{i+1/2,j,k+1/2} \left(D_z[v_x]_{i+1/2,j,k+1/2}^n + D_x[v_z]_{i+1/2,j,k+1/2}^n \right) + (F_{xz})_{i+1/2,j,k+1/2}^n \tag{6h}$$

$$D_t[\tau_{yz}]_{i,j+1/2,k+1/2}^n = \{\mu\}_{i,j+1/2,k+1/2} \left(D_z[v_y]_{i,j+1/2,k+1/2}^n + D_y[v_z]_{i,j+1/2,k+1/2}^n \right) + (F_{yz})_{i,j,k}^n \tag{6i}$$

where the parameters of the effective medium are defined as arithmetic averages at nodes of half integer value

$$\langle f \rangle_{i+1/2,j,k} = 0.5(f_{i+1,j,k} + f_{i,j,k}),$$

$$\langle f \rangle_{i,j+1/2,k} = 0.5(f_{i,j+1,k} + f_{i,j,k}), \tag{7}$$

$$\langle f \rangle_{i,j,k+1/2} = 0.5(f_{i,j,k+1} + f_{i,j,k}),$$

or averages in harmonic form [18] for nodes $(i + 1/2, j + 1/2, k)$

$$\{f\}_{i+1/2,j+1/2,k} = \begin{cases} [(1/f_{i,j,k} + 1/f_{i+1,j,k} + 1/f_{i,j+1,k} + 1/f_{i+1,j+1,k})/4]^{-1}, \\ \quad \text{if } f_{i+p,j+p} \neq 0, \ p = \overline{0,1}; \\ \\ 0, \quad \text{if any } f_{i+p,j+p} = 0, \ p = \overline{0,1}. \end{cases}$$

In our numerical experiments we use absorbing boundary conditions to constrain the computational domain. To do this, we surround all boundaries except the free surface with a convolutional perfectly matched layer (CPML) [16].

The boundary conditions on the free surface must also be reformulated for numerical calculations. Since the normal stresses ($\tau_{xx}, \tau_{yy}, \tau_{zz}$) are at integer nodes, their values at the zero point (corresponding to the free surface) are zero. The shear stresses ($\tau_{xy}, \tau_{xz}, \tau_{yz}$) must also be zero at this point, but they are located at half integer nodes. In order to satisfy the required conditions, stress components with the numbers $-1/2$ and $1/2$ must possess identical absolute values and opposite signs.

4   Description of Algorithm

To solve many problems of geophysics and seismology, it is necessary to reconstruct a seismic source from seismograms obtained at a free surface. Reconstructing the location and type of a seismic source is a complex issue, necessitating the use of specific techniques. In this regard, we evaluate the effectiveness of an algorithm based on TRM.

The TRM technique relies on the physical principle of time reversibility in the geological medium, without any attenuation. This means that the signal registered in the receivers can be reversed in time and used as a function of sources located at the same points. With such an operation, the simulated wave field at the moment corresponding to the wave generation is localized at the source. The success of the reconstruction of the position of seismic sources, inhomogeneities is confirmed by studies [12,13]. However, it remains uncertain whether the calculated wave field contains information about the nature and orientation of the seismic source.

To test this assertion, we divided the algorithm into two stages. In the first stage, we simulate seismograms recorded on a free surface. For this purpose, we determine the position and type of the source and use the selected initial data to solve the system of Eq. (1) through the finite difference method. At each time point, we write down the normal components of the elasticity tensor at the points corresponding to the chosen observing system and thus obtain seismograms. The results of the first step are simulated seismograms.

At the second stage we forget about the location of the source. Now the only information available is the coordinates of the receivers and the seismograms recorded in them. According to the principle of time reversibility, we unfold seismograms in time and place them at the same points where they were recorded as source functions.

To enhance the effect of source localization, instead of visualizing individual wavefield components, we calculate the total energy function for each time moment t^i

$$E(x_i, y_j, z_k, t^i) = \tau_{xx}(x_i, y_j, z_k, t^i)\varepsilon_{xx}(x_i, y_j, z_k, t^i) +$$

$$+\tau_{yy}(x_i, y_j, z_k, t^i)\varepsilon_{yy}(x_i, y_j, z_k, t^i) + \tau_{zz}(x_i, y_j, z_k, t^i)\varepsilon_{zz}(x_i, y_j, z_k, t^i) +$$

$$+2\tau_{xy}(x_i, y_j, z_k, t^i)\varepsilon_{xy}(x_i, y_j, z_k, t^i) + 2\tau_{xz}(x_i, y_j, z_k, t^i)\varepsilon_{xz}(x_i, y_j, z_k, t^i) +$$

$$+2\tau_{yz}(x_i, y_j, z_k, t^i)\varepsilon_{yz}(x_i, y_j, z_k, t^i), \tag{8}$$

where x_i, y_j and z_k denote the spatial grid points within the computational domain, while the time moment in the finite difference scheme is indicated by t^i. The stress and strain components are indicated by τ and ε, respectively.

Using this procedure, the most significant amount of energy concentrates at the source when the wave appears and then begins to dissipate. To determine the moment of energy concentration accurately, the sum of total energy E_{sum} is calculated for all previously computed time moments t^i:

$$E_{sum}(x_i, y_j, z_k, t^m) = \sum_{t^i \leq t^m} E(x_i, y_j, z_k, t^i). \tag{9}$$

We assumed that the distribution of the total energy in the wave field E_{sum} varies for different sources and thus can identify their types.

To confirm this hypothesis, we conducted a series of numerical experiments. These experiments involved studying the spatial distribution of energy E_{sum} and the polar plot of directional diagrams (also known as radiation patterns), which were obtained through the numerical solutions of the direct dynamic seismic and inverse TRM problems. The subsequent sections present our results.

5 Numerical Test

A region of $3020 \times 3020 \times 3020 \, \text{m}^3$ with a sampling step of 20 m was chosen as the computational model. The computational domain is surrounded by a PML layer with a thickness of 400 m. Within the domain, the medium parameters are constant and have the following values: $\rho = 2000 \, \text{kg/m}^3$, $v_p = 3000 \, \text{m/s}$,

$v_s = v_p/\sqrt{3}$. The computation was carried out up to a time of 13.5 s. A volumetric source with a frequency of $f_0 = 5$ Hz is placed in the centre of the simulation domain. Seismograms are required for the second step of the algorithm. For this purpose, the components of the normal stress $(\tau_{xx}, \tau_{yy}, \tau_{zz})$ are recorded at each time instant at receivers located near the free surface on a small burial at a distance of 20 m from each other.

In the first step of the algorithm we calculate the total energy E_{sum} of the wavefield for the direct wave. We use the functions corresponding to the different sources in the right-hand sides of the Eq. (1). In our study, we examined sources directed at specific angles (30°, 45°, 60°, 90°) towards the free surface in a plane perpendicular to (yz). In a three-dimensional volume it is quite difficult to visualise the calculated wave field. Therefore, we look at sections of the 3D volume along the planes containing the source (Fig. 2). It may be necessary to look at multiple slices to get a complete representation (Fig. 3).

The second stage of the algorithm is then carried out as described in the previous section. The result of the TRM procedure is the total wave energy of the reconstructed wave field (Fig. 2). In addition, the radiation pattern is also taken into account. This is plotted in a polar coordinate system and uses the energy values at points at a given distance from the source. Such a flat graph is easier of perception.

It can be seen that the radiation patterns and energy distribution diagrams have the same shape (Fig. 2). Therefore, it does not make sense to consider them in the same plane. In addition, the distribution of energy from the direct and reconstructed waves in a plane parallel to the plane containing the receivers has the same shape, which makes it possible to reconstruct the direction to the source with confidence. The angle to the free surface of the source direction increases with the higher energy distribution in the horizontal direction.

Let us also examine the energy diagram in the plane perpendicular to the plane containing the receivers (Fig. 3). Obviously, the shape of the reconstructed energy is more elongated due to the location of the receivers only on the free surface. Taking this into account, when comparing diagrams or energy distributions, one can see that the shape remains unchanged.

The analysis of the images obtained (Fig. 2–3) shows that the energy distribution and the direct waveform based on it depend on the type of source. In the plane perpendicular to the free surface (Fig. 2 e–2 h), the general direction of the shape is vertical and shifts to horizontal when the source direction is deflected. The reconstructed waveform does not coincide with a straight waveform, but has the same general direction. In order to clarify the information it is necessary to look at the shape or energy distribution in other sections, for example in a section parallel to the free surface (Fig. 2 a–2 d). In this plane, the shape of the energy distribution is the same for the direct wave and the reconstructed wave, and when combined with data from the vertical plane, the source direction can be reconstructed with reasonable confidence.

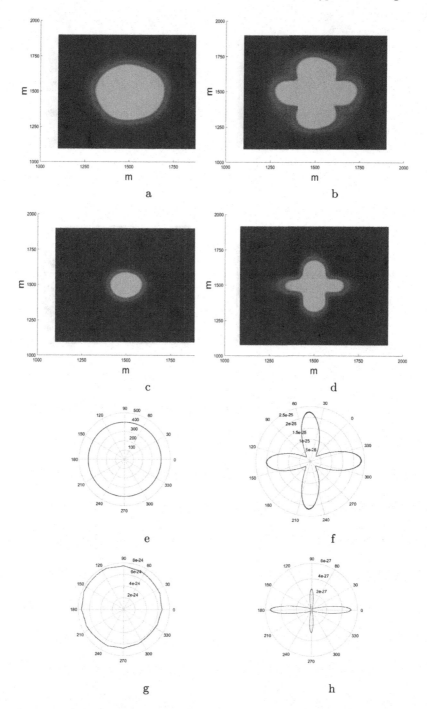

Fig. 2. Total direct wave energy E_{sum} distribution: (a) vertical source; (b) 30° source; E_{sum} distribution according to TRM: (c) vertical source; (d) 30° source; Radiation pattern of the direct wave: e) vertical source; (f) 30° source; Radiation pattern according to TRM: (g) vertical source; (h) 30° source in plain xy (z fixed).

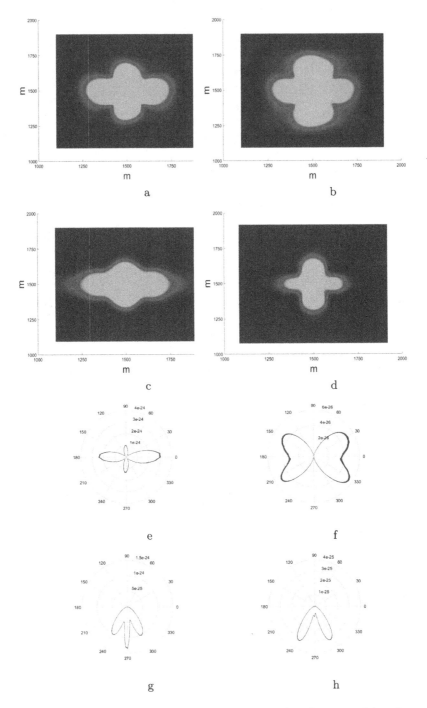

Fig. 3. Total direct wave energy E_{sum} distribution: (a) $45°$ source; (b) $30°$ source; E_{sum} distribution according to TRM: (c) $45°$ source; (d) $30°$ source in plane xy (z fixed); Direct wave radiation pattern: (e) $45°$ source; (f) $30°$ source; Radiation pattern according to TRM: (g) $45°$ source; (h) $30°$ source in plane xz (y fixed).

6 Paralleling Technique

Implementing the computational algorithm in three dimensions necessitates a significant memory allocation. Memory is also required to store the input data in the form of acquired gathers recorded on a free surface. For example, if the model in question is doubled in size, the computational volume and RAM must be increased eightfold, resulting in a significant computational load. Thus, the parallelisation of the computational algorithm described in Sect. 2 is a precondition for the solution of the presenting problem. The parallelization technique follows directly from the structure of the computational algorithm. Experience in solving problems in dynamic elasticity theory using finite difference methods

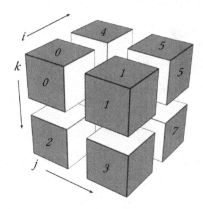

Fig. 4. A sample distribution of data between eight processes.

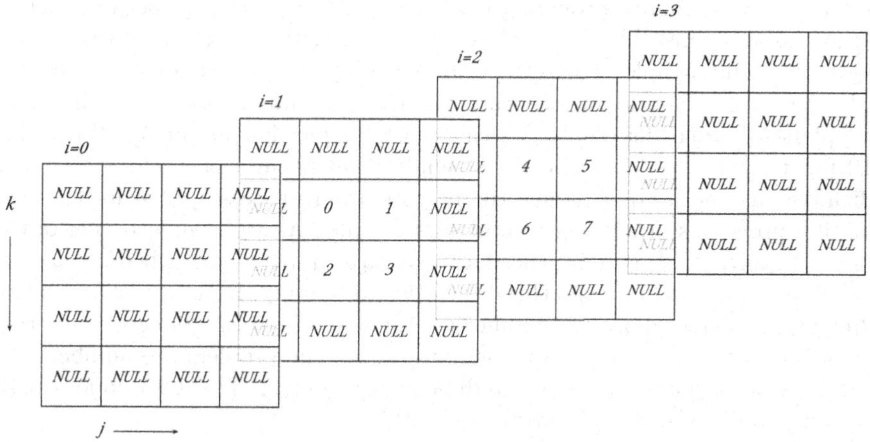

Fig. 5. An example 8 process grid with 2 processes in each of the three dimensions.

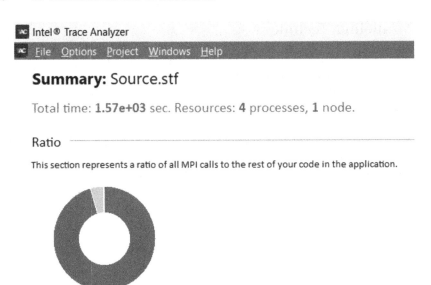

Fig. 6. Ratio of all MPI calls for 4 processes on 1 node using Intel® Trace Analyzer and Collector example.

shows that the most effective way of parallelizing is to use the domain decomposition method. The idea of this method is simple and consists in dividing the computations in the initial domain into a number of smaller subproblems in overlapping subdomains, providing the necessary data exchange between neighbouring subdomains. The Fig. 4 shows the distribution of data between eight processes as an example, where the number indicates the rank of the process.

In the three-dimensional case, each process communicates in three directions (two planes in each direction). Writing code for parallel communication using MPI functions in the three directions simultaneously can cause purely technical difficulties, as one needs to know the neighbouring processes in each direction. Also, if a process is processing a subdomain located at the edge or corner of the entire computational domain, the data exchange must be described separately for each such process. To avoid this difficulty and to unify the data exchange algorithm, we use a special process numbering, the so-called *itable* process numbering [19]. All processes involved in the computation of the problem are numbered in a special way in the form of a three-dimensional matrix. This technique is used to quickly find neighbouring processes.

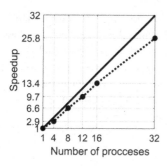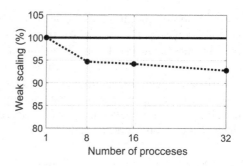

Fig. 7. Weak scaling efficiency and strong scaling speedup. The dashed line represents measured speedup and efficiency while the solid line represents the ideal speedup and efficiency.

A special enumeration matrix of 8 processes *itable* for $2 * 2 * 2$ domain decomposition is shown in Fig. 5. In the figure, *NULL* stands for the *MPI_PROC_NULL* operator. Executing *MPI_PROC_NULL* means that no data will be transmitted when a message is sent to it. For example, the coordinate vector of process 5 is $(2,2,1)$. Each process has its neighbours *itable(myranki±1, myrankj±1, myrankk±1)*. The use of the *MPI_PROC_NULL* operator allows us to unify the process of sending and receiving data for all processes, whether they are inside the domain, on the edge or in the corner. In fact, if the subdomain is on an edge, then data will only be sent or received towards the inside of the domain. There is no exchange from the outside, because the argument is *MPI_PROC_NULL*.

The direct use of the domain decomposition method does not always lead to the writing of an efficient parallel programme. The bottleneck in this parallelization approach is the data exchange process between adjacent processes. The efficiency of the program can be very low when using MPI *Send/Recv* subroutines which lock the data exchange together with synchronising processes at each time step of the difference scheme. Nevertheless, we use several simple but effective approaches to speed up the parallel algorithm. The first thing we do at each new time step of the difference scheme is to have each process start the computation from inside the subdomain and continue it to the boundaries. Second, simultaneously with the start of the computation, each process sends data to neighbouring processes and requests the necessary data using non-blocking procedures *Isend/Irecv*, which allow data transferring in the background while performing computation within a subdomain [20]. The computations within each subdomain take some time, and when the computations reach the boundaries where data from neighbouring processes is required, the data exchange procedures are usually completed. Thus, such simple techniques allow communication processes to overlap. To test the parallel program we used Intel Xeon X5670, 2.93 GHz (Westmere) resources of the Siberian Supercomputing Centre NKS-1P SB RAS [21]. Using the test computations outlined in Sect. 5, the performance of the parallel algorithm was analysed by executing it with varying numbers of processes. The communication overhead was evaluated and visualised through the use of the Event Timeline trace from Intel®Trace Analyzer and Collector.

The findings from the Event Timeline analysis are illustrated in Fig. 6 and demonstrate the ratio of MPI calls across four processes on a single node. It can be seen that the calls take about 4 percent of the total parallel program time. We also plotted the strong and weak scalability graphs to estimate the overall performance of the parallel program. The results are shown in Fig. 7, where the dashed line represents measured speedup and efficiency while the solid line represents the ideal speedup and efficiency. The resulting curves show a good performance of our parallel programme.

7   Conclusions

The investigation focuses on identifying the seismic source type from the observed seismic data. To resolve this problem, we propose an approach based on the Time Reverse Mirror method. Numerical simulations on a series of synthetic models were used to verify the algorithm. To describe wave processes in three-dimensional inhomogeneous media, the system of dynamic elasticity theory was used. A finite difference method on staggered grids with second-order accuracy in both time and space was selected as the numerical solution approach. The results of numerical simulations have shown that the Time Reverse Mirror approach allows us to determine both the spatial position of the source and its orientation. A research version of the parallel program was created to solve the problem. Parallel data exchange was implemented using domain decomposition and MPI library functions. Matrix numbering of *itable* processes was used for unified data exchange between processes, which simplified the process of parallel code writing. Some simple approaches were used to increase the efficiency of the parallel program, among which we highlight the non-blocking data exchange of MPI functions Isend and Irecv together with a special organization of calculations within subdomains. These methods allowed us to exchange data in the background. The strong and weak scalability graphs presented in the paper showed good performance of our parallel program.

Acknowledgements. This work was financially supported by the Russian Science Foundation, grant No. 22-21-00759, https://rscf.ru/en/project/22-21-00759/. The study was conducted using the equipment of the Siberian Supercomputer Center [21].

References

1. Maxwell, S.C., Urbancic, T.I.: The role of passive microseismic monitoring in the instrumented oil field. Geophysics **20**, 636–639 (2001)
2. Kim, K., Fee, D., Yokoo, A., Lees, J.M.: Acoustic source inversion to estimate volume flux from volcanic explosions. Geophys. Res. Lett. **42**(13), 5243–5249 (2015). https://doi.org/10.1002/2015GL064466

3. Bleibinhaus, F.: Full-waveform inversion of controlled-source seismic data. In: Beer, M., Kougioumtzoglou, I., Patelli, E., Au, I.K. (eds.) Encyclopedia of Earthquake Engineering. Springer, Heidelberg (2016). https://doi.org/10.1007/978-3-642-36197-5_376-1

4. Iezzi, A.M., Fee, D., Kim, K., Jolly, A.D., Matoza, R.S.: 3-D acoustic multipole waveform inversion at Yasur Volcano, Vanuatu. J. Geophys. Res. Solid Earth **124**(8), 8679–8703 (2019). https://doi.org/10.1029/2018JB017073

5. Fink, M., Wu, F., Cassereau, D., Mallart, R.: Imaging through inhomogeneous media using time reversal mirrors. Ultrason. Imaging **13**, 179–199 (1991)

6. Fink, M., Prada, C.: Acoustic time-reversal mirrors. Inv. Problems **17**(1), R1–R38 (2001)

7. Wapenaar, K., Thorbecke, J.: Review paper: virtual sources and their responses, Part I: time-reversal acoustics and seismic interferometry. Geophys. Prospect. **65**(6) (2017). https://doi.org/10.1111/1365-2478.12496

8. Larmat, C., Montagner, J.-P., Fink, M., , Y., Tourin, A., Clevede, E.: Time-reversal imaging of seismic sources and application to the great sumatra earthquake. Geophys. Res. Lett. **33**(19) (2006) https://doi.org/10.1029/2006GL026336

9. Larmat, C., Tromp, J., Liu, Q., Montagner, J.-P.: Time reversal location of glacial earthquakes. J. Geophys. Res. **113**(B9), B09314 (2008). https://doi.org/10.1029/2008JB005607

10. Montagner, J.-P., et al.: Time-reversal method and cross-correlation techniques by normal mode theory: a three-point problem. Geophys. J. Int. **191**(2), 637–652 (2012)

11. Aslanov, T.G.: Definition of earthquake focus coordinates using a combined method. Herald of Dagestan State Technical University. Tech. Sci. **44**(2), 118–125 (2017). (in Russia). https://doi.org/10.21822/2073-6185-2017-44-2-118-125

12. Givoli, D.: Time reversal as computational tool in acoustics and elastodynamics. J. Comput. Acoust. **22**(3) (2014). https://doi.org/10.1142/S0218396X14300011

13. Reshetova, G.V., Anchugov, A.V.: Digital core: simulation of acoustic emission in order to localize its sources by the method of wave field reversal in reverse time. Geol. geophys. **62**(4), 597–609 (2021)

14. Aki, K., Richards, P.G.: Quantitative Seismology, Theory and Methods, vol. I. W.H. Freeman, San Francisco (1980)

15. Virieux, J.: P-SV wave propagation in heterogeneous media: velocity-stress finite-difference method. Geophysics **51**, 889–901 (1986)

16. Komatitsch, D., Martin, R.: An unsplit convolutional perfectly matched layer improved at grazing incidence for the seismic wave equation. Geophysics **725**, sm155–sm167 (2007)

17. Samarskii, A.A.: The Theory of Difference Schemes. CRC Press, Boca Raton (2001)

18. Moczo, P., Kristek, J., Vavrycuk, V., Archuleta, R.J., Halada, L.: 3D heterogeneous staggered-grid finite-difference modeling of seismic motion with volume harmonic and arithmetic averaging of elastic moduli and densities. Bull. Seism. Soc. Am. **92**(8), 3042–3066 (2002)

19. Aoyama, Y., Nakano, J.: RS/6000 SP: Practical MPI Programming. IBM Redbooks (1999)

20. Reshetova, G., Cheverda, V., Koinov, V.: Comparative efficiency analysis of MPI blocking and non-blocking communications with Coarray Fortran. In: Voevodin, V., Sobolev, S. (eds.) RuSCDays 2021. CCIS, vol. 1510, pp. 322–336. Springer, Cham (2021). https://doi.org/10.1007/978-3-030-92864-3_25

21. Novosibirsk Supercomputer Center of SB RAS. http://www.sscc.icmmg.nsc.ru

Recognition of Medical Masks on People's Faces in Difficult Decision-Making Conditions

Oleg Miloserdov⬤ and Andrey Makarenko$^{(\boxtimes)}$⬤

V. A. Trapeznikov Institute of Control Sciences of Russian Academy of Sciences,
Moscow, Russia
avm.science@mail.ru

Abstract. The paper proposes and tested an approach to the video data formation processing pipeline that solves the problem of automating the control of the presence and correctness of wearing personal protective equipment by personnel in difficult conditions of filming by CCTV cameras. The proposed solution is based on neural network algorithms and is flexibly configured for specific conditions and tasks, including when generating operational alerts. The approach is demonstrated on the example of recognition of medical masks. The solution is based on: an automated markup system for training a detector based on AlphaPose, a YOLOX neural network detector, a ByteTrack tracking system, and a classifier based on a lightweight CNN, the input of which is minitracks of people's faces, 8 frames each. The collected dataset consists of over 260,000 minitracks. Achieved the quality of classification $F_1 = 0.86$ to determine the presence and $F_1 = 0.79$ to determine the correct wearing of the mask.

Keywords: Neural networks · Detection · Classification · Tracking · Pose estimation

1 Introduction

Neglecting safety requirements while working at the enterprise or in the event of quarantine restrictions is dangerous and leads to injuries, loss of life and financial costs. Thus monitoring the availability and the correctness wearing of personal protective equipment (PPE) has long been an urgent task for many industrial enterprises and medical institutions. There are different types of PPE: respirators and masks are used for respiratory protection and are among the most common PPE, hard hats are mandatory for head protection, specialized goggles protect the eyes, gloves and special suits protect against aggressive environments. The onset of the COVID-19 pandemic exacerbated the need to control the wearing of PPE; during the pandemic, medical masks and gloves became mandatory in many countries when visiting any public places and organizations.

Automation of PPE wearing control allows not only to reduce financial costs, but also improves the quality of control, which has a positive effect on the

V. Voevodin et al. (Eds.): RuSCDays 2023, LNCS 14389, pp. 282–298, 2023.
https://doi.org/10.1007/978-3-031-49435-2_20

employee safety in the enterprise and reduces the number of accidents. Deep neural networks are actively used in video analytics tasks as an automation tool, however, the difficulty of implementing such developments in business processes is well known, so it is important not only to develop an integrated approach to solving such problems, but also to search for methods to simplify the implementation process and integration with production and/or organizational processes/systems.

This paper proposes an complex approach to solving the problem of recognizing the presence of PPE on the personnel of an enterprise. The proposed approach has been tested and demonstrated on the example of medical masks recognition. Among the main components of the developed solution, an approach is proposed for creating a dataset for training a detector based on YOLOX using a pre-trained neural network AlphaPose for pose estimation. A trained neural detector based on YOLOX allows efficient detection of a human head, and the ByteTrack tracking system allows tracking a specific person, which makes it possible to use a set of consecutive face frames as an input to a neural classifier developed on the basis of a lightweight CNN. Such a solution is complex and can be implemented on objects with different shooting conditions, since the proposed approach allows you to further train a set of neural networks for specific cameras and their operating conditions.

2   Related Works

Existing methods for monitoring compliance with PPE requirements can be generally divided into two types: based on sensors and based on computer review methods, which, in turn, also have several types. This section is focused on modern approaches based on the processing of deep conversion methods for video data coming from machine vision and CCTV systems.

The most common papers are related to the hard hats recognition, as well as construction and medical masks in various conditions. For example, [8] proposed an automatic hard hats detection system based on YOLOv5x with good ability to detect small objects and objects in low light images. The "Hard Hat worker image dataset" [1] was used as the dataset, which contains 5000 images. Also one can single out the work [11], where, using the combination of several datasets and obtaining more than 12,500 images, the authors developed a Multiscale Segmentation and Feature Fusion Network (MSFFN) at the feature processing stage in order to increase the reliability of the algorithm when detecting objects at different scales, and also proposed an improved version of the attention mechanism. The proposed helmet detection network shows $mAP = 93.5\%$ quality and 42 FPS performance.

In the paper [10], the authors, in addition to solving the problem of determining the presence of a hard hats and a safety hook using Yolov5, solve the problem of classification the correct wearing the listed PPE. To determine the correct wearing of PPE, they use the OpenPose [3] pose estimation neural network to extract key points, which are then fed into a 1D-CNN to solve a classification problem. Paper [4] presents a novel solution for detecting PPE misuse by combining deep learning-based object detection and individual detection using geometric relationship analysis. Experimental results show that the proposed approach is able to identify the hazards of inappropriate use of PPE with an accuracy of 94.47% at a rate of 15.62 FPS.

The tasks associated with the detection of medical masks are somewhat more complex in their implementation, since the masks themselves have smaller size and it is easier to overlap them with objects in the frame, so let's consider several examples of such papers. [15] proposes a method that takes advantage of a combination of deep learning and local binary patterns (LBP) for masked face recognition using RetinaFace. In addition, the authors extract local features of the binary pattern from the areas of the eyes, forehead, and brow ridges of the masked face and combine them with the features obtained from RetinaFace into a single structure for face recognition in masks. The authors offer their COMASK20 dataset, which contains about 300 objects. Recognition results of 87% by the F_1 measure in the COMASK20 dataset and 98% by the F_1 measure in the Essex dataset were obtained. In the paper [12], the authors use the widespread ResNet-50 neural network to train a classifier that determines the mask presence on a face. Using the public dataset "Real-world masked face recognition dataset" (RMFRD) from [16], which contains 5,000 masked faces and 90,000 unmasked faces, has achieved classification quality $F_1 = 0.897$ on unmasked faces and $F_1 = 0.447$ on masked faces.

The main disadvantage of such works [8, 11, 12, 15, 16] is the lack of a complex approach to recognizing the presence of masks on people's faces, as well as quite "comfortable conditions" in which models are trained and tested. The papers propose approaches to training classifiers for the mask presence, and use data with already detected faces, but miss the real problems associated with face detection and tracking. In addition to the lack of an complex approach, the works use artificially obtained (or even synthesized, for example, in the Essex dataset) data with ideal shooting angles, lighting and location of subjects, with no blurring, defocusing and noise in the image. However, when trying to use such solutions in a real system for detecting face masks, there is a risk of encountering a large number of errors due to changes and complication of shooting conditions (lighting, angle, angle, scale, presence of collars, etc.).

As an example of papers with a complex approach to solving the problem, one can cite the work [13], which presents three approaches for checking the compliance with safety regulations by employees based on the use of convolutional neural networks (CNN). The authors propose to use YOLO-v3 as a detector and VGG-16, ResNet-50 and Xception as classifiers assembled in a Bayesian structure. In the first approach, the algorithm detects workers, hard hats, and vests, and then the machine learning model checks to see if each detected worker is wearing a hard hat or vest correctly. In the second approach, the algorithm simultaneously detects individual workers and checks for PPE compliance. In the third approach, the algorithm detects only workers in the input image, which are then cropped and classified by CNN-based classifiers. A distinctive feature of the work is the training on its own Pictor-v3 dataset, which contains about

1,500 annotated images and about 4,700 workers wearing various combinations of PPE components. The second approach is shown to provide the best performance (average mAP accuracy is 72.3%) and good speed at 11 FPS. However, the first approach is the fastest of all and can handle 13 FPS at 63.1% mAP.

It is also worth highlighting the work [5], in which three tasks are solved in a complex way: counting the number of people in the frame, maintaining social distance, and determining the mask presence. A dataset of more than 7,000 faces was collected based on PUC CCTV cameras with various shooting conditions. To create a dataset, the author uses a neural network to evaluate the HRNet posture, with the help of which he receives selected areas with a human head. Based on the obtained dataset, the author trains a neural network classifier using the BiT approach, the accuracy of which reaches about 90%.

3   Complex Approach to Solving the Problem of Recognizing the Presence and Wearing Correctness of PPE

Modern tasks of video analytics are extremely rarely solved using a single neural network and, as a rule, the solution pipeline consists of a whole complex of different neural networks and decision-making rules. The globally proposed processing pipeline for PPE presence recognition can be divided into two main components: detector&tracker and classifier. At the first stage, with the help of the pose estimation neural network, the parts of the body are flexibly adjusted to detect which the detector is trained. Next, a video (a sequence of frames) is fed to the input of the processing pipeline, the detector selects the specified parts of the image, the tracker allows you to track a specific person in time, and the classifier (or a set of classifiers) allows you to determine the presence or the correctness of wearing one or another PPE. Next, a decision rule is used that combines all the information on the track and the responses of the classifiers to display the final answer on the track. Additionally, blocks for measuring social distance, control over the movement of the target (for example, infected) object, and a visualization block are used. Let's consider the necessity of using each element in more detail.

The implementation of an complex solution requires retraining or additional training of the pipeline for the conditions of video filming and the tasks set. Somewhere it is important to wear hard hats, therefore, it is necessary to detect the head area, on other objects it is necessary to wear only gloves, which means that it is necessary to detect hands. For each of the above tasks, it is necessary to detect different parts of the body, and, consequently, to search for data, mark them up and train the detector again. In this regard, it will be useful to automate the markup of areas of interest for further solving the detection problem. Based on the problems described above, the pipeline uses a pose estimation mechanism to obtain key points on the human body and a rule for constructing an area of interest according to these coordinates. For this, a neural network for pose estimation is used, in which the detector detects the entire human figure. To

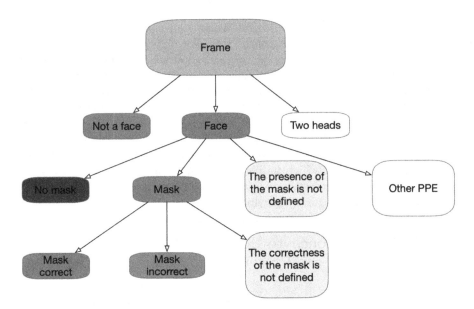

Fig. 1. Decision tree for classifying problem of the presence and correctness of wearing masks. Target nodes at each stage of decision making are highlighted in green. The node is highlighted in red, orange and yellow according to the degree of decrease in their criticality for the operator to make a decision. A node that does not affect the decision is highlighted in gray. White highlighted nodes are not implemented in the system, but are important for data markup. (Color figure online)

create an automatic markup system, human figure detector and pose estimation errors are not critical, since the some objects gap on some frames during head detector training will be perceived as noise and will not have a strong impact on the quality of work. Errors in the pose estimation network, expressed in the key points gap, can also be smoothed out by the algorithm for calculating the target area of the head. This approach makes it possible to use a pre-trained pose estimation neural network as an automatic markup system, almost regardless of the shooting conditions.

The detector used in the pipeline is trained using an automated markup system. If it is necessary to improve the quality of detection and refine the details, the stages of manual data labeling are used.

It is worth dwelling on the need to use a tracker. The use of the tracker allows the system in its reports to exclude duplication of violators of the mask regime, make decisions on the track, which means to increase the accuracy and stability of the decision, and also use information about the objects movement to implement the contact tracing functionality along the violator's track.

The final block in the pipeline is a set of neural network classifiers, in which the decision to classify a particular frame is carried out according to the decision scheme shown in the Fig. 1.

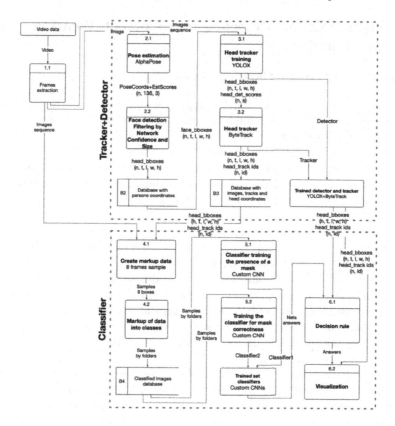

Fig. 2. Structural-functional scheme of the developed software package.

The decision on one frame classification is made by successive answers to the questions:

– on the frame is a face/not a face/"Two heads" (and more),
– if face, then class variants "Mask present"/"Mask not present"/"Unable to detect presence of mask"/"Other protections",
– if "Mask exists", then the options are "Mask is correct"/"Mask is incorrect"/"Unable to determine correct mask wearing".

By this stage, we have target areas in relation to a specific person for the entire time period when the subject is in the frame. This means that it is possible to submit to the classifier not only one frame, on which it is often impossible to make a decision about the class, but a frames sequence or some *minitrack*. This approach makes it possible to use additional information in the time interval for a more accurate classification problem solution.

The complete structural-functional scheme of the developed computational pipeline for PPE presence recognition is shown in the Fig. 2. All the elements of a functional diagram are described below, and their importance and effectiveness are demonstrated.

4   Recognizing the Presence and Correct Wearing of Medical Masks

4.1   Data and Dataset Characteristics

Modern deep neural networks require huge training datasets. The data in the existing open sources is not enough to train the detector (in our head detector problem) for three reasons.

Firstly, at the system implementation site, the shooting conditions can be very different from those on which the neural network from open sources was trained. For example, the angle of the cameras, the lighting, the presence of street clothing, and etc. Thus, the variability and amount of data in open sources does not allow obtaining a complete and universal solution.

Secondly, as a rule, existing detectors are aimed either at detecting a person completely, or at detecting only faces. Detection of a human figure is not enough for further work, since at some camera viewing angles, another person can get into the detected area, and confusion will arise during further detection of body parts of interest to us (in particular, the face, in the case of medical masks). Detectors trained to detect only faces have typically been trained on unmasked faces, resulting in performance degradation on masked faces. Also, face-only detection does not allow the use of tracking systems (tracking) due to the fact that a person moves and changes positions.

Thirdly, even a person cannot always determine the presence and correctness of wearing a mask from only one photo, therefore, there will be errors when marking up the data. In real video filming, it is necessary to analyze several angles to make a decision.

Video data from 20 surveillance cameras at the enterprise were used as the main data sample for training and testing. The cameras have variable viewing angles, are located in different lighting conditions, and also have different shooting scales. The data was taken for several full days of shooting during working hours from 8 am to 9 pm, which made it possible to obtain frames both in daytime and at night. Video clips are also selected under various weather and climate conditions, which allows you to cover people from the moment when they are in winter jackets and hoods, to summer clothes: T-shirts, caps and etc. None of the publicly available datasets have characteristics close to those mentioned above.

The Fig. 3 shows complex cases of determining the presence or correctness of mask wearing. In the Fig. 3(a), a cloud of cigarette smoke covers the person's face, and in the Fig. 3(b) the sunlight is directed onto the face in such a way that even a data markup person with only one frame cannot make out whether it is a mask or a light. Frames Fig. 3(c) and 3(d) use scarves instead of medical masks, while frame Fig. 3(e) shows an example of night shots. It is worth paying attention to the owners of the beard (drawings Fig. 3(f), 3(g), 3(h)), due to poor resolution, it is often difficult to recognize a beard or a white, black or grey mask. Naah Fig. 3(i) and 3(j) are frames of examples where objects have something in their teeth. Frames Fig. 3(k) and 3(l) demonstrate the variability of viewing angles.

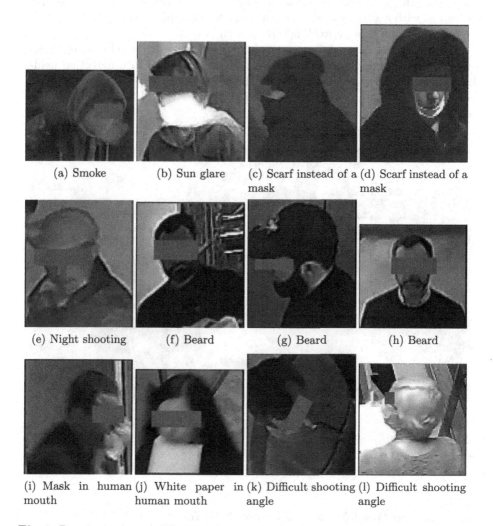

(a) Smoke   (b) Sun glare   (c) Scarf instead of a (d) Scarf instead of a
                                          mask   mask

(e) Night shooting   (f) Beard   (g) Beard   (h) Beard

(i) Mask in human (j) White paper in (k) Difficult shooting (l) Difficult shooting
mouth   human mouth   angle   angle

Fig. 3. Demonstration of difficult cases to determine the presence or correct wearing of the mask.

4.2 Automatic Data Markup System for the Detection Task

Neural networks capable of solving the pose estimation problem, such as Alpha-Pose [6] and OpenPose [3], applicable for implementing automatic data labeling for the detection task. AlphaPose was chosen due to its more flexible software implementation. AlphaPose is pre-trained on data from various cameras taken under various shooting conditions, which allows it to be used in this processing pipeline. It is important to note that AlphaPose copes with difficult cases such as overlapping a person with interior parts or other people, crowds of people, as well as with a variety of shooting angles. An example of the operation of the pretrained AlphaPose network is shown in the Fig. 4.

Using a neural network for pose estimation allows us to develop a rule based on the obtained coordinates, so one can create a markup with detection fields. In this pipline It was required to train the human head detector, however, such automatic data markup system can be applied to PPE for hands, feet and other parts of the body.

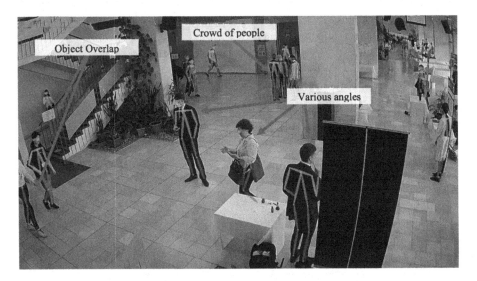

Fig. 4. An example of the work of the pre-trained AlphaPose network on a frame from the video. Examples of overlapping objects, crowds of people, various poses and angles of shooting are given.

4.3   Human Head Neural Network Detector

As a neural network detector, a modern YOLOX [7] neural network is used, which is an improved (in terms of quality and speed) version of the latest generations of YOLO (You Only Look Once) series networks, showing high results in the detection field. YOLOX is trained from scratch on the dataset obtained using AlphaPose. The ByteTrack [17] approach is used as a tracker, the main distinguishing feature of which is the tracking of all detection boxes, regardless of their metrics. This approach allows you to quickly and accurately track objects over a long time period, which is necessary for this task.

Using a neural network to estimate poses for the detection task turns out to be ineffective, due to a threefold loss in speed (YOLOX 60 fps versus 20 fps for

AlphaPose), since in most networks the same detector is used to estimate poses to highlight a human figure.

Figure 5 shows an example of the work of the YOLOX head detector and the ByteTrack tracker, trained on a dataset that was created using an automatic markup system. The frame shows, among other things, detector errors, and you can notice missed objects. Such errors are related to the nuances of learning based on AlphaPose data and, if necessary, are corrected by additional manual data labeling and additional training by YOLOX. It is worth noting that such a fix is not always relevant, for two reasons. Firstly, the ByteTrack algorithm allows skipping detector errors, and secondly, the decision to classify an object is made according to the track, which will be described in more detail below.

Despite the different camera angles and shooting conditions from the training set, the YOLOX + ByteTrack bundle gives a good result, regardless of whether the person is wearing a mask or not.

Fig. 5. An example YOLOX head detector in conjunction with the ByteTrack tracker work on a video with a crowd of people in various poses, scale and shooting angles.

4.4   Classifier

The first attempts to train the neural network classifier, which received one frame as input, showed rather low results in terms of the quality of functioning, in this regard, it was decided to apply several consecutive frames to the input. At the output of the YOLOX and ByteTrack bundle, we get a sequence of frames (15 frames per second) for one person, then *track*. As an input, 8 frames are fed to the neural network classifier - *minitrack*, corresponding to 1 s, thus the neural network receives more information about the object. Examples of minitracks from the received selection are shown in the Fig. 6 (faces are covered for confidentiality).

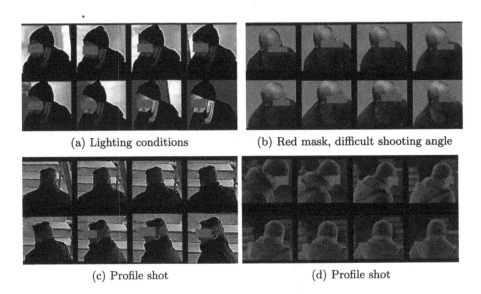

(a) Lighting conditions   (b) Red mask, difficult shooting angle

(c) Profile shot   (d) Profile shot

Fig. 6. Random examples of 8-frame minitracks.

The same structure was used as in the complex approach during data markup (see Fig. 1). The classification decision is made on the basis of a minitrack consisting of 8 frames. Thus, there may be situations when in 8 frames there are different classes defined according to the structure Fig. 1. In this case, the markups were guided by the list below for the main cases.

- If 8 frames contain at least one frame of the "No mask" class, then these 8 frames must be assigned to the "No mask" class.
- If 8 frames contain at least one frame of the "Mask incorrect" class and there are no frames of the "No mask" class, then these 8 frames must be assigned to the "Mask incorrect" class.
- If at least one frame of the "Mask correct" class is present on 8 frames and there are no frames of the "No mask" and "Mask incorrect" classes, then these 8 frames must be attributed to the class "Mask correct".
- If 8 frames contain at least one frame of the class "Unable to determine correct wearing of mask" and there are no frames of the classes "No mask", "Mask incorrect" and "Mask correct", then these 8 frames should be categorized as "Unable to determine correct wearing of mask".
- If 8 frames contain at least one frame of class "The presence of the mask is not defined" and there are no frames of classes "No mask", "Mask incorrect", "Mask correct" and "Unable to determine correct wearing of mask", then these 8 frames must be assigned to the class "The presence of a mask is not defined".

The pivot Table 1 presents the data obtained after several markup steps. It is worth noting that there is an imbalance of classes in the dataset. The pivot table also shows the classes that were not included in the training sample. The "Two heads" class includes images that contained two heads represented by faces. The class "Other PPE" contains images of people in such PPE as: a protective screen, a special suit, a gas mask, and etc. The "Incorrect" class includes images on which there is no face or it is impossible to determine its presence.

Table 1. Pivot table for training and validation sample classes.

Class name	Training set	Validation set	Total
Not fase	113883	16045	129928
No mask	52718	3703	56421
Mask correct	30460	4227	34687
Mask incorrect	26394	3564	29958
The correctness of the mask is not defined	3446	506	3952
Two heads	3435	237	3672
The presence of the mask is not defined	2612	278	2890
Other PPE	1150	175	1325
Incorrect	112	4	116
Total	234239	28739	262978

The classification task was divided into two stages. The task of the first classifier is to determine the presence of a mask, and the task of the second classifier is to determine the correctness of wearing a mask. The dataset for training the first classifier is divided into 4 classes: "Not a face", "Mask", "No Mask" and "The presence of the mask is not defined". The "Not a face" class includes minitracks where there are no signs of a face on all frames (nose, eyes, mouth, etc.). The class "Mask" includes minitracks where there is a mask on the face (regardless of whether it is worn correctly), thus frames with the classes "Mask correct", "Mask incorrect" and "The correctness of the mask is not defined". The "No mask" class includes minitracks where at least one frame with a face has no mask on the face.

The dataset for training the second classifier is divided into three classes: "Mask correct", "Mask incorrect" and "The correctness of the mask is not defined". It is assumed that the input of this classifier will receive frames classified at the output of the first classifier as class"Mask".

In total, the dataset is represented by over 262,000 minitracks, or over 2 million frames. Datasets for classifiers are divided into two subsets: training and validation. The division was carried out in accordance with the date of shooting and camera number to avoid data leakage.

The image classification solution is built on the basis of three successive layers: convolutional layer - Conv2D, batch normalization - BatchNorm [2], activation function - ReLu or LeakyRelu. Let's call such a sequence a cell (see Fig. 3(a). In this paper, we have replaced the Conv2D convolution with SeparableConv2D [14], which consists of two steps. The first part of SeparableConv2D is spatial depth convolution, which acts separately on each input channel. This step reduces the number of operations and saves computing resources. The second part is a point convolution intended for mixing the output channels. In this work, 8 frames are simultaneously fed to the input of the neural network, therefore, a multihead subnet with common weights (Multihead) is used for preprocessing, which consists of 3 cells connected in series. Then the cells are connected in sequence (a subsampling layer - MaxPooling can be embedded between the cells) to form a neural network feature extractor. At the output of the neural network, after using the global average pooling operation (GAP), there is a fully connected layer with 4 outputs. A distinctive feature of this architecture is its small size (41,460 weights), which allows it to be implemented in mobile robots. Training was performed for 200 epochs using the strategy of decreasing the learning rate (from 0.001 to 0.00001). Adam [9] was chosen as the optimizer. The size of the minibatch was 1500 samples. The weighted crossentropy was chosen as the error function. To improve the stability of the neural network, training was performed with the injection of normal noise into the resulting feature vector. This made it possible to stabilize the learning process, as well as slightly improve the quality of the network.

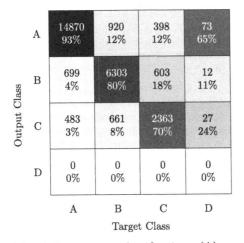

(a) Mask presence classification. (A) – "Not a face", (B) – "Mask", (C) – "No Mask", (D) – " The presence of the mask is not defined".

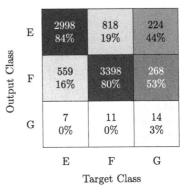

(b) The correctness of mask wearing classification. (E) – " Mask correct", (F) – "Mask incorrect", (G) – "The correctness of the mask is not defined".

Fig. 7. Confusion matrices of neural classifiers on validation sets.

The confusion matrix for the first classifier, that is responsible for the presence of the mask, showed in the Fig. 7(a). The weighted F_1 measure on the validation set increased to 0.86. The error matrix for the second classifier, shown in Fig. 7(b). The weighted F_1 measure on the validation set is estimated at 0.79. According to the confusion matrix, the class "The presence of the mask is not defined" is never defined correctly. There is a similar result for the class "The correctness of the mask is not defined" on the second classifier. This is primarily due to lack of data in the training set. Secondly, in accordance with the analysis of the confusion matrix and the impact of error analysis, the neural network refers most of the validation data to the "Not a face" class (in the case of the first classifier) due to very blurry frames, the markers were important as faces. Visual analysis of errors showed that some of the answers of the neural network turned out to be correct, and there are errors in the markup. Also, confusion matrices can be considered taking into account the system operation scenario. When choosing the class "The presence of the mask is not defined" as "Not a face", 65% re-identified or requested an additional frame, and choosing "No mask" will add some work to the system operator. At the same time, only in 11% errors are critical, when choosing this class as a "Mask".

Attempts were made to take into account the imbalance of classes and train the neural network with mini-packets of data with evenly distributed classes, however, this approach showed a similar quality or lower.

To improve the quality of the neural network classifier, in the future, the training samples will be increased for small classes, since there is a clear dependence of the classification quality on the size of the training dataset. But the general conclusion is that it is necessary to improve the quality of video recording in order to exclude cases in which it is impossible to correctly classify the presence or correctness of the mask.

It is also worth noting that in real systems the classification decision is made not by the minitrack, but by the full track of the object. This approach allows you to smooth out errors on minitracks, but at the same time retains the ability to track the exact moment in time at which the mask was removed or lowered.

4.5   Examples

The Fig. 8 shows an example of the processing pipeline operation on of several close frames. The observation objects are highlighted in color in accordance with the decision tree Fig. 1. The frame Fig. 8(a) shows an example of how the AlphaPose network works for pose estimation. It is important to note that the pretrained AlphaPose is not able to give out all the coordinates which is visible on the frame without errors. However, as one can see in the Fig. 8(b), the trained YOLOX detector overcomes this disadvantage of automatic markup. Figure 8(c) demonstrates how the classifier works on cropped images with heads. The violators of the mask mode are highlighted in red, while it is important to note that on this frame many violators turned away from the camera, and at the current time the system recognizes them as "Not a face", however, highlighting in red on the frame shows that the system has previously recorded a violation mask mode for these objects. Objects in incorrectly dressed masks are highlighted in orange, and tracked objects in gray, for which a decision has not yet been made due to lack of information (face is turned away all the time of observation).

(a) AlphaPose   (b) YOLOX&ByteTrack   (c) Classification   CNNs. Colors   according   to   the decision tree 1.

Fig. 8. An example of the operation of a computational pipeline using the example of several close frames.

It is possible to implement the functionality of tracking contacts along the track of the offender. Figure 9 shows the visualization of frames with current contacts and contacts during the track's lifetime (contact radius can be set). As additional functionality, you can add the absence or violation of the rules for wearing a mask for contacts. Thus, it is possible to track possible contacts with the infected after the fact, estimate the time of contact and, by adding an identification mechanism, notify and isolate the likely carriers of the infection.

Fig. 9. The functionality of contact tracing with a violator of the mask regime. The violator is highlighted in red, contacts with the violator during the life of the track are highlighted in yellow, contacts on this frame are highlighted in orange. (Color figure online)

5   Conclusion

The paper proposes an approach to the formation of a video data processing pipeline, which is able to solve the problems of automation and control of the presence and correct wearing of PPE. The developed processing pipeline was tested on the example of medical masks recognition in real difficult shooting conditions with CCTV cameras at the enterprise. The proposed solution is based on neural network algorithms, can be flexibly configured for specific conditions and tasks, and can also be supplemented with other algorithms to improve functionality, for example, with people identification system. The computational pipeline consists of an automated markup system (for detector training) based on Alpha-Pose, a YOLOX neural network detector, a ByteTrack tracker, and a two neural network classifiers based on a lightweight CNN. The ByteTrack tracker allows one to track a specific person during the time he is in the camera's field of view, which allows one to use a set of 8 consecutive frames at the input of trained neural network classifiers to increase the stability and accuracy of their work. A dataset with more than 262,000 minitracks was created and marked up. Dataset is marked into 6 classes to solve the problem of determining the presence and correctness of wearing a mask on a person's face. Set of work done made it possible to solve the problem and train a neural network classifier for the presence of a mask with a quality of $F_1 = 0.86$ and a neural network classifier for the correctness of wearing a mask with a quality of $F_1 = 0.79$ in low light conditions, generating blur, defocusing and significant noise in the image.

The authors thank the anonymous referees for their helpful comments.

References

1. Hard Hat Workers Dataset makeML - create neural network with ease. https://makeml.app/datasets/hard-hat-workers. Accessed 30 Sept 2023
2. Awais, M., Iqbal, M.T.B., Bae, S.H.: Revisiting internal covariate shift for batch normalization. IEEE Trans. Neural Netw. Learn. Syst. **32**(11), 5082–5092 (2021). https://doi.org/10.1109/tnnls.2020.3026784
3. Cao, Z., Simon, T., Wei, S.E., Sheikh, Y.: Realtime multi-person 2D pose estimation using part affinity fields. In: 2017 IEEE Conference on Computer Vision and Pattern Recognition (CVPR). IEEE (2017). https://doi.org/10.1109/cvpr.2017.143
4. Chen, S., Demachi, K.: Towards on-site hazards identification of improper use of personal protective equipment using deep learning-based geometric relationships and hierarchical scene graph. Autom. Constr. **125**, 103619 (2021). https://doi.org/10.1016/j.autcon.2021.103619
5. Cota, D.A.M.: Monitoring COVID-19 prevention measures on CCTV cameras using deep learning. Ph.D. thesis, Pontifícia Universidade Católica do Rio de Janeiro, Rio de Janeiro, Brasile (2020). http://webthesis.biblio.polito.it/id/eprint/15970
6. Fang, H.S., Xie, S., Tai, Y.W., Lu, C.: RMPE: regional multi-person pose estimation. In: 2017 IEEE International Conference on Computer Vision (ICCV). IEEE (2017). https://doi.org/10.1109/iccv.2017.256

7. Ge, Z., Liu, S., Wang, F., Li, Z., Sun, J.: Yolox: exceeding yolo series in 2021 (2021)
8. Hayat, A., Morgado-Dias, F.: Deep learning-based automatic safety helmet detection system for construction safety. Appl. Sci. **12**(16), 8268 (2022). https://doi.org/10.3390/app12168268
9. Kingma, D.P., Ba, J.: Adam: a method for stochastic optimization (2017)
10. Li, J., Zhao, X., Zhou, G., Zhang, M.: Standardized use inspection of workers' personal protective equipment based on deep learning. Saf. Sci. **150**, 105689 (2022). https://doi.org/10.1016/j.ssci.2022.105689, https://www.sciencedirect.com/science/article/pii/S0925753522000297
11. Liang, H., Seo, S.: Automatic detection of construction workers' helmet wear based on lightweight deep learning. Appl. Sci. **12**(20), 10369 (2022). https://doi.org/10.3390/app122010369
12. Mandal, B., Okeukwu, A., Theis, Y.: Masked face recognition using resnet-50 (2021)
13. Nath, N.D., Behzadan, A.H., Paal, S.G.: Deep learning for site safety: real-time detection of personal protective equipment. Autom. Constr. **112**, 103085 (2020). https://doi.org/10.1016/j.autcon.2020.103085
14. SIfre, L., Mallat, S.: Rigid-motion scattering for texture classification (2014)
15. Vu, H.N., Nguyen, M.H., Pham, C.: Masked face recognition with convolutional neural networks and local binary patterns. Appl. Intell. **52**(5), 5497–5512 (2021). https://doi.org/10.1007/s10489-021-02728-1
16. Wang, Z., et al.: Masked face recognition dataset and application (2020)
17. Zhang, Y., et al.: ByteTrack: multi-object tracking by associating every detection box. In: Avidan, S., Brostow, G., Cissé, M., Farinella, G.M., Hassner, T. (eds.) ECCV 2022. LNCS, vol. 13682, pp. 1–21. Springer, Cham (2022). https://doi.org/10.1007/978-3-031-20047-2_1

Use of Different Metrics to Generate Training Datasets for a Numerical Dispersion Mitigation Neural Network

Elena Gondyul, Vadim Lisitsa$^{(\boxtimes)}$ (iD), Kirill Gadylshin, and Dmitry Vishnevsky

Institute of Petroleum Geology and Geophysics SB RAS, Novosibirsk, Russia
{gondyulea,lisitsavv,gadylshinkg,vishnevskydm}@ipgg.sbras.ru

Abstract. The numerical dispersion which occurs in seismic data due to use of coarse meshes in numerical modeling is reduced using a neural network. The training dataset is a sample of wave fields that have been modeled on a fine grid. The trained NDM-net (Numerical Dispersion Mitigation neural network) is applied to the entire set of seismic data corresponding to all of the source positions. This approach makes it possible to obtain seismic data with suppressed dispersion at a lower cost compared to numerical modeling on a fine mesh. The use of a neural network for test cases confirms the approach's effectiveness. We present several approaches to generate a training dataset. All of them are based on the minimization of the Hausdorff distance, however, they use different element-wise metric. In this research, we provide the global sensitivity analysis of the network accuracy on the choice of the metrics. It is shown that the training dataset formed using the properties of the seismic data itself has the greatest weight for the resulting error.

Keywords: Seismic modelling · Numerical dispersion · Deep learning

1 Introduction

Artificial neural networks have recently become widely popular as a method of processing seismic data. They are used for the interpolation of seismograms [1,4] their interpretation and various types of post-processing [2,3,15]. Also, a neural network was used for ground-roll noise attenuation [5]. In the article neural convolutional networks are used to suppress the numerical dispersion that results from modeling seismic fields on a coarse grid using difference schemes.

Numerical dispersion can lead to significant inaccuracies in the numerical solution of the system of elastodynamic equations. Several pre-processing and post-processing algorithms have been proposed to reduce this numerical dispersion [6]. These approaches, however, require a lot of computational effort and are limited by the correction of the dispersion caused by the discretization of time derivatives. The problem of suppressing spatial dispersion using these algorithms is still open.

© The Author(s), under exclusive license to Springer Nature Switzerland AG 2023
V. Voevodin et al. (Eds.): RuSCDays 2023, LNCS 14389, pp. 299–313, 2023.
https://doi.org/10.1007/978-3-031-49435-2_21

Additionally, more sophisticated algorithms can be used, but they come at a cost. For example, finite-difference schemes with a high order of approximation, optimization schemes that suppress dispersion [7], the discontinuous Galerkin method, and spectral element methods can improve accuracy [8–10] but they do not necessarily lead to a decrease in computational complexity. The number of operations and memory use expand with the order of approximation.

In our previous study [11,14], we proposed using neural network called NDM-net (Numerical Dispersion Mitigation) based on U-net architecture, and also provided one of the ways to optimize the training dataset. In this study, we describe in more detail the methods of creation and analyze them using the global sensitivity method. Neural networks are suggested as a method for approximating a nonlinear transition operator from data with a significant numerical error to data with a smaller one. In comparison to previous methods, this method enables the reduction of dispersion and artifacts to a great level while requiring less memory and time.

There are difficulties in developing neural networks, such as choosing hyperparameters and creating a training sample. We selected appropriate hyperparameters by trial and error in the process of a large number of experiments. At the same time, the choice of the optimal training sample is practically not currently investigated. Although, this is the biggest factor in the quality of the neural network. An insufficiently representative data set leads to incorrect decision-making and a decrease in the effectiveness of learning algorithms. In this study, it is shown how the error depends on the choice of a training sample, which was developed based on the properties of the model or the data itself. Also, a rough analysis of statistically accumulated results is shown to assess the impact of input data on output.

The rest of the paper is organized as follows. The NDM-net architecture and the loss function that is reduced over the training process is introduced in Sect. 2. In Sect. 3 we describe the seismic data. In Sect. 4 we detail three algorithms for constructing a training dataset and discuss the results of training on them. In Sect. 5 we apply the global sensitivity analysis. Finally, we present our conclusion in which we say which sample is the most relevant.

2   Neural Network Architecture

The NDM-net architecture is based on one of the simple neural networks - U-net. Such a fully connected neural network (FCNNs) has performed well not only in image segmentation [13], but also data generation, approximation of nonlinear operators. The U-net architecture consists of an encoder that uses several convolutional layers to obtain high-level features of input images and a decoder that restores the original spatial resolution. The dimension of the input data and their quantity determined the depth of the network. NDM-net consists of 8 layers of upsampling (encoder) and 8 layers of downsampling (decoder). Layers consist of convolutional operator and batch normalization. The convolution layer produces the sum of the element product of the input data fragment and the convolution kernel. The weighting coefficients of the convolution core are determined during the training of the NDM-net. LeakyReLU (Leaky Rectified Linear Unit) is used as an activation function for the first eight convolutional layers, which has a slope coefficient of −0.2 and ReLU for the decoder. The neural network configuration is schematically depicted in Fig. 1.

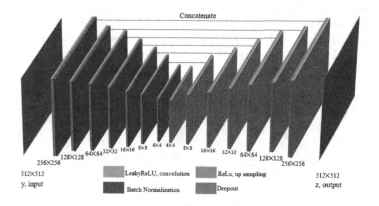

Fig. 1. NDM-net architecture

The advantage of this neural network is the use of skip connections to solve the problem of accuracy degradation. The method of early stopping is used to avoid overfitting.

A set of seismograms calculated on a coarse grid is used as input data and is denoted here as $X = \{x\}_{i=1}^{N_s}$, where N_s seismograms in total. The output data of the NDM-net is denoted as $G(x)$. Also, we need to introduce the exact solution $Y = \{y\}_{i=1}^{N_s}$, which is the seismograms computed on a fine grid.

During NDM-net training, the following loss function is minimized:

$$L = \sum_i \|G(x_i) - y_i\|_1,$$

where is $G : x_i \rightarrow y_i$ is the transition operator approximation with the neural network.

The neural network itself updates its parameters according to the chain rule:

$$\theta_l = \theta_l - \gamma(\delta l / \delta \theta_l),$$

where θ_l−neural network parameters on the l layer, γ−learning rate coefficient, the value of which changes during training.

3   Input Data

In this research, it is worth introducing data before describing the methods, because it will let us to illustrate the difference between the metrics.

Consider an elastic BP model (Fig. 2), which has a contrasting salt body and the right part smoothly changing its velocity values. The model is 67 km by 12 km in dimension. The seismic data set consists of 2696 sources, which are located at a distance of 25 m from each other. For each source at a 15 km distance, 2401 receivers record the wave field. The receivers are placed at a distance of 12.5 m. The source is described by a Ricker wavelet with a central frequency of 30 Hz.

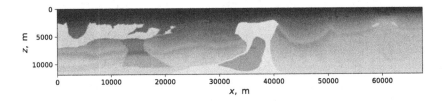

Fig. 2. BP model

As input data for the neural network, two sets of seismograms calculated on two different grids, one with a coarse step size of $h_x = 6$ m and the other with a fine step size of $h_x = 3$ m. Synthetic sets were calculated using schemes on shifted grids of the fourth order [16]. The seismic data was cropped in such a way that the direct wave did not enter the seismic images and had a size of 512×512.

4   Methods for Creating Training Dataset

Making a representative training sample is a crucial step in neural network training. The training sample should contain all possible features of the dataset, as well as have a sufficiently large size. There are three ways of forming a training sample, as well as their comparison.

4.1   Distance Between the Sources

The most obvious way to form a training sample is an equidistant arrangement of sources:

$$J^{eq} = 1, k, 2k, ..., q(k)k,$$

where J^{eq} is the indexes of sources that are included in the training dataset, $k \in \mathbf{N}, k > 1$ and $q(k) = \frac{N_s}{k}$. It means that we use only a part of the sources equidistantly distributed in space, for example each tenth, each twentieth source in the line or others. If we introduce the Hausdorff distance between the set of all sources J and $J^{eq} \subset J$:

$$\delta_d = \max_{j \in J} \min_{i \in J^{eq}} |i - j| d,$$

where d is the distance between two neighbouring source positions. It is evident that using equally spaced sources to create the training dataset ensures that $\delta_d = \frac{kd}{2}$, where k comes from the definition presented above. Construction of such dataset is trivial and not discussed here.

4.2 Dataset Based on the Velocity Model

Construction of the dataset based on the equally distributed sources is based on the assumption, that in horizontal direction, the model varies slowly, thus, the simulated seismogramms are also similar, if they correspond to the neighbouring sources. This assumption is essentially based on the model properties. In particular, if a horizontally layered media is considered; i.e., the model is independent of the horizontal direction, all the seismogramms will be the same. Thus, it is natural to introduce the metrics of model similarity/dissimilarity and build the training dataset according to this metric. We have a set $M = M_1, ..., M_{N_s}$ with the same number of models as sources. A distance matrix was constructed (Fig. 3) for a set of such velocity models using the nMSE distance:

$$nMSE(M_i, M_j) = \frac{1}{2} \frac{\|M_i - M_j\|_2}{\|M_i\|_2 + \|M_j\|_2}.$$

Such a matrix shows how the model varies in response to the distances between the sources. In the case when a part of the model coincides with itself, the value of the distance matrix is zero (the main diagonal). Low values of the distance matrix indicate that if the sources are close enough, the distance between the sources grows slowly. This occurs, for instance, near the main diagonal and in the area of a smooth change in the velocity model. To illustrate this effect, we depict a few of the distance matrix's columns in Fig. 4. The distance between this model and all the others is shown by each line on the graph.

Using metrics in the model space we may introduce the Hausdorff distance between the set of models corresponding to the training dataset and the entire set as:

$$\delta_m = \max_{j \in J} \min_{i \in J^m} nMSE(M_i, M_j),$$

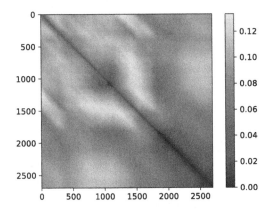

Fig. 3. Distance matrix

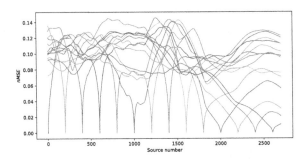

Fig. 4. The distances for 14 parts of velocity model

where J is the set of all indices to denote the seismogramms and J^m is the set of indices of the seismogramms from the training dataset. After that, training dataset can be constructed to limit the Hausdorff distance δ_m between the training set and the entire data set. Algorithm 1 presents the training sample constructing pseudocode.

The algorithm makes it so that similar parts are collected in clusters, and to form a representative set, the central seismograms included in each of the clusters are taken. Here, the indexes j_0 and j are used to indicate the first elements of the newly produced cluster and the current element, accordingly, N_{cl} is the number of clusters or the amount of data in the training dataset. The J^m sheet is a collection of model indexes that will be included in the training data. The central elements of the clusters are included in J^m, thus forming an index sheet of size N_{cl}. Also, an important parameter H_0 is used, which is the limiting Hausdorff distance based on $nMSE$, which we strive to preserve. The choice of the H_0 value strictly depends on the data set. By compression the training dataset size it is possible to reduce the neural network's training time.

Algorithm 1. An algorithm of L_2 preserving dataset construction based on velocity model properties

---

$J^m \leftarrow \varnothing$
$N_{cl} \leftarrow 0$
$j_0 \leftarrow 1$
$j \leftarrow j_0$
while $j < N_s$ **do**
    while $\min_{k=j_0...j} \max_{l=j_0...j} nMSE(M_k, M_l) \leq H_0$ **do**
        $j \leftarrow j + 1$
    end while
    $j \leftarrow j - 1$
    $J_{N_{cl}+1} \leftarrow \arg\min_{k=j_0...j} \max_{l=j_0...j} nMSE(M_k, M_l)$
    $J^m \leftarrow J^m \cup J_{N_{cl}+1}.$
    $N_{cl} \leftarrow N_{cl} + 1$
    $j_0 \leftarrow j + 1$
end while

4.3   Dataset Based on Distances Between Seismograms

As well as dataset based on conserving of the Hausdorff distances between the part of the velocity model we can introduce dataset based on preserving of the Hausdorff distances between seismograms. We have an assumption that the nearest seismograms are similar and have a small distance between each other. Consider a conventional 2D acquisition system with sources located at $r_j^s, j = 1, ..., N_s$. We use the entire set of seismograms obtained using a coarse grid to estimate the measure of similiarity:

$$X = \bigcup_{j=1,...,N_s} x(r_j^s)$$

In order to see the distances between each seismogram , we build a distance matrix (Fig. 5) using nMSE distance:

$$nMSE(x_i, x_j) = \frac{1}{2} \frac{\|x_i - x_j\|_2}{\|x_i\|_2 + \|x_j\|_2}.$$

The distance between the sources grow quite sharply near the main diagonal. However, the dependence of the distance between the seismogram and all the others shows that nMSE grows almost linearly near the source and reaches the limit value, after which it practically does not depend on the distance between the source coordinates. We plot a several of the distance matrix's columns to demonstrate this effect (Fig. 6). Depending on the sources, each line shows how the distance varies.

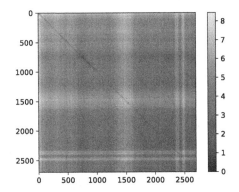

Fig. 5. Distance matrix

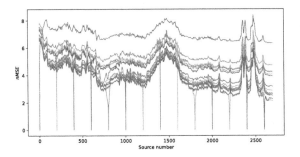

Fig. 6. Several columns of the distance matrix between seismograms for 14 sources.

Also, as in the previous case, the training sample is built using the Hausdorff distance between the training dataset and the entire set of inaccurate seismograms that is available:

$$\delta_s = \max_{j \in J} \min_{i \in J^s} nMSE(x_i, x_j),$$

where J^s represents the set of seismogram indices from the training dataset. To construct the training dataset we limit the Hausdorff distance δ_s. The pseudocode for such a process is presented in Algorithm 2.

The structure of the algorithm is almost the same as in the previous section, except that we use a set of seismograms rather than a velocity model.

You can also look at our previous study [14], in which a training dataset is created using the NRMS metric, which is often found in seismics.

Algorithm 2. An algorithm of L_2 preserving dataset construction

---

$J^s \leftarrow \varnothing$
$N_{cl} \leftarrow 0$
$j_0 \leftarrow 1$
$j \leftarrow j_0$
while $j < N_s$ **do**
    while $\min_{k=j_0...j} \max_{l=j_0...j} nMSE(\boldsymbol{x}(\boldsymbol{r}_k^s), \boldsymbol{x}(\boldsymbol{r}_l^s)) \leq H_0$ **do**
        $j \leftarrow j + 1$
    end while
    $j \leftarrow j - 1$
    $J_{N_{cl}+1} \leftarrow \arg \min_{k=j_0...j} \max_{l=j_0...j} nMSE(\boldsymbol{x}(\boldsymbol{r}_k^s), \boldsymbol{x}(\boldsymbol{r}_l^s))$
    $J^s \leftarrow J^s \cup J_{N_{cl}+1}.$
    $N_{cl} \leftarrow N_{cl} + 1.$
    $j_0 \leftarrow j + 1$
end while

4.4 Numerical Results

In this section, the results of neural network training on each of the above samples are presented (Fig. 7). We have constructed several training samples with an equidistant distribution of sources and denoted them as $D_{2.9}^{eq}, D_{6.2}^{eq}, D_{10}^{eq}$ with a training dataset size of $2\%, 6.2\%, 10\%$ respectively. We built optimized training datasets based on velocity model properties $D_{2.4}^M, D_{6.4}^M, D_9^M$ with $65, 173, 245$ sources respectively. And finally, we built optimized training samples based on seismic data distance $D_{2.5}^S, D_{6.4}^S, D_{10.5}^S$ with $68, 146, 283$ sources respectively.

Figure 7 shows how the learning outcomes change with respect to each source for approximately the same size of the training sample. It is worth noting that the results of applying NDM-net to samples depend on the distribution of sources. In Fig. 7(a, b) the learning error for D^S is equal to or less than the learning error for D^{eq}, despite the fact that the size of D^S is smaller. Below the 2000th source, where the model has smooth velocities and the distance between seismograms is somewhat smaller than between other sources, the optimized samples are more sparse, so they show similar results with training on D^{eq}.

The training time of a neural network is highly dependent on the training dataset size. For 300 sources, the training time was 40 min, and for 55 sources - 7 min. While the generation time of seismic data by a neural network is negligible, about 10 s for the entire test set.

Two NVIDIA GeForce RTX 3090 graphics cards each with 8 GB of memory and an Intel Core CPU with 256 GB of RAM are used to train the networks. Calculations were carried out in parallel on two GPU's using the Pytorch library.

5 Global Sensitivity Analysis of Operator G

We are interested in how many training samples are needed and how to make them representative. To investigate this issue, we generate sets of random indexes

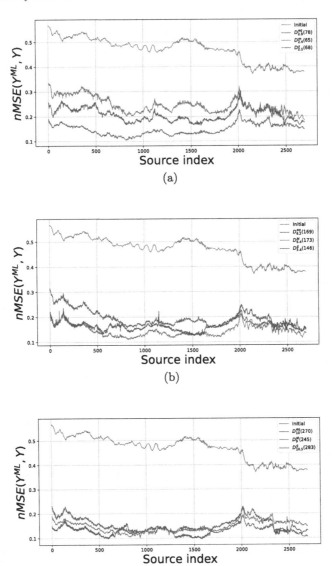

Fig. 7. Distances between seismic data with dispersion and accurate seismic data (Initial), as well as the NDM-net results for D^{eq}, D^s, D^M approximately: (a) 70 sources; (b) 160 sources; (c) 270 sources

that correspond to the training samples. We use binomial distribution which generate sequence of N_s random experiments whose output is either 1 with a probability p or 0 with a probability $1 - p$. The units in the sequence determine which data indices are taken into the training set. Next, we trained a set of neural networks for each of these samples and calculated the errors between all generated seismograms and seismograms modeled on a fine grid such that:

$$\varepsilon(Y^{ML}, Y) = \frac{1}{N_s} \sum_{i=1}^{N_s} nMSE(y_i^{ML}, y_i),$$

where $Y^{ML} = \{y^{ML}\}_{y=1}^{N_s}$ is the neural network generated data set. Figure 8 depicts the results of this experiment.

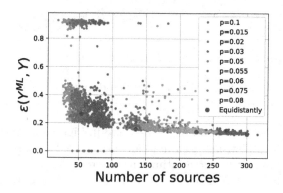

Fig. 8. Random sample and mean error

There are aberrations, most likely related to the features of the neural network architecture or the location of the sources that are used as training data in space. Such artifacts are easily filtered and are of little value in the study, although they should be kept in mind. Additionally, we have demonstrated that among all outcomes with a fixed number of seismograms in the training dataset, the results of a neural network training on the equidistant dataset D^{eq} provide nearly the lowest error.

We have deduced the trend of error that has an exponential dependence, and also showed how the deviation changes (Fig. 9). We see that a large variation occurs when the size of the training sample is small, while a large number of sources in the dataset gives us a more guaranteed result.

Next, for each randomly generated dataset we considered three types of distances, introduced above: Hausdorff distance based on the velocity model δ_m, Hausdorff distance between the seismograms δ_s, and Hausdorff distance between the source positions δ_d. We provide plots of these distances over the sample size in Fig. 10. First, we see that the distance δ_m has a linear dependence on the number of sources, and the variance has almost the same value on the entire trend line. Next, we see the exponential dependence of both the distances $\delta_s(N_s)$ and $\delta_d(N_s)$ from the number of sources. It is possible that the dependence may still be linear, but with a few sources included in the sample, the variation increases sharply.

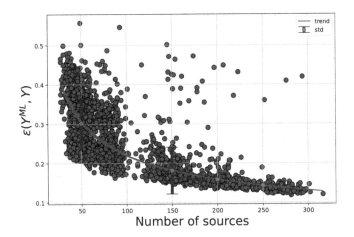

Fig. 9. Error trend and deviation

As it follows from numerical tests presented in Figs. 9 and 10, for a fixed N_{cl} the deviation of the NDM-net accuracy can vary, as well as the considered Hausdorff distances. Thus, it is worth estimating the relations between the distances variability and the overall NDM-net error. To do so, we suggest using the global sensitivity analysis [17–19].

If applied to multi-parametric data, global sensitivity analysis (GSA) allows one to determine significant parameters, which affect the final result. This helps to reduce the number of necessary experiments and allow us to understand how to form a training sample. We fix the training sample size: $N_{cl} = const$ to study the effect of each of the distances. In the global sensitivity analysis we look for the poly-linear approximation of the error within the entire domain of interest

$$\mathcal{E}_{J_k}(\delta_s, \delta_m, \delta_d) \approx \mathcal{E}_0 + \frac{\partial \mathcal{E}}{\partial \delta_s}(\delta_s - \delta_0) + \frac{\partial \mathcal{E}}{\partial \delta_m}(\delta_m - \delta_0) + \frac{\partial \mathcal{E}}{\partial \delta_d}(\delta_d - \delta_0)$$

For a fixed number of seismogramms in the training dataset we have several statistical implementation of the dataset. Each implementation can be considered as a single point in 3D parameter space. Thus, for each pair of points we may estimate the directional derivatives as

$$\frac{\partial \mathcal{E}}{\partial \boldsymbol{n}} = \nabla \mathcal{E} \cdot \boldsymbol{n} = \frac{\partial \mathcal{E}}{\partial \delta_s} n_{\delta_s} + \frac{\partial \mathcal{E}}{\partial \delta_m} n_{\delta_m} + \frac{\partial \mathcal{E}}{\partial \delta_d} n_{\delta_d},$$

where $\boldsymbol{n} = (n_{\delta_s}, n_{\delta_m}, n_{\delta_d})$ is normal to the direction. If all possible pairs of implementations are considered together one obtains a system of linear equations with partial derivatives as unknowns. The problem is in general overdetermined, however its generalized solution is composed of the averaged derivatives.

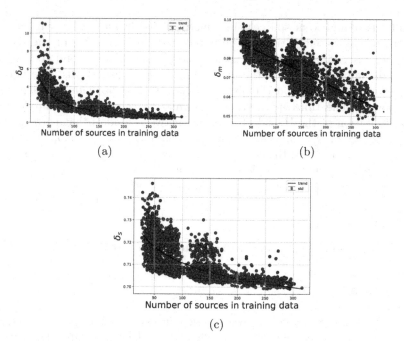

Fig. 10. Dependence of the distances on the size of the training sample: (a) δ_d;(b) δ_m; (c) δ_s

Next, we vary the N_{cl}, compute the derivatives, and average them over the number of different cardinality of the dataset. Consider the effect of each term from the expression for $\mathcal{E}_{J_k}(\delta_s, \delta_m, \delta_d)$ by multiplying partial derivatives by the spread of each of δ_k, where $k = \{\delta_s, \delta_m, \delta_d\}$:

$$\frac{\partial \mathcal{E}}{\partial \delta_s} \Delta \delta_s \approx 0.1, \tag{1}$$

$$\frac{\partial \mathcal{E}}{\partial \delta_m} \Delta \delta_m \approx 0.01, \tag{2}$$

$$\frac{\partial \mathcal{E}}{\partial \delta_d} \Delta \delta_d \approx 0.0005 \tag{3}$$

It can be seen from the results that the sampling based on the distance between the seismograms affects the results the most. That is, the D^S is the most significant in comparison with others, which is confirmed by experiments.

6   Conclusion

The training results showed that neural networks can be used to suppress numerical variance in seismic data. The NDM-net network was used, that converts seismic data with numerical dispersion into data calculated on a fine grid (accurate solution). Three ways of constructing a training sample are shown. The first way is to use equidistant sources. This method has shown that we can suppress the variance by about 5 times. The extent to which the size of the training sample affects training quality is also demonstrated. The second technique is optimized sampling based on the limitation of the Hausdorff distance between seismograms, assuming that the distance between them depends on the position of the source. The third method is the formation of a training sample based on the limitation of the Hausdorff distance between models that correspond to the coordinates of the sources. The last two samples were developed and used for NDM-net training. In the course of applying global analysis, it became clear that the most significant sample is an optimized dataset based on the properties of the seismic data itself. The above three methods of forming a training dataset can be generalized to other seismic data since such methods deal with the properties of the data and the velocity model.

Acknowledgements. The research is supported by the RSCF grant no. 22-11-00004.

References

1. Kaur H., Fomel S., Pham N.: Overcoming numerical dispersion of finite-difference wave extrapolation using deep learning. SEG Technical Program Expanded Abstracts, 2318–2322 (2019). https://doi.org/10.1190/segam2019-3207486.1
2. Yu, S., Ma, J., Wang, W.: Deep learning for denoising. Geophysics **84**(07), 1–107 (2019). https://doi.org/10.1190/geo2018-0668.1
3. Li, H., Yang, W., Yong, X.: Deep learning for ground-roll noise attenuation. SEG Technical Program Expanded Abstracts, 1981–1985 (2018). https://doi.org/10.1190/segam2018-2981295.1
4. Oliveira, D.A.B., Ferreira, R.S., Silva, R., Vital Brazil, E.: Interpolating seismic data with conditional generative adversarial networks. IEEE Geosci. Remote Sens. Lett. **15**(12), 1952–1956 (2018). https://doi.org/10.1109/LGRS.2018.2866199
5. Virieux, J., Calandra, H., Plessix, R.-E.: A review of the spectral, pseudo-spectral, finite-difference and finite-element modelling techniques for geophysical imaging. Geophys. Prospect. **59**(5), 794–813 (2011). https://doi.org/10.1111/j.1365-2478.2011.00967.x
6. Mittet, R.: Second-order time integration of the wave equation with dispersion correction procedures. Geophysics **84**(4), T221–T235 (2019)
7. Liu, Y.: Optimal staggered-grid finite-difference schemes based on least-squares for wave equation modelling. Geophys. J. Int. **197**(2), 1033–1047 (2014)
8. Kaser, M., Dumbser, M., de la Puente, J., Igel, H.: An arbitrary high-order Discontinuous Galerkin method for elastic waves on unstructured meshes III. Viscoelastic attenuation. Geophys. J. Int. **168**(1), 224–242 (2007)
9. Lisitsa, V.: Dispersion analysis of discontinuous Galerkin method on triangular mesh for elastic wave equation. Appl. Math. Model. **40**(7–8), 5077–5095 (2016)
10. Pleshkevich, A., Vishnevsky, D., Lisitsa, V., Levchenko, V.: Parallel algorithm for one-way wave equation based migration for seismic imaging. In: Voevodin, V., Sobolev, S. (eds.) RuSCDays 2018. CCIS, vol. 965, pp. 125–135. Springer, Cham (2019). https://doi.org/10.1007/978-3-030-05807-4_11

11. Gadylshin, K., Lisitsa, V., Gadylshina, K., Vishnevsky, D., Novikov, M.: Machine learning-based numerical dispersion mitigation in seismic modelling. In: Gervasi, O., et al. (eds.) ICCSA 2021. LNCS, vol. 12949, pp. 34–47. Springer, Cham (2021). https://doi.org/10.1007/978-3-030-86653-2_3
12. Gadylshin, K., Vishnevsky, D., Gadylshina, K., Lisitsa, V.: Numerical dispersion mitigation neural network for seismic modeling. Geophysics **87**(3), T237–T249 (2022)
13. Ronneberger, O., Fischer, P., Brox, T.: U-Net: convolutional networks for biomedical image segmentation. In: Navab, N., Hornegger, J., Wells, W.M., Frangi, A.F. (eds.) MICCAI 2015. LNCS, vol. 9351, pp. 234–241. Springer, Cham (2015). https://doi.org/10.1007/978-3-319-24574-4_28
14. Gadylshin, K., Lisitsa, V., Gadylshina, K., Vishnevsky, D.: Optimization of the training dataset for numerical dispersion mitigation neural network. In: Gervasi, O., Murgante, B., Misra, S., Rocha, A.M.A.C., Garau, C. (eds.) ICCSA 2022. LNCS, vol. 13378, pp. 295–309. Springer, Cham (2022). https://doi.org/10.1007/978-3-031-10562-3_22
15. Yang, F., Ma, J.: Deep-learning inversion: a next generation seismic velocity-model building method. Geophysics **84**(4), R583–R599 (2019)
16. Levander, A.R.: Fourth-order finite-difference P-SV seismograms. Geophysics **53**(11), 1425–1436 (1988)
17. Sobol, I.M.: Global sensitivity indices for nonlinear mathematical models and their Monte Carlo estimates. Math. Comput. Simulat. **55**(1–3), 271–280 (2011). https://doi.org/10.1016/S0378-4754(00)00270-6
18. Saltelli, A., et al.: Global Sensitivity Analysis. The Primer. Wiley, Chichester (2018)
19. Kucherenko, S., Iooss, B.: Derivative based global sensitivity measures. Monte Carlo and Quasi-Monte Carlo Methods, pp. 455–469 (2016)

Validity and Limitations of Supervised Learning for Phase Transition Research

Diana Sukhoverkhova[1,2] , Vladislav Chertenkov[1,2] , Evgeni Burovski[1,2] ,
and Lev Shchur[1,2(✉)]

[1] Landau Institute for Theoretical Physics, Chernogolovka, Russia
lev@landau.ac.ru
[2] HSE University, Moscow, Russia

Abstract. We analyze the Ising model and the Baxter-Wu model in
two dimensions using deep learning networks trained to classify paramagnetic (PM) and ferromagnetic (FM) phases. We use the usual Metropolis
Monte Carlo algorithm to create uncorrelated snapshots of spin states.
The images used as training data are labeled as belonging to the PM
state or the FM state using analytically known phase transition temperatures depending on a given set of parameters. The main result of
the paper is that the widely used technique for extraction of the critical
temperature directly from the dependence of the output function is not
universal. The value of the output function at the critical temperature
really depends on the anisotropy of the model under study, the architecture of the deep network, and some parameters of the deep network
application.

Keywords: Machine learning · Anisotropic models · Ising model ·
Baxter-Wu model · Phase transitions · Critical temperature · Critical
exponents

1 Introduction

Machine learning has become the *fourth* paradigm of scientific research, following the historically introduced 1) *experiment*, based on practical experience
in contact with nature, 2) *theory*, which developed models and mathematical
methods to explain some experiments, and 3) *computer simulations*, which is an
extended application of models and applied mathematics to situations in which
the theory could not make any clear predictions due to mathematical limitations. From about 2015 A.D. it became clear that data-driven science based on
deep machine learning is a powerful research tool and can complement the other
three paradigms.

It seems relevant to conduct research on the application of new methods of
deep machine learning to the problems of natural science in order to verify the
accuracy of the extracted results and search for the possibility of obtaining new
knowledge. It is also important to conduct a comparative analysis of the amount

© The Author(s), under exclusive license to Springer Nature Switzerland AG 2023
V. Voevodin et al. (Eds.): RuSCDays 2023, LNCS 14389, pp. 314–329, 2023.
https://doi.org/10.1007/978-3-031-49435-2_22

of use of computer resources when using already proven methods and algorithms and when using methods based on deep machine learning.

In this paper, we report the results of such an analysis within the framework of the "statistical mechanics and machine learning" direction. We choose two basic models of statistical mechanics for which there is a deep knowledge of the nature of the phase transition and a number of precise results, including a full set of analytical knowledge and reliable computational methods. These are the Ising model with a number of parameters and the Baxter-Wu model. These models belong to different classes of universality. For two of these models, a complete mathematical description of phase transitions is known, including the dependence of the critical temperature on the model parameters and a set of critical exponents that describe the universal behavior of thermodynamic quantities near the critical temperature. We choose three network architectures, CNN, FCNN and ResNet for model analysis.

The paper is organized as follows. Section 2 summarizes previous major work on applying machine learning to statistical mechanics models. The Sect. 3 presents the analytical knowledge that will be used to generate data and analyze the output of the deep network. Section 4.2 describes the deep learning networks used in the analysis. Section 6 presents the results of testing the Ising model taking into account the anisotropy of spin interactions, which leads to a deviation from the critical temperature prediction. Section 7 discusses how the number of epochs affects the shape of the output function. Section 8 summarizes the results obtained and discusses further work.

2   Previous Work

The first paper in the field [1] reports on the application of CNN to classify the paramagnetic (PM) and ferromagnetic (FM) phases of the Ising model. The main results are: 1) the output function is equal to $1/2$ at the critical temperature and 2) the data collapse of the output function obtained for various lattice sizes gives an estimate of the correlation length exponent.

The number of papers follows which use that idea with application to Potts model at second order and first order phase transitions [2]. The determination of the Berezinsky-Kosterlitz-Thouless phase transition and the second-order phase transition in XXZ models was recently reported [7], and the CNN network from the Keras library was used to classify the PM and FM phases to estimate the critical temperature. Therefore, they used the same network architecture and the same analysis as in the article by Carrasquilla and Melko [1].

Various network architectures, training protocols, and deep learning neural networks (NNs) have been used [3–6] to solve multiple physics problems and using supervised or unsupervised learning.

They all use the approach presented in the pioneering article [1], and the main purpose of this article is a thorough and detailed analysis of the applicability of the approach. In our previous article [8], we report a preliminary study of two-dimensional Ising and Baxter-Wu models. We have found that variation of the output function is more informative than the output function itself.

3   Models

We consider two two-dimensional models: the Ising model and the Baxter-Wu model. In addition, we consider two versions of the Ising model given on a square lattice and solved by Onsager [9], and on a triangular lattice and solved by Houtappel [10]. The difference between the Ising model and the Baxter-Wu model, which is defined on a triangular lattice, is that in the Ising model there is a coupling between two spins, while in the Baxter-Wu model there is a coupling between three spins.

3.1   Ising Models on Square and Triangular Lattices

Two-dimensional Ising model on a *square lattice* is defined by the Hamiltonian [9] with spins $\sigma_{x,y}$, which takes two values $\sigma_i = \pm 1$ and placed at the vertices of the lattice shown on the left side of Fig. 1

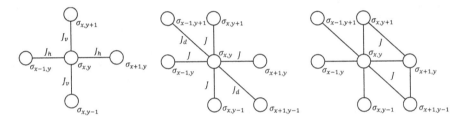

Fig. 1. Illustration of the spin positions and couplings. Left: Ising model on the square lattice, Expr. (1). Center: Ising model on the triangular lattice, Expr. (3). Right: Baxter-Wu model on triangular lattice, Expr. (5).

$$\mathcal{H} = - \sum_{(x,y)} \left(J_h \sigma_{x,y} \sigma_{x+1,y} + J_v \sigma_{x,y} \sigma_{x,y+1} \right), \tag{1}$$

where (x, y) denotes the summation over all vertices, J_h is the coupling constant between the horizontal bonds, and J_v is the coupling constant between the vertical bonds of the square lattice. The couplings J_h and J_v are positive, which leads to ferromagnetic ordering of neighboring spins. We use periodic boundaries in both directions.

The critical temperature T_c of the Ising model with Hamiltonian (1) is known [9] from the expression

$$\sinh \frac{2 J_h}{k_B T_c} \sinh \frac{2 J_v}{k_B T_c} = 1, \tag{2}$$

where T is the temperature and k_B is the Boltzmann factor.

Two-dimensional Ising model on *triangular lattice* defined by the Hamiltonian [10] with the spins $\sigma_{x,y}$, taking two values $\sigma_i = \pm 1$ and placed at the vertices of the lattice shown on the right side of Fig. 1

$$\mathcal{H} = -\sum_{(x,y)} \left(J\sigma_{x,y}(\sigma_{x+1,y} + \sigma_{x,y+1}) + J_d\sigma_{x,y}\sigma_{x+1,y+1} \right), \tag{3}$$

where J is the coupling constant between the horizontal and vertical bonds of the square lattice and J_d is the coupling constant between the spins along the diagonals. The J coupling is positive, which leads to ferromagnetic ordering of neighboring spins, while the J_d coupling can be positive, zero, or negative. In the latter case, it will try to make the antiferromagnetic ordering of the spins along the diagonal. For the lack of simplicity, we fix $J = 1$ and vary J_d as a model parameter. We use periodic boundaries in both directions.

The critical temperature of the Ising model with Hamiltonian (3) is known [10] from the expression

$$\left(\sinh \frac{2J}{k_B T_c} \right)^2 + 2\sinh \frac{2J}{k_B T_c} \sinh \frac{2J_d}{k_B T_c} = 1. \tag{4}$$

In what follows, we will measure the temperature in units of energy (or bond, since spin is a dimensionless quantity) and omit the factor k_B.

3.2   Baxter-Wu Model

Two-dimensional Baxter-Wu model on the *triangular lattice* defined by the Hamiltonian [11] with spins $\sigma_{x,y}$, taking two values $\sigma_i = \pm 1$ and placed at the vertices and with three-spin interactions, as shown on the right side of Fig. 1,

$$\mathcal{H} = -\sum_{(x,y)} J \left(\sigma_{x,y}\sigma_{x+1,y}\sigma_{x+1,y-1} + \sigma_{x,y}\sigma_{x+1,y}\sigma_{x,y+1} \right), \tag{5}$$

where the sum in the first term goes over triangles with one orientation, and the sum in the second term goes over triangles with the other orientation, as shown on the right side of Fig. 1. The coupling J is positive, which leads to ferromagnetic spin ordering. We use periodic boundaries in both directions.

The critical temperature of the Baxter-Wu model with the Hamiltonian (5) is known [11]

$$k_B T_c = J\frac{2}{\ln(\sqrt{2}+1)}. \tag{6}$$

3.3   Phase Transitions and Universality

All three models demonstrate a second-order phase transition - the internal energy E is a continuous function at all temperatures, but the heat capacity C has a singularity at the critical temperature and diverges to infinity on both sides of the critical temperature. The difference between the models is in the different law of divergence. The specific heat of the Baxter-Wu model diverges according to a power law [11] $C \propto 1/|\tau|^{\alpha_{bw}}$, where $\alpha_{bw} = 2/3$. The specific heats of two Ising models, the square lattice Ising model, Expr. (1), and the square lattice Ising model, Expr. (3), diverge logarithmically [9] $C_{is} \propto \ln|\tau|$, where the reduced temperature $\tau = \frac{T-T_c}{T}$ is the dimensionless distance of temperature T from critical temperature T_c. Therefore, it is assumed that $\alpha = 0$ for the Ising model.

The correlation length ξ [12] between the spins (the distance is measured in lattice units $a = 1$) diverges at the critical point with the exponent ν, and $\xi \propto 1/|\tau|^{\nu}$, and the value of ν for the two models is different, for the Baxter-Wu model it is equal to $\nu_{bw} = 2/3$. For both Ising models, the divergence is the same and $\nu_{is} = 1$.

Two critical exponents, α and ν, determine the class of universality of models [13]. Both Ising models, Expr. (1) and Expr. (3), belong to the same universality class named after the Ising model. While the Baxter-Wu model, Expr. (5), belongs to the universality class of the four-state Potts model [14]. It should be noted that the thermodynamic quantities of the four-state Potts model states have an additional logarithmic dependence on reduced temperature [16], while the Baxter-Wu model does not [11,15]. The absence of logarithmic corrections makes the analysis of the Baxter-Wu model more reliable [17].

4   Data Generation and Deep Learning

We generate data using the Monte Carlo Markov Chain (MCMC) approach and the generated data is used for supervised training and testing.

4.1   Data Generation

We use Metropolis algorithm for data generation [18]. Each set is generated with the fixed lattice size L and temperature of thermostat reservoire T. The unit of time for the data generation is 1 MCS (Monte Carlo Step) which is L^2 local Metropolis updates. The correlation time [19] between spin states estimated [8] $t_{corr} = L^{2.15}$. We drop out the first 20 t_{corr} MCS giving system to thermalize at the temperature T, and than save spin distribution each $2 \times t_{corr}$ MCS as an black-white image, associate black with spin pointing up ($\sigma = 1$) or white with spin pointing down ($\sigma = 0$). Thus saved images are not correlated and do not produce any systematic bias to the future research.

4.2   Neural Network Architectures and Output Data

We use three neural network (NN) architectures: fully connected NN (FCNN) architecture, convolutional neural network (CNN) architecture, and ResNet [20] architecture. The details was reported in our previous paper [8].

The NN parameters does depend on the system size of the statistical mechanics model. For example, for investigation of the Ising models defined by Expr. (1) and Expr. (3) we use NN consisting with following layers – Conv2d (N64, K2x2, S1) (see Ref. [21]), MaxPool2d (2x2), ReLU, Linear (64x(L/2-1)x((L/2-1),64), ReLU, Linear (64,1), Sigmoid. The outputs of each layer are shown in the table 1 and the last fully connected layer have one output neuron which used as prediction of the tested snapshot to the ferromagnetic (FM) state.

Table 1. Output of CNN layers used to analyze Ising models, where bs is a batch size.

Layer	Output Shape
Conv2d	[bs, 64, $L - 1, L - 1$]
MaxPool2d	[bs, 64, $L/2 - 1, L/2 - 1$]
ReLU	[bs, 64, $L/2 - 1, L/2 - 1$]
Linear	[bs, 64]
ReLU	[bs, 64]
Linear	[bs, 1]
Sigmoid	[bs, 1]

5 Learning and Testing

We form training datasets of size N_d and test datasets of size N_t. Typical values of N_d and N_t are several hundred, the actual value depends on the task and will be given below. Each set contains data generated with specific values of coupling constants J, J_v, J_h, J_d, snapshot temperatures T, lattice size L, and a class corresponding to temperatures within FM phase (Class = 1) or PM phase (Class = 0) of statistical mechanics models. The Class value is used for supervised learning of the NN.

All samples are randomly divided into batches of four snapshots ($bs = 4$) for each training iteration. The loss function is binary cross entropy (BCE).

$$Q(\hat{f}_i, f_i) = -\frac{1}{N_d} \sum_{i=1}^{N_d} \left[\hat{f}_i \ln f_i + (1 - \hat{f}_i) \ln(1 - f_i) \right], \tag{7}$$

where $\hat{f}_i$ is the correct class, f_i is the NN prediction, $\hat{f}_i \in \{0, 1\}$, $f_i \in [0; 1]$. The Adam algorithm is used for weight optimization [22].

The functions of interest for analysis are the average $F(T; L)$ of the output function $f_i(T; L)$, which is the prediction that sample i with lattice size L generated with temperature T, belongs to FM phase

$$F(T; L) = \frac{1}{N_t} \sum_{i=1}^{N_t} f_i(T; L) \tag{8}$$

and its variation, $V(T; L)$,

$$V(T; L) = \sqrt{\frac{1}{N_t} \sum_{i=1}^{N_t} (f_i(T; L))^2 - \left(\frac{1}{N_t} \sum_{i=1}^{N_t} f_i(T; L) \right)^2}. \tag{9}$$

6   Influence of Anisotropy

In this section, we present an analysis of the output function $F(T; L)$ and varia-tions of the output function $V(T; L)$ for two Ising models with Hamiltonians (1) and (3). We train the NN on the symmetric case of links $J_h = J_v$ for the first model and the zero value of the diagonal link J_d in the second model. Therefore, the training sample in both cases has the symmetry D_4, the lattice is invariant under rotation through the angle $\pi/2$. The test sets have D_2 symmetry, and the lattice is invariant under rotation through the angle π.

6.1   Ising Model on Square Lattice

Ising model on a square lattice with Hamiltonian (1) solved exactly by Onsager [9]. The critical temperature is given in Onsager's article [9]. The NN was trained on 2048 images of the Ising model with symmetrical coupling con-stants $J_h = J_v$. Testing was carried out on 512 images of Ising models for different values of the couplings $J_v = J_h$.

The pseudo-critical temperature is obtained in two ways, following the meth-ods proposed in [1] and in [8]. The pseudo-critical temperature depends on the lattice size [24] and converges to the critical temperature T_c in the thermody-namic limit of the infinite size of the system. This fact allows us to estimate the critical temperature from the behavior of the pseudo-critical point, which depends on the size of the system as $\propto 1/L^{1/\nu}$, where ν is equal to the critical length exponent (see discussion in Subsect. 3.3). In addition, this dependence allows us to estimate the exponent of the correlation length ν.

The first [1] method for calculating the pseudo-critical temperature $T^*(L)$ for a fixed lattice size L estimated as the intersection point of the functions $F(T; L)$ and $1 - F(T; L)$, which are the FM and FM phase predictions, respectively. We estimate $T^*(L)$ for each value of the ratio of coupling constants $J_v/J_h = 1, 0.75, 0.5, 0.25, 0.125,$ and 0.625, and take limit of the infinite system size using the formula [25]

$$T^* = T^*(L) + \frac{A}{L^b}, \tag{10}$$

where b is an estimate for $1/\nu$, and found visible deviation of the predicted critical temperature from the exactly known one [9] at small values of the ratio J_v/J_h, as shown in the Fig. 2. This deviation can be explained due to the dependence of the correlation length dependence on the ratio J_v/J_h. In the paper [26] the spin-spin correlation function was analytically calculated for the Ising model on the square lattice in the thermodynamic limit

$$C\left(\sigma(0)\sigma(R)\right) = \frac{F_{\pm}}{R^{1/4}} + O(1/R^{5/4}),$$ (11)

where R is the distance between any two spins $\sigma(0)$ and $\sigma(R)$, and F_+ and F_- are the amplitudes in the FM and PM phases, respectively. The Fig. 1 of the paper [26] shows dependence of the ratio of the amplitudes F_+/F_- which is similar to those deviation shown in the Fig. 2.

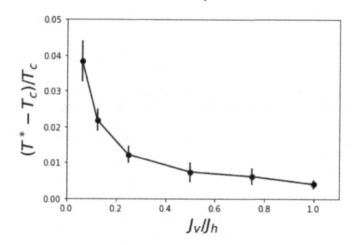

Fig. 2. Deviation of the critical temperature prediction T^* from T_c as function of the coupling ratio J_v/J_h. T^* estimated using method of output functions intersection [1].

The second method for estimating the pseudo-critical temperature [8] is based on the analysis of the variation of the output function $V(T; L)$ (Expr. 9). Approximation of $V(T; L)$ by a unnormalized Gaussian function gives the mean value μ, standard deviation σ (not to be confused with spin) and scale k. The value can be related to the pseudo-critical temperature $T^{\oplus}(L)$ and an approximation using Expr. (10) gives an estimate of the exponent ν and the critical temperature T_c. The deviation of $T^{\oplus}$ from the exact T_c is shown in the Fig. 3.

It is noteworthy that the deviations $(T^* - T_c)/T_c$ and $(T^{\oplus} - T_c)/T_c$ behave qualitatively in the same way, although the second estimation method gives somewhat smaller values.

Table 2 shows estimates of the inverse correlation length exponent $1/\nu$ obtained from the σ variance and demonstrating fairly good agreement with the exact value $1/\nu = 1$ for all ratios of coupling constants J_v/J_h.

6.2   Ising Model on Triangular Lattice

Another interesting and non-trivial model belonging to the universality class of the Ising model, which exhibits the same behavior near the critical point

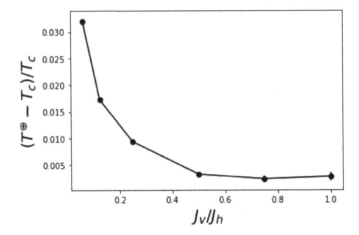

Fig. 3. Deviation of the critical temperature prediction $T^{\oplus}$ from T_c as function of the coupling ratio J_v/J_h. $T^{\oplus}$ estimated using approximation of the function $V(T; L)$ [8].

Table 2. The $b^{\oplus}$ estimate for the inverse correlation length exponent $1/\nu$ obtained from the σ variance.

J_v/J_h	$b^{\oplus}$
1.0	1.12(3)
0.75	1.09(3)
0.5	1.07(4)
0.25	1.06(6)
0.125	0.98(14)
0.0625	1.02(9)

in terms of critical exponents, is the Ising model on a triangular lattice with Hamiltonian (3). It was found [27] that the diagonal term, which is proportional to the coupling constant J_d, violates the universality of the Binder cumulant due to significant anisotropy. This case differs from that described in the previous section, for which the Binder cumulant retains a universal value for all ratios of the coupling constants J_v/J_h. The Fig. 4 shows the dependence of the ratio $(T^{\wedge} - T_c)/T_c$ on the change in the value of the coupling constants J_d/J. The deviation of the predicted critical temperature $T^{\wedge}$ from the exact one T_c systematically increases with the value of the anisotropy coupling constant.

7   Influence of Number of Epochs for Training

In the previous sections, we have considered the problem of correctly extracting the critical temperature and the correlation length exponent from the output classification function and have analyzed some properties of transfer learning

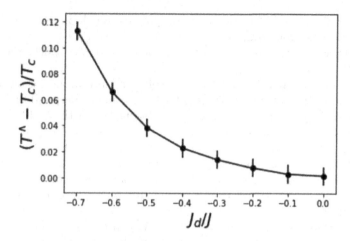

Fig. 4. Deviation of critical temperature prediction $T^\wedge$ from exact T_c depending on the coupling ratio J_d/J. Estimation of $T^\wedge$ by the intersection of output functions [1].

related to the same problem. The analysis of the previous section is presented in the language of statistical physics. This section is more related to machine learning itself, and primatily deal with the effect of the length of training: the number of training "epochs".

Transfer learning is a technique commonly used in applications to enable neural networks (NNs) to solve more than one task. This is sometimes referred to as NN pre-training. With pre-training, you don't have to train a new network for every problem you encounter. Instead, you train NN only once on a wide range of data and then you can use it as a specific layer. This layer, *the backbone*, is a network trained to extract important features. It usually has a deep architecture with millions of parameters and consists of complex layers such as convolutional layer blocks, encoder-decoder blocks, skip connections, attention maps, etc. Often the end layer of a backbone is a vector (embedding vector) that represents various aspects of input object.

The way to learn the critical behavior of spin models with NN classification pre-training translates the problem into multitasking. This study and related works demonstrate the property of the output function that it carries information about the ordered phase, critical temperature, and correlation length exponent. A more detailed study shows that this property is not stable and depends on the quality of NN training.

In previous sections, we analyzed the Ising model. In this section we use the Baxter-Wu model, (5). We expect that the qualitative conclusions for the NN learning process are similar.

7.1   Ordered Phase Prediction in Spin Systems

We have demonstrated that the critical exponent ν can be extracted from a linear approximation on the logarithmic scale of the standard deviation of the V(T) curve, the variance of a ferromagnetic output neuron. It is worth mentioning some aspects of network training that we did not study in the previous sections. The question is how to choose the batch size and how many epochs the training should last.

In [8] we used a batch size of 36. The rule of thumb is that increasing the batch size results in faster learning in terms of CPU time and a sharper decrease in the loss function. The extracted ν values were obtained from the V(T) curve after the first epoch of training, even though the training lasted 10 epochs. Training for more than 1 epoch was necessary in order to make sure that the mean value of the BCE loss function does not grow, and we are not in danger of overfitting.

We challenged the approach used in [8] and ran more experiments with different batch sizes and longer training times in epochs, as shown in Fig. 5. It seemed that 10 epochs was enough to train the network and that the error rate of 0.25 would not drop much in the future. As can be seen from Fig. 5, by the 50th epoch, the error drops 10 times relative to that level to a value of 0.025. A larger batch size results in a faster decrease of the loss function.

This observation raises the question of what would have happened to the functions F(T) and V(T) in epochs 10, 20, 30, 30+ since these functions were used to extract the exponent ν. The Fig. 6 shows the $F(T)$ and $V(T)$ functions predicted on the test data for the Ising model for different epochs with ResNet-10, lattice size 72 and batch size 512. The errors in the figures are less than or equal to the size of the markers.

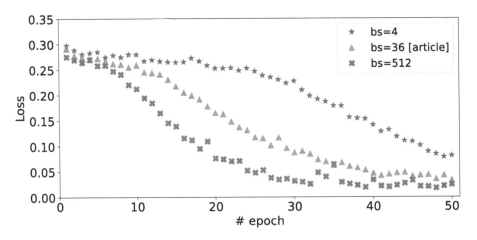

Fig. 5. Validation loss per epoch for different batch sizes (*bs*) for the Baxter-Wu model, 5.

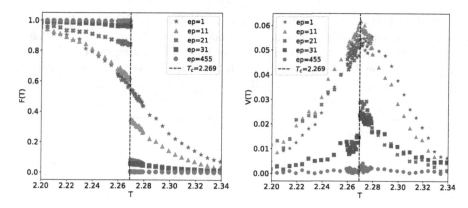

Fig. 6. (left) $F(T)$, the average of the output function, and the variance of output function, $V(T)$, (right) for different numbers of epochs 1, 11, 21, 31, 455. Dashed black vertical line indicates the critical temperature T_c.

The left image in Fig. 6 shows that the output function $F(T)$ turns into a step function as the number of epochs increases. Similarly to $F(T)$, the variance of the output function $V(T)$ in the right image decreases as the number of epochs increases. The direct interpretation is that the NN quality of classification improves. The NN is getting better and better at separating snapshots for the ferromagnetic phase from the paramagnetic ones. The output values f_i become close to 0 or 1. The measure of uncertainty of NN, which is expressed in the function $V(T)$, is reduced. For epochs greater than 1, it becomes difficult and even impossible to analyze the function $V(T)$ using the approximation of the unnormalized Gaussian function mentioned in Sect. 6.1.

This observation about the behavior of the output function $F(T)$ raised another question: what if we train the NN to classify configurations relative to the critical point T_c from the finite-size scaling (FSS) of the thermodynamic quantities. Is the NN able to determine the transition point and whether the step of $F(T)$ is observed near T_c with an increase in the number of epochs?

Let us investigate how the output function $F(T)$ would change from the epoch of the NN and train temperature $\hat{T}_c$, at which we train NN to classify into ferromagnetic $(T < \hat{T}_c)$ and paramagnetic $(T > \hat{T}_c)$ phases. Compare the results for different values of $\hat{T}_c$: a) $\hat{T}_c = 2.269$ from the exact solution, b) $\hat{T}_c = 2.274$ from intersection $F(T)$ with the level $1/2$, c) $\hat{T}_c = 2.28$ from the FSS of heat capacity C, and d) $\hat{T}_c = 2.295$ from the FSS of magnetic susceptibility χ. Figure 7 shows the $F(T)$ function predicted on the test data trained at different $\hat{T}_c$. The errors in the figures are smaller than or equal to the size of the markers.

The NN classifies snapshots with respect to the shifted critical temperature $\hat{T}_c$. If we select a classification threshold at which all values above are assigned to a positive class, and values below to a negative one, we get the accuracy of correctly classified snapshots close to 100% for epochs greater than 1. The output function $F(T)$ displays the step at the $\hat{T}_c$ used for training for epochs greater than 1. However, for temperatures $\hat{T}_c = 2.274, 2.28, 2.295$, as the number of epochs increases, $F(T)$ does not turn into a clear step, as at $\hat{T}_c = 2.269$, at which the step at epoch 10 and epoch 30 can be distinguished. At these temperatures, the $F(T)$ function do not differ much between epochs 10 and 80 and does not exhibit a systematic shift as they do at $\hat{T}_c = 2.269$.

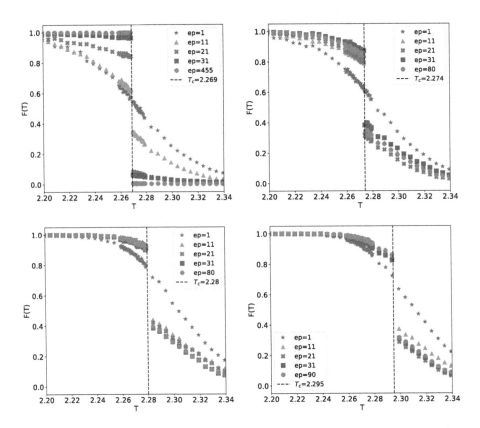

Fig. 7. The output function $F(T)$ for different epochs. Dashed vertical black lines correspond to train temperatures $\hat{T}_c = 2.269, 2.274, 2.280,$ and 2.295 in figure order.

8   Discussion

The paper discusses an important issue of applicability of *transfer learning* to critical temperature estimation in statistical mechanics models. Careful analysis using several neural network architectures, several statistical mechanics models, and various methods for extracting the critical temperature estimate from the NN output leads to the following facts.

First, the anisotropy of the interaction of models of statistical mechanics leads to a deviation of the critical temperature estimate from the actual value.

Second, we distinguish two cases of anisotropy – 1) a trivial case of orthogonal anisotropy that can be corrected by an aspect ratio: this case corresponds to the Ising model with Hamiltonian (1); 2) a trivial case of diagonal anisotropy not related to the problem of aspect ratio [27]: this case corresponds to the Ising model with Hamiltonian (3); the critical temperature estimate with the different methods, proposed in [1,8], coincide well within the statistical and systematic errors of the methods. Third, the critical temperature estimates by different methods proposed in [1,8] are in good agreement within statistical and systematic errors of the methods. Fourth, the estimate of the correlation length exponent by the method of the article [8] is more reliable than that proposed in the article [1]. Fifth, the estimate of the correlation length exponent for all anisotropic models agrees well with the value of the critical exponent of the correlation length of the Ising universality class, $\nu = 1$.

The batch size and the number of epochs should be chosen to pre-train the classification NN, as they affect the quality of NN predictions. The step function on Fig. 6 is the result of a long training. It should not be treated as overfitting of the model. Most likely, the classification trained NN, loses its generalizing ability, while training, and focuses on optimizing the quality of separating the phases. In Fig. 6, the phases are progressively more accurately separated as the number of epochs increases, and both the NN output, $F(T)$, and its variance, $V(T)$, become unsuitable to extract the critical exponent ν.

Another possible explanation that the output layer of a single neuron is limited by the amount of aspects it contains. An embedding vector of few neurons probably would have greater generalizing ability. A more thorough study is needed, since the huge number of NN parameters makes it impossible to interpret such vectors.

It may be worth focusing on finding more efficient ways to pre-train a NN, in addition to classification. For example, pre-training of language models is often based on understanding the context of a sentence, rather than sentiment classification. The BERT model [23] uses masking of an input for which the network tries to recover a masked part, by itself determining which features should be extracted.

Summing up, there are three main messages of the article. The first positive point is that neural networks trained on an isotropic model predict well the class of universality of anisotropic models. The second negative point is that NN predicts the critical temperature of an anisotropic model with a visible displacement. The third point is that there is some optimum number of epochs for a good estimate of the critical exponent. Therefore, transfer learning is valid for checking the class of universality, and care should be taken if there is no certain knowledge about the anisotropy of the system.

Acknowledgements. Research supported by the grant 22-11-00259 of the Russian Science Foundation.

The simulations were done using the computational resources of HPC facilities at HSE University.

References

1. Carrasquilla, J., Melko, R.G.: Machine learning phases of matter. Nat. Phys. **13**(5), 431–434 (2017)
2. Bachtis, D., Aarts, G., Lucini, B.: Mapping distinct phase transitions to a neural network. Phys. Rev. E **102**(5), 053306 (2020)
3. Van Nieuwenburg, E.P., Liu, Y.H., Huber, S.D.: Learning phase transitions by confusion. Nat. Phys. **13**, 435–439 (2017)
4. Morningstar, A., Melko, R.G.: Deep learning the Ising model near criticality. J. Mach. Learn. Res. **18**(163), 1–17 (2018)
5. Westerhout, T., et al.: Generalization properties of neural network approximations to frustrated magnet ground states. Nat. Commun. **11**, 1593 (2020)
6. Walker, N., Tam, K.M.: InfoCGAN classification of 2-dimensional square Ising configurations (2020). arXiv preprint arXiv:2005.01682
7. Miyajima, Y., Mochizuki, M.: Machine-learning detection of the Berezinskii-Kosterlitz-Thouless transition and the second-order phase transition in the XXZ models. Phys. Rev. B **107**, 134420 (2023)
8. Chertenkov, V., Burovski, E., Shchur, L.: Deep machine learning investigation of phase transitions. In: Voevodin, V., Sobolev, S., Yakobovskiy, M., Shagaliev, R. (eds.) RuSCDays 2022. LNCS, vol. 13708, pp. 397–408. Springer, Cham (2022). https://doi.org/10.1007/978-3-031-22941-1_29
9. Onsager, L.: Crystal statistics. I. A two-dimensional model with an order-disorder transition. Phys. Rev. **65**(3–4), 117–149 (1941)
10. Houtappel, R.M.F.: Order-disorder in hexagonal lattices. Physica **16**(5), 425–455 (1950)
11. Baxter, R.J., Wu, F.Y.: Exact solution of an Ising model with three-spin interactions on a triangular lattice. Phys. Rev. Lett. **31**, 1294 (1973)
12. Goldenfeld, N.: Lectures on Phase Transitions and the Renormalization Group. Addison-Wesley, Reading (1992)
13. Privman, V., Hohenberg, P.C., Aharony, A.: In: Domb, C., Lebowitz, J.L. (eds.) Phase Transitions and Critical Phenomena, vol. 14. Academic Press, New York (1991)
14. Potts, R.B.: Some generalized order-disorder transformations. Proc. Cambridge Philos. Soc. **48**, 16 (1952)
15. Joyce, G.S.: Analytic properties of the Ising model with triplet interactions on the triangular lattice. Proc. R. Soc. London A **343**, 45 (1975)
16. Cardy, J.L., Nauenberg, M., Scalapino, D.J.: Scaling theory of the Potts-model multicritical point. Phys. Rev. B **22**, 2560 (1980)
17. Shchur, L.N., Janke, W.: Critical amplitude ratios of the Baxter-Wu model. Nucl. Phys. B **840**[FS], 491 (2010)
18. Metropolis, N., et al.: Equation of state calculations by fast computing machines. J. Chem. Phys. **21**, 1087 (1953)
19. Sokal, A.: Monte Carlo methods in statistical mechanics: foundations and new algorithms. In: DeWitt-Morette, C., Cartier, P., Folacci, A. (eds.) Functional Integration NATO ASI Series, vol. 361, p. 131. Springer, Boston (1997). https://doi.org/10.1007/978-1-4899-0319-8_6
20. He, K., Zhang, X., Ren, S., Sun, J.: Deep residual learning for image recognition. In: IEEE Conference on Computer Vision and Pattern Recognition, pp. 770–778 (2016)

21. Le Cun, Y., Bottou, L., Bengio, Y.: Reading checks with multilayer graph transformer networks. In: IEEE International Conference on Acoustics, Speech, and Signal Processing, vol. 1, p. 151 (1997)
22. Kingma D., Ba J.: Adam: A Method for Stochastic Optimization, arXiv:1412.6980
23. Devlin, J., Chang, M.W., Lee, K., Toutanova, K.: BERT: pre-training of deep bidirectional transformers for language understanding (2018) arXiv preprint arXiv:1810.04805
24. Fisher, M.E., Ferdinand, A.E.: Interfacial, boundary and size effects at critical points. Phys. Rev. Lett. **19**, 169 (1967)
25. Ferdinand, A.E., Fisher, M.E.: Bounded and inhomogeneous Ising models. I. specific-heat anomaly of a finite lattice. Phys. Rev. B **185**, 832 (1969)
26. Wu, T.T., et al.: Spin-spin correlation functions for the two-dimensional Ising model. Exact theory in the scaling region. Phys. Rev. B **13**, 316 (1976)
27. Selke, W., Shchur, L.N.: Critical Binder cumulant in a two-dimensional anisotropic Ising model with competing interactions. Phys. Rev. E **80**(4), 042104 (2009)

Author Index

V. Voevodin et al. (Eds.): RuSCDays 2023, LNCS 14389, pp. 331–332, 2023.
https://doi.org/10.1007/978-3-031-49435-2